ON EARTH PEACE

Discussions on War/Peace Issues
Between Friends, Mennonites, Brethren,
and European Churches, 1935-75

Edited by Donald F. Durnbaugh

THE BRETHREN PRESS, ELGIN, ILL.

Copyright © 1978, The Brethren Press
Printed in the United States of America

Cover design by Ken Stanley, based on a sculpture by Ralph Holdeman in a collection by LeRoy Kennel, photographed by Glenn Mitchell

Acknowledgements

The editor and the publisher are grateful to the owners of copyrighted material who have granted permission for their use in this book, including the Publications Office of the World Council of Churches, for selections from WCC publications; Association Press, for excerpts from *New Delhi Report,* edited by W. A. Visser 't Hooft; Harper and Row, for selections from *The First Assembly of the World Council of Churches* and *The Evanston Report* (Second Assembly), both edited by W. A. Visser 't Hooft; *Christianity and Crisis,* for "God Wills Both Justice and Peace," by Angus Dun and Reinhold Niebuhr; Friends World Committee for Consultation, for "The Quaker Peace Testimony"; and Gütersloher Verlagshaus Gerd Mohn, for "On Divine and Human Justice," by John H. Yoder. Complete identification of sources of materials is provided in the bibliographical notes beginning on page 397.

Library of Congress Cataloging in Publication Data
Main entry under title:
On earth peace.
    Includes index.
    1. Peace (Theology)—Addresses, essays, lectures.
I. Durnbaugh, Donald F.
BT736.05   261.8'73   78-538
ISBN O-87178-600-5

Foreword

In 1935 the term "Historic Peace Churches" was coined to describe the collective pacifist convictions of the Society of Friends, the Mennonites, and the Church of the Brethren. After World War II, M. R. Zigler brought together in Europe representatives of these churches, along with the International Fellowship of Reconciliation, to consult on their shared concerns. This was expanded to include spokesmen from the European churches in a series of theological discussions often known as the "Puidoux Conferences" after the small.Swiss village where the first meeting was held in 1935. These talks had a weighty influence on the stance of the European churches on military issues in the reconstruction period.

At the same time the Historic Peace Churches co-operated in bringing the peace witness to the newly-formed World Council of Churches. Over the years this testimony has aided in raising the consciousness of the ecumenical movement to the urgency of peace concerns. In 1975 the World Assembly of the WCC called specifically on the Peace Churches to share their experiences as part of a drive to confront the growing power of militarism.

This book contains major documents from the discussions ranging from 1935 in Newton, Kansas to 1975 in Nairobi, Kenya. They provide an important resource for all those eager to think about war/peace issues on a serious and substantive level. An introduction provides the over-all framework for understanding the discussion, and briefer statements aid in placing each document in its historical setting.

Although not a participant in the series of early Puidoux conferences, I met with the group in Geneva which planned the first conference in 1955. Ten years later I was asked to prepare an overview and assessment of the first decade of dialogue. A number of persons involved in these peace discussions were invited to the large consultation held at the Ecumenical Institute at Bossey, Switzerland, in early summer, 1965. During the consultation, those who had contact with the Puidoux conferences met to lay plans for the future. At that time I urged that the materials already produced be given wider circulation in some printed form, because of their high quality and perceptiveness. To my surprise, I was asked to undertake the task.

Subsequently, I collected as much documentation about the series of conferences as possible and sought some means of publication. There seemed, however, for many years to be no open avenue for such a complicated and costly venture. In 1974 a movement emerged in the life of the Church of the Brethren known as "On Earth Peace." It was inspired and promoted by M. R. Zigler, long-time peace activist and administrator. Zigler believed that a new initiative was needed "to clarify the issues that a Christian church must face . . . regarding violence." The method chosen was the holding of conferences, often organized along vocational lines, at the Brethren Service Center, New Windsor, Maryland; the conferences sought common purposes on peace and practial ways to work for peace.

At a meeting of theologians at New Windsor in March, 1975, I proposed that the On Earth Peace movement might take on the responsibility of making the materials from Puidoux and other ecumenical discussions available to a larger public. The suggestion was warmly received; later on it was approved by the On Earth Peace assembly. In this way the idea first presented in 1965 is now reaching fulfillment.

Several persons deserve warm appreciation for their aid to the publication. M. R. Zigler had long been associated with the Puidoux meetings and was naturally keenly interested in making the book possible. Dan Raffensperger made a significant financial donation. Kenneth I. Morse, book editor of The Brethren Press, saw the value of the documentation, despite its technical nature, and gave helpful counsel in solving production problems. Two successive executives of the General Services Commission—Galen B. Ogden and Joel Thompson—gave their support. H. Lamar Gibble, peace consultant for the Church of the Brethren, made his files available and encouraged the project. The European representative of the Brethren, Dale Ott, was helpful in many ways. John H. Yoder made a number of suggestions which strengthened the manuscript and wrote a thoughtful epilogue from the viewpoint of one of the key discussants in the ecumenical dialogue. Copyright-holders of previously published materials generously gave permission for republication here, specific acknowledgement of which is found elsewhere.

Selecting items to be included was not easy, given the wealth of substantial papers and articles during the forty years covered. Much that was valuable had to be omitted. Another editor would certainly have made other choices. Those statements here published, it is hoped, fairly represent and illustrate the important contributions made by many scholars and churchmen during the course of these theological encounters.

                Donald F. Durnbaugh
                December, 1977

Left to right: M. R. Zigler, formerly executive secretary, Brethren Service Committee; L. W. Shultz, formerly chairman, Brethren Service Committee; E. Raymond Wilson, formerly executive secretary, Friends Committee on National Legislation; Henry A. Fast, formerly executive secretary, Peace Committee of the General Conference of the Mennonite Church of North America. Taken at the Historic Peace Church Conference, New Windsor, Maryland, May, 1975.

View of the Protestant retreat center, Crêt Bérard, Puidoux, Switzerland, where the first large conference on the Lordship of Christ over Church and State was held (August, 1955).

Participants in the first Puidoux Theological Conference (August, 1955). Seated on steps, from left to right: Dr. E. L. Allen, Newcastle-on-Tyne, England; Prof. Götz Harbsmeier, Lüneburg, Germany; Dean Harold S. Bender, Goshen, Indiana; A. J. Muste, New York, N.Y. Seated on or leaning against wall: Colin Fawcett, Reading, England; Dean William Beahm, Chicago, Illinois; Dr. Hendrik Bremer, Amsterdam, Netherlands; Pastor Jean Lasserre, Saint-Etienne, France; Pastor Emile Jéquier, La Chaux-de-Fonds, Switzerland; Pastor Walter Dignath, Düren/Rhineland, Germany; Esko Loewen, Amsterdam, Netherlands; André Trocmé, Versailles, France. Standing at right of wall: Graydon F. Snyder, Princeton, N.J.; Mrs. Percy Bartlett, London, England; Albert J. Meyer, Valdoie-Belfort, France; Percy Bartlett, London, England; M. R. Zigler, Geneva, Switzerland. Standing in back row: Prof. H. G. Wood, Birmingham, England; Pastor Fritzhermann Keienburg, Gelsenkirchen-Schalke, Germany; Prof. Ernst Wolf, Göttingen, Germany; Doris Neff, Mannheim, Germany; John H. Yoder, Basel, Switzerland; Prof. Culbert G. Rutenber, Philadelphia, Pa.; W. Harold Row, Elgin, Illinois; Dr. Alvin Pitcher, Chicago, Illinois; Pastor Edouard Theis, Le Chambon-sur-Lignon, France; Prof. John W. Harvey, Leeds, England; Oberkirchenrat Heinz Kloppenburg, Dortmund, Germany; Oberkirchenrat Joachim Beckmann, Düsseldorf, Germany; Dr. G. Hartdorff, Amsterdam, Netherlands.

Table of Contents

Prefatory Statements: M. R. Zigler, Eric S. Tucker, Albert J. Meyer . 13
Introduction: Donald F. Durnbaugh 17

1. **Principles of Christian Peace and Patriotism—Historic Peace Churches,** (Newton, Kansas, October 31-November 2, 1935) 30
2. **World Conference on Church, Community and State** (Oxford, United Kingdom, July 12-26, 1937) 33
3. **The First Assembly of the World Council of Churches** (Amsterdam, The Netherlands, August 22-September 4, 1948) 38
4. **War Is Contrary to the Will of God—Historic Peace Churches and the International Fellowship of Reconciliation** (Zeist, The Netherlands, July 12, 1951) 46
5. **Peace Is the Will of God—Historic Peace Churches and the International Fellowship of Reconciliation** (Geneva, Switzerland, October 1953) 73
6. **The Second Assembly of the World Council of Churches** (Evanston, Illinois, August 15-31, 1954) 91
7. **God Wills Both Justice and Peace** (Angus Dun and Reinhold Niebuhr, June 13, 1955) 100
8. **God Establishes Both Peace and Justice** (Paul Peachey and Members of the Continuation Committee of the Historic Peace Churches, 1955 and 1958) 108
9. **The Lordship of Christ Over Church and State I** (Puidoux, Switzerland, August 15-19, 1955) 122

    Introduction to a Discussion on "Church and World" with Reference to Luther, Ernst Wolf
    Theses on the Relevance of the Authority of Scripture and the Church to the Responsibility of the Individual, Götz Harbsmeier
    The "Good" of Romans 13:4, Jean Lasserre
    The Theological Basis of the Christian Witness to the State, John H. Yoder
    Resumé of the Conference
    The Church and Peace (Declaration)

10. **The Lordship of Christ Over Church and State II** (Iserlohn, Germany, July 28-August 1, 1957) 146
    Discipleship as Witness to the Unity in Christ as Seen by the Reformers, Ernst Wolf
    Discipleship as Witness to the Unity in Christ as Seen by the Dissenters, Paul Peachey
    Protestant Preaching on Peace, Hans-Werner Bartsch
    Justice and Love, Richard Ullmann
    Report to the *Landeskirchen*

11. **Christians and the Prevention of War in an Atomic Age—A Theological Discussion** (Geneva, Switzerland, August 27, 1958 excerpt) 185

12. **The Lordship of Christ Over Church and State III** (Bièvres, France, August 2-7, 1960)... 196
    On Divine and Human Justice, John H. Yoder
    The Sixth Commandment: Its Significance for the Christian as Citizen and for the Statesman, Warren F. Groff

13. **The Third Assembly of the World Council of Churches** (New Delhi, India, November 19-December 3, 1961) 223
    The Report of the Section on Service: The Churches' Involvement in World Affairs and World Order
    An Appeal to All Governments and Peoples

14. **The Lordship of Christ Over Church and State IV** (Oud Poelgeest, The Netherlands, July 9-14, 1962) 229
    Fundamental Problems of Evangelical Social Ethics, Part 1, Hendrik Van Oyen
    Social Ethics in the Bible, André Dumas
    The Significance of Historical Events for Ethical Decisions, Jan M. Lochmann
    The Social Aspects of the Teachings of the Early Church, Hans-Werner Bartsch
    War and the Christian Ethic, Jean Lasserre

15. **The Authority of Government and the Lordship of Christ** (Chicago, Illinois, Faculty of Bethany Theological Seminary, 1962) 272

16. **God's Reconciling Work Among the Nations Today** (Bossey, Switzerland, June 28-July 3, 1965) 277
    The Biblical Message of Peace, Hans-Werner Bartsch
    Church and State According to a Free Church Tradition, John H. Yoder
    The Task of the Church, Heinz Kloppenburg

17. **World Conference on Church and Society** (Geneva, Switzerland, July 12-26, 1966) 292

    Report of Section III. Structures of International Cooperation: Living Together in Peace in a Pluralistic World Society (excerpts)

18. **The Quaker Peace Testimony** (Guilford College, North Carolina, 1966) 300

19. **Consultation on the Christian Witness to Peace** (Bossey, Switzerland, May 28-June 1, 1968) 306

    A Pacifist/Non-Pacifist Discussion of Its Theological Bases, Division of Studies

20. **The Fourth Assembly of the World Council of Churches** (Uppsala, Sweden, July 4-20, 1968) 313

    Towards Justice and Peace in International Affairs
    The Martin Luther King Resolution

21. **Puidoux 1955-1959: Report of a Dialogue about the Theological Foundation of a Christian Peace Witness** (Heinold Fast, 1969) ... 319

22. **Report of the Consultation on Violence, Nonviolence and the Struggle for Social Justice** (Cardiff, Wales, September 3-7, 1972) . 329

23. **Response to the Cardiff Report by Brethren, Friends, Mennonites** (Richmond, Indiana, April 21-23 and December 15-17, 1972) 353

24. **Jesus and Power** (John H. Yoder, October, 1973) 365

25. **Violence, Nonviolence and the Struggle for Social Justice** (Church and Society Working Committee, August 28, 1973) 373

26. **The Fifth Assembly of the World Council of Churches** (Nairobi, Kenya, November 23-December 10, 1975) 386

    An Appeal to the Churches
    Pacifist Minority Still to Be Heard

Epilogue: The Way Ahead, John H. Yoder 390

Notes: Introduction 395

Notes: Documents 397

Index 401

List of Contributors

(The identification is of current occupation, which in some cases is different from that of the time of writing.)

Hans-Werner Bartsch, Professor, University of Frankfurt/Main, Germany

André Dumas, Professor, Protestant Theological Faculty, Paris, France

Angus Dun, Bishop, Protestant Episcopal Church, Washington, DC, USA (deceased)

Donald F. Durnbaugh, Professor, Bethany Theological Seminary, Oak Brook, Illinois, USA

Heinold Fast, Pastor, Emden, Germany

Warren F. Groff, President, Bethany Theological Seminary, Oak Brook, Illinois, USA

Götz Harbsmeier, Professor, University of Göttingen, Germany

Heinz Kloppenburg, Editor, Bremen, Germany

Jean Lassere, Formerly Pastor, Lyons, France

Jan M. Lochmann, Professor, University of Basel, Switzerland

Albert J. Meyer, Executive Secretary, Mennonite Board of Education, Elkhart, Indiana, USA

Reinhold Niebuhr, Professor, Union Theological Seminary, New York, New York, USA (deceased)

Paul Peachey, Professor, Catholic University, Washington, DC, USA

Eric S. Tucker, Formerly Secretary, Friends Peace Committee, London, UK

Richard Ullmann, Editor, Society of Friends, London, UK (deceased)

Hendrik Van Oyen, Professor, University of Basel, Switzerland

Ernst Wolf, Professor, University of Göttingen, Germany

John H. Yoder, Professor, Associated Mennonite Biblical Seminaries, Elkhart, Indiana, USA; University of Notre Dame, South Bend, Indiana, USA

Zigler, M. R., Formerly Director in Europe, Brethren Service Commission, Geneva, Switzerland

Prefatory Statements
Brethren

In 1935 Mennonites, Friends, and Brethren met unofficially at Newton, Kansas, in an interchurch convocation. The purpose of the meeting was to discuss peace and war and the position of the three Historic Peace Churches facing the future. I did not attend this meeting, but in 1936 and 1937 I became identified with a long list of meetings jointly arranged and followed through by the three parties. These meetings were designed to inspire our churches independently as far as our programs were concerned.

In 1948 I was asked to go to Europe to represent the Church of the Brethren in the World Council of Churches and to establish Brethren Service programs along with other relief agencies. The last meeting I attended in the States was held in Chicago, Illinois. It was decided there that in Europe I should call together Mennonites, Friends, and Brethren to form a continuation committee or some organization similar to that which had served us in the United States since 1935. There I found Angie Newlin at Geneva, Switzerland, for the American Friends and Robert Kreider in Berlin for the Mennonites; together we decided that we should invite the British Friends. Eric Tucker accepted that invitation and then the International Fellowship of Reconciliation accepted an invitation to be represented through Percy Bartlett. This group, as in the States, held many meetings, some of which are reported in this volume.

Because of our being in Europe at the time we were eager to have contacts with other church bodies through representatives who might be interested to discuss peace even though they did not take the position of the Historic Peace Churches regarding war. This developed into a fellowship that was an inspiration to the Historic Peace Churches and the Fellowship of Reconciliation. The relief programs in the interest of peace and the presence in Europe of young volunteers from the Historic Peace Churches were the most convincing evidences of our being interested in making peace among people who had just gone through a World War. Through this combination of activities we gave our testimony to governments and to churches in the interest of peace on earth through service.

M. R. Zigler

Mennonites

The Puidoux theological conferences of the fifties and sixties were the first extended theological conversations in over four hundred years between the Historic Peace Churches, who date from the Anabaptists of the early days of the Reformation, and the official churches of Central Europe.

The issues between them have not fallen away with the passing of the centuries. The alliance of the large churches with the powers-that-be has continued to our own time. The Western "Christian" nations have engaged in a chain of conflict and violence which has led in this century to the bloodiest wars the world has yet known and the threat of nuclear catastrophe.

There has been a change in recent decades. After more than a millennium under the sign of the victory of Christianity in the Roman Empire, the Western world is entering a post-Constantinian era. Western Christian leaders, shaken by the fact that National Socialism could rise in the heart of Christian Europe and further unsettled by the depths of insensitivity and immorality into which Christian America could stumble in Vietnam, have been asking some new questions—or, from another stance, some old questions from a new perspective.

Twenty and thirty years ago, the interests of the peace churches took the form of marginal comments and hardly-noticeable footnotes on the main agenda of the World Council of Churches, a body at that time representing primarily the larger politically or culturally established churches of the West. With the recent rise in Third World consciousness and representation in world Christian bodies has come an increasing awareness of the experience and message of the Free Churches, who have for centuries lived and witnessed as non-establishment movements.

What, indeed, should be the shape of the life of God's people among the nations? What is the word of those committed to the Lamb's War to warring peoples? Is there good news for nations apparently inextricably mired in civil and international conflict?

It was to these issues that World Council of Churches leaders suggested—was it formal ecumenical courtesy or did someone really think there might be a genuinely helpful word from the Lord?—the Historic Peace Churches might wish to speak.

These were the Puidoux issues. The peace churches had to confer with each other and with representatives of other traditions to test and clarify their own thinking and message. They found an extraordinary resonance with official European churches, and the Puidoux work on the issues began.

Interest in a new word on these issues is growing. Indeed, the concluding words of a 1958 *Christian Century* editorial seem more prescient now than when they were first penned eighteen years ago: "Puidoux conferences may be the beginning of a conversation which will one day involve us all."

Albert J. Meyer

Quakers

The Society of Friends in Great Britain came out of the Second World War bruised and shaken. Whilst a majority of its young men and women had resisted the demands of the state for their compulsory enrollment in the military machine, the evils perpetrated by the National Socialist regime in Germany and throughout temporarily conquered Europe revealed an unbelievable depth of depravity to which men could sink. The Quaker relief workers arriving on the continental mainland found it necessary to question their previously accepted belief in the element of the divine in all men, and as their reports came back to their home bases, doubts and uncertainties arose in the minds of many Friends as to the continuing validity of the Quaker peace testimony.

In the United States, the situation of Friends was different. There had been no experience of the bombing of their cities, of spending night after night in dark clammy underground shelters, of rigid food rationing, all of which contributed in Britain to a weakening of will power, of the will to believe, of belief in the fundamental love of God for all his creatures. In the USA, too, the Historic Peace Churches had already forged a close relationship before the war broke out and this served to strengthen and uphold their united membership. But in Britain something new and invigorating was needed.

It was provided, first, by the arrival in Europe of American Mennonite, Brethren, and Quaker relief workers, full of commitment and vigour, and then by the drawing together of them with British Quakers in conference and fellowship out of which came the desire to establish a joint witness for peace before the churches of the world.

The two documents which emanated from these discussions were widely circulated and read, and formed the basis of many a discussion group. As a result, and despite the hardships of the recent past, Friends found that their historic positions could be maintained, could again say that in their faith and understanding war is contrary to the will of God, and, more positively, could reaffirm their belief that peace between all men everywhere is the will of God.

Eric S. Tucker

Introduction

Donald F. Durnbaugh

An appeal to the churches was issued at the conclusion of the Fifth Assembly of the World Council of Churches meeting at Nairobi (November-December 1975). It asked the churches to "take a significant initiative in pressing for effective disarmament" and to urge their respective governments to "ensure national security without resorting to the use of weapons of mass destruction." The Assembly called on the Central Committee of the World Council of Churches to organize an international consultation on disarmament. The purpose of the consultation would be to develop a strategy which could limit ever-increasing military expenditures. Among other points proposed for the strategy was the sharing "of the experience of the Historic Peace Churches." This is the term used since 1935 to speak collectively of the Mennonite churches, the Society of Friends, and the Church of the Brethren, all of which have held, since their inceptions in the sixteenth through eighteenth centuries, to a witness for peace and conscientious objection to participation in war.[1]

M. R. Zigler, veteran Church of the Brethren peace leader and the oldest person present at the Nairobi conference, commented that this was the first time, to his knowledge, that the Historic Peace Churches were named as an ecclesiastical entity in a formal document of the World Council. His memory goes back to the landmark conferences in 1937 at Oxford and Edinburgh, out of which came the present ecumenical organization. In reporting on the Fifth Assembly, Zigler challenged the peace churches to respond to this "unique opportunity" to share their experience.

One of the purposes of this volume is to aid in that response. Its intent is to bring together in one place the most significant and also typical documents which have emerged in forty years of ecumenical discussion on peace/war issues. An additional purpose is to make available to a wider public some of the papers produced in a series of theological conferences on peace known popularly as the Puidoux Conferences, after the village in French Switzerland where the first assembly was held in 1955. The formal theme of the series of four conferences (1955-1962) was "The Lordship of Christ Over Church and State."[2]

Concern for world peace has been ever present in the modern ecumenical movement. As early as 1908 the British Quaker J. Allen Baker called for an international conference of the churches to discuss universal cooperation for peace through the churches. A continental associate, Dr. Friedrich W. Siegmund-Schultze, can be singled out as a European champion of peace. He was at the heart of several organizations working for peace, as a cofounder of the International Fellowship of Reconciliation and the World Alliance for Promoting International Friendship Through the Churches.[3]

Archbishop Nathan Söderblom of Sweden must also be named as a leading ecumenical figure working for world peace. He was behind numerous initiatives for peace during and after World War I, especially in the Life and Work movement among the churches, culminating in the Stockholm conference of 1925. Although the propaganda machines of the governments contending for military dominance were very effective in spreading fabrications and tendentious reports of the opposing regimes, there were still voices raised among the churches which spoke for sanity, justice, and peace.

The post-1918 reaction to the wartime hysteria brought renewed energies to bear on peace proposals. The period was characterized by great optimism about the possibilities of spreading the benefits of peace and democracy across the world as Wilsonian ideology had promised. This was undergirded by a regnant Anglo-Saxon theological liberalism which provided most of the ecumenical leaders with powerful motivation for their institution-building. The kingdom of God was for them not some distant, eschatological dream but a lively reality, given enough good-will and enough organization.[4]

This mood gave way to a more sober analysis in the troubled thirties. The dual impact of the growth of totalitarian states and the shift to Neo-Reformation theology associated with the names of Reinhold Niebuhr and Karl Barth can be clearly documented in the Oxford Conference on Church, Community and State (July 1937). Conference planners, chief among them J. H. Oldham, were concerned that the churches regain their historic foundations and renewed biblical realism so as to gird themselves for the tests looming on the horizons. The Oxford Message and pertinent sectional reports pronounced solemn "condemnations of war unqualified and unrestricted." Yet the Oxford delegates confessed to perplexity in arriving at a unified stance vis-a-vis Christian participation in war. They saw the lack of unity as "itself a sign of the sin in which its members are implicated." Oxford listed three positions held by Christians on war—ranging from Christian pacifism to the classic "just war"—and called for further study.[5]

The constitutive assembly which marked the formation of the World Council of Churches (WCC) was held at Amsterdam in 1948. Again the Amsterdam delegates found themselves repeating the pluralism of positions seen at Oxford—what has been called the ecumenical "trilemma." After stating that "war is contrary to the will of God" the Assembly report described three positions held by Christians, similar to but not identical with the Oxford trilogy. The Assembly called on theologians "to consider the theological problems involved" and urged upon all Christians the "duty of wrestling continuously with the difficulties" of the perplexing issue.[6]

A continuation committee of representatives of the Historic Peace Churches (HPC) responded to the plea, made more specific by a communication from the WCC general secretary, W. A. Visser 't. Hooft. They arranged for statements to be made by the Friends, the Mennonites, and the Brethren. They also asked the International Fellowship of Reconciliation (IFOR) for a statement. These four, with a joint introductory message, were published in the booklet, *War Is Contrary to the Will of God* (1951). The groups forthrightly asserted that they were "convinced that Christian pacifism and non-resistance is the true interpretation of the teaching and example of Jesus as recorded in the New Testament." They contended that "this teaching is intended as a guide for his disciples here and now . . . ." In so doing, they squarely rejected the popular interpretation of pacifism as a legitimate minority position for those Christians given that vocation.

It must be noted that the HPC were not at this point prepared to issue a joint declaration, despite their common witness on peace. As the editors of the booklet noted, "It is agreed that the four statements written in *different idioms* and reflecting *different traditions* and each having a character of its own, ought to be considered individually" [emphasis added]. This underscored a fact not always recognized by other Christian groups. The peace churches had been influenced by different historical factors, despite their basic agreement on the nature of the church. Their traditions are not identical, especially in terms of theological expression and conviction. The failure to recognize widely differing beliefs and ideologies among those who call themselves or who are called pacifists has often muddied the waters of ecumenical discussion. This lack of typological clarity has caused faulty communication and misperceived signals. What has been lacking in this process is a stage of "comparative ecclesiology" akin to what was engaged in by the Faith and Order movement.[7]

When the booklet was presented to the ecumenical leadership it was graciously received. However, the HPC were asked how they expected so diverse a group as the WCC membership to come to unity on the peace issue when even the peace churches could not come to a common mind. Thus chastened, the European continuation committee of the HPC went back to the drafting boards and came up two years later with a joint document—*Peace Is the Will of God* (1953). This was presented to delegates at the Second Assembly of the World Council, held in Evanston, Illinois (August 1954). It was also given to WCC staff members in the hope that a continuing study process might be initiated. This did not happen, partly because the Study Department thought that such issues fell under the purview of the Commission of the Churches on International Affairs (CCIA). Subsequently, the CCIA did deal seriously with the document.[8]

The CCIA was a joint formation in 1946 of the World Council and the International Missionary Council. Although its charter as subsequently revised did call for basic theological study of the issues, in practice its work was limited to high-level interventions and sophisticated lobbying among governments and international organizations in the cause of world peace and reconciliation. Several of the CCIA meetings did make pronouncements on peace and war issues. Typical, perhaps, was the statement issued by the Executive Committee in 1951 under the title "Christians Stand for Peace." It read, in part: " . . . we must neither purchase peace at the price of tyranny nor in the name of justice look on war as a way to justice or as a ground of hope." The basic ideological stance could be identified as that of the "responsible society," coined by J. H. Oldham. The underlying assumption was that the business of concerned Christians was to be deeply involved in the processes of governments, either by personal participation in high office or by judicious application of the churches' influence at appropriate times and places.[9]

The Evanston Assembly did not go beyond Amsterdam in theological clarification (observers criticized the paucity of theological development generally) of the "trilemma" on peace. The *Christian Century* editorialized about the pertinent section of the report:

> . . . the total document is more a reflection of tortured consciences trying to make their "agonized reappraisals" than of confident moral direction. The nature of modern war, and most of all the nature of the H-bomb, grows in immensity as a baffling problem for the Christian conscience.

It was noted that the tone in reference to pacifists was more friendly at this conclave than had been the case at earlier meetings. In commenting on the results of the Evanston Assembly, Jesuit Edward Duff, who wrote a pioneer study of the social thought of the WCC, commented that the greatest hope was placed in the limitation of national sovereignty and narrow nationalism: "The most effective action to prevent war is judged to be the constructing of a world government through the strengthening of existing instruments of international cooperation."[10]

The years 1954-55 brought some response to the HPC document, *Peace Is the Will of God.* A Danish theologian, N. H. Söe, wrote a lengthy analysis. More important was the reaction of two leading American churchmen, Reinhold Niebuhr—the foremost critic of pacifism—and Angus Dun. Their statement appeared in *Christianity and Crisis* with an editorial statement that the lack of response to the HPC document demanded some non-pacifist answer. This statement, in turn, brought a counter-analysis from the peace groups, later to be published along with the Dun-Niebuhr article.[11]

In 1955 there began also a more fruitful encounter, the first of the so-called Puidoux Conferences. This has been characterized as the resumption of disputations and discussions between members of the left-wing churches and the territorial churches interrupted by persecution several centuries previously. The plan for the first conference came from an enlarged meeting of the continutation committee of the HPC with members of the WCC staff at Geneva—Robert Bilheimer, Paul Abrecht, and Philip Potter; this was early in 1955. The original plan was to try bringing the peace groups more closely together in theological stance with the aid of some sympathetic and academically qualified European theologians. As plans for the conference developed, and at the actual meeting, something more significant took place. This was a direct encounter between peace church theologians and spokesmen from the formerly established churches from several countries. This encounter was to set the course for three following major "Puidoux" conferences.

These took place as Iserlohn, Germany (July-August 1957), Bièvres, France (August 1960), and Oud Poelgeest, The Netherlands (July 1962). Smaller meetings related to the series were held at Vallecrosia, Italy (April 1956), and Askov, Denmark (August 1957). In addition another group of conferences were held bringing together churchmen from East and West under Puidoux auspices. There was also linkage here with the Christian Peace Conferences in Prague. Following 1965 it was decided that more progress could be made by a more regular series of meetings of a small working group which would remain constant in membership. This took place under the umbrella of the Research Institute of the Protestant Study Fellowship at Heidelberg from 1967-1969, with meetings at the study center of Höchst, Germany.[12]

Although the Puidoux discussions have been credited with making a definite impact on theological attitudes toward peace on the continent generally, it was in Germany that they had the most impact. They became a part of the ongoing theological dialogue within the churches, particularly among the left-wing of the former Confessing Church movement. As the German church showed an increasingly restorationist mentality with little interest in major restructuring or rethinking of its pre-1933 status, the radical faction led by Martin Niemöller was open to making common cause with the descendants of the Radical Reformation. The nuclear threat also played a large role in the reassessment within the German churches as they faced the nightmare of West Germans fighting East Germans in a potential new war and the possibility of the German area becoming the frontline of the East-West conflict and hence a nuclear graveyard.[13]

It is also in West Germany that the rise of conscientious objection has been the most marked. Although not totally absent in German history prior to the formation of the German Federal Republic—German Mennonites were allowed to serve in the Prussian medical corps through World War I—the role of conscientious objection was anchored in the new constitution and has grown remarkably. It is reported that currently forty thousand young Germans are freed from military service under German law, which allows political and philosophical objection as well as religious objection as a basis of refusal for conscience' sake to join the military.

In the Puidoux discussions the predominant figures on the German side were Ernst Wolf, professor of systematic theology at Göttingen University, and Hans-Werner Bartsch, professor in biblical studies at the pedagogical university in Frankfurt. On the side of the peace churches, two persons making key contributions were Jean Lasserre, friend of Dietrich Bonhoeffer and longtime French IFOR leader, and the American Mennonite John Howard Yoder, professor of theology at the Associated Mennonite Biblical Seminaries, Elkhart, Indiana. Yoder became involved in the discussions while a graduate student in theology at Basel and has continued to be a central figure in the series of conferences and those he held since. Many of the ideas first brought forward in the Puidoux papers prepared by Yoder have been given more systematic formulation in recent books, especially in his well-known study on *The Politics of Jesus*.[14]

As the Puidoux conferences were being carried out, several ecumenical consultations took place centering on the same subject matter. Three WCC studies (1956-1959) were organized around a theme very similar to that of Puidoux—"The Lordship of Christ Over the World and the Church." Although the peace issue as such was not directly addressed, these meetings dealt with the same basic hermeneutical and ecclesiological problems which emerged in the minds of Puidoux participants as central to the question. Despite a specific assertion in the last document produced that the study was not ended but that the paper should be seen as "a contribution to an ongoing study process," the series was discontinued after 1959 without announcement of the reason for cessation.[15]

The year 1958 saw the publication of a highly controversial WCC paper, *Christians and the Prevention of War in an Atomic Age,* produced by a task force over a three-year period. The drafters included a distinguished company of scientists, statesmen, theologians, and churchmen. The Central Committee received the document in a gingerly fashion, and allowed its publication only with extraordinary reservations. The paper itself was called a "Provisional Study Document"; a statement was printed on the cover and again in the resolution of the Central Committee introducing the study which emphasized that "No point here expressed is to be understood as an official view of the World Council of Churches. This document is in no sense a statement of World Council policy." As with the Lordship of Christ study, it was stressed that the statement was "but the first step in a continuing study process" offered to the churches for "their reflection and discussion."[16]

What was the reason for the disclaimers? The working party, although it numbered only a few expressed pacifists, came to the conclusion that "all-out war" would be so destructive of human life that nuclear weapons dared not be used. In fact, in the face of this threat, they advised that surrender to an enemy would be preferred to destruction. The paper is best understood as an updating of the just-war theory to take cognizance of the terror of nuclear weapons. The announced study process was not continued in a major way, although the document was published, in revised form, in 1961.[17]

Also fitting into this time period was the Third Assembly of the Council in New Delhi (November-December 1961). Opinions differ as to whether the work of the Council marked an advance in the position of the ecumenical movement in regard to peace/war issues. One might have expected that an assembly held in the nation most strongly influenced by Gandhi might have a definite word to speak to the churches and to the world on peace. In fact, the Assembly did issue an appeal for peace which one scholar called a "high-water mark" of ecumenical statements on peace until that time. Others criticized the apparent hesitation of the assembly to speak out against nuclear war. In one publicized incident, the accusation was made that through staff influence a more strongly-worded resolution was moderated behind the scenes to avoid offending Western politicians.[18]

The 1961 Assembly did direct the Division of Studies to sponsor a week-long consultation on the biblical and theological bases of the peace witness. The rationale given was that the new atomic context demanded rethinking of former Christian attitudes and options regarding war. For reasons never fully explained, the WCC staff did not completely comply with this directive. It did sponsor a small gathering in Switzerland in the early summer of 1968 shortly before the next full assembly which was to meet at Uppsala. The Ecumenical Institute at Bossey also carried out a study conference on "God's Reconciling Work Among the Nations Today" in 1965, but this did not meet the New Delhi prescription.[19]

A significant turn in the whole nexus of discussion came about in the summer of 1966. This watershed was the Conference on Church and Society held at Geneva in July. The conference was thoroughly prepared for and well organized, although the entire procedure was later criticized by such observers as Paul Ramsey for its lack of true deliberation. Be that as it may, there is no question that the Geneva conference set the course for the future development of the WCC. It was here that the theologies of liberation received their first major hearing, that the justification of revolution for the sake of oppressed peoples was announced. A carefully worded statement in the conference's report dealt pointedly with the values of nonviolence but even more pointedly raised the issue of "invisible violence" perpetrated by unjust systems. Revolution against such oppression was said to be justifiable as an "ultimate recourse," after all other measures had failed; at the same time it was granted that the resolution itself was not without its ambiguities and dangers.[20]

The Uppsala Assembly (August 1968) has come to be remembered for its critique of racism, but that was in fact only a small part of its work. More basic was a shift in attention to concerns on the "horizontal" or social level as opposed to "perpendicular" concerns which had been traditionally within the purview of the churches. Right practice became as important as right doctrine.

A group of interested persons was able to present to the Assembly a memorial resolution for the late Martin Luther King, Jr., who was to have addressed the meeting. In addition to its memorialization, the resolution as passed by the Assembly asked the "Central Committee to explore means by which the World Council could promote studies on non-violent methods of achieving social change." It was hoped that by emphasizing the way in which the slain civil-rights leader had been able to appropriate nonviolent means for social amelioration and achieving the rights of minorities, a new start could be made in discussion of and action on peace concerns. It was thought that part of the reason for the reluctance of the Geneva staff to move on the peace issue was the feeling that it was a tired issue, about which all of the important points had been made already. By linking the discussion to nonviolent means of social change the impasse might be sidestepped.[21]

An ad hoc group of HPC members, largely Quakers from the United States, linked with other interested groups, worked intensively with the WCC staff following Uppsala in planning ways of implementing the King resolution. Partly as a result of their efforts, the Central Committee, meeting at Canterbury in August 1969, authorized the Department of Church and Society (with other interested units) to

> follow closely the discussion of violence and nonviolence in rapid social change already taking place in various departments of the World Council of Churches, in view of the Martin-Luther-King resolution of Uppsala and related discussion by other organizations.

The committee urged that financial resources be sought to enable the holding of consultations on key theological issues and suggested that attention to Gandhian views might be fruitful. A staff member at WCC headquarters had this assignment added to his portfolio.

This relatively low-key item took on much greater importance when a related initiative of the post-Uppsala era received wide attention. The decision to work against racist structures was given widespread publicity after the Notting Hill meeting in May 1969. The decision was made there to attack racism, among other means, by aiding liberation movements in the Third World, especially in Africa. It was agreed that

> all else failing, the Church and the churches [should] support resistance movements, including revolutions, which are aimed at the elimination of political or economic tyranny which makes racism possible.

Prodded by often inaccurate journalistic coverage, there were intense reactions, predictably among the churches of South Africa, but also in Germany, Great Britain, the United States, and other countries.[22]

One line of reaction—which has proved bothersome for the advancement of peace concerns—was that of critics of the liberation movements among the "establishment" churches which counsel minorities living in oppressed areas to practice nonresistance and nonviolence in their stance toward their political superiors. This could only be considered hypocritical when it came from the same church leaders who had so loudly proclaimed the righteousness of just wars against totalitarianism or whose own countries had been formed by violent revolutions, such as the USA. This "instant pacifism" has tended to discredit the ongoing discussion because it has seemed to be a cloak for those antagonistic to the concerns of minorities in the Third and Fourth Worlds. Ironically, as has been pointed out, the peace groups themselves were largely supportive of the WCC Program to Combat Racism, although they did not by that token give up their own pacifist principles.

The effect of the controversy, institutionally, was to bring about on the staff level what the peace groups had been urging for years—the creation of a staff assignment specifically concerned with nonviolence/violence problems. The Central Committee meeting in Ethiopia (January 1971) directed that a staff member of the Church-and-Society group give half time to the nonviolence study. This was done so that the Department could

> give particular attention to the development of this programme; in collaboration with other relevant units of the World Council of Churches and with study centres, institutes, and action groups working in this field in various parts of this world.

David Gill, who had been earlier involved with the study, was given the assignment.[23]

The Department of Church and Society understood the assignment to be essentially twofold: "furthering the churches' reflection on the ethical dilemmas caused by violence and non-violence in the struggles for peace and justice"; and "contributing to the search for strategies of action which will minimize the sum total of violence in conflict situations." (The latter formulation was originally developed at a meeting of the newly created SODEPAX, a joint effort of the WCC at Geneva and the Vatican.) The outcome of the proposed two-year study was a statement on "Violence, Nonviolence and the Struggle for Social Justice" which has been the key ecumenical document to emerge in recent years in the general area of peace. A preliminary conference of experts was held in Nemi, Italy (June 1971) to help outline the study. A larger consultation brought together fifty persons from several nations in Cardiff, Wales (November 1972). Many of the participants had long years of experience in nonviolent actions, others were concerned theologians. The task assigned was to "delineate the issues of our study and to clarify the concepts of 'violence' and 'nonviolence.'" One of the problems which emerged from the expansion of the parameters of violence after Geneva 1966 to "invisible violence" and "structural violence" was that there was an ever present danger that "violence" could be said to be practiced on any person in any situation at any time, and hence the concept could become useless for serious discourse.

The Cardiff report received wide circulation and stimulated a number of responses although not as many as the staff had wished for. One of the most thorough critiques came from an ad hoc committee of American representatives of the HPC which had met once before Cardiff to discuss the issues and another time afterward to criticize the report. A smaller group of biblical scholars and theologians was called together at Geneva in the summer of 1973 to prepare a supplemental report on the topic of "Jesus and Power." The reason was that there were so many opinions afloat about the way in which Jesus actually responded himself to the situation of violence.[24]

The results of the two-year study process went to the Central Committee meeting at Geneva in August 1973 with a list of recommendations. The report was approved for circulation, largely as received, but the recommendations were largely bypassed. The thrust of the recommendations of the working committee was to continue with the impetus of the study and to broaden WCC involvement in the areas of peace education and action. Intervention ministries to tension spots were proposed. The paper itself was widely publicized in the pages of the *Ecumenical Review* and as a separate booklet. A summary of responses received from churches and individuals was published for the use of the Nairobi Assembly.[25]

Again, the HPC were eager to cooperate with the Geneva staff in facilitating and implementing the nonviolence paper. To do so they committed themselves to raise money to underwrite (in part) a staff position. Sums of money were given to the Council for this purpose. Although the directives of the Central Committee did ask the staff to develop fresh initiatives in their respective programs and to assist the Christian churches around the world to engage in more study of and more courageous engagement in nonviolent action, little was accomplished. A staff committee of WCC units related to the study was formed, but in the view of the HPC not much was accomplished between 1973 and 1975.

An HPC-written survey of the developments since Uppsala pinpointed some possible reasons for the non-action, despite numerous interventions on their part with Geneva:

> (1) The increasing shortage of funds and pressure to reduce staff and program rather than to expand program.
>
> (2) Suspicion expressed by liberationists who tend to regard the "violence-nonviolence" effort as a new form of western imperialism designed to keep oppressed people in their place.
>
> (3) The view of many in the WCC that much of the work already

being done is fundamentally nonviolent in character and that significant "intervention ministries" are already being carried on in various countries of the world.

(4) The question whether the staff has a mandate to engage in new program between Assembly meetings, or whether such a mandate would have to come from the Fifth Assembly at Nairobi in 1975.

It might also be suggested that WCC energies invested in the SODEPAX program tended to divert attention from the nonviolence program.[26]

It was therefore with great anticipation that the HPC looked forward to the Fifth Assembly. Some low-key effort was made prior to and at the Assembly to urge the WCC to press forward on the actions agreed upon by the Central Committee in 1973. While not wishing to lobby, the peace advocates did want to register their concerns. John H. Yoder was invited by the Assembly planners to attend as a special consultant. Although many references to the broader nonviolence area were made in Assembly reports and hearings (one analysis counted more than thirty), it remains unclear what action will emerge as part of the work of the WCC.

It was decided that the Assembly was too bulky to allow for a prioritizing of the many issues raised at the conference, especially in the face of the financial crisis. This was assigned to the staff and to the Central Committee. It is important that one of the sixteen points established by the Program Guideline Committee to shape priorities was "the need to exercise a ministry of peace and reconciliation and to explore further the significance of nonviolent action for social change and the struggle against militarism."

Militarism and the associated arms race seem likely to be the focus of new WCC initiative. Staff is now preparing the groundwork for the consultation asked for by the Assembly. Another area which may receive attention is a further explication of how "just revolution" is to be understood. An African writing his reactions to the Assembly in *One World* said that blacks were "generally agreed that there can be a just war, such as that waged by the liberation movements in Southern Africa, but what happens when nationals subjugate nationals in an independent country?" He referred to Philip Potter's call for a theology of the "just rebellion."[27]

It thus remains to be seen where several decades of intense and sometimes frustrating discussion on peace/war, violence/nonviolence issues will now lead. That attention is desperately needed is underscored by a glance at the daily newspapers with their coverage of the agonies of war, civil and international. A review of the four decades of dialogue covered in this volume leads to the following conclusions, phrased here in the form of theses which may stimulate discussion:

(1) The Historic Peace Churches—though hampered by the fact that not all of their constituent bodies are members of the WCC and limited by other sociological factors—have made a persistent and consistent effort to enter into dialogue with other Christians within the framework of the ecumenical movement.

(2) The ecumenical movement—though directing its attention to the peace/war issues from its formative stages to the present—has never been able to reach an agreed-upon position on how individual Christians or how churches should respond to the actuality of war or the question of military participation.

(3) The WCC staff—though at times given specific directives to pursue the theological study of peace and war in vital fashion—has (with notable exceptions in 1968 and 1971-1973) generally given this low priority.

(4) Since the Fourth Assembly at Uppsala (1968)—though the real impetus came from the controversial Program to Combat Racism—there has been much greater interest among ecumenical circles on the issues of violence and nonviolence.

(5) Whereas under the rubric of the "responsible society"—though this was never given full-scale theological development as a system of social ethics—the dominant ecumenical ethos was some variation of the "just war" which had the essential thrust of preserving a stable political order, the focus of ecumenical attention has now shifted to the "just revolution" with its aim of liberating oppressed peoples.

(6) It is possible—though it would be regrettable for several reasons—that the concerns of the Historic Peace Churches which were once given only passing attention because of the dominance of the "responsible society" concept, will in the future be neglected once again because of the emphasis now placed on justice and autonomy for oppressed minorities.

After all of the words spoken and all of the ink spilled, the call of the Oxford Conference of 1937—forty years ago—remains appropriate as it addressed the variance of views on the subject of war and peace:

> [The church] . . . cannot rest in permanent acquiescence in the continuance of these differences but should do all that is possible to promote the study of the problem by people of different views meeting together to learn from one another as they seek to understand the purpose of God as revealed in Jesus Christ.[28]

1. Principles of Christian Peace and Patriotism — Historic Peace Churches (Newton, Kansas, October 31-November 2, 1935)

Brethren, Friends, and Mennonites had met six times between 1922 and 1931 in "Conferences of Pacifist Churches" initiated by Friend Wilbur K. Thomas. The Newton meeting, called by Mennonite H. P. Krehbiel, was the first to use the phrase "Historic Peace Churches" which has since found wide acceptance. It was likely coined for this conference because of Mennonite discomfort with the liberal theological connotation of "pacifist."

Besides the following statement, agreed upon by the fifty-seven delegates and twenty-four visitors in the three-day meeting, the conference set up a "Continuation Committee" with two members from each of the peace groups. The committee was to foster peace education and discussion and to coordinate their own peace activities. One of the early joint efforts was a message, which received fairly wide attention, to the Methodist General Conference held in June 1936. More significant were the testimonies to government made by representatives from the three churches which paved the way for cooperation during World War II. The National Service Board for Religious Objectors and the Civilian Public Service camps for conscientious objectors to war both emerged from this background.

In historical perspective, the separate histories and variant theological positions of the three churches have sometimes caused distance if not strain. The threats of world war seen clearly by the participants in the Newton conference and the later actuality of conflict brought the groups together in common tasks and Christian fellowship.

Principles of Christian Peace and Patriotism With Scriptural Basis

STATEMENT OF POSITION

We, Friends, Brethren, and Mennonites, assembled in the Conference of the Historic Peace Churches at Newton, Kansas, October 31 to November 2, 1935, remembering in gratitude to God the historic war testimony of our churches, desire, in absolute renunciation of war for the wholehearted practice of peace and love, to state the basis of our common position.

1. Our peace principles are rooted in Christ and his word.

2. Through Jesus Christ, who lived among men as the incarnation of the God of love, we become partakers of the spirit and character of our Lord, and thereby are constrained to love all men, even our enemies.

3. Christ has led us to see the value of human life and personalities, and the possibilities in all men, who by spiritual rebirth from above may become sons of God.

4. The spirit of sacrificial service, love, and goodwill promotes the highest well-being and development of men and society, whereas the spirit of hatred, ill will, and fear destroys, as has been demonstrated repeatedly in human experience.

5. Since good alone can overcome evil, the use of violence must be abandoned.

6. War is sin. It is the complete denial of the Christian spirit of love and all that Christ stands for. It is wrong in spirit and method, and destructive in results. Therefore, we cannot support or engage in any war or conflict between nations, classes, or groups.

7. Our supreme allegiance is to God. We cannot violate it by a lesser loyalty, but we are determined to follow Christ in all things. In this determination we believe we are serving the interests of our country, and are truly loyal to our nation.

8. Under God we commit ourselves to set forth in the true way of life this statement of position and assume the obligations and sacrifices attending its practice.

OUR CONCEPT OF PATRIOTISM

As members of the Historic Peace Churches we love our country and sincerely work for its highest welfare. True love for our country does not mean a hatred of others. It is our conviction that only the application of the principles of peace, love, justice, liberty, and international goodwill will make for the highest welfare of our country; and the highest welfare of our country must harmonize with the highest welfare of humanity everywhere. Our faith is in security through love, protection through goodwill; and for such we are willing to make the necessary sacrifice. We are opposed to war as a method of settling disputes because it is unchristian, destructive of our highest values and sows the seed of future wars. We feel that we are true patriots because we build upon the eternal principles of right which are the only foundation of stable government in our world community. [The scriptural basis is omitted.]

2. World Conference on Church, Community and State (Oxford, United Kingdom, July 12-16, 1937)

It has been said that the statements on Christianity and war made at the Oxford Conference have not been surpassed in their theological perception and literary clarity. The finding of the conference that there existed no unified position on the question of the Christian's participation in military service was accurate at that time and, unfortunately, remains true today. Nevertheless, it marks the first time that Christian pacifism was acknowledged as a legitimate position.

The conference was held in an era of totalitarian threat and increasing secularism. Churches were under mounting pressure to shape their witness to the needs of politics; especially in Germany the linking of nationhood and soil was fostered by the Nazi government and accepted by a large number of Christians in the so-called German-Christian movement. Representatives of the German Evangelical Church were denied state permission to attend the Oxford Conference. The planners of the conference, led by J. H. Oldham, wished to address these tensions directly by focusing the delegates' attention on the theme, "Church, Community and State."

With this background, the slogan which emerged from the conference—"Let the Church Be the Church"—was no antiquarian and narrow appeal to ecclesiastical busyness. Rather it was a clear call to Christians to take seriously the foundation of the church upon the lordship of Christ and to draw the practical implications for action from this basis. In the words of the message of the conference,

> The first duty of the church, and its greatest service to the world, is that it be in very deed the church—confessing the true faith, committed to the fulfillment of the will of Christ, its only Lord, and united in him in a fellowship of love and service.

In the message, the problem of war was addressed squarely: "The universal church . . . must pronounce a condemnation of war unqualified and unrestricted. War can occur only as a fruit and manifestation of sin." If, notwithstanding, war were to break out, "then preeminently the church, still united as the one body of Christ, though the nations wherein it is planted fight one another . . . " must retain unbroken its fellowship of prayer. To a surprising degree this did happen during World War II. The organizational form of the ecumenical movement, the World Council of Churches in Process of Formation, was set up soon after the Oxford Conference. It provided a way for many Christians to keep in touch despite the war; moreover, it played a decisive role in reestablishing warm relationships immediately after the war among citizens of nations which had been wartime enemies.

World Conference on Church, Community and State
Oxford, United Kingdom, July 12-26, 1937

Report of the Section on the Universal Church and the World of Nations

7. THE CHURCH AND WAR

We approach this part of our subject with a profound sense of its urgency and of the inadequacy of the best that we can say. We know that multitudes are oppressed by the actual menace of war. While we may seek to influence actions which may avert the immediate danger, our main task is to probe the underlying sources of the evil and point to the ultimate remedy.

Here again our starting point is the universal fellowship of Christians, the *una sancta*. All Christians acknowledge one Lord, whose claim upon them is such as to transcend all other loyalties. Here is the first obligation of the church, to be in living fact the church, a society with a unity so deep as to be indestructible by earthly divisions of race or nation or class.

Wars, the occasions of war, and all situations which conceal the fact of conflict under the guise of outward peace, are marks of a world to which the church is charged to proclaim the gospel of redemption. War involves compulsory enmity, diabolical outrage against human personality, and a wanton distortion of the truth. War is a particular demonstration of the power of sin in this world and a defiance of the righteousness of God as revealed in Jesus Christ and him crucified. No justification of war must be allowed to conceal or minimize this fact.

In all situations the Christian has to bear in mind both the absolute command, "Thou shalt love thy neighbor as thyself," and the obligation to do what most nearly corresponds to that command in the circumstances confronting him. His action may be but a poor expression of perfect love; the man is caught in a sinful situation, to the evil of which he may have contributed much or little. The best that is possible falls far "short of the glory of God" and is, in that sense, sinful; each man must bear his share of the corporate sin which has rendered impossible any better course; and we all have to confess that "our righteousnesses are as filthy rags." Yet to do what appears as relatively best is an absolute duty before God, and to fail in this is to incur positive guilt.

The search for the will of God is a matter of agonizing perplexity for the Christian whose country is involved in war. We have to recognize two widely divergent views regarding war, along with several that are intermediate. One view hopes for the elimination of war by the power of God working in history through the religious and moral enlightenment of men and the exercise of their free wills; the other view regards man as so bound in the necessities of a sinful world that war will be eliminated only as a consequence of the return of Christ in glory.

In practice this divergence issues in three main positions which are sincerely and conscientiously held by Christians:

(1) Some believe that war, especially in its modern form, is always sin, being a denial of the nature of God as love, of the redemptive way of the cross, and of the community of the Holy Spirit; that war is always ultimately destructive in its effects, and ends in futility by corrupting even the noblest purpose for which it is waged; and that the church will become a creative, regenerative and reconciling instrument for the healing of the nations only as it renounces war absolutely. They are therefore constrained to refuse to take part in war themselves, to plead among their fellows for a similar repudiation of war in favor of a better way, and to replace military force by methods of active peacemaking.

(2) Some would participate only in "just wars." Here there are at least two points of view, depending upon the definition of "just war." The first view holds that Christians should participate only in such wars as are justifiable on the basis of international law. They believe that in a sinful world the state has the duty, under God, to use force when law and order are threatened. Wars against transgressors of international agreements and pacts are comparable with police measures and Christians are obliged to participate in them. But if the state requires its citizens to participate in wars which cannot be thus justified, they believe that Christians should refuse, for the state has no right to force its citizens to take part in sinful actions. Many would add that no war should be regarded as "just" if the government concerned fails to submit the subject of dispute or *casus belli* to arbitration, conciliation or judgment of an international authority.

Those who hold the second view would regard a "just war" as one waged to vindicate what they believe to be an essential Christian principle: to defend the victims of wanton aggression or to secure freedom for the oppressed. They would urge that it was a Christian duty, where all other means had failed, to take up arms. In so doing they would look to the verdict of conscience as their ultimate sanction. While recognizing the general importance of supporting civil or international order, the maintenance of such order in the present imperfect state of society cannot be a final obligation. The Christian, though he must be willing to accept martyrdom for himself, cannot expose others to it by refusing to fight for them.

(3) Some, while also stressing the Christian obligation to work for peace and mutual understanding among the nations, hold nevertheless that no such effort can end war in this world. Moreover, while recognizing that political authority is frequently administered in a selfish and immoral way, they nevertheless believe that the state is the agent divinely appointed to preserve a nation from the detrimental effects of anarchic and criminal tendencies among its members, and to maintain its existence against the aggression of its neighbors. It is therefore a Christian's duty to obey the political authority as far as possible and to refrain from everything that is apt to weaken it. This means that normally a Christian must take up arms for his country. Only when he is absolutely certain that his country is fighting for a wrong cause—for example, in case of unjustifiable war of aggression—has the ordinary citizen a right to refuse military service.

Of those who hold this view, some would admit that individuals may be called directly by God to refuse categorically to take part in any war and so draw attention to the perverted nature of a world in which wars are possible. In either case the individual must recognize in principle the significance of the state and be willing to accept punishment by the authorities for violating the national law.

We do not affirm that any one of these positions can be held to represent the only possible Christian attitude. The church must insist that the perplexity itself is a sign of the sin in which its members are implicated. It cannot rest in permanent acquiescence in the continuance of these differences but should do all that is possible to promote the study of the problem by people of different views meeting together to learn from one another as they seek to understand the purpose of God as revealed in Jesus Christ. Recognizing that its members are also called to live within the secular state or nation and that in the event of war a conflict of duties is inevitable, it should help them discover God's will, should honor their conscientious decisions, whether they are led to participate in or to abstain from war, and maintain with both alike the full fellowship of the body of

Christ. It should call them to repent and to seek together that deliverance from the entangling evil which can be found in Christ alone.

The church must call its members to confess their share in the common guilt of mankind for the continuance of war and the spirit of war among the nations. Notwithstanding the notable efforts for peace which have been made within the church, clergy and laity alike have not done what they ought to have done to remove the causes of war by raising their voices against attitudes and policies making for war, and have not proclaimed with boldness the word of truth in time of war. Moreover, they have often been guilty of greed, selfishness, distrust, and pride of race and nation, thus contributing to the embittering of relations among the nations. At the same time, the church must call its members to give "diligence to keep the unity of the Spirit in the bond of peace." Church members should earnestly strive to remove in their own lives every attitude and practice deriving from political, social and racial differences which are the seeds of war, and should seek the fruit of the Spirit, "love, joy, peace, long-suffering, kindness, goodness, faithfulness, meekness, self-control."

The church should remind its members that the principle of the unconditional supremacy of the state or nation, advanced either in time of peace or of war, is incompatible with the church's faith in Jesus Christ as its only Lord and is therefore unacceptable as the final norm of judgment or action. It is the church's duty to serve the nation in which it is placed, but the greatest service which it can render is to remain steadfast and loyal to its Lord and to test rigorously all claims of national interest by his gospel.

The church, confessing its faith in redemption through Jesus Christ, sees in every man a "brother for whom Christ died." In time of war, as in time of peace, it should pray not only for the nation in which God has placed it, but also for the enemies of that nation. If Christians in warring nations pray according to the pattern of prayer given by their Lord, they will not be "praying against" one another. The church should witness in word, in sacramental life and in action to the reality of the kingdom of God which transcends the world of nations. It should proclaim and obey the commandment of the Lord, "Love your enemies."

3. The First Assembly of the World Council of Churches Amsterdam, The Netherlands, August 22—September 4, 1948)

The coming of World War II postponed the foundational assembly of the World Council of Churches until 1948. At that time 147 churches became members of the Council, representing some of the ancient communions—Coptic, Orthodox, Syrian, some of the largest—Orthodox, Anglican, Presbyterian, Lutheran, and some of the youngest—daughter churches of Anglo-Saxon missionary concern.

The Historic Peace Churches were represented, but not in totality. The Church of the Brethren was a charter member, as were the German Mennonites and three of the American bodies of the Society of Friends.

The slogan emerging from this inaugural conference was: "We intend to stay together." Added to the long-standing churchly and doctrinal questions which had caused tension were the post-war political strains resulting from the sharpened East-West conflict. This was dramatized by the personal confrontation of John Foster Dulles and J. L. Hromadka.

In the following statement which deals with the problem of war, the criticism pronounced by Oxford was heightened by the phrase, "War is contrary to the will of God." Having made such a sweeping claim, the conference delegates found themselves in a "trilemma," reminiscent of but not identical with the Oxford determination. The three positions on war blocked out could be classed as (1) an unjust necessity; (2) a lawful duty; (3) an impossibility for Christians. Confessing their "deep sense of perplexity," the conference members urged "upon all Christians the duty of wrestling continuously with the difficulties." A special call was issued to theologians to "consider the theological problems involved."

The conference message reported that, so soon after the end of World War II, there still "hangs the peril [over all mankind] of total war." They confessed that they had at times "put other loyalties before loyalty to Christ, confused the gospel with our own economic or national or racial interests, and feared war more than we have hated it." Yet, there was a sense of joy in the accomplishment of forming an ecumenical body despite the host of unresolved issues.

The First Assembly of the World Council of Churches
Amsterdam, The Netherlands, August 22—September 4, 1948

Report of Section IV
The Church and the International Disorder

The World Council of Churches is met in its first Assembly at a time of critical international strain. The hopes of the recent war years and the apparent dawn of peace have been dashed. No adequate system for effecting peaceful change has been established, despite the earnest desire of millions. In numerous countries, human rights are being trampled under foot and liberty denied by political or economic systems. Exhaustion and disillusionment have combined with spiritual apathy to produce a moral vacuum which will be filled, either by Christian faith or by despair or even hatred. Men are asking in fear and dismay what the future holds.

The churches bear witness to all mankind that the world is in God's hands. His purpose may be thwarted and delayed, but it cannot be finally frustrated. This is the meaning of history which forbids despair or surrender to the fascinating belief in power as a solvent of human trouble.

War, being a consequence of the disregard of God, is not inevitable if man will turn to Him in repentance and obey His law. There is, then, no irresistible tide that is carrying man to destruction. Nothing is impossible with God.

While we know that wars sometimes arise from immediate causes which Christians seem unable to influence, we need not work blindly or alone. We are laborers together with God, Who in Christ has given us the way of overcoming demonic forces in history. Through the churches, working together under His power, a fellowship is being developed which rises above those barriers of race, colour, class, and nation that now set men against each other in conflict.

Every person has a place in the Divine purpose. Created by God in His image, the object of His redeeming love in Christ, he must be free to respond to God's calling. God is not indifferent to misery or deaf to human prayer and aspiration. By accepting His Gospel, men will find forgiveness for all their sins and receive power to transform their relations with their fellowmen.

Herein lies our hope and the ground of all our striving. It is required of us that we be faithful and obedient. The event is with God. Thus every man may serve the cause of peace, confident that—no matter what happens—he is neither lost nor futile, for the Lord God Omnipotent reigneth.

In this confidence we are one in proclaiming to all mankind:

I. *War is contrary to the will of God.*

War as a method of settling disputes is incompatible with the teaching and example of our Lord Jesus Christ. The part which war plays in our present international life is a sin against God and a degradation of man. We recognize that the problem of war raises especially acute issues for Christians today. Warfare has greatly changed. War is now total and every man and woman is called for mobilization in war service. Moreover, the immense use of air forces and the discovery of atomic and other new weapons render widespread and indiscriminate destruction inherent in the whole conduct of modern war in a sense never experienced in past conflicts. In these circumstances the tradition of a just war, requiring a just cause and the use of just means, is now challenged. Law may require the sanction of force, but when war breaks out, force is used on a scale which tends to destroy the basis on which law exists.

Therefore the inescapable question arises—Can war now be an act of Justice? We cannot answer this question unanimously, but three broad positions are maintained:

(1) There are those who hold that, even though entering a war may be a Christian's duty in particular circumstances, modern warfare, with its mass destruction, can never be an act of justice.

(2) In the absence of impartial supranational institutions, there are those who hold that military action is the ultimate sanction of the rule of law, and that citizens must be distinctly taught that it is their duty to defend the law by force if necessary.

(3) Others, again, refuse military service of all kinds, convinced that an absolute witness against war and for peace is for them the will of God and they desire that the Church should speak to the same effect.

We must frankly acknowledge our deep sense of perplexity in face of these conflicting opinions, and urge upon all Christians the duty of wrestling continuously with the difficulties they raise and praying humbly for God's guidance. We believe that there is a special call to theologians to consider the theological problems involved. In the meantime, the churches must continue to hold within their full fellowship all who sincerely profess such viewpoints as those set out above and are prepared to submit themselves to the will of God in the light of such guidance as may be vouchsafed to them.

On certain points of principle all are agreed. In the absence of any impartial agency for upholding justice, nations have gone to war in the belief that they were doing so. We hold that in international as in national life justice must be upheld. Nations must suppress their desire to save "face." This derives from pride, as unworthy as it is dangerous. The churches, for their part, have the duty of declaring those moral principles which obedience to God requires in war as in peace. They must not allow their spiritual and moral resources to be used by the state in war or in peace as a means of propagating an ideology or supporting a cause in which they cannot wholeheartedly concur. They must teach the duty of love and prayer for the enemy in time of war and of reconciliation between victor and vanquished after the war.

The churches must also attack the causes of war by promoting peaceful change and the pursuit of justice. They must stand for the maintenance of good faith and the honouring of the pledged word; resist the pretensions of imperialist power; promote the multilateral reduction of armaments; and combat indifference and despair in the face of the futility of war; they must point Christians to that spiritual resistance which grows from settled convictions widely held, themselves a powerful deterrent to war. A moral vacuum inevitably invites an aggressor.

We call upon the governments of those countries which were victors in the second world war to hasten the making of just peace treaties with defeated nations, allowing them to rebuild their political and economic systems for peaceable purposes; promptly to return prisoners of war to their homes; and to bring purges and trials for war crimes to a rapid end.

II. *Peace requires an attack on the causes of conflict between the powers.*

The greatest threat to peace today comes from the division of the world into mutually suspicious and antagonistic blocs. This threat is all the greater because national tensions are confused by the clash of economic and political systems. Christianity cannot be equated with any of these. There are elements in all systems which we must condemn when they contravene the First Commandment, infringe basic human rights, and contain a potential threat to peace. We denounce all forms of tyranny, economic, political or religious, which deny liberty to men. We utterly oppose totalitarianism, whenever found, in which a state arrogates to itself the right of determining men's thoughts and actions instead of recognising the right of each individual to do God's will according to his conscience. In the same way we oppose any church which seeks to use the power of the state to enforce religious conformity. We resist all endeavours to spread a system of thought or of economics by unscrupulous intolerance, suppression or persecution.

Similarly, we oppose aggressive imperialism—political, economic or cultural—whereby a nation seeks to use other nations or peoples for its own ends. We therefore protest against the exploitation of non-self-governing peoples for selfish purposes; the retarding of their progress towards self-government; and discrimination or segregation on the ground of race or colour.

A positive attempt must be made to ensure that competing economic systems such as communism, socialism or free enterprise may co-exist without leading to war. No nation has the moral right to determine its own economic policy without consideration for the economic needs of other nations and without recourse to international consultation. The churches have a responsibility to educate men to rise above the limitations of their national outlook and to view economic and political differences in the light of the Christian objective of ensuring to every man freedom from all economic or political bondage. Such systems exist to serve men, not men to serve them.

Christians must examine critically all actions of governments which increase tension or arouse misunderstanding, even unintentionally. Above all, they should withstand everything in the press, radio or school which inflames hatred or hostility between nations.

III. *The nations of the world must acknowledge the rule of the law.*

Our Lord Jesus Christ taught that God, the Father of all, is Sovereign, We affirm, therefore, that no state may claim absolute sovereignty, or make laws without regard to the commandments of God and the welfare of mankind. It must accept its responsibility under the governance of God, and its subordination to law, within the society of nations.

As within the nations, so in their relations with one another, the authority of law must be recognized and established. International law clearly requires international institutions for its effectiveness. These institutions, if they are to command respect and obedience of nations, must come to grips with international problems on their own merits and not primarily in the light of national interests.

Such institutions are urgently needed today. History never stands still. New forces constantly emerge. Sporadic conflicts East and West, the attainment of independence by large masses of people, the apparent decline of European predominance, the clash of competing systems in Asia, all point to the inevitability of change. The United Nations was designed to assist in the settlement of difficulties and to promote friendly relations among the nations. Its purposes in these respects deserve the support of Christians. But unless the nations surrender a greater measure of national sovereignty in the interest of the common good, they will be tempted to have recourse to war in order to enforce their claims.

The churches have an important part in laying that common foundation of moral conviction without which any system of law will break down. While pressing for more comprehensive and authoritative world organisation, they should at present support immediate practical steps for fostering mutual understanding and goodwill among the nations, for promoting respect for international law and the establishment of the international institutions which are now possible. They should also support every effort to deal on a universal basis with the many specific questions of international concern which face mankind today, such as the use of atomic power, the multilateral reduction of armaments, and the provision of health services and food for all men. They should endeavour to secure that the United Nations be further developed to serve such purposes. They should insist that the domestic laws of each country conform to the principles of progressive international law, and they gratefully recognise that recent demands to formulate principles of human rights reflect a new sense of international responsibility for the rights and freedoms of all men.

IV. *The observance of Human Rights and Fundamental Freedoms should be encouraged by domestic and international action.*

The church has always demanded freedom to obey God rather than men. We affirm that all men are equal in the sight of God and that the rights of men derive directly from their status as the children of God. It is presumptuous for the state to assume that it can grant or deny fundamental rights. It is for the state to embody these rights in its own legal system and to ensure their observance in practice. We believe, however, that there are no rights without duties. Man's freedom has its counterpart in man's responsibility, and each person has a responsibility towards his fellows in community.

We are profoundly concerned by evidence from many parts of the world of flagrant violations of human rights. Both individuals and groups are subjected to persecution and discrimination on grounds of race, colour, religion, culture or political conviction. Against such actions, whether of governments, officials, or the general public, the churches must take a firm and vigorous stand, through local action, in cooperation with churches in other lands, and through international institutions of legal order. They must work for an ever wider and deeper understanding of what are the essential human rights if men are to be free to do the will of God.

At the present time, churches should support every endeavour to secure within an international bill of rights adequate safeguards for freedom of religion and conscience, including rights of all men to hold and change their faith, to express it in worship and practice, to teach and persuade others, and to decide on the religious education of their children. They should press for freedom of speech and expression, of association and assembly, the rights of the family, of freedom from arbitrary arrest, as well as all those other rights which the true freedom of men requires. In the domestic and in the international sphere, they should support a fuller realisation of human freedom through social legislation. They should protest against the expulsion of minorities. With all the resources at their disposal they should oppose enforced segregation on grounds of race or colour, working for the progressive recognition and application of this principle in every country. Above all it is essential that the churches observe these fundamental rights in their own membership and life, thus giving to others an example of what freedom means in practice.

V. *The churches and all Christian people have obligations in the face of international disorder.*

The churches are guilty both of indifference and of failure. While they desire more open honesty and less self-righteousness among governments and all concerned with international relations, they cannot cast a first stone or excuse themselves for complacency.

Therefore, it is the duty of the Christian to pray for all men, especially for those in authority; to combat both hatred and resignation in regard to war; to support negotiation rather than primary reliance upon arms as an instrument of policy; and to sustain such national policies as in his judgment best reflect Christian principles. He should respond to the demand of the Christian vocation upon his life as a citizen, make sacrifices for the hungry and homeless, and, above all, win men for Christ, and thus enlarge the bounds of the supranational fellowship.

Within this fellowship, each church must eliminate discrimination among its members on unworthy grounds. It must educate them to view international policies in the light of their faith. Its witness to the moral law must be a warning to the state against unnecessary concession to expediency, and it must support leaders and those in authority in their endeavor to build the sure foundations of just world order.

The establishment of the World Council of Churches can be made of great moment for the life of the nations. It is a living expression of this fellowship, transcending race and nation, class and culture, knit together in faith, service and understanding. Its aim will be to hasten international reconciliation through its own members and through the cooperation of all Christian churches and of all men of goodwill. It will strive to see international differences in the light of God's design, remembering that normally there are Christians on both sides of every frontier. It should not weary in the effort to state the Christian understanding of the will of God and to promote its application to national and international policy.

For these purposes special agencies are needed. To this end the World Council of Churches and the International Missionary Council have formed the Commission of the Churches on International Affairs. The Assembly commends it to the interest and prayers of all Christian people.

Great are the tasks and fateful the responsibilities laid on Christians today. In our own strength we can do nothing; but our hope is in Christ and in the coming of His Kingdom. With Him is the victory and in Him we trust. We pray that we may be strengthened by the power of His might and used by Him for accomplishing His design among the nations. For He is the Prince of Peace and the Risen and Living Head of the Church.

4. War Is Contrary to the Will of God—Historic Peace Churches and the International Fellowship of Reconciliation (Zeist, The Netherlands, July 12, 1951)

Upon the initiative of M. R. Zigler, director of Brethren Service programs in Europe after 1948 and representative to the World Council of Churches, there was established in May 1949 a continuation committee of the Historic Peace Churches in Europe. Those participating in a series of meetings called by this committee came from American relief agencies— the American Friends Service Committee, the Brethren Service Commission, and the Mennonite Central Committee—and from European churches—the Society of Friends in Great Britain and continental Mennonites. In addition, members of the International Fellowship of Reconciliation were invited to take part regularly.

At the first meeting it was agreed to hold subsequent conferences and to study several points: (1) how to engage in discussions with pacifists from other church bodies; (2) how to make an approach on peace to the World Council of Churches; and (3) how to approach governmental and intergovernmental leaders in the interests of peace. Action on the second point intensified after October, 1949 when W. A. Visser 't Hooft, general secretary of the WCC, invited the peace churches and the IFOR to produce statements on the Christian basis of pacifism. Each of the groups developed a draft, copies of which were circulated fairly widely. Thus, although the papers were not formally approved by church assemblies, care was taken to "ensure the representative character of the statements accepted."

After careful appraisal, it was decided at a meeting held in England in April 1951, that the papers should stand separately when published but be accompanied by an introduction written jointly. This was because "the four statements written in different idioms and reflecting different traditions" could best be considered individually by readers. The final document was approved in July 1951, and was published shortly thereafter. It was also published in German translation for wider circulation. The Quaker statement was published separately in Great Britain by the Friends Peace Committee.

War Is Contrary to the Will of God

Introduction

Section IV of the report of the World Assembly of the Churches (Amsterdam, 1948) contained a sub-section headed "War is contrary to the Will of God." It acknowledges a deep sense of perplexity in face of the conflicting opinions expressed on this subject and urges on all Christians the duty of wrestling continuously with the difficulties they raise and of praying humbly for God's guidance. It adds, "We believe there is a special call to theologians to consider the theological problems involved."

The subject of peace and war will certainly be raised again, both in its theoretical and in its practical aspects, at the next Assembly of the Churches, to be held at Evanston, U.S.A. It is hoped that the response now made by the three Peace Churches and The International Fellowship of Reconciliation will serve to draw fresh attention to the whole question and to the ethical and theological issues involved. For this reason it is further hoped that the four documents, together with this introduction, will be printed in full for consideration by both pacifists and non-pacifists throughout the Ecumenical Movement and used as preliminary study material. To the following jointly agreed paragraphs, the four separate statements are appended.

We believe that God is seeking to express his will in relation to international affairs, now, through the Churches and in each individual Christian.

The will of God was made known in the life of Christ, beginning at Bethlehem and reaching its fullest significance on Calvary. His teaching and example provide clear guidance for refusal to participate in war, even if ordered by governments or justified by jurists or theologians. God continues to speak, giving insight into his purposes and methods, by his grace, and in virtue of the light of Christ shining in man's heart.

We are convinced that Christian pacifism and non-resistance is the true interpretation of the teaching and example of Jesus as recorded in the New Testament. We believe that this teaching is intended as a guide for his disciples here and now, and that the Christian is called to follow Christ along the same path of forgiveness and redemptive love.

We believe that this is the only principle consistent with the Gospel and we desire to lay it upon the consciences of all.

From the human standpoint this may appear to lead only to failure and extinction, but in the sight of God and in the conscience of man, the immediate question is not so much the results of the action as the character of the action itself. Good aims cannot be achieved by bad means. The Cross of Christ was his triumph. The way of the Cross must be trodden in faith and confidence, and through the power of Christ it becomes for us the road to victory.

In order to bring God to men, and men to God, Christ, as a priest, made himself one with man, with both victim and oppressor. He calls all his disciples to adopt the same attitude, and in so doing to realise the priesthood of all believers. Christian pacifism is therefore not a calling only for the select few, either clerics or laymen.

No man can separate himself wholly from the action of the rest of mankind but must share its suffering and guilt. None the less, the Christian is directly responsible to God, and has not only the right, but the duty, to stand out if necessary against the state, and against the popular will, and also against any argument justifying war on grounds of policy, expediency, or military necessity, whatever the cost.

We do not believe that Christ who is the way, will leave his disciples with a choice only between two courses both wrong. Unless Christians take the lead in rejecting both wrong alternatives, mankind will not be able to see and accept God's guidance as to the next right step.

The next right step may involve grave risks. It may well place in jeopardy the lives and liberties of our families and our neighbours, as well as the cultural heritage and moral values of our civilization. It may even leave our children and those who look to us for protection open to death or moral perversion. It can, however, never be the duty of a follower of Christ to take the lives of some of God's children in the hope of protecting others. Christ gave us clear warning that the cost of following him is indeed heavy and may even include a sacrifice of those nearest and dearest to us.

To the Church, to the individual Christian, Christ's call is to overcome evil with good. In the end, this will have more effect than any kind of violence. Throughout the New Testament the duty to resist evil in the moral and spiritual sense is proclaimed, and the Christian is enabled continually to rediscover and to reconstruct in modern terms, and in concrete situations, the strategy and tactics of our Christian warfare against evil.

The fact that we speak with assurance does not imply that we assume the right to elevate ourselves above others who in many respects may live nearer to God than we. We are painfully aware of our personal unfaithfulness and weakness in both negative and positive aspects of pacifism. We are convinced, however, that God has given light as to his will in regard to war—light which has led our Churches, which has been known in our own experience, and must be passed on. We are but a small number and cannot expect to reach the ears and hearts of all mankind. We therefore appeal to all other Christians, especially to the Churches, fearlessly to preach the gospel of peace and goodwill to all men, and energetically to exercise the ministry of reconciliation of man to God, and man to man, entrusted to all the followers of Jesus Christ.

Conference of representatives of the Historic Peace Churches and the International Fellowship of Reconciliation. Heerewegen, Zeist, Netherlands.

(signed) Robert Zigler
Chairman.

Finally adopted July 12, 1951.

Mennonite Church

Basic Central Truths

The peace principles of the Mennonite Church, including its historic four century old witness against all war, are an integral part of the way of Christian discipleship which it believes the Lordship of Christ requires. They derive directly from a Christian faith which holds as central truths:

(1) That one is our Master, even Christ, to whom alone supreme loyalty and obedience is due, who is our only Saviour and Lord. Christ and Christ alone is the basis for our faith and commitment to the non-resistant way of life, "For other foundation can no one lay than that is laid, which is Jesus Christ."

(2) That by the atoning and renewing grace of God which makes us new creatures in Christ, and alone thereby, we can, through the power of the indwelling Spirit, live the life of holy obedience and discipleship to which all the children of God are called, for his grace does forgive and heal the penitent sinner.

(3) That redeeming love is at the heart of the Gospel, coming from God and into us to constrain us to love him and our neighbour, and that such love must henceforth be at the center of every thought and act.

(4) That the life of love and peace is God's plan for the individual and the race, and that therefore discipleship means the renunciation of hatred, strife, and violence in all human relations, both individual and social.

(5) That Christ has established in the church which is his body, a universal community and brotherhood of the redeemed, within which the fullness of Christ's reign must be practiced and from which must go out into all human society the saving and healing ministry of the Gospel.

Scriptural Basis

Holding firmly to the authority of God's revelation of his nature and will as it is found in the Holy Scriptures both in the spirit, life, and redemptive work of Christ, and in the direct teachings of Jesus and the Apostles, and believing that war is altogether contrary to this revelation, Mennonites hold that all war is sin, as is all manner of carnal strife, and that it is wrong in both spirit and method.

Christ

In the life of Christ who in his incarnation was made in the likeness of man becoming one with man, and who "surely bore our griefs and carried our sorrows," is the full revelation of God's will, beginning at Bethlehem and reaching supreme meaning at Calvary. Integral to this divine-human life of our Lord was his innocent and defenceless enduring of the evil inflicted upon him, his identification of himself in his suffering with both victim and oppressor, thus bearing man's sin in his own body on the tree, and his triumphant victory over sin by this very means. What he taught in the Sermon on the Mount he fulfilled in his life and practice, including the cross. As those who believe in this Christ are united with him, they also will of necessity become identified with him in his way of non-resistant suffering and triumphant overcoming. Christ is the High Priest; his disciples endeavour to realize the priesthood of all believers. In this "way" of Christ, war and its sister evils can have no place.

New Testament Passages

Among the many New Testament passages which directly support the conviction of the sinfulness of war Mennonites point to the following: "Love your enemies"; "Do good to them that hate you"; "Resist not him that is evil"; "My kingdom is not of this world: if my kingdom were of this world, then would my servants fight"; "Put up thy sword into its place; for all they that take the sword shall perish with the sword"; "Dearly beloved, avenge not yourselves"; "If thine enemy hunger, feed him; if he thirst, give him drink; for in so doing thou shalt heap coals of fire on his head"; "Be not overcome of evil, but overcome evil with good"; "The servant of the Lord must not strive; but be gentle to all men"; "The weapons of our warfare are not carnal"; "Christ also suffered for us, leaving us an example, that ye should follow his steps, who did no sin, neither was guile found in his mouth; who, when he was reviled, reviled not again; when he suffered, he threatened not"; "Not rendering evil for evil, or railing for railing; but contrariwise blessing"; "If a man say I love God and hateth his brother, he is a liar . . . and this commandment have we from him, that he who loveth God loveth his brother also."

The Way of the Cross

But over and above these specific words, Mennonites hold that the whole tenor of the Gospel, being redemptive, forbids the destructiveness of war. The very cross of Christ itself, the heart of our faith, the means by which God's love operates redemptively in a world of sinful men, speaks against war, for it stands for the acceptance of unlimited suffering, the utter denial of self, and the complete dedication of life to the ministry of redemption for others. This is the cross which Christ has made our cross, the symbol and method of the Christian way of discipleship, of self-denial, and of suffering love. This is the way which from a human standpoint seems to lead only to failure and extinction but which through Christ has become and remains the road to victory, for the disciples of Christ suffer with him that they may reign with him. "We are accounted as sheep for the slaughter, but in all these things we are more than conquerors through him that loved us."

The Old Testament Subordinate to Christ

Believing that the Scriptures of the Old Testament are likewise divine in origin and authoritative in character, Mennonites hold that these Scriptures are a record of the progressive revelation of the nature and will of God, leading to the full and final revelation found in the New Testament. Therefore, Old Testament Scriptures which are sometimes cited in support of Christian participation in war may not be used to contradict clear New Testament teaching, but must be interpreted in the light of the teaching of Christ and the Apostles, for in Christ we find the norm for the whole of Scripture. The national history of Israel as recorded in the Old Testament cannot have normative significance for us, for much in it contradicts Christ. It is significant to note that Israel rejected Christ, at least in part, because he refused the Messiahship in a national and therefore coercive sense.

Added Grounds for Rejection of War

Added grounds for this complete rejection of war, Mennonites believe, are: (1) the impossibility, as demonstrated in human experience, of permanently controlling or limiting the use of large-scale force in human society because of the depth and power of individual and corporate sin; (2) the destructiveness of violence and hatred which, once applied, inevitably begets more of its own kind, and cannot be overcome except by redemptive love; and (3) the treachery of victory which so often betrays the victor into arrogance and oppression of the vanquished, and incapacitates him for that redemptive love which alone will save both groups of sinners in the struggle, the victor and the vanquished.

Not Humanitarianism

Mennonites do not hold that the application of Christian love to evil men will automatically overcome the evil, but consider such love to be primarily a witness to God's grace and love by which alone evil can be overcome. Christian love demonstrated in spirit and action, and applied to the concrete situation, can serve as an instrument to awaken consciousness of sin and a desire for the holy life which the grace of God alone can create. This position is thus necessarily not one of belief in the simple power of man's good will and humane action to transform human nature and thus to make the use of force unnecessary in society; on the contrary, it depends upon the grace and power of God to operate in the hearts of evil men to produce the life of love.

The Way of Discipleship the Way of Victory

Seeing this vision of God's judgment of war and his call to the way of love, a vision which many other Christians also see, Mennonites call upon all Christians to commit themselves to this way in holy discipleship, for they believe that this vision is to be appropriated for the here and now, and is not given merely as a foretaste of the heavenly world to come. When we are united with the suffering Christ, we also know that we are united with him who conquered death. We venture to accept a way of life which may seem hopeless, because of a firm faith in the victory of the Lamb, a faith that is more certain than trust in all the kings of the earth. We are assured that God's ways differ from man's ways; that if we endeavour to maintain ourselves and our communities by the human impulse of self-preservation with means which are not from God, we shall perish. On the other hand, if we are willing to lose our lives in following after Christ we shall find them. Therefore, we do not consider our non-resistant Christianity a faith of despair but a joyful belief in the reality of God's Kingdom, and we forthrightly establish our lives on the power of Christ. There is here no merely negative attitude towards life, but rather a very positive attack on evil, which proceeds from that power and love of Christ which is the means by which human hearts may be redeemed from a life of sin to a life with God. With faith based on the power of the victorious Christ we remain firm in the belief that evil can and will be overcome by good, even when this involves the "foolishness" of suffering and the cross. The Mennonite is convinced that the teachings of Jesus and the power of the Gospel are the solution to the problems of sin in man and society, but only if applied. He declares that the reason society is still in its broken state is that professing Christendom has either not comprehended or not obeyed these teachings.

A Realistic Action Program

Mennonites hold that true social construction and reconstruction is the result of the redemptive and creative forces of divine love operating through regenerated human nature and its expression in Christian love. Mere operation in theological dialectics with the problem of the redemption of human society is completely illusory without the personal application of the redemptive forces of the Gospel by individual Christians and groups in their own behaviour. The Christian pacifist comes down out of the clouds of theological and ethical theory into the real world of sin and need and there applies the Gospel in its fullest extent, uncompromisingly, and in and through his own life. This calls for an action program of the highest potential and requiring the full unfolding of divine grace and power through man, but it is the only hope of the world. At times it may seem that military and political programs are the most significant, but history has often proved otherwise. An illustration of this is the achievement of early (and pacifist) Christianity in the days of the Roman Empire whose very genius was law and order based on military prowess and political administration. In the light of the ultimate complete disintegration of this ancient great military world, while Christianity conquered, the words of a modern scholar seem fully warranted: "The more one thinks about the early Christian communities and the Roman Empire, the more one is convinced that the only permanent piece of social building was that carried on by the Christian community in the face of the Roman Empire" (Arthur E. Holt).

Unrestricted Obedience to Christ

The heart of our position is that once having been laid hold of by God through Christ in a regenerating experience, the Christian cannot withhold his unrestricted obedience, but must follow Christ in all things regardless of consequences. He cannot buy "cheap grace," as a recent writer calls it, but he must pay the price of complete discipleship, without calculating in advance what this may mean for his behaviour and for society. He cannot withhold his own obedience merely because many of his fellow Christians do not obey, nor can he determine his response to Christ's commands by an estimate in advance as to their practicability. He considers the commands of Christ and the principles of the Gospel not to be mere counsels to be accepted or rejected as may seem good at the moment, but rather imperatives which must be followed to the end. Once the premise is accepted that Christ speaks with authority from heaven, only one thing remains, that is to obey his command.

Means Must Conform to Ends

If in testifying to this position we must pronounce judgment, it must, in the first place, be directed against the sinful inclination and the will to maintain self at all costs. It is this selfish attitude which leads to the greatest possible disasters, particularly that of war. We must also pronounce judgment against striving for goals which are good and right but using means which are contradictory to such goals. We submit that there must be absolute conformity between ends and means, and that one of the greatest sins of society is the lack of this consistency. It is a fallacy to believe that good ends can be achieved by bad means. Jesus warned that evil cannot be combatted with evil, that it is impossible to cast out the devil by Beelzebub. When Jesus said, "For all they that take the sword shall perish with the sword," he indicated that ultimately the outcome is inevitably determined also by the means employed. History demonstrates the dreadful reality of this axiom. Our modern world, in trying to avoid catastrophe by the employment of all kinds of violence, is forging the arms with which divine and human judgment will be executed.

The Problem of the Use of Force in a Sub-Christian World

It has been charged against this position that it ignores the necessity for the sanction of force in an imperfect and sinful world, and that it is a counsel of perfection totally unrealistic in facing the actual world, but this is not so. Mennonites recognize that in a sub-Christian world order, there is—by the will of God—some place for the use of force for the maintenance of law and order, though never to the extent of taking human life and always under restraints deriving from the higher laws of God and with the awareness of the implicit sinful tendencies of its use. Yet in Christ they see the beginning of a new order, that of the Kingdom of God. The task of the church is to herald and by the grace of God to seek to realize this new order. Being citizens in a sense of both old and new orders, Christians owe obedience and submission to the authorities of the old though within the limits of the principles of the new, but cannot take part in the use of force, a basic method of the old. It is the calling of the Christian rather to operate on the basis of love, the method of the new. If he reverts to the old, he effectually destroys the only hope of the world, for force can never create righteousness or a Christian society; it can only restrain the evil in varying degrees. The dreadful danger is that once the sanctions of force are approved and employed, men come to trust in them and abandon the higher level of action.

Total Discipleship Needed

These declarations of faith and convictions give no blueprint for permanent peace nor do they assume that human endeavour alone can bring about a warless world within history, for only when men come under the Lordship of Christ can they make peace and fulfill the prayer of our Lord, "Thy kingdom come, thy will be done on earth as it is in heaven." They do however require certain positive attitudes, duties, and ministries by Christian disciples toward all men which have far larger scope than only a testimony against war and which call for consistent demonstration of sacrificial Christian love in all relationships. The total demands of this genuine Christian pacifism upon its advocates and practitioners are tremendous, for they are the demands of total love and total discipleship. Mennonites believe however that they by God's grace can be met. If war and its allied evils are not wiped out of human society, it will not be because the Gospel and cross of Jesus Christ could not accomplish it, but either because men reject the Gospel or because those who have taken the name of Christ will not live that Gospel and take up the cross of utter discipleship laid upon them by their Lord. The fact that we seem to speak here with a great measure of assurance, does not mean that we seek to elevate ourselves above others who also call themselves Christian, for we are convinced that they may perhaps in other respects live nearer to God than we and we would not question the sincerity of their desire to follow Christ. But we are convinced that the Christ of nonresistant love confronts us all and that all who claim his name must give their answer.

Appeal to Witness to the Gospel of the Cross

Mennonites humbly confess their inadequacies and failures both in understanding and in following the way of peace set forth in this statement, knowing well that they have come short both in demonstration and proclamation of Christian love and thus also fall under the judgment of God. As they renew their commitment of discipleship and ambassadorship for Christ, they know how much they need God's grace and the help of their brethren in the fellowship of Christ's body in learning and obeying. To the end that the ears and hearts of all mankind may be reached, they appeal to the whole Christian church fearlessly to preach the Gospel of the

Cross and earnestly to exercise the ministry of reconciliation of man to God and man to man entrusted to all the followers of Jesus Christ.

This declaration of faith is submitted in the name of the International Mennonite Peace Committee representing Mennonites of both Europe and North America, particularly those cooperating in the Mennonite Central Committee Peace Section (North America) Akron, Pennsylvania, and the Dutch Mennonite Peace Group (Netherlands) "Heerewegen," Zeist, and affiliated individuals in other countries.

Society of Friends

A Christian Testimony

It is emphatically on Christian grounds that the Religious Society of Friends maintains its historic testimony against all war and its concern for service in the cause of reconciliation and peace-making. The Society of Friends is not content to urge a merely ethical principle of non-violence or to assert only a social and political doctrine of good relations. Friends naturally share with others an abhorrence of the ravages of war, a humane regard for its victims and a longing for the quiet, the order and the constructive cooperation of peace and are willing to work with others for these ends; but they base their pacifist thinking on fundamental conviction that was is wrong in itself and wrong in the sight of God. They certainly desire to apply their pacifism constructively to concrete situations in the service of mankind as well as to remove all occasions of war and in particular to eliminate the economic and political causes of the outbreak of war; but they are clear that their actions in this regard must be an attempt to express love in realistic forms and an expression of a sense of religious responsibility and of a deep reverence for the Will of God as revealed by Jesus Christ.

Taught by the Spirit

Friends believe that their witness and service are a response, however imperfect, to the promptings and movings of the Spirit of God in the hearts of individuals and in the fellowship and communion of groups meeting for worship, prayer and waiting on God. They believe that through a divinely given insight man is made aware of the vital distinction in the sight of God between good and evil, right and wrong; aware that the practical problem of good and evil is inextricably involved in the problem of man's relationship with his brother man; and aware increasingly that the overcoming of evil with good and the establishment of relationships of love and cooperation with his fellow man are possible to him only by the power of God working within him. Friends are persuaded that it is by the grace of God and in virtue of the light of Christ shining in his heart that this power and this insight into God's purpose are open to every man, veiled though his sight may be too often by fear and passion. They are persuaded also that God seeks to accomplish His will in the contemporary world through those who are ready to be led by His Spirit.

The New Testament

The Society has always held that the Christ whose light shines in every man is the Christ of the Gospels. It is convinced that Christian pacifism is the true interpretation of the teaching, experience and example of Jesus Christ as recorded in the New Testament, that pacifism is, indeed, an attempt to translate into modern human terms something of the divine attitude and action toward evil men which are demonstrated in the crucifixion of Jesus Christ. It believes that in Christianity alone, as thus interpreted, is to be found the solution of the moral problem of mankind, a problem presented in acute form in war and in all that war involves.

Competent Christian scholars, for example Harnack, Heering, Macgregor and some members of the Society of Friends, have repeatedly examined all the passages of the New Testament commonly quoted in discussion of the peace and war issue—including those popularly regarded as justifying the use of violence. In the result, it seems clear that the words and spirit of the Gospels fully warrant the statement that war is incompatible with the teaching and example of Jesus Christ. And certainly there is nothing in the New Testament to justify modern warfare. Friends rely, as already said, on Christian perception and conviction and on the authority of the light and law of Christ known within the heart of man, but appeal also to the unmistakable tenor of the New Testament.

The Relevance of Christianity

While abstaining from judgment of those who hold another view, and of course conceding to them the same right and duty of obedience to conscience as they claim for themselves, Friends believe it right to enunciate a general principle which seems to them the only principle consistent with the Gospels, and to lay it on the consciences of all. Friends hold that all physical war, including "cold war," even if ordered by governments or justified by jurists and theologians, is contrary to the Will of God, and that on this ground it is wrong for the Christian to engage in war, or for the

Church to sanction it. The Society of Friends insists that Christians are required to act on the principle that the ethics of Christianity apply now to all the relationships of men, their group and international, as well as their individual relationships. It therefore claims that Christianity is strictly relevant to the political situation of the present time. It maintains that the Christian must not only say, as did the Amsterdam Assembly of the Churches in 1948, that war is contrary to the Will of God, but must accept the practical consequences of this principle, both in refusing arms and in seeking peace through social and political action.

The Cost

But Friends take this position well aware that faithful Christian service of any kind is costing, and that following the way of the Cross rather than that of the world may mean utter destruction for man and state and even for civilisation at the hands of evil men. But in the sight of God and in the conscience of man, the immediate question for the present time is not so much the results of the action, as the character of the action itself. The way of the Cross must be trodden, in faith and in confidence.

Man's Responsibility

Friends agree, of course, that a man is in some measure responsible to his fellow-man for the consequences of his deeds. They are aware also that when he takes part in an activity which is social, or in the case of a mass movement almost instinctive, he can bear but a fraction of the total responsibility for it. They recognise, too, that he cannot in any case separate himself wholly from the action of the rest of mankind but must share its suffering and its guilt. None the less, they believe that he is before all things a being directly responsible to God. With all other Christians, they acknowledge man's over-riding obligation to live by a higher law, known through the grace of God, and recognised inwardly by its own divine authority. They are convinced that under this authority the Christian has not only the right but the duty to stand out if necessary against the state and against the popular will, and also against any argument justifying war on grounds of policy, expedience or military necessity, whatever the cost. Man's continued existence has no meaning except as a continuing and continuous response to the Will of God.

The Claims of the State

The Society maintains, then, that man's primary responsibility to God should never be clouded by the claims of the state and its subordinate loyalties. Remembering that the Roman state killed Paul and many other early Christians, as well as their Master, Friends do not think that the oft-quoted words to the Romans (Rom. 13:1) can be pressed in defence of military service. If they could, they would mean that as Roman soldiers Christians could be required to assist at crucifixions.

Nor can Friends accept the purely vocational view of Christian pacifism, that is the view that it is the religious calling of a select few, whether clerics or laymen, to refrain from warfare, while the rest shall bear arms at the command of the magistrate and with the concurrence of the church.

Friends further decline to allow the issue to be obscured by secular arguments for the maintenance of the law and the defence of the state by force. The euphemism "police action" applied to military operations such as those in Indonesia and Korea, whether by one government or by a union of governments, seems to Friends to cloak an intellectual and moral confusion. The false analogy between soldier and policeman has been too often exposed to require full discussion here. Perhaps it is sufficient to remark that the policeman is required to do no more than bring the individual criminal alive before an impartial court, which will try him by an accepted code of law, first providing him with facilities for defence. The soldier, on the other hand, is required to destroy innocent and guilty alike in the mass and to impose the will of the stronger, too often with small regard even to such international law as exists or to the rights of the case as they might have been seen by a really impartial court. In any case, the justice of the lawcourt, in so far as it is based on force cannot be a substitute for the righteousness of the Kingdom of God.

Friends freely acknowledge the claims of patriotism. The community in which a man is born, properly commands his love and devoted service. But his response must be governed by the dictates of morality and conscience. His finest service is found in seeking for his country the righteousness that exalteth a nation. And for the Christian, the true service of his fellow-man is an expression of his obedience to God.

The Problem of Evil

Some Christians feel that, in a moral as well as in a theological sense, they share the ultimate responsibility for the death of Jesus Christ, and that they are both personally and corporately guilty. But this is a reason for repentance and amendment of life, not an argument for continuance in an evil way. The extreme pessimism of certain theological positions with regard to the evil and sin in which a man is involved is inconsistent with the Christian doctrines of the power, goodness and grace of God and the salvation of man.

Again, some Christians think that evil is inherent in the world and that war, as a part of that evil, is inevitable. This position cannot be accepted as a justification either for doing nothing or for taking part in war. Being a soldier of God's Kingdom of righteousness, the Christian is required to oppose himself to evil, not to surrender to it. He must indeed fight evil wherever it is found, but he must fight this spiritual battle with weapons other than physical. It is a false reading of the New Testament that uses apocalyptic metaphor regarding the fundamental conflict of good and evil to justify physical warfare, as if that could in any sense replace the spiritual struggle and victory to which the Church is called.

Whatever our theory of it, we know that in practice evil lives in the heart and will of man: it lies in his pride, in his perversion of his freedom, and in his denial of his responsibility to God. Evil is not something external to man, such as can be struck and smashed or carted away and burned up. It is within man, and cannot be cast out by inflicting pain or death on his body.

Though the problem of society is not in all respects the same as the problem of the individual, it remains true that moral evil has no existence in a community except as the effect of the evil will of members of the community, and consequently that social evil cannot be resolved by violence. The fact that the violence of war often arises out of the spirit of greed, ambition and lust for power, and that these are sometimes explained by centuries of injustice so that war seems to be the only possible resort for an oppressed people, is itself an argument for the use of moral and spiritual weapons which alone can reach the fundamental evil.

Friends are convinced that the principle of deterence cannot be justified morally and that war preparation to meet the threat of aggression is therefore wrong. The idea that men can be frightened out of their evil ways is not the teaching of the Gospel of love and forgiveness. Still less can resort to war, if the aggression becomes actual, be justified as a Christian response to collective wickedness, for it does not represent the antidote to evil in other men so much as its reflection in ourselves, the response of our own fear and anger in the presence of evil. Weapons and war are therefore not really relevant to the solution of the actual problem of evil.

The "Lesser Evil"

Friends cannot accept the argument that justifies war as "the lesser evil." They do not believe that God requires men to choose between two courses both wrong. They believe that there is a third way more in accord with the will of God, though admittedly men are too often unable to see or to follow it: but unless Christians take the lead in rejecting both wrong alternatives, it is hardly to be expected that man will look for and be able to accept God's guidance as to the next right step.

Nor must it be assumed that war, with its unending heritage of wrong, is the lesser evil. It may be that victory—if it is achieved—means for the victor less suffering than would defeat and occupation; but for the Christian, evil means guilt rather than pain, and to inflict wrong is clearly evil, while to suffer it undeservedly may be a true following of Christ.

Defence

Friends find themselves obliged to deny that the so-called "right of self-defence" against the evil of attack can be a justification for war. They believe that in the light of the Gospel of Christ no such supposed right to defend oneself at the cost of the life of an "enemy" will stand examination. It is one thing for a Christian to surrender his own life, it is quite a different matter to take the life of another man by virtue of a "right" nowhere recognised in the New Testament.

But closely connected in men's minds with this assumed right of self-defence, is the duty, regarded as equally obvious, of defending from destruction the lives and liberties of our families and our neighbours and the cultural heritage and moral values of our civilisation. Friends, however, do not believe that these things can be defended by war: war inevitably involves devastation, both in its course and in its consequences, an immeasurable devastation that not only destroys millions of lives and countless treasures and instruments of civilisation, but also destroys the very moral and spiritual values which war seeks to defend.

Furthermore, Friends believe that, even if it could be shown that a particular war was likely to defend more of these things than it would destroy, that would not justify participation in it. At this point the Christian pacifist faces the crux of his position. He may be sincerely willing to endure suffering himself rather than betray his principles; but an acute tension arises when it becomes a matter of preserving them at the cost of suffering inflicted on others, especially those who look to him for protection; and if he has to envisage the death of his children or, still worse, their moral perversion carried out as a matter of policy by the agents of an occupying power, the tension becomes almost intolerable. And yet he knows that it can never be the duty of a follower of Christ to take the lives of some of God's children in the hope of protecting thereby the lives and liberties of others. In the face of this dilemma, he recalls the clear warning given by Christ that the cost of following Him is, indeed, heavy and may even include a sacrifice of the claims of those nearest and dearest to him (Luke 14:25-33).

In this spirit Friends would declare to their fellow Christians today, as they declared to King Charles II in 1660: "The Spirit of Christ by which we are guided is not changeable, so as once to command us from a thing as evil, and again to move unto it, and we certainly know and testify to the world that the spirit of Christ ... will never move us to fight or war against any man with outward weapons, neither for the Kingdom of Christ nor for the kingdoms of this world."

They hold that the words written a hundred years later by the American Friend John Woolman (1720-1772) are perfectly apposite today: "It requires great self-denial and resignation of ourselves to God, to attain that state wherein we can freely cease from fighting when wrongfully invaded, if, by our fighting, there were a probability of overcoming the invaders. Whoever rightly attains to it does in some degree feel that spirit in which our Redeemer gave His life for us" (*Journal*—Rancocas Edition, p. 207).

The Christian Alternative to War

Friends believe that there is a solution to the problem of evil, a "third way" between failing to answer its challenge and multiplying it by answering in kind.

While Christians are not to use even defensive violence against the evil man—the apparent meaning of the Sermon on the Mount saying recorded in Matthew 5:38 and 39—they are certainly required throughout the New Testament to resist evil in the moral and spiritual sense. They are in short to overcome evil with good. Clearly it is not sufficient to quote these texts and to do nothing. But Friends believe that by prayer the Christian is enabled continually to rediscover and to reconstruct in modern terms and in concrete situations the strategy and tactics of our Christian warfare against evil (Eph. 6:13ff.).

Knowing both themselves and their "enemies" to be children of God and brethren of one another, Friends believe that Christians are required to reject war and to work out the ethics and politics of peace on the basis of forgiveness, generosity and active goodwill with sacrifice. They are required to build a world community based on friendship, understanding and co-operation, which are the fruits of Christian love, and to draw into its fellowship even those who have hitherto relied on falsehood, self-aggrandisement and violence.

Personal Witness to Teaching of Jesus Christ

But Friends acknowledge that they have failed to live up to their ideals and, in particular, have too often compromised with the social conditions that produce war. Neither through refusal of arms nor through ambulance and relief work, neither in propaganda nor in direct effort at reconciliation, has the Society succeeded, either in speech or in act, in giving full expression to the spirit that takes away the occasion for all war. But we dare to call on our fellow Christians everywhere to exercise that ministry of reconciliation which is committed to the Church of Christ, and fearlessly to proclaim the Gospel of the Cross, the foolishness of God which is wiser than men.

Prepared by a group of the Friends Peace Committee, London, after consultation with the Friends World Committee for Consultation, Friends House, Euston Road, London, N.W.I.

CHURCH OF THE BRETHREN

The Church of the Brethren emerged out of a century of conflict. With the background of the terrible Thirty Years War, the wars of Louis XIV and repeated invasions of their lands, the founders were familiar with war and its attendant evils. They became convinced that it was incompatible with the Christian way. Our Lord and Master had taught that the mark of discipleship is the love Christians have for one another, but the early Brethren had witnessed the slaying of Christian by Christian each presumably acting in good faith. Some of their contemporaries, the Pietists, who had also lived through these experiences, had come to believe that the creeds did not matter so much as behavior and inward attitudes. The founders of the Church of the Brethren, strongly influenced by the Pietists, believed that Christianity was primarily a way of life. They believed that to discover what this life requires, they must study again the New Testament, and then endeavor to follow Jesus' teaching as faithfully as they could, wherever it would lead them.

They developed the convictions that:

> Jesus' life as a whole, his teachings, and his death reveal an emphasis on forgiveness, and a redemptive love that led him through service and sacrifice even to the Cross.
>
> Christians should follow in this pathway. The instructions given in the Sermon on the Mount are intended as a guide for his disciples here and now; therefore, they are not to retaliate with "an eye for an eye and a tooth for a tooth" as Moses had allowed, but like Jesus, who endured suffering rather than inflict it, they are to seek to overcome evil with good.

Jesus' teaching on forgiveness, as set forth in the eighteenth chapter of Matthew, must be used as the method of settling disputes among his followers. So important did this seem to the Brethren that they felt it necessary to set up a church organization in order to carry out the instructions effectively.

Christians should follow more closely the example of Jesus who came to minister, not to be ministered unto. The greatest, he said, is the one who is servant of all. He had washed the disciples feet to show them that no service is too menial for love to perform. The hungry are to be fed, the naked to be clothed, the sick and those in prison to be visited.

God, as revealed in Christ and the Scriptures, is the Creator and sustainer of all men. He made of one blood all nations of men, and he is not far from any one of us, for "in him we live and move and have our being." He is our Father, who cares for all and is ever ready to receive his prodigal children when they turn home. He is just, but his justice is always tempered with mercy.

God continues to speak to men. Through the enlightened Christian conscience he enables men to interpret his ways. The individual's first concern must be to find and obey the will of God. Brethren recognized, however, that not all individuals will have reached the same stage of discernment of God's will at the same time. Therefore, they must respect each individual's interpretation of God's will for his life, so long as he is sincerely striving to bring his will into harmony with the Divine will.

As to the social and economic implications of these religious convictions they believe that:

Governments are instituted for man's good, and Christians must act as law-abiding citizens except when the laws of the land conflict with the higher law. Then "we must obey God rather than men." In the midst of conflict and persecution we must continue to preach God's message of good will to men, to witness to his concern for everyone, even our "enemies," and to try to bring his healing mercies to those who are the victims of catastrophe.

The Christian way of life necessitates living simply, without pride and ostentation. One is to live in the world but not to be of the world. "Be ye not conformed to this world, but be ye transformed by the renewing of your spirits."

These few principles Brethren have cherished as the most precious part of their heritage. Some of our number have borne testimony to them at great cost, risking not only their property but their lives.

As they believed, so do we. We are aware, however, that many of us have not lived up to these high standards of discipleship. We have failed to teach our children sufficiently by our lives, often presenting a reserved or erratic commitment to these standards. Nor have we been sufficiently concerned about sharing these ideals with our neighbors. However, though we have fallen short in our conduct, we believe that these principles are eternally true, and now as always we offer the world a way of deliverance.

We believe that Christ's teachings and his death upon the Cross provide clear guidance for a refusal to participate in war. But we recognize that merely to refuse to kill does not reflect the whole essence of Christ's example of redemptive love. Jesus' teaching on non-resistance was only the reverse side of a positive way of life which Christians must follow. Our lives are to be transformed. We are to leave behind the old ways and venture on the new paths which he pointed out. Even the most painstaking righteousness of the old law must be transcended by the gospel of love.

No statement of faith is ever adequate in itself; it needs to be accompanied by a living demonstration. In order to give material expression to the doctrine of Christian love, we have attempted to carry on a service and reconciliation program which has taken various forms, from simple, sacrificial living in the local community to international relief and rehabilitation projects. We admit that our efforts in these fields have not represented an adequate implementation of our philosophy of love. But our purpose is clear. We pray for an intensification of effort, and a more sacrificial expression of our peace concern for all men everywhere.

We believe that some day Christians will renounce war, in keeping with the record of the earliest Christians, and that his disciples will be one, even as Jesus prayed. We appeal to our fellow Christians in the World Council of Churches to use their great influence to hasten the day. Acknowledging our shortcomings, and pledging the renewal of our faith in these abiding truths, we invite all men to join together in the determination to follow Jesus more perfectly, and to make his will the first consideration in their lives.

This statement was prepared by the Brethren Service Commission and approved by the General Brotherhood Board of the Church of the Brethren, 22 South State Street, Elgin, Illinois, U.S.A.

The International Fellowship of Reconciliation

The I.F.O.R.

The International Fellowship of Reconciliation is an international body of Christian pacifists with larger or smaller groups in some 25 countries. It is not a Church, and it has no claim to representation on the World Council of Churches. But it is definitely and by confession a Christian body, and its membership is drawn from many branches of the Christian Church. It is concerned for many of the values that concern the World Council of Churches. Eighty of its members attended the Amsterdam Assembly of the Churches in 1948 in one capacity or another.

Dr. 't Hooft's Invitation

The I.F.O.R. welcomes Dr. Visser 't Hooft's letter of October 19, 1949, addressed to Dr. Robert Zigler, in which the Historic Peace Churches are invited to submit "an agreed statement as to the Christian basis of Pacifism . . . for purposes of study and discussion within the ecumenical movement." It appreciates also Dr. Visser 't Hooft's further suggestion in the same letter that any statement provided by the Historic Peace Churches "would be even more valuable, if it would at the same time represent the position of some of the International Christian Peace movements." In response to this last suggestion, the officers of the International Fellowship of Reconciliation, who feel confident that they speak in the name of their membership throughout the world and for the "International Christian Peace Movement," and who themselves are ministers of the Protestant Episcopal Church of the United States, the Lutheran Church of Germany, the Reformed Church of France, the Remonstrantse Broederschap of Holland, the Quakers of Japan, etc., submit the following paragraphs, indicating their understanding of the Christian basis of the pacifist conviction. It may, however, be convenient to regard this submission as an addendum to the statement or statements submitted by Friends, Brethren and Mennonites.

Oxford, 1937, and Amsterdam, 1948

Both the Oxford and the Amsterdam Assemblies of the Churches declared that war was contrary to the will of God and to the mind of Christ. But they proceeded to state three differing positions on the question of individual Christian duty in peace and war, though both urged on all Christians the duty of wrestling continuously with the difficulties and perplexities raised by this conflict of opinion. Neither Assembly was ready to proceed from its theoretical condemnation of war in general to the practical conclusion that Christians should not participate in war. It should be noted that, while the Oxford statement of the Christian pacifist position was a good one, that of Amsterdam, limited to four lines and open to interpretation as involving only so-called "vocational pacifism," cannot be regarded as adequate. But it should further be noted that the first position there stated, admitted that, while the occasion for a war might be regarded as "just," the means by which modern war was carried on made it intolerable to the Christian conscience.

The Law of God
The Christian pacifist is far from rejecting the concept of vocation; but, accepting also the declaration that war is contrary to the will of God, he believes that obedience to God's will in this matter also is incumbent on all Christians, and indeed on all men, whether they acknowledge God or not. That war, the organised slaughter of men to compel their submission, is wrong, should in the Christian pacifist's view be accepted as part of the Law of God for the whole world.

The Law of God is known by the witness of his Spirit in the heart of man, and is declared in the New Testament. The relation of man to God makes God's will obligatory on man. Jesus Christ did not legislate in detail, but his brief restatement of the Law of God for man makes clear its unique character and its unlimited scope (Mark 12:30-31).

The Law of God is a judgment of evil; and under it the task of the Christian is to resist and abolish evil in society, though not to fight the evil man (Matt. 5:39). But the Law of God is also a constructive law of righteousness; and it calls the Christian to be, not a man of war, but a peacemaker. The Christian is in fact to overcome evil with good. The new and ill-understood weapon placed in his hands by Jesus Christ for this purpose is that of forbearing and suffering love.

The Grace of God
The Law of God is completely reinterpreted in the New Testament (John 1:17, Rom. 6:14, etc.). Jesus Christ transformed man's vision of God and revealed him as a father of mercies rather than a judge, a God who by his grace forgives the evildoer and draws him back into sonship and fellowship with newness of life. In Christ man is a new creation. Moreover, the grace given to man through Jesus Christ is not only a saving force for the individual man, but a new power which makes possible the reconciliation of conflict and provides a means by which men may live at peace and establish a new basis for society. Reconciliation of man to God involves

reconciliation of man to fellow-man and nation to nation. It will be objected that this Utopia is impossible, at least until, in a new age, all men shall have surrendered themselves by and to the Grace of God. But the Law of God is for this present age. And it is by the methods, spirit and power of Jesus Christ that his followers must conquer evil. The first step to the conversion of the world, as well as to the abolition of war, is that Christians and the Church should live by the Grace of God rather than by the laws of states, and that they should disarm men's fear and violence by their own fearlessness and trust in God.

The Lord's Prayer, the essential document and experience of our common membership of the family and Kingdom of God, requires us all to pray for divine forgiveness, as we also forgive (cf. "First be reconciled . . . "). But we dare not pretend to forgive privately and individually while we exact the uttermost farthing officially and as serving an institution. Forgiveness is an essential element in the Grace of God, not known to human law as ordinarily defined, but the secret of life in community. It is noteworthy that a department of state will on occasion do something explicitly as "an act of grace" which it is not required to do by the letter of its law. Here is a distinct step towards recognition of love as a fulfilment of that fundamental justice to which human law is but a rough approximation.

The State

The state cannot be recognised as possessing an absolute law of its own; for if so it becomes a rival god, and the first of the Commandments is broken. The state and its law are under the judgment of God. Ultimately it is the Law of God that the magistracy must administer. But the Law of God is still too commonly understood by the officers of the state in an Old Testament sense and in terms of merely human law—the command of a sovereign, sustained by his forces and effective mainly through the principle of terror. It is on this basis that the case for war is put forward, the case that a (good) state or a union of states has the responsibility and the obligation to restrain evil men and evil states by force, even at the cost of the slaughter of the innocent with the guilty. (Cf. the second position stated in the section of the Amsterdam report dealing with peace and war.)

The state has no moral authority or power, only that of force, except as it administers the Law of God, but the law of the New Testament rather than the Old. The utterly new version of the divine law enunciated by Jesus Christ, the law of grace, based on love and characterised by forgiveness, cannot be quoted as authority for any attempt to enforce by war either the law of any state or the decisions of the United Nations.

International law cannot be sustained in practice, it will rather be destroyed, by the indiscriminate mass destruction of cities and peoples which is part and parcel of the modern military method, and which, unlike proper police action under municipal law, makes no distinction between innocence and guilt of persons and is unlimited in its destruction. And these things cannot be defended from the Christian point of view. International law can only be established in a world community which has been freed from the threat of great armaments. It must therefore be quite different in character from a law dependent on force. Its sanction must be the consent of the governed, in recognition of the righteousness and moral authority of its law, a law based ultimately on the Word of God. The world is now suffering under efforts to maintain a lesser law by force. The establishment of a true international law is the problem of our time, the problem for the Christian statesman. It is one with the problem of peace, but not in the way generally understood, the way of victorious war. Whether evil can be abolished by violence or peace reached by way of war are still matters of public controversy, but the immediate point is that, as interpreted by the life and death of Jesus Christ, the Law of God is not vindicated by force.

International relationships are the responsibility of statesmen, men often entitled to respect for their personal character and deep sense of Christian as well as social responsibility. The Church must not usurp their responsibility, but neither must it abdicate its own ministry, prophetic or pastoral: it has the duty of supporting and guiding the statesman spiritually when he can see no right way out of a complex situation and a tangle of conflicting claims, the result, perhaps, of a long history, lest he be tempted to adopt an official policy that his personal conscience would not approve. Even in such circumstances there must be a way, perhaps a way of the Cross, which is in accordance with the mind of Christ.

The Task of the Church

Both the statesman and the Church must be reminded that a ministry of reconciliation has been committed to the Church, and that peacemaking is peculiarly the task of the Christian. From the beginning of Christianity it has been the Church's duty to testify before kings and governors. It is for the Church, which is sometimes regarded as the conscience of the state, to prophesy and witness against the state in situations where the rejection of the New Testament law of neighbourliness, generosity, service and forgiveness and the adoption of a policy of the group self called "national honour and vital interests" threaten to drag the world into conflict again. The Churches and the whole Ecumenical Movement must take responsibility, both in refusing support to governments which resort to arms in international disputes, and also in themselves striving to overcome evil in the power of the divine love. It is for the whole body of Christians, not only to recognise that war is contrary to the will of God, but to attack its causes by working to relieve tensions, to disperse fear and suspicion, and constructively to reconcile international differences and to build up between peoples the relations of good faith, mutual trust and peace.

The immediate task of the Church is to help the natural man to overcome that fear which expresses itself in instinctive violence and leads to war. Such a result can be accomplished only as specially qualified representatives of the Church cross frontiers, as evangelists have long done, mingle with strangers, show understanding of the circumstances and problems of communities different from their own, offer real tokens of generosity of spirit, and enable those who at first instinctively shrink from them as foreigners to realise that their suspicions are groundless, and that friendliness and co-operation in political and economic terms are not only possible but to be desired. Such a change of spirit is the indispensable basis of the technical instruments of international peace.

If the Church does not bring its peacemaking influence to bear to avert the "peril of total war" which, says the Amsterdam report, hangs over all mankind, the whole of civilisation and many of the values of Christianity itself will, humanly speaking, be-involved in cataclysm. And because the ordinary man has come to realise that there is no solution of the problem in war, but only an expression of despair, this is the moment for real peacemaking.

Christian Pacifism

The New Testament records may be incomplete, or to some extent obscure, but there can be no question that discipleship of Jesus Christ involves a spirit contrary to that which the making of war demands. In spite of some controversy over a few particular passages, the New Testament is its own evidence that "the Gospel excludes all violence, and has nothing in common with war, nor will permit it." The authority and confirmation for the Christian pacifist position is found in the work and words of Jesus Christ himself.

Christian pacifists in all Churches are united in the conviction that because war is contrary to the mind of Christ individual Christians and Churches ought, in obedience to the will of God, both to refuse and to oppose participation in war in all circumstances. This conviction is based on a sense of responsible discipleship, deepened both in private prayer and intercession for all sorts and conditions of men, and at the Communion table, where disciples of all nationalities, but of one Master, kneel side by side. Not only is war between the members of various Churches completely inconsistent with their Christian profession, but they know that the Church herself cannot, while remaining in obedience to her Lord, fight even the enemies of the Church, the enemies for whom also Christ died. It is impossible for the Christian to prefer citizenship before discipleship, or to argue that any part of his relations with his neighbour should be based otherwise than on obedience to his Lord. If the Son of Man is lord of the sabbath, he is lord also both of eternity and of the workaday world. The ethic of the Gospel cannot be set aside or so restricted as to excuse war. Refusing to support war against the enemies of the nation, it is the Christian's part to show how they may be forgiven and reconciled and won for friendship and peace. The solution of the problem of inter-state relations must require no less an attempt to apply the divine principle of grace.

Christian pacifists do not accept the paralysing fatalism, pessimism and despair which declare that the Christians can do little or nothing positive in an evil world. They believe that the Church, the whole company of Christians, is called to carry on the fight against the forces of evil and for the enthronement of love in the spirit and by the strength of Jesus Christ himself. It is apostate if it resigns the task of saving the world to goverments and armies. That way lies utter catastrophe. Governments must indeed be held responsible to their peoples; but the Church must warn them that they are under the judgment of God, and must make clear on the authority of the Gospel both the method and the cost of saving the world. "For whosoever will save his life shall lose it, but whosoever shall lose his life for my sake and the Gospel's, the same shall save it" (Mark 8:35).

Clearly the positive task lying before Church and individual Christian, the task of showing the nations and governments of the world the way to the conquest of evil and the establishing of a real community of peoples depends upon our readiness for a fresh visitation of the Holy Spirit and for a new sense of call to the work of reconcilation. The masses, the forces, the inertia of the world can be overcome by the Christian Church only by virtue of the power and purpose of God.

Summary

We sum up this brief statement of the Christian foundation of our position by declaring our conviction that war is the negation of Christianity and that pacifism is the sound and inevitable response to the call of God as known in the hearts of men, a true interpretation of the mind of Jesus Christ and of the spirit and ethic of the whole of the New Testament.

Christian pacifism is the positive way to reconciliation between man and man and to real victory in man's conflict with evil. Especially in the atomic age do we consider that the Church is challenged to renounce war totally, to learn herself and to teach her members what forgiveness and love of enemies can mean in present day conditions, to teach them to refuse to kill their neighbours, and so to lead the nations in the spirit of the New Testament to relations of positive peace throughout the world.

On behalf of the International Fellowship of Reconciliation. John Nevin Sayre, Chairman.

5. Peace Is the Will of God—Historic Peace Churches and the International Fellowship of Reconciliation (Geneva, Switzerland, October 1953)

When the publication War Is Contrary to the Will of God—*the title of which picked up the assertion of the Amsterdam Assembly of the World Council of Churches—was presented to the staff of the World Council of Churches, there was mixed reaction. On the one hand, ecumenical leaders expressed appreciation to the peace churches and the IFOR for following the appeal of the assembly to direct theological attention to the problem. On the other hand, regret was expressed that the publication was not a unified statement. If the peace churches themselves, it was said, could not unite on a position, how could they reasonably expect a council as diverse in denominational and political backgrounds as the WCC to arrive at a common mind?*

The continuation committee, therefore, addressed itself to this task. At a meeting held in The Netherlands in September 1952, it was agreed: "This conference recognizes that the challenge [to produce a unified statement] of the World Council of Churches is an opportunity which should not be lost and . . . reaffirms the decision . . . that we attempt to prepare such a statement."

With heavy drafting involvement by younger Mennonite scholars and British Friends, the continuation committee was able to produce an agreed-upon statement within one year's time. This was published as a response to the "special call" of the Amsterdam Assembly for theological attention to war/peace issues. It was presented with this attitude:

> We do not profess to have a detailed solution to the international problems of today's world, but we believe that our conviction confirmed by several centuries' experience of the full pacifist position, deserves more thorough consideration than has yet been accorded to it.

It concluded with the "hope and in the conviction that the perplexity acknowledged by the Amsterdam report must not remain the Church's only answer to the world's great need . . . ." It was also published in German and French translation.

Peace Is the Will of God

I. THE COMMON CHRISTIAN FAITH

The World Council of Churches was constituted on the confession that the "Lord Jesus Christ is God and Saviour." The Christian men and women who met in Amsterdam, representing millions of Christians from every corner of the earth, were deeply conscious of man's failure and despair apart from God and of the serious crises of our own time. But they had met to proclaim that "there is a word of God for our world. It is that the world is in the hands of the living God, Whose will for it is wholly good; that in Christ Jesus, His incarnate Word, Who lived and died and rose from the dead, God has broken the power of evil once for all, and opened for everyone the gate into freedom and joy in the Holy Spirit; that the final judgment on all human history and on every human deed is the judgment of the merciful Christ; and that the end of history will be the triumph of His Kingdom, where alone we shall understand how much God has loved the world" (Amsterdam, 10).

The Council's proclamation that "War is contrary to the Will of God" thus rested on a clear conviction of the supremacy and finality of Christ. It sensed the incompatibility of war with his "teaching and example." Eleven years earlier the Conference on Church, Community and State at Oxford had expressed the same conviction thus: "The universal Church . . . must pronounce a condemnation of war unqualified and unrestricted. War can only occur as a fruit and manifestation of sin" (Oxford, 59). This Conference, under deep realization of the transcendence of the Christian community over earthly social divisions, had urged that our starting point in consideration of war be "the universal fellowship of Christians, the Una Sancta." And at another point it had pleaded: "The first duty of the Church, and its greatest service to the world, is that it be in very deed the Church—confessing the true faith, committed to the fulfilment of the will of Christ, its only Lord, and united to Him in a fellowship of love and service (Oxford, 57).

Whatever may be our judgment as to particular credal statements, we are in agreement with the consensus of Christian faith as expressed at Oxford and Amsterdam. It is on this basis that we for our part have come to reject war. Since "war is contrary to the Will of God" it would seem to be incumbent on every Christian to abstain from it. We are convinced that the unreadiness of most Christians to come to this practical conclusion reflects the thinking quite general within Christendom, in which alongside of Scripture certain pseudo-Christian or secular attitudes and assumptions have gradually and at times unconsciously been accorded axiomatic status. A number of these will be briefly examined here.

II. SOME EXTRANEOUS PRESUPPOSITIONS INFLUENCING CHRISTIAN THOUGHT

a. The inviolability of natural social bonds

While there can be no doubt of the essential unity of mankind, a man's personal experience of community is limited to the very small number of individuals with whom he can share life. World society is therefore built up by social groupings of infinite variety in kind and size. This structure, however distorted it may become at times, is rooted in the order of creation, as is seen in the divine establishment of the conjugal tie and the family which grows up around it. Yet this is the very structure whose distortions are an immediate cause of war, for from time immemorial the needs and desires as well as the pride of one social group have come into conflict with those of another. In these conflicts each group has a self-consciousness which is expressed by the instinctive sense of loyalty which each member of the group feels. Perhaps nothing has ever seemed more detestable socially than that a member of a community in time of common danger should flee or should betray the common cause. Indeed, the right and duty of group self-defense is considered axiomatic in every society.

The problem then arises whether Christ accepted this group solidarity as an axiom, consequently implying that his new ethic was to be practised within the limits of natural community, leaving its absolute claims inviolate, or whether the ethic of the clan was to be supplanted as ultimate norm by that of the Christian brotherhood. Is *agape* intended in the final analysis to transcend all other impulses of social cohesion? In other words, Can the Christian at the moment when his nation is faced by military attack from without refuse his social responsibility to fight in its defence on the grounds that Jesus said, "Love your enemies"?

At first thought the answer to this question seems obvious. Christ confirmed the created order of society; he strengthened, for example, the marriage relationship and lifted it to an even more inviolate level. Some would conclude that the tendency among Christians to accept the claims of the natural community, including military service, as axiomatic and as absolute can therefore be justified.

On the other hand, however, we encounter in various settings the "dark" sayings of Christ, in which he seems openly to contradict his general attitude. "Think not that I am come to send peace on earth: I came not to send peace, but a sword. For I am come to set a man at variance against his father . . . and a man's foes shall be they of his own household. He that loveth father or mother more than me is not worthy of me . . . " (Matt. 10:34-37). "Who is my mother? and who are my brethren? And he stretched forth his hand toward his disciples, and said, Behold my mother and my brethren! For whosoever shall do the will of my Father which is in Heaven, the same is my brother, and sister, and mother" (*ibid.,* 12:48-50). To this might be added his own attitude at the moment of supreme danger, when Peter, "moved by the natural instinct of group loyalty and the ethic of the natural community," drew his sword in defence, only to hear from his Master, "Put up again thy sword into his place; for all they that take the sword shall perish with the sword" (*ibid.,* 26:53). In all this we learn that Christ consciously subordinated the imperfect ethic of the natural community to the perfect ethic of the Christian brotherhood, although he fully realized the inevitable hostility that arises within the natural community when one of its members subordinates his group loyalties to the transcendent ethos, the *agape* of the Christian community. We therefore believe that Christian participation in war can be justified neither by the natural instinct of loyalty nor by the ethical norms of the natural community. It is impossible for the Christian to prefer citizenship before discipleship or to argue that any part of his relations with his neighbour should be based otherwise than on obedience to his Lord.

To us it seems clear then that in the light of the Gospel of Christ neither the right nor the duty of the defence of self or of others at the cost of the life of an "enemy" will stand examination. Furthermore we do not believe that those values of liberty and cultural heritage which are often unconsciously identified with Christianity and cited to justify wars of "defence," can be defended by war. War, even when conducted against an agressor or an occupying power, inevitably involves the destruction not only of human life and of instruments of civilization but also of the very moral and spiritual values which it seeks to defend. But even if a particular war were likely to preserve more lives and values than it would destroy (leaving aside the impossibility of such calculation) it could never be the duty of a follower of Christ to take the lives of some of God's children in the hope of protecting the lives and liberties of others.

The interpretation of "solidarity" according to which the Church's or the Christian's ethical duty is identification with a particular class or with the interests of a particular nation is in truth a contradiction of the distinctively Christian solidarity with all of mankind, demonstrated by Jesus when he answered the question, "Who is my neighbour?" with a parable about a Samaritan, thus showing a startling disrespect for Jewish national sentiment. Christian love is distinguished from customary human behaviour precisely in this, that it overreaches the bounds which natural group solidarity sets to unselfishness. The distinctively Christian ethical teaching is not that we should love our neighbour, but that *every man* is the neighbour whom we must love. "For if ye love them which love you, what thank have ye? For sinners also love those that love them" (Luke 6:32).

b. The mediaeval Christian concept of society

In the great but mistaken mediaeval vision of the *corpus christianum* the kings of the earth were thought to have been brought into the Kingdom of Christ, the natural and religious communities being regarded as conterminous, synthesized in the universal empire and the universal church. Though that *corpus* has largely disintegrated, its social and political ethos still persists today. Influenced in part by subconscious mediaeval attitudes, the Church is unwilling to break with the political and even economic *status quo* of the social order within which she finds herself, maintaining the delusion that in some fashion she is salvaging that order or discharging her responsibility for it by this very dilution of her own substance. We are grateful that the Oxford conference called attention to this problem in the following words: "The Church has not yet faced the new situation with sufficient frankness. With the conservative instincts of all institutions of long standing and influence, it has fought a defensive—and on the whole a losing—battle for the maintenance of as much as possible of the old ideal of the *corpus christianum* and of the privileges and authority which that implies" (Oxford, 200).

The persistence of this mediaeval attitude is seen also in the Church's readiness to support the military operations of the nation in which she finds herself, identifying the cause of the fatherland with the cause of God. Another vestige of this tradition is the survival of the concept of the divine right of kings in the form of the readiness of Christians to take up arms in obedience to the state, to which they have transferred the absolute authority once erroneously attributed to the monarch.

c. The concept of the "just war"

Within the mediaeval tradition was developed the Augustinian-Thomistic concept of the "just war," a concept resting on the premises of *theologia naturalis*. Whatever our attitude toward "natural theology" as such, the concept of the "just war" represents a construct of human reasoning which is at a variance with revealed truth. Furthermore, it disregards the distinction, to which we shall refer [later] between the dispensation of preservation (or providence) and that of grace (or redemption). It is reasoned that since the state is responsible for the common weal and since the war in question is fought in its defence, such war is just—just not only politically speaking, but also in the sense that its execution is not sin. In other words we have here a suspension of the divine absolute law and will. Whether and under what circumstances St. Paul in Romans 13 would permit a state to engage in war in execution of its responsibility to maintain order is an open question; that such action could ever be "just" in the sense of involving no guilt is untenable.

It is of no mean importance that the validity of the "just war" concept for our time is being challenged, even by the tradition most closely bound to Thomas Aquinas. In *Institutiones Iuris Publici Ecclesiastici,* a recent Vatican publication, appears the following remarkable assertion: "Today a just war which would permit a state to attack in the interest of obtaining its right no longer exists" (translation ours), though under certain conditions defensive wars might still occur. This modification of mediaeval Catholic doctrine is justified according to this view by the fundamental change in character of modern warfare. In other quarters similar trends in thinking can be noted. Nevertheless, the limited validity of this argument must be recognized, since its basis is not the absolute evil of all war, but certain pragmatic considerations according to which in its present extreme form it has become too costly and dangerous. The moral issue is thus obscured. Furthermore such reasoning tends to exaggerate the distinction, qualitatively speaking, not only between offence and defence but also between earlier and present wars. Whether there exists a difference other than quantitative between the sacked cities of the Crusades and Hiroshima is not self-evident. At any rate though every contribution which this theory can make to the prevention of war is to be welcomed, we dare not forget that rejecting war because it no longer "pays," no more constitutes Christian pacifism than being honest because it is the best policy, makes an honest man.

d. *The concept of Christian pacifism as a vocation*

Since the "gathered" character of the early Church began to disappear, the discrepancy between the Christian ideal and the conduct of the nominally Christian masses has disquieted the earnest disciple. The resultant monasticism eventually led to a "normalized" dualistic ethic distinguished between the *consilia,* which constituted the "maximal" monastic norm, and the *praecepta,* which constituted the "minimal" norm of the masses. Against this dichotomous ethic the Reformation protested vigorously, but it still moved fully in the ethical atmosphere of the *corpus christianum.* Luther, for instance, in his concept of the two kingdoms, transferred this ethical tension from the social community into the anguished breast of the individual Christian. The Christian now followed, as it were, the *consilia* in his "private" life, while in political or military matters he maintained his former conduct which had supposedly met the demands of the *praecepta*. And so the Christian still serves in the army today: privately the *consilia* forbid him to kill, but the *praecepta* permit him to do so at the bidding of the state.

This same sort of dichotomy appears in the current view that God may call certain people to the pacifist position, just as He may call certain others to be preachers or teachers, or may give some other *charisma*. Since their 16th century dissent from this Reformation view, pacifist churches have held that this dichotomy belongs, not between higher and lower Christians, but between Christian and non-Christian, between Church and world, where the New Testament placed it originally. We therefore reject the concept of vocational pacifism, which is the view often taken of our position by those who can neither accept nor reject it; for this concept is essentially a monastic one. While here is not only a place but also an urgent need for prophetic effort in the promotion of peace, we must maintain firmly that to put pacifism aside as a special "calling" for a few to keep the conscience of Christendom alive is a misinterpretation of the Gospel ethic.

e. An antinomian concept of grace.

It has been felt by some that the absolutist position of the pacifist represents a return to legalism inconsistent with Christian justification by faith, and that it creates a delusion of innocence equivalent to self-righteousness. On the other hand, it is assumed that the true Christian who admits his sin in going to war, and yields to God in penitence, is justified by God's grace. We readily admit that pacifism can contain elements of self-deception, legalism and hypocrisy, and that pacifists can mistakenly suppose that they have fulfilled their responsibility simply by refusing to fight. But such dangers beset all areas of Christian living and are not peculiar to pacifists. The charge laid against pacifists seems rather to be based on two serious misreadings of the New Testament view of law and grace. First, since we are justified by faith and free from the law it is assumed that we are no longer subject to absolute norms but rather make our choices in the freedom of Christ, so that what may be sin for one need not be sin for another, since all live above the law. Now there is an element of truth in this view, for indeed we meet God no longer on the level of human merit and legalism but of grace; the power of sin and the judgment of the Mosaic law against us have been nullified; by writing the law in our heart God has placed us above it so that we obey because we will, not because we must. Nevertheless it is fundamentally false in supposing that the absolutes of the divine will are in any way suspended. Every man is still responsible to God for his works, good or bad.

In the second place, the above accusations seem unwarrantedly free in their application of grace. "What shall we say then? Shall we continue in sin, that grace may abound? God forbid. How shall we, that are dead to sin, live any longer therein?" (Rom. 6:1, 2). "For if we sin wilfully after that we have received the knowledge of the truth, there remaineth no more sacrifice for sins" (Heb. 10:26). Does not the assumption that we can deliberately go to war, because we go penitently realizing it to be sin, constitute a most serious abuse of the doctrine of grace? Can we really countenance the many conference resolutions that never go beyond the meaningless admonition that when we are implicated in a war we must at least fight penitently? As Christian pacifists we realize keenly that only by the grace of God and not through our pacifism can we stand in his sight. But we realize with equal keenness that justification is the door to a discipleship from which there is no turning back, and that deliberate sin nullified the efficacy of grace for us.

f. The concept of war as the lesser evil

A very current line of non-pacifist reasoning regards war as a lesser evil than conquest and oppression. War is thus envisaged as a resistance to enemy invasion. Apart from the fact that this is obviously not a true picture of the behaviour of both sides in all wars, we note at the outset that valid comparison must be between two things of the same kind: it is valid to compare the infliction of one evil with the infliction of another, or the suffering of one evil with the suffering of another, but it has no moral meaning to say that one evil which a man may inflict is greater or less than another evil which he may suffer. If therefore this concept of the "lesser evil" means that a nation will inflict less evil on its enemies if it goes to war with them than it will suffer if it does not, it may or may not be a correct prediction, but in any case it gives no moral justification for going to war.

If the concept is taken as a comparison of two evils of which one or the other is to be suffered, it means that a nation will suffer less evil if it resists the invaders than if it does not. This may be true if it turns out that the defenders win the war, but it takes no account of the possibility that they may lose the war and so suffer not one of the two evils but both. In any case it is a purely prudential calculation, and as such it offers no guidance on the moral question whether it is or is not right to resort to war. The avoidance of suffering is no criterion of good: on the contrary, we are warned, as disciples of Jesus, to expect suffering, and we know that our free acceptance of suffering may have a redemptive value that no positive action of ours could have had.

To have any moral significance, the concept of the "lesser evil" must be intended as a comparison of evils inflicted, either directly or indirectly, on others. It may be a quantitative comparison, meaning that although resorting to war admittedly inflicts suffering on one's enemies, this is less than the suffering of one's friends under enemy oppression, for which one would be responsible in refusing to go to war. Or it may be a qualitative comparison, meaning that it is a less evil thing to inflict suffering on one's enemies than to allow it to be inflicted on one's friends. Whichever kind of comparison it is, it means that he who resorts to war does evil, but he who does not does a greater evil, and thus the only choice is between two evil courses of action. This apparent inevitability of sin is expressed, in somewhat different terms, in the Oxford declaration: "In all situations the Christian has to bear in mind both the absolute command, 'Thou shalt love thy neighbour as thyself,' and the obligation to do what most nearly corresponds to that command in the circumstances confronting him. His action may be but a poor expression of perfect love; the man is caught in a sinful situation, to the evil of which he may have contributed much or little. The best that is possible falls far 'short of the glory of God' and is, in that sense, sinful; each man must bear his share of the corporate sin which has rendered impossible any better course; and we all have to confess that 'our righteousnesses are as filthy rags.' Yet to do what appears as relatively best is an absolute duty before God, and to fail in this is to incur positive guilt" (Oxford, 178-179).

This statement no doubt reflects faithfully the thinking of many, perhaps the majority of Christians, who assume that in our world of mutually related values ethical absolutes can be applied only relatively and that consequently the norm of conduct is not the absolute good but the "relatively best." In this way war, while wrong in an absolute sense, is thought to be the "relatively best" course in a particular situation. Sober reflection, however, will indicate at once that such an ethic moves on an entirely different level from that proclaimed by Christ.

To admit the possibility that a man may be placed in a position where he has no choice but to sin is to shut God out of his own world. We are God's children, and it is inconceivable that our Father, who loves us and wants us to behave as his children, could ever so abandon us. Christ himself, when seemingly faced with the choice of imposing his leadership by violence or permitting the extinction of his nascent kingdom, did not justify violence as a lesser evil, as the "relatively best" course, or as a means to a good end: he chose the way of God's will and his own nature, even though it was the way of the cross. And by that choice there came a release of God's power that could have come in no other way, and the situation was startlingly transformed so that the way that Christ chose was not after all the way to the extinction of his kingdom but the way, and the only way, to its triumph.

While we may recognize that human conduct does not attain absolute perfection in this life, such recognition is entirely different from the deliberate postulation of ethical norms different from those set up by Christ, or the admission that obedience is a relative matter. That certain absolutes apply to our own time is the obvious intent of Christ as seen in the Scriptures. Even though we cannot achieve absolute perfection as human mortals, the only star given us to steer by is the perfect will of God.

g. The compatibility of war with Christian love

Some hold that a Christian spirit of love toward the enemy may be maintained even in the act of killing. But such a benevolent sentiment, even if it could be preserved by the killer, is not love, for "love worketh no ill" (Rom. 13:10). Furthermore a "love" that expresses itself in violence is *for the victim* indistinguishable from hatred, and can only call forth hatred and violence in return. Indeed, the higher the values in the name of which violence is done, the deeper will be the resentment of the victims against the "love" that kills them or their loved ones. The unhappy effect of colonial exploitation on Christian missions is sufficient demonstration that according Christian sanction to violence compromises the communication of the Gospel of love.

III. THE CHRISTIAN NON-RESISTANT PACIFIST POSITION

a. Love and the way of the cross

Christians all agree that the essence of the Gospel is the love of God reaching down to redeem and transform the imperfections and sin which mar the life of men, and further, that this love must call forth in a man a like expression of redemptive love for his fellow man. "This is my commandment that ye love one another, as I have loved you" (John 15:12).

Those who read the New Testament in this perspective will find themselves in agreement with the numerous competent Christian scholars who have examined the passages commonly quoted in discussion of the peace and war issue, studying them objectively and with no attempt to read meanings into them. They will recognize that the words and spirit of the Gospels fully warrant the Amsterdam statement that "war is incompatible with the teaching and example of Christ"; furthermore, that the cross of Christ, the heart of our faith, the means by which God's love operates redemptively in a world of sin, speaks against war, for it stands for the acceptance of unlimited suffering, the utter denial of self, and the complete dedication of life to the ministry of redemption.

But that cross is not merely exemplary, nor is the love to which it gives expression only redemptive, for beyond the cross lies the resurrection, and the moral renewal of the believer, "that like as Christ was raised up from the dead by the glory of the Father, even so we also should walk in newness of life" (Rom. 6:4). Thus through the Scriptures and the light of Christ shining into the human heart man is made aware of the vital distinction in the sight of God between good and evil, right and wrong: aware that the problem of good and evil is bound up with the problem of his relationship with his brother; and aware increasingly that the overcoming of evil with good and the establishment of relationships of love and cooperation with his fellow man are possible to him only by the power of God working within him. The clear teachings of Christ: "Love your enemies"; "Do good to them that hate you"; "Resist not evil"; etc., bear the unmistakable authority both of his spoken word as recorded in Scripture and of the inner witness of his Spirit. The Sermon on the Mount is in spirit declarative as well as imperative—such *is* the natural conduct of the children of God.

These assertions do not mean that we can achieve an easy perfection nor do they assume that human endeavour alone can bring about a warless world within history. Sin and violence will remain with us as long as man continues to abuse his moral freedom. The Christian himself is still subject to sin and to human limitation and still beset by the violence of the world. It is only the miracle of divine love that lifts him up, enabling him to realize the divine purpose of his existence. But he cannot claim that love without accepting the discipleship it entails with all its consequences. It is the heart of our position that once having been laid hold of by God through Christ the Christian owes him unqualified obedience. He may not calculate in advance what this may mean for himself or for society and obey only so far as seems practicable. The Christian is thus placed in a position of inevitable and endless tension. Though he lives in the world and participates in the activities that belong to human life, he must recurrently face situations where loyalty to Christ, to the new "aeon" in which he already stands, means refusal to the world, "in which" he is, but "of which" he is not. Perhaps nowhere does this conflict of loyalties become more articulate or more acute than in the question of war. But here as elsewhere in life the Christian has but one weapon, to "overcome evil with good." His whole life must be one of unflinching fidelity to the way of redemptive love, even though it be the way of the cross.

b. The Church

In his discipleship, however, the Christian is not an isolated individual whose faith is a matter merely of private interest. He is a member of the Church, the universal community established by Christ in which his Spirit must reign and his will must be done, and from which must go out into all society the saving and healing ministry of the Gospel. "Nothing stood out more clearly in the thought and work of the Oxford Conference than the recognition that the Church in its essential nature is a universal society, united in its one Lord, and that in Him there can be neither Jew nor Greek, Barbarian nor Scythian, bond nor free" (Oxford, 31). Further, "the Church should witness in word, in sacramental life, and in action to the reality of the kingdom of God which transcends the world of nations" (Oxford, 13). In her transcendent life the Church already lives in the new aeon which she is called to manifest. As his body she lives according to the new "law of liberty," and we who are her members are called to "stand fast in the liberty wherewith Christ hath made us free" (Gal. 5:1), a freedom which no exercise of earthly authority can ever impair or usurp. Her source of life is the final and absolute reality of God in Christ, who in her existence manifests that power which will ultimately triumph over all the forces of darkness. To her has been entrusted the ministry of reconciliation, and henceforth neither she nor her members can engage in activities contrary to that mission. She is the herald of the new order, the kingdom of God, and her members must live within that order. Where in the supposed interest of the new order they revert to the methods of violence characteristic of the old they thwart the very process of redemption to which as Christians they are dedicated, for righteousness cannot spring up from unrighteousness, nor love from strife.

For Christians to allow themselves to be drawn into taking sides in war is a denial of the unity of the Body of Christ. The Christian Church is not provincial or national, it is universal. Therefore every war in which churches on each side condone or support the national effort becomes a civil war within the Church. Is not this state of affairs where Christian kills Christian an even greater breach of ecumenical fellowship than the deplorable confessional differences that have rent our unity? Indeed, can we Christians expect the Lord to restore our unity in worship as long as we put one another to death on the field of battle? Therefore we humbly submit: The refusal to participate in and to support war in any form is the only course compatible with the high calling of the Church of Jesus Christ.

c. Church and State

The Church has to fulfil her mission not in a perfect society but in a world of men and nations who are free to spurn the will of God, in an aeon which Scripture itself recognizes will be marked by the continuing presence of evil. In the face of social disharmony both the Old and the New Testament recognize the authority of the state, as instituted to maintain order by force. This seeming contradiction of the ethic of love is clearly the heart of the problem of the Christian attitude toward war.

The classic New Testament passage dealing with this question, Romans 13, says unequivocally that the state is "ordained of God" as an institution of order, the role in which it is "a minister of God to thee for good."

In the same breath, however, this passage asserts that "there is no power but of God." The state has therefore only a delegated and limited authority. It possesses nothing of a mystical or metaphysical quality, no autonomous norms or existence, no ultimate source of justice. Indeed this passage appears in a context where St. Paul had quoted God's words from the Song of Moses, "Vengeance is mine, I will repay" (Deut. 32:35, Rom. 12:19). Thus it is clear that whatever authority the state exercises, whatever justice it may be called upon to achieve, is purely of a delegated, relative and provisional nature. At no point may its functions presume a suspension of the divine will.

Furthermore, the New Testament, and particularly the Apocalypse, sees in the state also a "demonic" quality. In this respect it is implicated in the usurped temporal power of the "prince of this world." This element, like a dominant trait in a biological organism, constantly seeks to assert itself, and leads a state, particularly one whose power is growing, to overstep its boundaries, to forget its derivative character, and to abuse its authority, as for example in the prosecution of modern warfare. In the eschatological vision of Scripture the kingdoms of this world are therefore visited with the righteous wrath of God. The authority which they are given becomes the very occasion of their downfall, and ultimately every functionary of the state stands before God as any other individual. For him therefore to kill men on the field of battle at the state's behest does not divest the deed of its sinful character, even though it appears to be a sin less heinous than private murder.

In the Old Testament, the first clear reference to the institution of justice in human hands follows the Noachic flood, where God declares: "Whoso sheddeth man's blood, by man shall his blood be shed" (Gen. 9:6), stating thus a maxim later formulated as "Eye for eye, tooth for tooth" (Ex. 21:24). In the course of Jewish history, God appears to legitimatize military action, in contrast to his own prohibition of murder: "Thou shalt not kill" (ibid., 20:13). But these behests stood in the context of human disobedience, where the people of Israel had to bear the consequence of their own wrongdoing. The resulting bloodshed was thus not God's original will for man but rather his judgment on human disobedience, whereby "sin was chastened by sin." We see this clearly in the great drama of Old Testament nations (e.g. Isaiah 10), where God uses the spontaneous evil designs of one nation to punish another only for the first to fall under divine judgment itself, often for that very act, even though he had made it subserve his purposes. This principle is still operative today in the achieving of justice and order on the level of divine preservation, on which level war occurs. Here we stand before that humanly impenetrable mystery whereby the wrath of men, while judged by God, is nevertheless so diverted as to serve his glory, a mystery which we encounter even more strikingly in the crucifixion itself.

The role which war plays in the Old Testament has been a source of difficulty for many people, particularly for those who are most deeply convinced of the unity of the Holy Scriptures. On the other hand the Old Testament especially has been a source book for many who have sought or felt called to give religious sanction to military enterprise. Obviously the various parts of the Bible cannot be examined here in regard to this question. The basic problem, however, constituted by the seeming contradiction between the Old and the New Testament, finds its answer in the progression of redemptive revelation which culminated in Christ and in the corresponding progressive preparation of man for his advent. The pre-Christian covenants provided for man's provisional pardon, but they did not alter his fallen state. When Christ said, "Ye have heard that it hath been said," he referred to the old dispensation, where provisional justice and order were achieved through the natural laws of "eye for eye" and "tooth for tooth," although this was contrary to God's real intent then as now. But for those who have been renewed and placed into the new dispensation he goes on to prescribe a wholly different sort of conduct. "I say unto you that ye resist not evil: . . . Love your enemies." In the new economy of grace this vicious cycle of human sin is broken; henceforth the Christian is restored from his sinful state and is lifted into the new aeon, "into the glorious liberty of the children of God" (Rom. 8:21).

A distinction hereby becomes apparent between the dispensation of providence on the one hand, where violence, including that exercised by the state, remains imbedded in the structure of unredeemed society, and the dispensation of redemption on the other, where man is restored to unity with God and made "a new creature in Christ," where "old things are passed away" and "all things are become new" (II Cor. 5:17), where he cannot "continue in sin" because he is "dead" to it (Rom. 6:1, 2). There is no provision for the Christian to revert, under force of circumstance, to the sub-Christian code of conduct. Hence it is clear that man's primary responsibility to God may never be annulled by the claims of the state. Under no circumstances, according to our understanding, may the Christian take the life of his fellow man, who also was created in the image of God and for whom Christ died.

War therefore presents itself to the Christian as a two-dimensional problem, not only because he himself stands in two "worlds," but also because in another sense the state too is of a dual character. In keeping with his conscientious affirmation of the state, he seeks through every legitimate secular or political means to help build the kind of society which can avoid war. Moreover, with war and its origin so intricately interwoven in the texture of social and particularly of economic life, the Christian conscience cannot renounce war while tolerating other abuses equally incompatible with the Christian ethic. In the highest sense, however, the Christian must regard his direct economic and political efforts as secondary, inasmuch as they are at best ameliorative and can never deal with the ultimate root of war, which is in the perverted human personality. Consequently, paradoxical as it may seem, he entertains no utopian illusions that the ethic of the Gospel will be applied in its real meaning in international affairs as long as men reject the basic claims of Christ, for their acceptance alone can produce that ethic as fruit.

It follows that the Christian endeavour to eliminate war by political and other secular means does not constitute the heart of the Church's peace effort. The task of the Church does not consist in the statements she makes on international affairs or in the influence she exerts on national policies. Whether or not the Church and Christians engage in war is not dependent on whether or not war can be avoided. The Church's most effective witness and action against war comes on a different level and consists simply in the stand she takes in and through her members in the face of war. Unless the Church, trusting the power of God in whose hand the destinies of nations lie, is willing to "fall into the ground and die," to renounce war absolutely, whatever sacrifice of freedoms, advantages, or possessions this might entail, even to the point of counselling a nation not to resist foreign conquest and occupation, she can give no prophetic message for the world of nations. As the Oxford report stated so aptly in another connection, "The first duty of the Church, and its greatest service to the world, is that it be in very deed the Church" (Oxford, 57, already quoted).

Such a position will admittedly often be misunderstood by the world as negativism, evasion of responsibility and even betrayal. Indeed this is precisely the point that even Christians find difficult to comprehend. We cannot hope to convince alone by appeal to reason, for the issue here is one of faith and obedience which the "natural man" cannot comprehend (I Cor. 2:4, 14). We can, however, point out that it is not a question here of evading responsibility but one of correct diagnosis and remedy. Certainly the Church is the first to oppose evil wherever it is found, but she cannot fight this spiritual battle with physical weapons. Even though the problem of society is not in all respects the same as the problem of the individual, it remains true that moral evil has no existence in a community except as the effect of the evil will of members of the community, and consequently that social evil cannot be resolved by violence. Whatever our theory of evil we know that in practice it lies in the heart of man. It is not something external to him which can be struck and smashed or carted away, or which can be destroyed by an atom bomb. The waging of war only aggravates and spreads the trouble, and the Christian must turn from this to the far more difficult and unpopular task of attacking evil at its root. The only way to end war is to cease to fight, for the devil cannot be driven out by Beelzebub.

IV. The Common Christian Task

In this statement we have endeavoured to set forth briefly the attitude of the Christian gospel toward war and to consider the present practices of the Christian Church in the light of her professed faith. Our conclusion is that the Church must reject war, not merely because of the disorder, waste, or suffering which it causes, but far more because it is contrary to the will of God. War is the negation of the Gospel itself, of the great redemptive truths proclaimed through the centuries by the Church, and of the ministry of reconciliation entrusted to her by her Master. We have seen further that "the first duty of the Church to the world is to be the Church," that the source of her strength, and of her impact on world affairs is not the ability to out-manoeuvre the world at its own game, using the world's methods, but in the fact that she is, for all her weakness, the instrument of God, the Body of Christ, the temple of the Holy Spirit. We have seen that Christians serve society not by being assimilated into society, but by being the salt of the earth and letting their light shine before men. Finally we have seen that the ultimate destiny of nations lies beyond human control, that whatever responsibility we carry, it is God who "removeth kings, and setteth up kings" (Dan. 2:21), and therefore the power of prayer and the working of God's Spirit through the faith and obedience of his servants are the only effective weapons against the forces of evil. If the Church is impotent in this time of crisis, it is as a judgment on her lack of faith, because she still compromises and even denies her own intrinisic nature—declining to follow her Lord to suffering and the cross.

The World Council said at Amsterdam in 1948: " . . . the part which war plays in our present international life is a sin against God and a degradation of man" (Amsterdam, 89). The reasoning by which, in spite of this admission of its sinfulness, Christians continue to justify participation in war, is based on presuppositions which we have seen to be questionable. If such reasoning leads us to persist in what we have admitted to be sin, for the sole reason that the ethic of the Gospel seems unrealistic, do we not behave as though this were not God's world, as though Christ had never given the Church his Holy Spirit? The confession that Jesus Christ is Lord proclaims that God in Christ has created new possibilities which are not nullified by the Christian's involvement in sinful society. We are never so involved in sin that it is impossible for us to return, never so lost in the maze that God cannot lead us out again. The prophetic exhortations to repentance which we find recorded in Scripture never promised that the way of obedience would be easy, or that to take it would avoid all personal and national loss; but they always insisted that there was a way. We affirm that Christ is that way; and that in this world of tension and these times of strife the only course compatible with the prophetic calling of the Christian Church is to renounce every complicity with materialism and national ambition, beginning with the rejection of war and refusing arms even for the defence of those values that the Gospel has produced in our civilization. Let her whose very being is of the Spirit cast aside the unbelief of despair together with the unbelief of trust in violence, and place full faith in the weapons of her warfare, which are not carnal but mighty, in the resources of mercy and power which are hers by grace.

We believe that God has set no limits to the new possibilities that would be given the Church to reconcile, to create, to pioneer, to relieve suffering, to alleviate tensions and to meet every human need with the love of the Gospel. Christians more than anyone else can bring to the social and political tensions which trouble our world, a spirit of understanding, of patient and sacrificial concern for all men. In this spirit there can develop new processes of mediation and negotiation for the peaceful settlement of disputes. In this spirit the Church can expand the help which she is already giving to the needy people of the world to overcome hunger, disease and illiteracy, and can arouse the conscience of men and nations to direct to this purpose resources now squandered in a never-ending arms race. A World Church entirely committed to a creative Christian pacifism could bring into world affairs a transformation as yet unimagined. Her own renunciation of warfare in favour of faith in the power of the Spirit would for the first time entitle her to call the nations to the act of faith which disarmament requires. We do not believe that war is inevitable, that it comes and goes as by an inexorable and arbitrary decree of fate. It cannot be avoided by armed might nor by compromise with evil, but only by the penitence, the faith, the obedience, the righteousness and the love that exalt a nation. Ultimately God controls and shapes the destiny of nations, in accordance with their response to his will, and he dwells, not with the "biggest battalions" as was once blasphemously suggested, but "with him that is of a contrite and humble spirit" (Isa. 57:15).

Finally, our plea is not a utilitarian one; it is not based on the calculation that war will be eliminated at once if the Church refuses to participate. We do not know "the times or the seasons, which the Father hath put in his own power" (Acts 1:7). But we do know assuredly from the promise of our Master that the gates of hell cannot prevail against the Church and that therefore her victory cannot be measured in terms of military victory, nor her survival by the survival of a civilization. Our faith rests alone in "Christ the power of God, and the wisdom of God. Because the foolishness of God is wiser than men; and the weakness of God is stronger than men" (I Cor. 1:24-25).

6. The Second Assembly of the World Council of Churches (Evanston, Illinois, August 15-31, 1954)

Although the Amsterdam Assembly had asked the churches to study the problem of war, the WCC itself sponsored no major consultation in the six years between 1948 and 1954, when the second assembly was held in Evanston. The message of the Evanston Assembly was also silent on the issue. As one scholar put it:

> ... it must be pointed out that the Message carried no word about war nor peace nor world understanding, except indirectly through the response of churches and the nations to the utterance's preachment. There was no cautionary word to the great political powers, no word of restraint to the power blocs, no word of guidance to the heads of states, no word of instruction for churchmen in the pews and in the pulpits.

The Assembly did speak to the issue of war in the report of Section IV on international affairs. Pacifism itself did not become the focus of a major debate in the working meetings of the sections, but observers noted a greater openness to the pacifist witness:

> In the face of the horrors of weapons of mass destruction, the delegates to the Second Assembly were prepared to accord the pacifists a more respectful and sympathetic hearing; in the face of threats to human freedom, the pacifists showed themselves at Evanston more realistic, less inclined to regard Gandhi as a Father of the Church.

In the report of Section IV the prior condemnation of war was heightened by calling it "insane"; weapons of war were "evil." An overall assessment of the report characterized it as having strengthened the ecumenical movement's pronouncements on war and peace.

Very conscious of the bitterness of the Cold War which made difficult the participation of socialist-bloc representatives of the churches, the Assembly urged in its resolution on international affairs "governments and the peoples to continue to speak to one another, to avoid rancour and malice, and to look for ways by which fear and suspicion may be removed."

Report of Section IV
International Affairs: Christians in the Struggle for World Community

Introduction

The Assembly of the World Council of Churches proclaims the Christian hope in an hour of grave international crisis. Social and political systems are in conflict. Opposing ideologies compete for the minds and souls of men. Rival power blocs imperil the peace of nations large and small. An arms race of unprecedented dimensions casts its ominous shadow over the face of the earth. Natural and human resources, intended by God for the enrichment of society, are diverted to purposes alien to His holy will. Science is conscripted. Hydrogen weapons carry the threat of mass destruction on a scale hitherto unknown.

2. Nations arbitrarily divided by war and the aftermath of war press for the restoration of their unity, as free and sovereign peoples. Millions of God's children are in revolt against economic deprivation, political bondage and social inequality. Other millions of God's children, uprooted from the land of their fathers, seek refuge from the storms by which they are beset. Curtains of disunity and divisiveness create situations of tension around the globe. Nations and peoples whose primary desire is to dwell in peace, live in fear lest they will be destroyed by the conflict of power.

3. This troubled world, disfigured and distorted as it is, is still God's world. He rules and overrules its tangled history. In praying, "Thy will be done on earth as it is in heaven," we commit ourselves to seek earthly justice, freedom and peace for all men. Here as everywhere Christ is our hope. Our confidence lies not in our own reason or strength, but in the power that comes from God. Impelled by this faith, all our actions will be but humble, grateful and obedient acknowledgment that He has redeemed the world. The fruit of our efforts rests in His hands. We can therefore live and work as those who know that God reigns, undaunted by all the arrogant pretensions of evil, ready to face situations that seem hopeless and yet to act in them as men whose hope is indestructible.

4. With this situation before us, and our hope in Christ within us, we commend to the 170 millions of our fellow Christians in the 163 member

churches of the World Council of Churches, the following concerns on which the common judgment of Christians should be exercised, with a view to our corporate and individual action in world affairs.

I. The Desire for Peace and the Fear of War

5. Deeply and persistently man longs for peace. He no longer finds any glamour in war; he has tasted the fruit of its insanity and found it bitter and poisonous. His ideals are mocked, his liberty curtailed, his possessions destroyed, and his future undermined by total war even as its high-sounding goals have eluded his grasp. He is sick of it, and wants to be at peace!

6. Christians everywhere are committed to world peace as a goal. However, for them "peace" means far more than mere "absence of war"; it is characterized positively by freedom, justice, truth and love. For such peace the Church must labour and pray.

7. Christians must also face the fact that such a peace will not be easily or quickly attained. We live in a world in which from generation to generation ignorance of God and rebellion against Him have resulted in greed and an insatiable lust for power. War and its evils are the consequences. Basically the problem is a spiritual one, and economic and political measures alone will not solve it. Men's hearts must be changed. This is always the supreme evangelistic challenge to the Church, although we must confess that our response has been tragically casual and feeble.

8. The development of nuclear weapons makes this an age of fear. True peace cannot rest on fear. It is vain to think that the hydrogen bomb or its development has guaranteed peace because men will be afraid to go to war, nor can fear provide an effective restraint against the temptation to use such a decisive weapon either in hope of total victory or in the desperation of total defeat.

9. The thought of all-out nuclear warfare is indeed horrifying. Such warfare introduces a new moral challenge. It has served to quicken public concern, and has intensified awareness of the urgency of finding means of prevention. War's consequences can no longer seem remote to any individual; all mankind is vulnerable to a disaster from which there may be no escape.

10. The foremost responsibility of the Christian Church in this situation is undoubtedly to bring the transforming power of Jesus Christ to bear upon the hearts of men. Christians must pray more fervently for peace, repent more earnestly of their individual and collective failures to further world order, and strive more urgently to establish world contacts for reconciliation, fellowship and love.

11. Lofty objectives so often invented to justify war cannot conceal the truth that its violence and destruction are inherently evil. Therefore Christians, in their respective countries, must not lend themselves to, but expose, this deceit.

12. It is not enough for the churches to proclaim that war is evil. They must study afresh the Christian approaches to peace, taking into account both Christian pacifism as a mode of witness and the conviction of Christians that in certain circumstances military action is justifiable.

Whatever views Christians hold in respect of these approaches, they must seek out, analyse, and help to remove the psychological and social, the political and economic causes of war. Without forsaking their conviction that all weapons of war are evil, the churches should press for restraints on their use. Christians in all lands must plead with their governments to be patient and persistent in their search for means to limit weapons and advance disarmament.

13. But even this is not enough. An international order of truth and peace would require:

(a) under effective international inspection and control and in such a way that no state would have cause to fear that its security was endangered, the elimination and prohibition of atomic, hydrogen and all other weapons of mass destruction, as well as the reduction of all armaments to a minimum;

(b) the development and acceptance of methods for peaceful change to rectify existing injustices.

14. However, it must be recognized that on the basis of current suspicions and distrust the nations at the moment have reached a stalemate on the issue of control of atomic and nuclear weapons, either through international inspection or by mere resolution. What constructive steps can be proposed in this impasse?

15. We first of all call upon the nations to pledge that they will refrain from the threat or the use of hydrogen, atomic, and all other weapons of mass destruction as well as any other means of force against the territorial integrity or political independence of any state.

16. If this pledge should be broken, the Charter of the United Nations provides for collective action and, pending such international action, recognizes the right of national self-defence. We believe that any measures to deter or combat aggression should conform to the requirements of the United Nations Charter and Christians should urge that both the United Nations and their own governments limit military action strictly to the necessities of international security.

17. Yet even this is not enough. The churches must condemn the

deliberate mass destruction of civilians in open cities by whatever means and for whatever purpose. The churches should press through C.C.I.A. and other channels for the automatic stationing of U.N. Peace Commission teams in areas of tension to identify any aggression if it takes place. Christians must continue to press for social, political and economic measures to prevent war. Among these should be the giving of strong moral support for the positive use of atomic power for the benefit of mankind.

18. We must also see that experimental tests of hydrogen bombs have raised issues of human rights, caused suffering and imposed an additional strain on human relations between nations. Among safeguards against the aggravation of these international tensions is the insistence that nations carry on tests only within their respective territories, or, if elsewhere, only by international clearance and agreement.

19. Above all, Christians must witness to a dynamic hope in God, in whose hands lie the destinies of nations, and in this confidence be untiring in their efforts to create and maintain an international climate favourable for reconciliation and goodwill. The specific problems and tasks will vary in each country according to circumstances. Civil authorities may be hostile to the Church or even avowed enemies of Christ. We know that the power of the Holy Spirit does work effectively through the witness of faithful and obedient and suffering Christians, and the purposes of God will not be denied but will be fulfilled in His time.

II. Living Together in a Divided World

20. The Assembly believes that an international order conformed to the will of God and established in His peace can be achieved only through the reconciliation which Christ makes possible. Only thus will those transformed attitudes and standards, agreements and practices which alone will ensure lasting peace become possible. Because of their belief in this gospel of reconciliation and their experience of its power, Christians can never accept, as the only kind of existence open to nations, a state of perpetual tension leading to "inevitable" war. On the contrary, it is the Christian conviction that war is not inevitable, because God wills peace.

21. From this it follows that the first responsibility of Christians is to live and work for the reconciliation of men to God and, therefore, as individuals and nations, to one another. Endeavours to secure that nations shall live together in peace on any basis less fundamental than this are always precarious; at any moment they may prove to be but frail expedients in a world which has not yet become subject to the power of the Cross.

22. Nevertheless, the preservation even of these "frail expedients," in a world where Christ's reign is not yet acknowledged, is morally imperative as a minimum condition of international order. Today there is urgent need for this moral imperative to be recognized and acknowledged. The clash of national interests, social systems and ideologies tends to dominate every phase of international life. Hostile propaganda, border incidents and a suicidal competition in arms more deadly than any hitherto used, characterize a situation which is unfit to be described as peace. Over all there moves the spectre of total war. Only as these current tensions are reduced and controlled will time be secured for bringing to bear the deeper and more creative influences of reconciliation.

23. A current political definition of such endeavours is "co-existence." We avoid the use of this term because of its unhappy historical significance and some of its current political implications. "Co-existence" as conceived by Christians cannot imply any willingness to disguise from themselves or others the vast difference which lies between the search for an international order based on belief in Christ and His reconciling work, and the pursuit of aims which repudiate the Christian revelation. There can be no abandonment of the right to assert this fundamental difference and the faith on which it rests.

24. We stand against submission to, engulfment by, or appeasement of, totalitarian tyranny and aggression. We also stand against the exploitation of any people by economic monopoly or political imperialism. In the world community we must stand for the freedom of all people to know the truth which makes men free and for the basic civil liberties of all people to struggle for a higher freedom.

25. Christians claim the right to propagate their faith, by proclamation and persuasion, by example and suffering, just as they uphold the same right for others. Nevertheless, conflicts of conviction about the origin and destiny of man have long existed within societies essentially peaceful and Christians must continue to condemn totalitarianism as false in doctrine and dangerous in practice. They will be no less firm in continuing to oppose atheistic materialism. Yet however deep the conflict may be it is not necessarily an insuperable bar to living together in a divided world. The same may be said of methods of political and economic organization, whether they be democratic or dictatorial.

26. Such living together does, however, require that certain minimum conditions be met on both sides:

(a) A conviction that it is possible for nations and peoples to live together, at least for a considerable periods of years.

(b) A willingness not to use force as an instrument of policy beyond the existing frontiers. This would not mean the recognition and freezing of present injustices and the unnatural divisions of nations, but it would mean renouncing coercion as a means of securing or redressing them.

(c) A vigorous effort to end social and other injustices which might lead to civil, and hence, international war.

(d) A scrupulous respect for the pledged word.

(e) A continuing effort to reach agreement on outstanding issues, such as the peace treaties and disarmament, which are essential to a broader stabilization and pacification of relations.

(f) Readiness to submit all unresolved questions of conflict to an impartial international organization and to carry out its decisions.

27. These are minimum requirements. This limited form of living together can only be a transitional stage or a point of departure. It must move, through untiring endeavour, beyond these minimum requirements into an order of genuine cooperation. The first move into such an order must surely be in the direction of peaceful competition with growing cooperation. This order will be facilitated and reinforced through the free exchange of persons, culture, information and goods; through common undertakings for relief and human welfare and through the growth of the United Nations as an instrument for peaceful change. Christians must go still farther. They must promote the reconciliation of the nations; they must work for the extablishment of justice based on a rule of law, so that a responsibile society, grounded in truth, may be possible.

28. For the Christian the ecumenical fellowship of the churches is evidence of progress towards this goal, and of God's use of the Christian Church as one of the foundation stones of world order. Further, by its supra-national character the Church also provides the point of meeting where the search for the truth as it is in Christ in its bearing on all the problems of human society may be pursued in faith and hope as well as in love's creative power. . . .

VI. Towards an International Ethos

49. Underlying the more obvious barriers to a genuine world community is the lack of a common foundation of moral principles. At the root of the most stubborn conflicts is the failure of governments and people to treasure any common set of guiding principles. Attempted settlements involving differing ideologies are essentially unstable and tend to produce new frictions, not only because of political differences but also because of underlying differences as to moral values.

50. The world of nations desperately needs an international ethos to

provide a sound groundwork for the development of international law and institutions. This requires not only attempts to find wider areas of common moral understanding, but also efforts to bring the guiding principles of international life into greater harmony with God's will. Christians should urge statesmen to devote more attention to this fundamental task. In order to do this with authority Christians must be clear in their own understanding of the essential principles. This can be done only by sustained study. Tentatively, we advance the following considerations:

(a) All power carries responsibility and all nations are trustees of power which should be used for the common good.

(b) All nations are subject to moral law, and should strive to abide by the accepted principles of international law, to develop this law, and to enforce it through common actions.

(c) All nations should honour their pledged word and international agreements into which they have entered.

(d) No nation in an international dispute has the right to be sole judge in its own cause or to resort to war to advance its policies, but should seek to settle disputes by direct negotiation or by submitting them to conciliation, arbitration or judicial settlement.

(e) All nations have a moral obligation to ensure universal security and to this end should support measures designated to deny victory to a declared aggressor.

(f) All nations should recognize and safeguard the inherent dignity, worth and essential rights of the human person, without distinction as to race, sex, language or religion.

(g) Each nation should recognize the rights of every other nation, which observes such standards, to live by and proclaim its own political and social beliefs, provided that it does not seek by coercion, threat, infiltration or deception to impose these on other nations.

(h) All nations should recognize an obligation to share their scientific and technical skills with peoples in less developed regions, and to help the victims of disaster in other lands.

(i) All nations should strive to develop cordial relations with their neighbours, encourage friendly cultural and commercial dealings and join in creative international efforts for human welfare.

51. The churches must, therefore, see in the international sphere a field of obedience to Jesus Christ. They cannot agree that it falls outside the range of His sovereignty or the scope of the moral law. Their first duty is to fulfil their calling to manifest the Kingdom of God among men. Their fellowship must be a bond of union among all, a bond both more patient and more resistant than any other. The Church must seek to be the kind of

community which God wishes the world to become. By virtue of its calling it must act as a redemptive suffering fellowship in the form and manner of its Lord Jesus Christ. Within it differences of sex, class, nation, colour or race are to become a source of mutual enrichment, and not of rivalry or antagonism. Its members must rise above the limitations of nationalism to a truly ecumenical outlook. It must carry into the turmoil of international relations the real possibility of the reconciliation of all races, nationalities and classes in the love of Christ. It must witness to the creative power of forgiveness and spiritual renewal.

52. All these things the churches must do as an essential part of their evangelistic task. But they can never be content with words. Through the life, service and sacrifice of their members, they must make their contribution to justice and peace, to the improvement of human conditions and to the care of the needy and of the refugee. They must serve humbly the needs of the less developed peoples. In persecution and oppression they still can witness to the spiritual freedom which their members enjoy, and which no human authority can take away. Thus they will testify, both by deed and word, to the hope which Jesus Christ has brought to the world.

7. God Wills Both Justice and Peace (Angus Dun and Reinhold Niebuhr, June 13, 1955)

There were few formal replies to the joint statement by the Historic Peace Churches and the International Fellowship of Reconciliation entitled Peace Is the Will of God *(1953)*. For this reason certain non-pacifists asked two outstanding American churchmen and theologians, Bishop Angus Dun of the Protestant Episcopal Church and Professor Reinhold Niebuhr, acclaimed ethicist of Union Theological Seminary in New York, to answer the peace churches.

This they did in an article called "God Wills Both Justice and Peace," published, appropriately, in Christianity and Crisis. It is a succinct presentation to the point of view articulated in the 1930s and 1940s by Niebuhr, drawing a neo-Lutheran distinction between an ethic of love for individuals and the needs of a sinful society for which justice is the most to be hoped for. To continue the discussion, the Historic Peace Churches in Europe, along with the IFOR, later reprinted their 1953 statement and the Dun-Niebuhr response.

Something of a comparable discussion was being held in the United States. In May 1950, a Conference on Church and War was held in Detroit which was attended by four hundred delegates and many visitors—members of the Historic Peace Churches, the Fellowship of Reconciliation, and "a dozen unofficial denominational peace or pacifist fellowships." At the meeting, a Church Peace Mission was organized which continued the work of peace education. One of its major results was a program of publication of pacifist literature. A significant publication was called The Christian Conscience and War *(1953),* authored by a team of American pacifists.

This book and the Peace Is the Will of God *statement were critically reviewed by Niels H. Söe, professor of systematic theology at the University of Copenhagen in an important article "War and the Commandment of Love,"* Ecumenical Review *(1954). Although sympathetic to many of the pacifists' concerns Professor Söe believed that war was sometimes necessary as an expression of Christian love. Essentially, he arrived at a position comparable to that of Dun and Niebuhr.*

God Wills Both Justice and Peace

Angus Dun and Reinhold Niebuhr

All Christians abhor war and the evils which stem from it. Non-pacifist Christians agree with their pacifist brethren on the duty to help reduce causes of conflict, and to help promote the positive conditions of peace with justice. They share the belief that the Christian should base his action in a war situation on the dictates of conscience, informed by the command of love, and that each is responsible to God for his acts. But non-pacifist Christians reject the position of absolute pacifism because it distorts the Christian concept of love and tries to apply an individual ethic to a collective situation. At the same time they recognize the moral hazards and complexities of the non-pacifist position, which are increased by the growing powers of mass destruction.

I. PACIFISM DISTORTS THE COMMAND OF LOVE

The Christian stands under the command of love, which challenges him in his relations with persons and with society. As a citizen of the Kingdom he knows the redeeming power of the love revealed by Christ. As a citizen of a sinful society, he is called, and judged, and renewed by the divine command.

This central principle of the Christian ethic provides both the dynamic for transforming personal relations and the mainspring for social responsibility. Love has what might be called two dimensions: the vertical dimension of perfection, of sacrificial love; and the horizontal dimension of concern for all people, of concern for social justice and the balances by which it is maintained. The pacifist comprehension of love seizes upon one of these two aspects. It makes an absolute of sacrificial love at the expense of social responsibility. The pacifist tends to regard the love command less as an over-arching principle which confronts the Christian in all his relations than as a neat formula to use in situations of violence. This is an inadequate, distorted view of the Christian concept of love.

This partial view leads the pacifist to exalt peace over the claims of justice, when a choice between the two must be made. Non-violence is regarded as a pure expression of love, while the struggle for justice is seen as a rough and inferior approximation of love. It is true that the Christian must wrestle with the ultimate possibilities of love. And justice, which depends upon the uneasy balances of social life, is not ultimate. On the other hand, justice is not essentially a compromise with evil or simply an approximation of love in an evil world. It expresses the social responsibility which stems from one dimension of love. Justice is an instrument of love in a sinful society. To abandon it, whenever violence is involved, is irresponsible.

The struggle for justice and the struggle for peace have the same sanction in the commandment of love. Both present a moral imperative. But justice has the prior claim, for while order may be conducive to justice, there can be no lasting peace without justice. The Biblical concept is expressed by Isaiah: "And the effect of righteousness will be peace" (Isa. 32:17) The just war position gains strength from the consideration that the triumph of an unjust cause would defeat both the ends of justice and the future hope of peace.

By making an absolute of non-violence, the pacifist is led to a position of social irresponsibility. Violence is regarded as sinful, no matter how just the cause or how great the wickedness which would follow its defeat. Non-violence is seen as an escape from sin, no matter how evil the consequences which may flow from it. Many pacifists naively believe that the consequences of non-violence can only be good. Some, however, recognize that the consequences for society in any particular situation may not be good, and find justification in the unqualified character of the command, that "under no circumstance . . . may the Christian take the life of his fellow man . . . ." (*Peace Is the Will of God*, p. 17) Identifying the pacifist position with obedience to Christ, these argue that the Christian "may not calculate in advance what this may mean for himself or for society." (*Ibid*, p. 14) Yet the calculation of consequences is part of a responsible moral decision. The "works," for which every man is "responsible to God," (*Ibid*, p. 9) include the results as well as the motives of our deeds.

II. PACIFISM APPLIES AN INDIVIDUAL ETHIC TO A COLLECTIVE SITUATION

The tendency toward social irresponsibility in the pacifist position also derives from the attempt to apply the personal ethic of sacrificial love to the social problems of war. Pacifists say that Christians must accept suffering instead of inflicting it. This is quite true, so far as personal relations are concerned. But the moral issues of war seldom present themselves in such simple terms. The issue often is whether or not to accept (and thus to inflict) suffering by others, as the victims of aggression or injustice. This issue cannot be resolved by a formula of non-violence, quite applicable to individual relations. A social ethic is required.

The same tendency is seen in reverse in the pacifist interpretation of the phrase of the Amsterdam Report, "War is contrary to the will of God."

As the context ought to make clear, this phrase is a condemnation of war as an institution, as a social evil. It does not say or mean that the aggressor and the victim are alike condemned. No, the predominantly non-pacifist group which approved this phrase did not assume that degrees of guilt and innocence had been wiped out by the increasingly catastrophic character of modern war. Yet pacifists move directly from the social evil of war to an individual ethic: "since 'war is contrary to the will of God' it would seem to be incumbent on every Christian to abstain from it." (*Ibid,* p. 4) Here the claims of justice disappear.

In the face of such criticism, pacifists find refuge in the unconditional demand of sacrificial love: "even if a particular war were likely to preserve more lives and values than it would destroy . . . it could never be the duty of a follower of Christ to take the lives of some of God's children in the hope of protecting the lives and liberties of others." (*Ibid,* p. 6) Whose duty then is it to protect the lives and liberties of others? Apparently pacifists who stop short of philosophical anarchism would say the state, whose primary task is to be the "guarantor of order," is responsible. (*Ibid,* p. 15ff) Non-pacifist Christians today would largely agree as to the "delegated, relative, and provisional nature" of the authority exercised by the state, and that it applies to "unredeemed society" under the "dispensation of providence" as compared with the "dispensation of redemption." (*Ibid,* pp. 16-17) The issue here is the relation of the Christian to the state.

The very limited concept of Christian citizenship held by pacifist Christians is one of the weaknesses of their position. The responsibility of the Christian to and for the state is recognized up to a point: "In keeping with his conscientious affirmation of the state, he seeks through every legitimate secular or political means to help build the kind of society which can avoid war." (*Ibid,* p. 18) But when the state has to exercise its admitted central function as guarantor of order, then the state is abandoned on the ground that the Christian has a higher loyalty and code of conduct. The Christian is thus "in the world" until coercion or violence enter the scene, when he becomes "not of the world."

This is a wrong concept of the tension in which the Christian stands, for the demands of the Gospel challenge him at every point, and not merely when the state resorts to force. And he is obliged to act responsibly in society at all times, and not merely when the state is at peace. Being in the world, but not of the world applies to the whole of life.

Moreover, pacifists not only refuse to support the state when it tries to preserve order. Many tend, by translating pacifist principles into political terms, to oppose or weaken the power of the state to maintain order or to defend justice. Thus, the church is urged to "renounce war . . . even to the point of counseling a nation not to resist foreign conquest and occupation" and to "refusing arms even for defense of those values that the Gospel has produced in our civilization." (*Ibid,* pp. 18, 20) The advocacy of unilateral disarmament and national non-resistance constitutes not a pacifist witness but an effort to impose a pacifist policy on the state itself, the "guarantor of order." Such aberrations of Christian pacifism spring not from the principle of sacrificial love, but from regarding it as the framework of a political strategy. The confusion between an individual and a social ethic is here compounded.

These, in brief, are reasons why non-pacifist Christians find pacifism an inadequate expression of the commandment of love, and are compelled to reject it. But it is easier for them to point out the weaknesses of the pacifist position than to work out a satisfactory formulation of their own more complex position.

III. The Concept of the Just War

There is no adequate definition of a just war which can surely be applied to the various conceivable war situations with which the nations may be confronted. Nor is such a definition likely to emerge. For the permutations of the international crisis, the shifting claims of justice and order, and the changing consequences of alternative courses, are endless. Consequently, for non-pacifist Christians unable to make the state the keeper of their consciences, there is no easy way or foolproof guide. In the end, each must weigh the conflicting claims for himself, in the light of the most objective information available. Each must decide whether, on balance, there is enough preponderance of moral value on one side of a conflict to justify conscientious participation. While the judgments of the Christian community can help, in the final analysis the individual conscience is the arbiter of the concept of a just war.

A heavy burden of responsibility is thus placed on the individual Christian. His access to accurate and objective information, particularly in a war situation, is limited. The principles he must strive to apply, while finding sanction in the commands of the Gospel, do not provide any infallible guide to his decision. There are no foolproof yardsticks for him to use. And the possibilities of erroneous conclusions in such complex situations are many. The hazards here, which are the hazards of the Protestant heritage, are real.

To help guide the conscience and to reduce the hazards, various formulas have been advanced. Each has its merits and its weaknesses. The three positions put forward at Oxford and Amsterdam may be referred to briefly.

The traditional concept of a just war, which is the official position of Roman Catholicism as well as of certain communions within the ecumenical fellowship, defines a just war as one in which just means are used to defend a just cause. This traditional concept calls attention to the importance of means appropriate to the ends sought and to the danger of excessive violence. But efforts to construct a precise guide through detailed elaborations of this definition result in a rigid and highly artificial structure, more likely to confuse than illumine the conscience.

An example of such confusion is the first position advanced in the Amsterdam Report, a position derived from this traditional concept:

> There are those who hold that, even though entering a war may be a Christian's duty in particular circumstances, modern warfare, with its destruction, can never be an act of justice.

This says in effect that because the excessive violence of atomic weapons does not fit the traditional formalistic definition of a just war, the term should be dropped. Yet since the problem of a just war remains, whatever the terminology, a new term must be used such as Christian duty. Here the effort to preserve an elaborate formula has gotten in the way of clear thinking. For what is the ground of Christian duty except the concern for justice and order?

A second approach to guidance for the Christian conscience is one which attempts to establish international law as the plumb line for the concept of a just war. This position was stated in differing ways at Oxford and at Amsterdam. The valid element here is recognition that the judgment of the international community can provide a corrective to the distortions of national interest and provide a factor of relative objectivity in determining the justice or injustice of a particular cause. Thus the presence in Korea of a U.N. Commission provided an important element of objectivity in determining the aggressor. It was on the basis of this report that the World Council's Central Committee urged support for the collective measures undertaken by the U.N.

The Oxford definition held that Christians are obligated to take part in wars, comparable with police measures, against transgressors of international agreements and pacts. But in recognition of the fact that many causes of conflict are not covered by such agreements, it was added that Christians should participate only in such wars as are "justifiable on the basis of international law." The Amsterdam definition is somewhat more general:

In the absence of impartial supra-national institutions, there are those who hold that military action is the ultimate sanction of the rule of law, and that citizens must be distinctly taught that it is their duty to defend the law by force if necessary.

Insofar as there is a "rule of law" in international affairs, that law does provide an aid to conscience. But it is clear that the rule of law in world affairs is both primitive and partial. Undue reliance on it as a guide leads to a false legalism. The United Nations provides the most objective collective judgment available, but it is not an "impartial supra-national" institution, nor is it infallible. To "defend the law" is part of the defense of justice and order, but it is no substitute for it.

The third approach to the concept of a just war, is the position advanced at Oxford that Christians, in obedience to conscience, have a duty to participate in war "waged to vindicate what they believe to be an essential Christian principle: to defend the victims of wanton aggression, or to secure freedom for the oppressed." In its stress upon conscience and its avoidance of elaborate formulas, this definition is closest to the idea of a just war here advanced. It has the merit of simplicity, and flexibility in the face of changing crisis. It also has the weakness of giving little precise guidance to the conscience. While aggression and oppression remain the chief targets of a just war, the formulation seems to breathe more of a crusading spirit than most non-pacifist Christians would find appropriate today.

IV. THE NEW DIMENSION OF WAR

The rapid development of weapons of mass destruction has enormously increased the destructive power in Soviet and Western hands. This has created a new dimension of catastrophe for any future global war. And because of the ramifications of the power blocs, and the tensions between them, there is grave danger that limited wars will become a global war. Obviously, the probability of tremendous, perhaps incalculable, destruction on both sides in a future war needs to be reckoned with in the moral calculations of the just war position.

The notion that the excessive violence of atomic warfare has ended the possibility of a just war does not stand up. Even the Amsterdam proposition, which rejected the concept of the just war, as traditionally defined, brought back the idea itself under the guise of Christian "duty in particular circumstances." The moral problem has been altered, not eliminated.

The threat of atomic destruction has heightened the criminal irresponsibility of aggression, the employment of war as an instrument of national or bloc policy. Correspondingly, the moral obligation to discourage such a crime or, if it occurs, to deny it victory, has been underscored. The consequences of a successful defense are fearful to contemplate, but the consequences of a successful aggression, with tyrannical monopoly of the weapons of mass destruction, are calculated to be worse. While the avoidance of excessive and indiscriminant violence, and of such destruction as would undermine the basis for future peace remain moral imperatives in a just war, it does not seem possible to draw a line in advance, beyond which it would be better to yield than to resist.

Resistance to aggression, designed to deny it victory and tyrannical control, is not to be equated with victory by those who resist the aggressor. In view of war's new dimension of annihilation, the justification for a defensive war of limited objectives, to prevent conquest and to force an end to hostilities, does not apply equally to the objectives of bringing an aggressor to unconditional surrender and punishment. Because the ultimate consequences of atomic warfare cannot be measured, only the most imperative demands of justice have a clear sanction.

For this reason, the occasions to which the concept of the just war can be rightly applied have become highly restricted. A war to "defend the victims of wanton aggression," where the demands of justice join the demands of order, is today the clearest case of a just war. But where the immediate claims of order and justice conflict, as in a war initiated "to secure freedom for the oppressed," the case is now much less clear. The claims of justice are no less. But because contemporary war places so many moral values in incalculable jeopardy, the immediate claims of order have become much greater. Although oppression was never more abhorrent to the Christian conscience or more dangerous to the longer-range prospects of peace than today, the concept of a just war does not provide moral justification for initiating a war of incalculable consequences to end such oppression.

While this position gives the claims of order a certain immediate priority over the claims of justice, the fact remains that no lasting peace is possible except on foundations of justice. Nor can the shorter-range prospects be improved unless remedial measures are taken in regard to social injustices likely to erupt as civil and hence international war. Consequently, the restraints imposed by the new dimension of war underline the importance of a vigorous development of methods of peaceful change. For God wills both justice and peace.

8. God Establishes Both Peace and Justice (Paul Peachey and Members of the Continuation Committee, 1955 and 1958)

After the publication of the Dun-Niebuhr article in 1955 the continuation committee of the Historic Peace Churches and the International Fellowship of Reconciliation asked Paul Peachey to draft a response. Peachey, at that point a professor in the Eastern Mennonite College, Harrisonburg, Virginia, had been earlier active in the committee's work while pursuing graduate studies in theology in Paris and Zürich.

His draft provided the basis for an expanded reply to the Dun-Niebuhr critique, with the writing assistance of another peace-church scholar and counsel of other members of the continuation committee. The revision was published in 1958—along with the 1953 statement, Peace Is the Will of God, *and the Dun-Niebuhr article. The three documents were now entitled* The Christian and War: A Theological Discussion of Justice, Peace and Love. *They made up a forty-seven-page booklet issued by the peace churches and the IFOR.*

A later incarnation of the same material under the last-named title, with the addition of a brief ecumenical study document, was published by the continuation committee in September 1970. The 1958 booklet had gone out of print and numerous requests for copies led to the new edition.

God Establishes Both Peace and Justice

... The article, "God Wills Both Justice and Peace," by Bishop Dun and Professor Niebuhr, published as a reply "for discussion purposes" to the pamphlet of the Historic Peace Churches, *Peace Is the Will of God,* augurs much good for the future. This is not because an early agreement between the divergent views expressed in the two documents is to be expected—the thoughtful reader of both will become quite conscious of this—but because serious conversation has finally been joined between traditions that have communicated far too little in modern times. And such conversations will be welcomed by all who recognize the value of dialogue in the development of Christian insights, regardless of their particular viewpoint.

This said, however, it must be added that "God Wills Both Justice and Peace," does not deal adequately with the main line of argument in the statement it purports to consider. (For brevity's sake and without disrespect, we may in the future refer to the statement argued by Bishop Dun and Professor Niebuhr as DN and *Peace Is the Will of God* as PWG.) Whatever the validity of its arguments or conclusions, PWG is primarily an attempt to put forth a distinctively Christian approach to war by the isolation and exclusion of a complex of axioms of other extraction, which through the centuries have become so deeply imbedded in the substratum of Christian thinking that, for most people, they are not required to answer critical muster. It is after a scrutiny of such presuppositions that the Peace Church document concludes with a call to Christians to live fully in the "new aeon," where lesser loyalties are subordinated to the *agape* of the Christian community. DN takes a position with respect to only one of these challenged presuppositions, namely, "the concept of the 'just war,'" and even then agrees that the concept offers little precise guidance to Christian individuals trying to decide what they should do in the various conceivable modern war situations. Whereas it would seem that, in order to reply clearly to PWG, convinced representatives of the nonpacifist position should be ready to explain for what reasons and under what conditions Christians are called to go to war with the assurance that it is God's will, the present reply satisfies itself with the demonstration that the problem is complicated; its last word is that every individual must decide with little help from its authors or from other Christians.

PWG recognizes that Christian individuals now find themselves in a complex of societies, each involving certain bonds of social obligation and responsibility, but this Peace Church statement goes further in clearly asserting that membership in the Body of Christ is membership in a social group whose bonds transcend other impulses of social cohesion. One indication of what pacifists regard as a failure to consider this point seriously is the fact that, although DN refers in many places to Christians as individuals and to society at large, it refers to the Church only once, and that is in connection with a quotation from PWG. In a word, it appears as though its authors are replying, not to PWG, but to a kind of individualistic pacifism that was current after the First World War—and with traces of the same individualism appearing in the argument. Although DN accuses the pacifism it attacks of "applying an individual ethic to a collective situation," its own conclusion is that, "in the end, each must weight the conflicting claims for himself . . . each must decide whether, on balance, there is enough preponderance of moral value on one side of a conflict to justify conscientious participation . . . in the final analysis the individual conscience is the arbiter of the concept of the just war." This is the neglect of the most important social dimension, the Church of Christ. The Peace Churches know from experience that Christians must sometimes follow their conscience in opposing social evil as individuals, when the voices of the churches are unclear and even conflicting, but they do not excuse this situation by calling it normative. While the authors of DN propose the application of an individual standard of choice to a social situation, the Peace Churches appeal to the Church to be faithful to her distinctive calling as Church, with a message that is desperately needed in the face of what all societies recognize as the world's most pressing social problem.

Let there be no doubt about the issues at stake. We are not talking only about border skirmishes, such as those of the *Pax Romana* at the time when the concept of the "just war" was first articulated. Neither can we apply the scholastic Roman Catholic "just-war" doctrine, where a war is not just unless it can be won, to the case of those modern wars where everybody loses. Some of these difficulties are recognized in the last two sections of DN in the following words: "There is no adequate definition of a just war which can surely be applied to the various conceivable war situations with which the nations may be confronted; the authors speak of the new dimensions of war arising from the enormous increase in the destructive power of modern weapons. We can only agree. This only makes the question the more urgent."

The Peace Church statement is cited in DN ("the Christian may not calculate in advance what this may mean for himself or for society'") to accuse pacifists of failing to regard the consequences. We would, indeed, be ready to begin a discussion on the consequences of a given modern war, although experience has indicated that proponents of war who want to discuss only consequences often fail to include all the consequences and to evaluate them from a distinctively Christian viewpoint. On the one hand, they attack pacifists for not making decisions by weighing the consequences; on the other hand, they themselves refuse to accept the responsibility for the consequences for past wars by contending the wars they favored were not the wars that were later actually fought. If we are to discuss "The War to End All Wars," we will insist on pointing out that one of the consequences was a second World War more terrible than the first. If we discuss World War II, the war to "establish the Four Freedoms," we will also discuss the consequences for millions of non-combatants who were direct victims of rockets, atomic bombs, and the later extension of Russian totalitarianism. From past experience, pacifists are led to wonder whether it is not inherent in the nature of war that military necessities which sacrifice the proposed ends continually arise. War may appear to achieve certain goals, but the chain of consequences does not stop at apparent victory. Modern war is not an instrument that can be used to achieve a given objective and then laid down at will.

But the real issue in this discussion of consequence is not the reluctance of pacifists to begin by speaking of consequences, but a disagreement concerning the standard by which the consequences are to be evaluated. Consequences cannot be meaningfully discussed until this last point is clear. The authors of DN contend that certain wars are "just"—but it is precisely their standard of justice by which they evaluate these wars and their consequences that must be called into question. Specifically, they must assure us that their concept of justice will lead to distinctively Christian decisions in accordance with the testimony of the Word of God. This, as we shall see, has not been done.

Lest we seem to evade the issues as they are phrased in DN, however, we shall comment on them more specifically before coming to the basic problem.

I. Does Pacifism Distort the Command of Love?

It is argued in DN that "love has what might be called two dimensions: the vertical dimension of perfection, of sacrificial love; and the horizontal dimension of concern for all people, or concern for social justice and the balances by which it is maintained. The pacifist comprehension of love seizes upon one of these two aspects." The pacifist is thus led "to exalt peace over the claims of justice." To insist on absolute nonresistance in a sinful society is to allow evil in the form of injustice to go unchecked and thus to defeat the very purposes of love, according to DN. Against pacifists, who would see the struggle for justice as a rough and inferior approximation of love, the authors of DN assert that "justice is not simply an approximation of love in an evil world . . . justice is an instrument of love in a sinful society." These authors do recognize, however, that "justice, which depends upon the uneasy balances of social life, is not ultimate."

This dialectic does not yield a clear conclusion on the factors which should finally determine the decision of the Christian or the content of the Church's message in practical situations. Near the beginning of the draft, in a comparison between the struggle for "justice," on the one hand, and for "peace" and "order," on the other, the authors assert that "justice has the prior claim." We are indeed surprised, then, to find that the last section of the draft, which discusses modern war, concludes with a position which "gives the claims of order a certain immediate priority over the claims of justice." Aside from the empirical fact that no real justice is possible without peace and order, it must be pointed out that the theological ambiguity at this point is very confusing for the Christian who wonders which of two alternative possibilities *does* have the priority in the immediate situation confronting him. PWG showed that a casuistry in which non-Christian presuppositions lead to the actual decision between the two "Christian" categories so indecisively balanced rests on precisely this kind of ambiguity.

The validity up to a certain point of the use of "justice" as a reference point in ethics is not to be denied. In a society where higher impulses of action are wanting it is necessary that certain men be entrusted with the task of maintaining a provisional and minimal justice (Isa. 10; Rom. 13). Furthermore, Christian love, with its concern for the well-being of the other, is not less but more concerned with the ordering of human relations than is the impulse of legal justice.

The question which must be faced, however, is whether or not justice, in the common legal sense, is a Christian value at all. Certainly the context of the term had been colored far more deeply by the classical Graeco-Latin tradition than by the Judeo-Christian heritage. "Justice," in current usage and whatever its particular religious interest, is primarily concerned with equality, with harmony among the parts, with rendering to each its own, and thus ultimately also with retribution. It is partly because of the use of the Latin *justitia* as a translation for Biblical terms that the principle of legal and equivalent retribution has come to be regarded as an absolute principle of moral behavior derived from God.

This is what is evidenced in DN when the authors introduce the undefined concept of "justice" as one of two perpendicular dimensions of Christian love in the third paragraph, criticize pacifists for not giving this "justice" the prior claim over peace and order in succeeding paragraphs, and then conclude with the statement that there are times when the claims of order do come first. Rather than to accept the parallel claims of the two "dimensions" and then to attempt in a pacifist counter-casuistic to establish conditions under which "justice" does *not* have the prior claim, we shall try to clarify the basic dilemma posed and answered in different ways in different sections of DN by examining the relationship between social rules and conventions concerning equity, on the one hand, and the righteousness of God in the Biblical concept of justice, on the other.

The modern Christian concept of justice had its origin in the Hebrew *tsedeq,* the Old Testament term regularly used to designate God's righteousness acting in judgment. The principal meaning of another word, *mishpat,* denoted the human justice present in social custom and formulated in judgments in courts of law. In Biblical usage, the *tsedeq* of God is differentiated from and, at the same time, related to the *mishpat* of men.

Exegetical studies have confirmed two important facts: (1) in Old Testament thought, God's righteous judgment (*tsedeq*) is intimately linked with His saving activity, and (2) the *tsedeq* of God is normative for all human justice (*mishpat*). God's *tsedeq* in the Old Testament is redemptive; it borders on His *chesed,* His sure love and mercy. And the repeated juxtaposition and even occasional poetic interchange of *tsedeq* and *mishpat* make it clear that the passion for human justice is to be rooted in the righteousness of God, and ultimately in His redemptive acts. Far from the *justitia* that could be contrasted with "the dimension of sacrificial love," it is itself the expression of redemptive love for all men, especially for those poor and needy to whom nothing at all is really "due."

The New Testament ethic is the culmination of this tradition of redemptive justice patterned after divine justice. God is seen as "faithful and just to forgive us our sins" (I John 1:9). Social justice in the teachings of Jesus involves giving "to him who begs of thee," "loving your enemies, and praying for those who persecute you," and again these fruits of grateful obedience are seen as obligations for those who would be "sons of the Father who is in heaven." Jesus was the "righteousness of God" for the early Christians, and the idea that their just obligations to their fellow men should be defined by any justice other than the righteousness of God revealed in Christ's self-abasement and love was unthinkable. God's justice and righteousness were viewed as ultimately redemptive.

In the Old Testament, the medium for the interaction of the righteousness of God and human justice was the covenant. It was through the miracle of the Exodus that God created the Israelite nation, and the covenant community was founded in the confidence that God would be faithful. The laws and customs of God's people were to have no foundation other than His righteousness and mercy, and the covenant community was to be the center from which all nations could learn of His justice and redemption. Redemption as awaited by Israel meant, particularly in the eyes of the late Jewish prophets, the restoration, the recreation of true community. One day, through God's saving righteousness, human relations would be so transformed that "the wolf should dwell with the lamb . . . " (Isa. 11:6).

References to the relationship between the Church of Christ and the Old Testament covenant people are frequent in the New Testament. In both cases, "God's people" is conscious of its difference from other societies; the primary choice before each individual aware of the existence of the covenant people is as to the group with which he wants to be identified. The radical implications of the dependence of the New Testament covenant community on the Lord are most clearly brought out in Paul's figure of the Body whose Head is Christ. Those who respond to His work in grateful obedience are united with Him; they are the continuing incarnation of His redemptive initiative. The social ethic of the early Christians was nothing other than the collective expression of the redeeming and sacrificial *agape* of their Master.

What, then, can be said about the "justice" of DN, the "social justice which depends upon the uneasy balances of social life"? In modern societies, there are certain ideas of "fair dealing" and "moral action" that are more or less generally accepted. What is the relationship between these standards of human justice and God's plan of redemption?

We have seen that, for the Old Testament, it is the *tsedeq* of God that is normative for all human justice. But, in the context of a society in its unredeemed state, the Old Testament realistically articulates a *lex talionis,* as well. Although vengeance as such is a prerogative retained by God (Deut. 32:35), a kind of justice characterized by retribution, vengeance, and the righting of wrongs, by coercion if necessary, is operative and has a deterrent value and objective in societies where the impulses of true community are wanting. This kind of relative justice "is not ultimate," as the authors of DN would agree; however, we can further say that it can only be measured in terms of a kind of justice which is not relative, the redemptive "*agape-justice*" revealed supremely in Christ.

Men are free to refuse the "*agape-justice*" of God—they were free to send Christ to the Cross—and still to retain a certain socially convenient concept of justice, which they often proceed to absolutize and make normative. But if the redemptive justice of God means nothing less than the re-creation of true community, all lesser concepts of justice are sub-Christian values. The *lex talionis* may be accepted as a principle and responsibility in fallen societies. But Christ, in the new age He has initiated, creates the true human community rooted in *agape* and within ordinary "social justice" is transcended by a higher impulse. In pointing to the ambiguity in DN's use of the term "justice," and in attempting to identify and use in this conversation a concept of justice with firm roots in Christian revelation, we do not mean to say that ordinary legal justice has no relation to *agape-justice*. Were there no relationship at all, we would object to any use of the term instead of seeking to articulate a distinctively Christian concept of justice. Further, in insisting that a critique of the church's life be phrased in Christian terms, we are in no way claiming that the Church is now characterized by such great love as to make impossible any critique from the level of a sub-Christian kind of justice. We of the Historic Peace Churches must confess that our own fellowships have not at all times presented a unanimous witness with respect to war; neither have we consistently lived out the radical economic and social consequences of our peace position. We would not, however, be deterred from recognizing the vocation to which God calls us, together with His whole Church, merely because our Christian behavior and that of our fellows is inferior to the standard. Rather would we plead with fellow Christians to join us in dedication to a deeper and more costly obedience.

We will have occasion to deal with certain specific types of perfectionism as misinterpretations of the Christian gospel later. But for the present we maintain that when "justice" is examined in the light of the Christian gospel, it either plainly reduces itself to something sub-Christian or it becomes synonymous with *agape*. The Church is not called to work for either justice or peace using methods not founded in God's righteousness and mercy. For God establishes both justice and peace in redemption.

II. Does Pacifism Seek to Apply an Individual Ethic to a Collective Situation?

The attention given in recent years to ethical problems in the sphere of intergroup relations has confronted pacifism with a challenge that has been wholesome. There have been pacifists who have naively refused to recognize commonplace realities concerning the behavior of modern subnational economic groups and national political units. They have been unaware that even in the Christian community, where the love relationship supposedly reaches its highest expression men often resort extensively to "justice" of a sub-Christian kind.

The misgiving arises here again, however, that the true complexity of the social situation is not given in DN, and that a rediscovered insight has been absolutized at the expense of other aspects of the same reality.

Already in their argument on "social justice," the authors of DN repeatedly accuse pacifists of "social irresponsibility"; they apparently think that the latter concept is sufficiently clear that it can be introduced without further comment as a basis for ethical judgments. They speak of the responsibilities of the Christian "as a citizen of a sinful society" without mentioning the fundamental questions: to whom is the Christian responsible, and for what is the Christian responsible? For the fact is that the Christian is not a member of *one* society that is characterized by the continued presence of sin; social problems are so complex precisely because the collective situation in which the Christian finds himself involves the presence of a *number* of social groups, each with its own norms and each making certain demands, with some of the demands and norms of one group in radical conflict with those of other groups. Saying that the individual in this situation is "responsible" to these groups may be true, in general, but it evades the real questions: what is implied in the responsibility to each group, and which of the societies has the priority when their demands conflict?

The Biblical record of the history of salvation is not as irrelevant to this question as DN would indicate when it limits truly Christian ethics, "the dimension of perfection, of sacrificial love," to the sphere of the individual and relegates all social groups to other norms, such as the concept of justice we have just examined. We live in a sinful world, a fact of which war is one evidence, but let this not be an argument for continuing in sin. Although the justice of human societies may fall from the Biblical norm — as, indeed, does the justice of many individuals, in spite of the "dimension of perfection" that everyone agrees is relevant for them — we have already observed that norms for men are not to be found in the claims or conventions or the social justice of any sinful society, but in the redemptive righteousness of God. Historic Peace Church pacifists, who look back on centuries of persecution from Christians and non-Christians alike, will hardly be lightly accused of optimism about the alternatives likely to interest a sinful society, but this is not because they are pessimistic about the possibilities of divine righteousness or because they believe that final hope can be placed in anything less. Paul indicates that ultimate pessimism is characteristic of men who are "without Christ and strangers from the covenants of promise." Failing to reckon with God's people and His promises, they are those "having no hope and without God in the world" (Eph. 2:12).

To be specific, there is certainly little in the Biblical record that would lend support to DN's extreme distinction between individual and group ethics. We cannot escape the strongly social frame of reference in which the whole drama of redemption is presented. What can be more highly structured than the kingdom which is central in the prophetic vision and the good news proclaimed by Jesus? The restoration of true community, as we have noted, is central in the whole redemptive scheme. In the Sermon on the Mount, the new dimension is not the prohibition of private vengeance — indeed this is not a unique Judeo-Christian insight — nor yet the proclamation of justice, but rather the transcendence of the *lex talionis* by a new dynamic of community. The relations of the Christian community thus stand in sharp contrast to those of the societies governed by the principle of "eye for eye" and "tooth for tooth."

In recent years, the importance of the life and death of Jesus for this question has been made increasingly clear. *The ethic of Jesus was not an individual ethic; His most "individual" actions carried social and political implications.* Suffering with His people under the Romans, He lived in a time of political unrest, and the Zealot movement was the background of His whole ministry. This underground resistance was well represented among those who followed Him; even the intimate circle of the Twelve seems to have included members of the party, to say nothing of the crowds who once wanted to make Him King. And why not, when the Zealots were those who represented in its purest form the old theocratic ideal? Establishing a human order where God would reign over the people of His choice—was not this, since David, the dream of every Israelite?

From His baptism to the arrest in Gethsemane, Jesus was faced with a real choice. If we are not to depreciate the humanity of Jesus, we can only conclude that the world domination offered Him by Satan (Matt. 4:8, 9) and a last-minute defence in the Garden (Matt. 26:53) were, for Him, real possibilities, and that He considered them in all seriousness before rejecting them as incompatible with His mission. And yet, even in the week of crisis, when He was hailed as a pretender to the throne and then condemned to death as a rebel against the Roman state five days later, He did not turn to defend Himself and His fellow victims of oppression. For Himself and His friends, the political consequences of His action were crucial; thenceforth, those who wanted to go with Him had to go the way of the Cross. A more categorical rejection of a "Christian politics of defense" would be hard to imagine.

Indeed, the central events of this history also contain several striking examples of misguided responsibility. Pilate was socially responsible first of all to the people and for doing what they wanted him to do. Peter felt himself responsible for Jesus, who certainly was an innocent man unjustly attacked if there ever has been one, but the record indicates that Peter fulfilled his responsibility in the wrong way. While it is not possible to discern any different principles of moral action guiding Jesus' life and mission toward the end of His life when He was acclaimed and then executed as a political figure, Annas and Caiaphas, who thought it expedient that one man should die for the people, are judged precisely because they sacrificed moral considerations to their calculations of what would best preserve the stability and order of society, and estimated political action by a standard we have every reason to suppose they would have shrunk from applying in private life.

It is clear that, of the various concepts of "social responsibility," some may be far from Christian. Specifically, the Chistian's social responsibility to his fellow men is grounded, not in the social conventions fixing what other societies might want him to do for them, but in the righteousness of God. Social responsibility to whom and for what? Responsibility first of all to God, a corollary of membership in His people, and for showing His redeeming and community-creating righteousness and love to all of His children, no matter in what society they may be found.

In all this, moreover, there is no suggestion that the community of love created through the work of Christ and proclaimed in the Church can be accomplished from without through legislation. What is announced in the Gospel is not merely formal in character; the conduct depicted in the Sermon on the Mount is descriptive of action which flows from real transformation. For this reason, when he is confronted with the possibility that abundance of grace might encourage antinomianism, Paul argues from the transformed character (Rom. 6:2). We are thus driven to ask whether the argument that Christian conduct is intended for relations across the garden fence and not across the ocean, does not involve us in an untenable contradiction. To argue that privately the Christian must love his enemy but in a group situation fight him is a denial, not of the possibility of transformation of life in the redeemed community, but also of the basic character of individual Christian experience itself.

III. The Inevitability of Dualism: The Basic Problem

Peace Is the Will of God is concerned with the contradiction between the insight of the Assembly of the World Council of Churches at Amsterdam that "War is contrary to the Will of God" and the conclusion obviously reached by the majority of that assembly that it nonetheless may become necessary and thus justifiable. In seeking to discover how this contradiction comes about, it was noted that a number of extraneous or non-Christian presuppositions had gained axiomatic status in Christian thought, which serve to modify or neutralize the basic Christian insights regarding war. Among these were some of the common arguments such as the sanctity of a given national group, the just war, and war as the lesser evil.

To this group we may now well add the arguments based on the priority of justice and on the distinction between the individual and the collective ethic. This is not an attempt to close the discussion on these two further points prematurely, but rather to urge that they be not accepted without more convincing evidence. When the emphasis of the whole New Testament and the peace testimony of the early Church is so clear, we may reasonably ask for a valid argument on the basis of which modern Christians would be commanded by God to participate in modern war. Christian churches have too often assumed that, once God's name has been invoked, the situation itself and the "necessities" thereof define the appropriate action for the Christian, quite irrespective of the relevance of the revelation of God in Christ for the question. Let us not be legalistic in deducing "neat formulas" from this revelation. Let us not begin with prohibitions, but by asking what indications we are given to guide us in what we should do to show the love of Christ to our fellow men. But, at the same time, let us not, in our fear of legalism, jump to a counterlegalism which would prove that, since the Bible is not a book of laws, indications in it relevant to the question of war—that we should "love our enemies" and "overcome evil with good," for example—cannot possibly mean what they clearly seem to say.

We have already seen that justice, in so far as it is a Christian value at all, is rooted in the righteousness of God. We can go farther and state that there is only one ethical good for the Christian, and that it is founded in and defined by God's self-revelation. "God is Lord over Church and World," to use a phrase current in present studies of the World Council of Churches, and His will for all men, whether viewed as *tsedeq* or *agape,* is one. The "World" may refuse to acknowledge God's Lordship, but it is not therefore subject to autonomous norms which would be unrelated to the "good" defined by God's self-revelation.

A basic problem has been confronting us throughout this discussion: the contradiction between the *ought* in life—this "good" or the will of God—and the *is* in human attainment. We are face to face with a duality that has plagued human history, for human freedom itself is one of its sources. In principle and in practice, we can and do say "No" to God. On the one hand stands the will of God revealed in Christ, with its lofty but "impossible" ideals, and on the other, the level of conduct that seems to be the most that can be demanded of men.

In every age this contradiction perturbs the sensitive spirits among Christians, and across the centuries one effort after another is made to overcome or resolve the tension. Familiar among these solutions are the counsels of perfection exemplified in monasticism and the less demanding precepts observed by Christians in ordinary walks of life. There is the two-kingdoms view of Luther. In historical Calvinism the conflict was forced into the individual, and we can see the personality-disintegrating effects of the attempt to force a puritanical standard on thinking individuals who did not accept the theological bases on which the standard was constructed. There is the familiar conflict between the "church ethic" and the "sect ethic," where the "sect" is willing to withdraw or be excluded from certain areas of social participation for the sake of purity, real or imagined, while the "church," embracing the multitudes, is willing to sacrifice quality to quantity in influencing human events. In DN, it appears, we are presented with the contemporary variant of the old theme. The contrast is now between the ethic of the primary and the secondary group, between the ideal of sacrificial love and the "socially possible" ethic of justice.

The basic tension which expresses itself in these different ways is indeed inescapable. The perusal of the New Testament reveals that Jesus and the circle which sprang up around Him and after Him were deeply conscious of the inevitability of a dualism. What is alike surprising and distressing, however, is that in many circles the duality of which they were conscious rarely gains a serious hearing today. For the duality of which they speak is the duality of Church and World, of those who say "Yes" and "No" to God, of those who are a people *in Christ,* and those who are not a people because they are *not* in Christ.

When the authors of DN fail to reckon with God's people and stress only the tension under which the individual Christian lives as a socially responsible citizen of a national society, they are quite naturally offended at the limited loyalty of the Christian to the State. Presumably they adopt this approach only in an attempt to generalize their community of discourse to include men who doubt the uniqueness of the Church. It is, however, a direct consequence of this limitation in the starting point of their logic that, in their description, the Christian pacifist appears to be a solid citizen who can be depended on to support his government consistently—that he is "in the world"—and, then, that he suddenly and apparently unreasonably abandons the State when he is asked to kill people of nations other than his own. Viewing the lives of Christ and His followers in this way, the historian would similarly conclude that they also were quiet citizens except for those times when they, quite inexplicably, became disturbers of the peace or revealed themselves in their preaching as public enemies.

The Christian can never view himself as the kind of harmless citizen DN would seem to expect him to be. He confesses from the start that, as a member of another society, the Church, his first loyalty is to *its* Ruler. The Christian is willing to make some adjustments to avoid unnecessary difficulties with his government in matters where his government adopts a policy of permitting and even sponsoring certain activities that Christians are called by God to engage in. We have repeatedly stated that the Christian will love and serve his fellow men. But for the content of his specific duty in any situation, he turns first to God, as revealed to him and to the

Christian community of which he is a member, and this first loyalty makes civil disobedience a constant possibility.

We of the Historic Peace Churches must confess in humility that we have not adequately demonstrated many of the radical consequences of our loyalty to God in our corporate life. Our humility must be all the greater because we cannot claim that God has not revealed His will. No one but a non-Christian outsider looking in should be able to claim that the Christian appears to be "'in the world' until coercion or violence enter the scene"; if Bishop Dun and Professor Niebuhr can say this, in viewing the Peace Churches, the latter can only reply that their witness must not be sufficiently clear and ask the help of these authors in pointing out other areas of their life in which a similar break with the modern world is a part of a faithful Christian witness. In any case, the normal assumption is that the Christian's physical presence "in the world" will not need to cloud the fact that the obligations which fall upon him are not derived from the world in which he lives, but from his primary commitment to the Kingdom that is "not of the world."

It is not true that all men are in only one society, or in societies of only one kind, and that God has two wills for them in their various relations with each other. God has one Word in Christ and men divide themselves into two groups according to their acceptance or rejection of God's message and will for them. The freedom to refuse God's will is a part of His *agape,* but God is still the Lord, even though His Lordship must be mediately expressed in the *lex talionis,* in allowing evil to break against evil. No war is just, but, even in time of war, the Church can proclaim the relevance of God's Lordship over the world by saying that all human justice is to be judged only with respect to God's agape-justice, and that all men, including those who refuse God's justice, are still responsible to Him.

The Church's positive duty, however, is to incarnate God's reconciling initiative. She is faced with the choice: she can reflect only an echo of the world's cry for help or she can be a channel of redemption by being true to her calling as Church—by living in the "new aeon" that never seems quite right in this world, by being the incarnation of a life that is possible only in faith, and by proclaiming a Gospel in which one saves his life only by losing it. It is only through the foolishness of this obedience unto death that the Church can live unto God.

9. The Lordship of Christ Over Church and State, I. (Puidoux, Switzerland, August 15-19, 1955)

At an enlarged meeting of the continuation committee held in Geneva on March 22-23, 1955, with significant participation by staff members of the World Council of Churches, plans were laid for a major conference on the theme, "The Lordship of Christ Over Church and State." The stated intent of the conference was to "attain a greater degree of unity in theological viewpoint among Christians who hold or sympathize closely with the Christian pacifist position, and to do this in the context of an ecumenical conversation on a broader scale" than that which had occurred thus far.

Heinz Kloppenburg of the IFOR was asked to become chairman and Albert J. Meyer to be the secretary. A. J. Muste, of the American FOR, who was present at the Geneva meeting, and John H. Yoder worked with Kloppenburg in securing leadership for the meeting. The response was beyond the committee's expectation. The two problem areas to be reflected in the program were: "What is the relationship of the people of God to the world and to the state in the Old Testament, in the New Testament, and in church history? Is there a Christian ethic for the state?"

Twenty-seven churchmen and scholars from seven nations came for the week's discussions in August. An elaborate portfolio of study documents was provided for the meeting; at Puidoux itself a heavy schedule of presentations, responses, and discussions resulted in intense and moving encounter. The chairman, Heinz Kloppenburg, reminded the gathering that this was the first time in hundreds of years that theologians from the Lutheran and Reformed Churches in Europe had met for dialogue with representatives from the peace churches on serious issues of theology and ethics. An account of the meeting stated:

> The willingness on behalf of all participants to learn from each other in true ecumenical spirit despite the variety of ecclesiastical traditions and theological conceptions represented constituted a promising basis for a continued study of these theological problems.

Those meeting concurred in a final statement:

With thankfulness and rejoicing we report that we have discovered again in a concrete way that the unity of the Church of our Lord Jesus Christ takes form, as we listen together to Scripture, in a fresh realization of our common responsibility for faithful witness to our Lord and for service in His name in the world.

A full report of the first Puidoux gathering was published in multilithed form; it includes all of the papers, summaries of the discussions, and the many preparatory workpapers as well. These are available for study in libraries connected with the peace churches.

Introduction to a Discussion on "Church and World" with Reference to Luther

Ernst Wolf

I.

When a German or Swedish Lutheran of today is asked how one should think on the subject "Church and World," the reply is: in terms of the doctrine of the *zwei Reiche*. The doctrine of the *zwei Reiche*, or the two governments, serves as the key for the answering of the question concerning the work of the Christian in the World. I do not want to give a detailed treatment of Luther's doctrine on both kingdoms; we know that it is a crucial point in the interpretation of Luther's thought. Neither do I want to try to give a treatment of the various interpretations. I would, however, just like to indicate the main points of this teaching.

Both governments, or kingdoms, are expressions of the love of God towards men; it cannot be said that one is an expression of God's goodness, and the other of His authority. This difference, which refers to the unified activity of God in Creation and Redemption, and which cannot be misunderstood as a separation of the two kingdoms—this difference is to make comprehensible the way the same God manifests Himself as Lord of the World and as Lord of His Kingdom of Heaven. The realm of worldly governments is therefore not abandoned to human selfishness and self-affirmation, but it also stands under the grace of God. Through this, we immediately have (1) the responsibility of the Christian for the World emphasized, (2) his earthly activity given importance as service at God's behest, and (3) despair and resignation, as well as arrogance and high-handedness, rejected.

2. The differentiation of the two kingdoms corresponds to the differentiation of the Christian (*Christ-Person*) from the man of the World (*Welt-Person*). When the two kingdoms are separated, as is frequently done in the newer Lutheranism, one comes to the idea that the Christian citizen is in two kingdoms. The Christian would then act on the basis of different principles: as a citizen of the Kingdom of God, according to his conscience, and, as a citizen in the worldly realm, according to his good judgment.

3. The statement that the Christian is a citizen of two kingdoms is false, even for Luther. The Christian has his *politeuma* in the Kingdom of God; he is a citizen of only the Kingdom of God, although he is commissioned by God as God's co-worker in His redemptive activity with respect to the World. The Concept of "co-worker" (co-operator)—not "co-creator"—is important for Luther and is in the center of his doctrine of vocation.

4. This is made clear to us in Matthew 5:13 ("You are the salt of the earth . . . "). This was said to the disciples—that is, to those called to discipleship in the Beatitudes, those who, worthy of the Kingdom of Heaven, are needed by the earth. It is through these disciples, for whom persecution is imminent, that the world is preserved. To be the salt of the earth is the function of the Christian. When Jesus calls His disciples, not Himself, the salt, he is charging them with effectiveness on the earth. The text reads, "You are . . . ," not "You should be." It is not a call to become salt of the earth. The disciples *are* the salt of the earth, whether they wish it or not. They are it, not only when they deliver the message—salt is the World of Life; they are it as those called of Christ. "He who, called of Jesus, is a disciple of Him is, through this call, salt of the earth in his whole existence" (Dietrich Bonhoeffer).

He who withdraws from being salt of the earth, he who wants to live as a Christian only for Heaven, only for his salvation, ruins himself. Disciples are also the light of the world, and this light is the light that comes forth from the mystery of the Cross. The "good works," the *kala erga* of Matthew 5, are the light of the disciples, and they are made up of the following, which are enumerated in the Beatitudes: the poor in spirit, the mourners, the meek, those who are hungry and thirsty for righteousness, the merciful, the pure in heart, the peacemakers, and those who endure persecution for Christ's sake. "The Cross is that strange light in whose shining alone all these good works of the disciples may be seen" (Bonhoeffer).

What does this mean for us, as disciples of Christ:

(a) We can no longer ask why we are here on the earth. That is the question of an impossible, absolute Existence.

(b) The answer that we are here in order that God might receive praise and thanks keeps the basic *raison d'etre:* that we are co-workers in God's work, in the work of reconciling the World with God. Or one could say that we are living in discipleship to Jesus—this is the same thing.

(c) This discipleship is by no means a life-ideal that may be chosen; it is the difference between being and not-being, between life and death. It has to do with the total and universal claim of Jesus. Being a Christian is never a private matter; responsibility for the earth, for the "world," is bound to being a Christian. There is therefore no exemption from any area of life as, for example, in the theory of the new Lutheranism on the autonomy of certain areas of culture. But there is also no retreat behind the theory of the *zwei Reiche* of God in the hope "that the Word (*Verbum*) will do it." The Word does it, but it is precisely the Word that has taken form in the Church that does it. There is also no holding back by referring to the theory of the "professional politician"; there is only the irrefutable concern for peace, law, and justice for God's creatures, for the neighbor, and for the enemy.

(d) In spite of everything, "politics" is the concern for what is best for the State. And, finally, what is decisive here is, not the facts of the matter, but the conscience, the love, and the obedience to which Christ has freed his chosen, the insight of the heart.

5. The Christian is not a private person; he humbles himself before the World, just as Christ did; he places himself in solidarity with the need of the World. This is the heart of Luther's treatise "On the Freedom of the Christian." Today this treatise would carry the title, "On Social Ethics"; *libertas christiana* is the medieval *terminus technicus* for this.

II.

6. If the Church is the preliminary representation of humanity sanctified in Christ, then Christians are the bearers of this representation. From this, two things follow for the relation of the Church to the World:

(a) The Church is (and should be) in solidarity with the needs of this world.

(b) The Church is (and should be) responsible to God for seeing that the World *as World* remains the creation of God called to reconciliation.

7. What does it mean to say, "The Church is (and should be) in solidarity with the needs of the World"?

(a) *Not* that the Church is the law of society or of the World. The Church is not the ideal for the structuring life in the World. In this sense, she is not, as for Augustine, *civitas dei*. Where the Church understands herself as law or ideal of society, she ends in utopias.

(b) Further, the Church exercises no lordship over the World. When Christ proclaims his might in our weakness and when He builds up His Kingdom, the Church testifies to His Lordship as to a hidden Lordship.

(c) The Church knows the World in a loving way, and she should know the World in a loving way. She knows the World, if she knows the needs that oppress the World. She must always concern herself about taking cognizance of these needs realistically; in this, she must better understand the World than the World understands itself.

8. The second sentence, "The Church is responsible to God for the World," means that the Church cares, not for her own matters. nor for those that engage the interest of the World, but in service for what God has to do with His mankind. What God has to do with men is always indicated in that place where the Church prays for justice and peace on earth. This prayer is the strength that leads to corresponding action. That is, the Church can not then hold fast to traditional denominational doctrines when the World has changed; on the contrary, starting with the Gospel and in discipleship to Christ, she will have to proceed ever anew to reflect on, examine, and carry farther her theological and confessional inheritance with reference to today's world.

Up to this point I have been trying to state briefly what I believe can be said on the subject "Church and World" from the standpoint of a rightly-understood Luther. In the ninth point, I will make this clear with an example.

9. In German Lutheranism today (and not only today), people are used to citing Luther's monograph entitled "*If* Soldiers Can Be in the State of Blessedness" *(Ob Kriegsleute im seligen Stand sein können)* as if the title

read "That Soldiers Can Be in the State of Blessedness" (*Dass* Kriegsleute . . .). The hypothesis behind the use of "Whether" or "That" is a hypothesis as to the possibility that the Christian may speak of war in a positive way. If Luther asks, "Whether Soldiers . . . ," he indicates that he is not sure that one can speak positively of war. He procured a certain assurance for himself in the form of the medieval theory of the *bellum justum*. This theory is untenable. We Lutherans of today should follow Luther only in making radical the uncertainty of the question, "Whether." We should know that war is *in no way a positive* possibility in legitimate Christian discourse in proclamation or pastoral work—or theology.

We must avoid everything that might give the impression that a person can speak as a Christian of an act that is included in the sins of the World as though it were a positive possibility. We must, for example, give up the theory that war is a "necessary evil," since we do not sit in the Council of God. When, for example, we in Germany are faced with the question of military service for pastors, we must give up the theory that the readiness to bear arms is indispensable to the manhood of a man. Furthermore, we must expose the conception that the soldier dies a hero, a conception that is supposedly to be explained on a Christian basis, and with this must go all the religious needs of our Churches that are attached to this conception.

10. Lutherans and Christians conditioned by Lutheranism (for example, the *Evangelische Kirche in Deutschland*) must arrive at a new position, a position between the former theology of orders (*Ordnungstheologie*), which pretended to have its origin in the Word of God, and an ethic of the situation (*Situationsethik*), which pretends not to need the instruction of the Word of God. The new position that is needed must ask about God's command in a new way/it must understand activity within this world as human activity that is responsible before this command—and thus free activity, and thus activity that gives form and order. This means that we must clearly see social, economic, and political institutions, not as "eternal order," but as human attempts at order. The primary function of the Christian is to take part in these attempts at order, since he as a Christian is free from the seduction of self interest.

With what I have here outlined, I believe I have indicated how an answer to the "Church and World" question can be given from the standpoint of a properly-understood Luther. In all of this, it is understood that, while Luther is a respected guide, the Bible is the final authority.

Theses on the Relevance of the Authority of the Scripture and the Church to the Responsibility of the Individual

Götz Harbsmeier

1. The authority of the Bible is not that of a practicable, religious-ideological "doctrine" or "program" about God and the world, but that of a message of God to man in the world.
2. The authority of this message comes from God. It cannot be derived from or grounded in man. It is an authority of fact, not of principle. "What stands in the Bible is not God's Word because it is in the Bible; it is in the Bible because it testifies to God's Word" (Grundtvig).
3. God Himself is the Initiator of the message, as well as its Content and the only One who guarantees its truth.
4. The message is God's revelation of Himself to the world. It contains the self-communication of God, as of the Creator, Redeemer, and Sanctifier. In other words, it actively contains God's grace in His judgment of the world.
5. The message is the testimony of the judging and saving Presence of God in the sense of His Lordship in Heaven and on earth.
6. Faith is the acceptance of this message. The acceptance of this message happens and is carried out in the thanksgiving of him who receives this out-going, life-giving message. It happens in the obedience that responds to the claims of the message, in the hope in the message's promise, and in the love of God's co-workers in the Church for the world.
7. The message directs all who are reached by it, and because they are reached by it, to the world as well to serve God's creatures. Those who are struck by the message are also responsible to the Lord of the message for the world. The realization of this responsibility for the world consists in the faithful delivery *(Ausrichtung)* of the message to the world.
8. For the faithful delivery of the message to it, the world is entrusted to the Christians. The latter are to see the world in the light of the message and to act towards men in accordance with its directions. The responsibility conferred on Christians before God is, in a comprehensive and unlimited sense, the active carrying out *(Ausrichtung)* of the message.
9. What does it mean to see the world in the light of the message of Jesus Christ? It means:

    a. To see the world, in spite of its fall, as God's creation and under His claim;
    b. To see the world as loved in Christ and therefore not lost (that

is, *not* to see the world in the light of its own interpretation of itself);

    c. To see the world as called to sanctification (but *not* to see the world as a field where so-called Christian principles are to be pushed through and enforced).

10. What does it mean to act in accordance with the directions of the Biblical message to the world? It means to love the world with that love with which it is loved in Christ.

11. What does this mean in the concrete case of military service? In what sense can the Christian refer to the message of the Lordship of God for his refusal of military service? He can do this only through a reasonable evaluation and examination of the situation in the light of the message, i.e., in the interpretation of Scripture—but not through the application of certain Scriptural instructions in the sense of the setting-up of a law for which not he (the Christian) but God would be responsible.

There are, however, possibilities which are excluded in the strictest sense. These have already been mentioned in the contribution of Ernst Wolf. The justification of war in the *bellum justum* sense is one of these excluded possibilities. The glorification of war and the proclamation of "Holy Wars" are others. But making conscientious objection in all times and under all conditions a part of the objective content of the message of Christ Himself is also an excluded possibility. For conscientious objection is not the content of the message of the Lordship of Christ but a consequence thereof, a consequence that is put before Christians at all times and in all circumstances and a consequence for which they have to give account to the Lord. The Kingship of Christ does not deliver us from, but rather charges us with, the responsibility for maintaining peace on earth and letting justice reign. Earthly peace and justice are not under the direct administration of Jesus Christ, but placed in our hands and entrusted to our freedom; that is, they are not at our discretion, but we are rather made responsible in freedom to Christ for seeing that, in the Church and through the Church, there should be peace and justice on earth. In this way our reason (*Vernunft*) is claimed, called, and mobilized for deciding and for acting according to the measure of enlightenment granted in those things that God has entrusted to us for faithful stewardship.

It is illusionary to think that through conscientious objection the church of Christ can keep herself clearly and distantly separated from the world. Indeed, the Church can really become conformed to the world in objecting to military service. For it is characteristic of the world to deify itself through absolute solutions. Conscientious objection is an act of humble obedience and responsible love only when it is not intended as the

Church's absolute realization of herself, but rather as daring testimony to the love of God here and now. In no case do principles dispense us from the necessity of examining the situation and acting on the basis of our examination.

The "Good" of Romans 13:4

Jean Lasserre

Theology is the knowledge *of God,* not of something else. That is why there can be no theology of the State; there is only a theology of our obedience to the State. It happens that almost all theologians who speak of the State maintain a discreet silence on the only thing that is important: our obedience to the State.

For centuries pacifists have based their position on the Sermon on the Mount, while non-pacifists have refuted their argument by citing Romans 13. We must avoid this sterile quarrel by basing our pacifism on Romans 13—and this not only because it is strategically adroit, but also because Romans 13 is actually the Biblical passage which treats the question of the Christian and the State most explicitly. We will consider three points.

1. The first evidence given in Romans 13 is that political authorities have been established by God. For centuries men have improperly concluded that authorities are situated above the ordinary human conditions, thereby giving an easy conscience to all statesmen, who are placed above the laws applied to ordinary citizens and outside the demands of God. How are we then to understand the establishment of the State by God? Exactly where must we place the State?

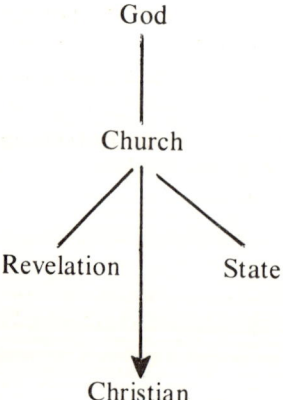

a. According to the Catholic viewpoint, God established the Church, whose interpretation of the Scripture is supreme and who sends Scriptural directives (encyclicals) to the State. The believer is subject to the Church directly and exclusively; the Church tells him how he is to understand Scriptural revelation and to what degree he is to obey the State (cf. the Belgian school wars). The Christian is not split by divided loyalties; everything is clear for him.

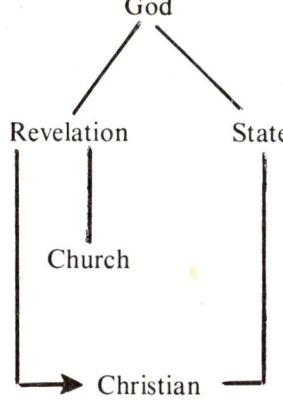

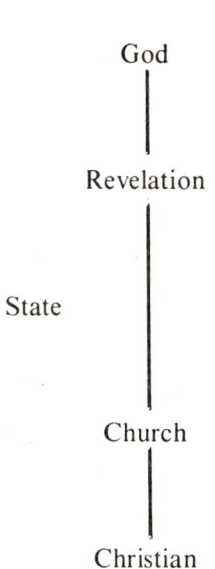

b. We now come to the traditional Protestant scheme: God has revealed Himself in Jesus Christ, the Church is under the supreme authority of Scripture, and the Christian is to be submissive to the Church to the degree to which the latter is faithful to the Scripture. But, on the other hand, God has established the State directly without making it subject to the Revelation. The believer is thus split between his obedience to the Scripture in the Church and his obedience to the State. Since the latter is in no way subject to Scriptural control, the Christian finds himself in a position as uncomfortable as it is indescribable.

c. Certain sects (the Jehovah's Witnesses, for example) have another scheme: they hold that God has revealed Himself in Scripture, and that the latter is interpreted by their church or leader, which the Christian must follow without asking questions. As for the State, it is frankly outside the plan of God, it is even the instrument of Satan, and believer considers it null and void..

The error of this scheme is in its failure to take into consideration the "establishment" specified in Romans 13, while the error of scheme "b" is in suggesting an "establishment" which contradicts the supreme authority of the Holy Scriptures and in removing the political obedience of the Christian from this authority to an astounding degree. Besides, how could God "establish" something if not *through* His Word and in the framework of His Revelation?

d. Calvin suggested another scheme, a scheme which I think is correct in spite of the fact that Calvinists have abandoned it: God has revealed Himself in Jesus Christ; both the Church, on the one hand, and the State, on the other, are subject to the authority of God as this becomes clear in the Scriptural revelation; and the believer is obedient to the Church and State under the control of Scripture and in the measure to which the Church and the State do not violate the will of God as this is expressed in the Scripture. From here on, the believer is no longer torn between demands that are often contradictory but a difficulty now arises in that what God demands of the Church is not identical with what He demands of the State. The scheme is valid, but it is now necessary to distinguish and define what God expects of the Church and what He expects of the State. In any case, the whole of human life, and, *a fortiori,* of the life of the Christian, is placed under the control of the Scriptural revelation.

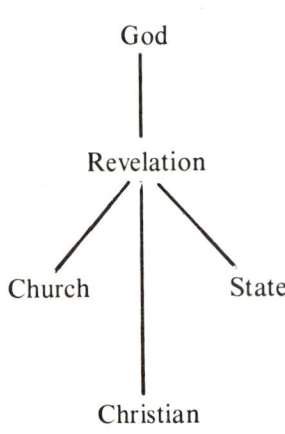

In the course of a recent public discussion with a good Barthian theologian, we were able to reach an agreement on the fact that, in the plan of God, the State is charged by God with seeing to it that citizens observe the Decalogue. But we remained in disagreement on the question as to whether or not the State and officers of the State should themselves be subject to the Decalogue. I said "yes." He said: "No, the State is subject to the Decalogue in a different way than is the private Christian; the State should see that the Decalogue is respected, but it is not forced to conform *itself* to the Decalogue." To which I replied to my interlocutor that he could speak of "a different kind of subjection" to the Decalogue only because he was speaking of the "State," a non-Biblical abstraction, instead of speaking, as the Bible does, of kings, magistrates, etc.—that is, of "men" charged with political duties. Now it is never said in the Bible that kings and magistrates are released from subjection to the Law of God. We see the serious danger that arises in the use of the abstract and erroneous term "State." Men have done quick work of making it a sort of hypostasis, a kind of half-god soaring at an altitude so high that the Law of God no longer concerns it. But 1 Peter 2:13, which resumes the teaching of Romans 13, rightly corrects this tendency to idealize the political authorities by calling them, no longer "authorities (*exousiai*)" but "creatures (*ktisei*)"—as if, to avoid a wrong interpretation of Romans 13, he wanted precisely to emphasize the fact that the political authorities are completely subject to the authority of God and can in no way avoid His demands.

2. The second basic indication that we find in Romans 13 is that the magistrates are *servants, ministers, of God.* Therefore their function as God sees it, is in no way placed outside the Revelation as though they enjoyed some kind of autonomy that they had to themselves. Very much to the contrary, they carry out a ministry—extra-ecclesiastical, to be sure—which is integral in the framework of Redemption. I think that the picture of Cullmann, who speaks of two concentric circles representing the Church and the *Regnum Christi,* is right. In the plan of God, the magistrates are placed, not in the circle of the Church, but in the larger circle of the "Reign of Christ." But there they are always under the control of the Revelation.

In what does the ministry of the magistrates consist? The words "good" and "evil" re-occur constantly and with insistence in the Biblical passages where the magistrates are discussed. And in such a way that there is no doubt about the fact that, in the plan of God, the magistrates (and State functionaries) are charged with punishing evil and approving and encouraging the good. It is thus that, according to God's will, they contribute to making human society human (or, at least, less inhuman). The magistrate is "God's servant with a view to the good *for you,*" specifies Romans 13. Thus the apparatus of the State is in the service of man, and the converse is anti-Biblical.

Since there are two concentric circles, we can well speak of two different realms in Christian ethics. However, this differentiation is not an easy one, and in any case it is not a question of clearly separating the two realms. Niebuhr, for example, distinguishes between an individual ethic and a collective ethic; the Sermon on the Mount concerns only the individual ethic. But, in this case, where will one place family ethics? And, if it is labelled "collective," is that to say that the Sermon on the Mount no longer concerns it? Since the magistrates are called "ministers of God," their function is within the realm of Christian ethics and can in no case get into contradiction with Christian ethics or be freed from it by intellectual speculation.

3. Romans 13 tells us that the magistrate is "God's servant with a view to the good (*eis agathon*)." Here is the third basic indication in our text. What is this "good"? Is it to be defined according to human wisdom or "natural theology"? That is the usual sleight-of-hand trick by which ideas foreign to the Revelation and often of pagan origin are introduced into

Christian theology. For our part, it seems certain that, when Paul was speaking of the "good," he was using a concept that could be defined only by referring to the Revelation, to the Word of God. But how are we to define this "good" according to the Bible?

There are two possibilities. First, there could be two kinds of good. The superior good would begin with the Ten Commandments as a minimum and would go to unlimited love, to forgiveness, sacrifice, and utter *agape*. For the political world, there would be another good, the "equity" of which Luther speaks, for example. This equity, which would be defined by the prince or by the social group in power, can sometimes be used to justify procedures worthy of Machiavelli (tortures, massacres, etc.). But the Bible justifies neither the notion of a good independent of the Revelation nor the idea that there are two different "goods."

| Machiavellianism | Agape | | 10 | Agape |

The other possibility consists in considering, not two goods, but two different, but not independent, directions. The two hairpins are not completely separated; the curved end of one is placed over the curved end of the other. Thus the two goods, the two ethics, are articulated with each

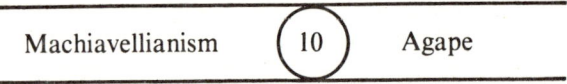

other, as the Scripture has this, and their common denominator turns out to be the Decalogue. This is the minimum that can be expected of the believer and the maximum that can be expected of the magistrate.

Thus the Decalogue has a two-fold significance: on the one hand, it is a "schoolmaster to bring us to Christ" by revealing my sin to me and urging me to repentance. But it also has a political meaning, as Luther and Calvin clearly saw. It is the Word that God addresses to *all* men and through which He gives His directives to the end that human society might be truly humane and just. That Christians, following theologians, have completely lost sight of this principle that the Reformers, on the other hand, firmly affirmed has been and is catastrophic.

Calvin's error was in making the Decalogue the norm (or matrix) or political life, instead of seeing in it only the criterion for the political obedience of the Christian. This nuance is extremely important. The "norms" for a railroad car are the specifications given to the manufacturer concerning its color and type of construction. But before the railroad car is used, it must be able to go through an underpass, thanks to which one can be sure that the car can be put into service without danger. The specifications are "norms," while the underpass is a "criterion." The danger in taking the Decalogue as a norm is that of introducing into society an artificial and ridiculous moralism and Puritanism. But the danger of forgetting the political significance of the Decalogue is even greater: Christians have neglected the very clear indications of God by which He sees to it that men themselves do not destroy the human character of their society.

Let us consider, for example, the problem of force and violence. On one hand, a state which would not have recourse to constraint is unthinkable; on the other, it is evident that very often the State uses force wrongly and, by its overuse, commits crimes (such as massacres) that cannot be justified. Where is the limit beyond which the force used by the State ceases to preserve social order and becomes an additional cause of disorder and injustice? At this point it seems to us impossible to overlook the Sixth Commandment, which says to every man, including the statesman: "As soon as you have started killing people, you have started making the disorder worse, even though you have apparently brought, by your murder, a temporary 'peace'; you have created more disorder than order, and your so-called peace is heavy with vengeance."

In conclusion, apart from faith no ethical decision is possible. And faith is unthinkable apart from a dialogue between the Living God and the believer. Faith is the believer's response to the Word of God. There can be no faith where God does not speak. There can only be faith when man seizes the Word of God, believes that it is the Word of God, listens to it, and obeys it. As for the war question, God has spoken. And, as in Genesis 3, the real temptation begins when the voice whispers to us: "Has God really said that?"

One last word. During the First World War, soldiers coming back from the front ridiculed and made sport of the arm-chair strategists who stayed in the rear, of those who "strategized" while leisurely sipping their glasses of wine . . . . Theology is always in danger of being a kind of "armchair strategy." We must remember that we are not the Commanding General. We are just soldiers—maybe corporals, but not much more—and soldiers never have the distance and competence needed for speculation on the progress of the battle. The true issue of the battle will always be out of our grasp. We must not put ourselves in the place of the Lord when we talk of the future of our country or of "Christian civilization." I do not mean that we must not think about our problems. But I mean that our study of the situation in which we find ourselves must not keep us from hearing what our Commanding General has said.

The Theological Basis of the Christian Witness to the State

John H. Yoder

... I think the most helpful thing will be for me to say what is to be said, from the general orientation of this paper, to all the debate which has gone on until now. That will give my remarks a more polemic form than would otherwise be the case, but, as we have heard before, it is possible for a debate to get more brotherly as it gets warmer, and I think our next step will have to be a step into polemic.

I. On the question, "Is the Christianization of the World possible?" we have seen four positions. There is that of Calvinism and of a certain modern pacifism (not to be calling names), which says: "Yes, a certain Christianization of the World is possible, and it consists in the application to the World of the same standards which apply in the Church." In the second place, there is a position which is, roughly speaking, more in the Lutheran line. This position, which I think was the one represented by Professor Harbsmeier this morning, would basically deny the possibility of a Christianization of the World because there are no principles which can be taken from the Church and applied to the World. We can completely discard the third position, which simply says the Church has nothing to say to the World. At some times and places this has been the Mennonite position, in practice, but it is not the historic Mennonite position or the New Testament position we are interested in here.

Finally, the fourth position, and the one which this paper represents, says: "Yes, the Christianization of the World is possible in the sense that there is a Christian influence on what happens in the World; but the real question is not whether, but *how* this Christian influence is to be exercised upon the World. Is this to be by a direct transfer from the Church to the World of some form of Christian ethics, or is it to be by the application of two sets or levels of ethics, such as the ecclesiastical ethics and the political ethics Lasserre has spoken about?"

What is, precisely speaking, the difference between the two kinds of ethics we are referring to? We have heard from Lasserre that they must be articulated, i.e., that they must be related to each other, Further, I do not think we can say that the difference is that God has an affirmative relation to Christians and a negative relation to the World, that God says "yes" to the Christians and "no" to the World. It is rather that God has a positive word of salvation and call to salvation which He addresses to both the Church and the World—He says "yes" to both the Church and the

World—but that the World says "no" to God, while the Church says "yes" to Him. And God respects the "no" of the World. This means that, in the realm of the World, which includes the State, God's requirements are adapted to the fact that man says "no" and that, for this reason, he cannot count on the power of the Holy Spirit, the power of forgiveness, and the miracles which are a part of Christian life. All that can be counted on is a certain basic minimum, a minimum which is valid in spite of man's "no."

II. This brings us to the second general question: "Are there valid generalizations *(gültige Lehrsätze, Denksätze, or Prüfungsmasstäbe)* concerning the 'good'?" This morning, in the paper of Harbsmeier, it sounded as though there were not; this afternoon, in the paper of Lasserre, we assumed that there were. This discussion must be carried further. This may not be the place to do it in detail, but we are forced to recognize that this is a part of our problem, and the point where a part of our future discussion will have to begin.

To be blunt we would ask whether there are "principles," if the word had not been given such a bad taste. But unless we are simply going to condemn ourselves to following the fashions of German theology like sheep, we have no right to accept this bad reputation the word "principles" has acquired as a consequence of the way it has been misused in certain circles. If we want to be thorough, we have no choice but to ask ourselves whether there are not valid generalizations concerning the good, generalizations which are valid as expressions and explanations of the Message, which we do not consider as impossible in advance, and for which we do not foresee exceptions. If there are such generalizations, then we will have to talk about them. If there are none, we will part company and will not talk ethics, since there is no possibility of conversation if one says it is impossible to make a general statement.

A second problem that arises when the word "principles" comes up is that it seems to be assumed that freedom exists only where there are no principles. But according to the witness of Scripture, freedom exists precisely when we are bound to Christ. And the binding to Christ is not undefinable—it involves, not only a Person whom we can grasp only momentarily, but a definite line which is always behind the moment to moment encounters. As George Fox said, "The Spirit of God never changes, and what the Spirit of God will say from day to day is always the same thing." God is free in the sense that I cannot tie Him down. But God has expressed His freedom in tying Himself down. There is no second Word, no second Christ, and no second Spirit. God said, "This is my Son; listen to Him." God has committed Himself, and there is a certain consistency in that commitment, which is the basis for certain generalizations. For we are permitted and commanded to search out the main lines in God's Self-Revelation. We must also look for those places where the general lines of God's Revelation limit themselves and their realm of application. But to say that there are no main lines is simply to extinguish all conversation.

The third thing to be said within this general area is that those who deny having principles simply have unexamined principles. (It's like the Baptists and the Brethren who want to have no doctrine, but who say that as the first point in a list of things which the Baptists or Brethren believe!) The question is never, *"Haben wir Denkweise?"* or "Are we saying anything consistent?" If we are not, we might as well quit. The question is: "Are we willing to test what we say for consistency? Are we willing to test our presuppositions, the rules of our logic and our grammar, and everything we say by Scripture?"

III. More could be said on the necessity of valid generalization but we must now turn to a related question: our insistence on visibility (*Sichtbarkeit*). It is immediately clear, from what we have already seen, that a part of the refusal to have principles is a belief in the invisibility of obedience. Obedience refuses to let itself be made visible in the form of a line or generalization, just as, in the case of the Reformers, the Church refused to let itself be made visible.

But the fact is that when the Reformers refused to teach the visible Church they were actually submitting the Church to a visible institution anyway—to the organizational Church, i.e., the office of preaching and to the State. And, since they refused to ask what the visible Church was, both of these elements became "visibilizations" (*Versichtbarungen*) of various functions of the Church in an uncontrolled and unchecked way. Our contention would simply be that visibility, the visibility of the Church and the visibility of obedience, is commanded.

IV. We now come to the main question: the duality. We have all said, in various ways—everyone since before the Reformation has said—that there are dualities. We see it in the two levels of Catholic morality; we see a duality however we describe the *zwei Reiche* of Luther. We see it least in original Calvinism, because there the two Testaments have exactly the same validity and the same morality is required of everyone; but what happens in Calvinism and in Puritanism is precisely that the duality is pushed within the individual, and the result is the breakdown Freud talks about. This is the same duality. Because Calvin refused to accept it outside as a matter of fact, the duality between the area where man says "no" to God and the area where man says "yes" to Him was pushed within the individual. We all agree that there is a duality. The only question is whether it should be formulated as the Catholics or the Lutherans or the Calvinists or the Anabaptists (or someone else) formulated it.

If our problem were one of understanding from scratch a message from God which said only that we were free to love (*"eine inhaltlose Botschaft"*), we would not know how to begin to grasp this duality. But it is our contention that this duality, which arises at the point where God respects man's "no," is defined constitutively by the content of the Christian message. It is the purpose of this paper, and in a certain sense, I believe, a purpose of this Conference to test and formulate the definition of this duality.

Its first characteristic is that faith, obedience, demands a break with human continuity, with the sociological, psychological, and moral unity of normal human existence. This applies to the race, the nation, the family—to the closest of human ties. "You have to hate your father and mother before you are worthy of Me." You have to be a traitor to the State at some point; you have to be willing to disobey somewhere. You have to break with culture and human togetherness somewhere in order to be a disciple.

This is actually what is meant by the condescension (*kenosis*), the emptying of Christ. It is *not* that He became a sinner with sinners. It is that He was ready, in obedience, to love until death, and never, through considerations of social togetherness, or of saving culture or freedom or order or peace, to become unfaithful to this *agape*. It is precisely that He, sinlessly, in order to remain sinless, and as a definition of sinlessness, was ready to break with human continuity. One of the problems we have to face is that there are people who think that becoming one with the World, and humiliating ourselves as Christ did, means that we have to become sinners with the World. Christ's humiliation was just the opposite.

The second constitutive element of the duality is the Resurrection. A new continuity, a new unity, is recreated by a miracle of God. the unity which Christ was willing to sacrifice in His death was recreated by the miracle of God in the Resurrection. The unity which we are ready to sacrifice when we make the full step of obedience in discipleship is reconstituted in the miracle of the Church.

The Church is the visible Body of Christ. God respects the "no" of man in the World, but the Church is the place where He no longer tolerates it. Man's "no" is overcome through His grace. When man says "no" within the Church, he is subject to discipline; if he insists on saying "no" within the Church, he finds himself no longer in the Church.

And finally, in speaking of the Church, we must say that the meaning of history and the significance of everything that happens in the world is, not the fate of Western culture, of civilization, of the human community of justice, or of the World, but the formation and building of the Body of Christ. In the first vision of the Apocalypse (Revelation 5), John is bitterly weeping "because no one could be found fit to open the scroll or look into it"; no one can explain the meaning of history. And then the angel comes and says: Do not cry! There is one Person who can open the scroll. It is the Lamb who was slain so that He might form from every tribe, tongue, people and nation a People." It is the formation of this new People that is portrayed as the meaning of history. This is a key to the basic problem we have with non-pacifists. The Christian pacifist believes that the Church is the meaning of history. That is why he is willing to make a break with civilization, with human continuity, to count on the Resurrection of the Church.

In the third place, we now assert that the two members of the duality we have been speaking of have the same Head. This is what Lasserre was saying when he told us that the two ethics have to be articulated with each other. Cullmann says this, too, in saying that the *Regnum Christi* and the Body of Christ have the same Head and can be represented as concentric circles. The two levels of ethics must have at least a common point of origin.

Lasserre has told us we cannot admit a theology of the State; we can only talk about our relation to the State, since we can have a theology only when we are talking about God. But it is the contention of this paper that, apart from the technical problems which arise in the discussion because the word "State" is an abstraction, there is a relation between God and the State such that, when we talk about the State, we are talking about God and it is theology. When we talk about the magistrate and the *exousiai* we are dealing with theological problems, since they are in a relation to God—not the same as our relation to Him, but it is a direct relation to God under the Lordship of Christ. These questions are not outside the realm of theology.

And now, fourthly, in this discussion of the nature of the duality, the Lordship of Christ over the World, to use Cullmann's concept, or the Order of God in which the State stands, to use the concept of the Anabaptists, is to be described in three ways. First of all, it is mediate. The Church has an immediate relationship to God in Christ and in the Spirit; the World has a mediate relationship to God in the sense that there exist the powers, the *exousiai*—we do not know exactly what they are or what they look like, but we do know that they exist somewhere between God and the World. Biblical thought simply said there were angels, which does not help those of us who use Western terminology very much, but that is what I mean to say. The World, because of its "no" to God, and because this "no" is respected by God is related to God only in a mediate way—through intermediate instances, one could say.

Secondly—and this is what is important when we say the relation is mediate—the powers (*exousiai*) have fallen. We are in a fallen World. The *exousiai* of which the Bible speaks are fallen angels. The angels are resisting. Their resistance has been broken; they have been defeated in Christ; but the victory has not yet come into effect. The angels are not fully obedient. As Lasserre showed us, the State does not even follow the States' norm, not killing. Pragmatically speaking, the State is always fallen. Briefly, then, because the State is subject to God mediately through the resisting *exousiai,* which are between God and the World, the submission of the State is relative. The State can be more or less submissive. It is never as submissive as it should be. We are concerned with our relation to a disobedient State.

There is thus a continuum of possible positions, degrees of "submittedness," of the State. It is in these relative degrees of submissiveness of the fallen State that we may speak of Christianization. A fully Christianized state would be one which did completely the work of the State. But that would be out of our stage of history. It is therefore always a question of asking relatively how far a given State is submissive. For example, I think we would have to say that a democracy like Switzerland or Holland is Christianized in comparison to Egypt or a South American republic or an Indian princely state, in the sense that it is relatively more submitted to the order God wants to impose on it. But the State is never so submitted that one could say there is anything but this qualitative duality. Our judgment is purely relative, and it never makes of the State a part of the Church.

The third and last thing we have to say about the Lordship of Christ is that its purpose is not redemptive but conservative. The purpose of Christ's dominion over the *exousiai* and over the states is not to bring in the Kingdom, but simply to keep things from falling apart so that the Church can do the work of the Kingdom. The reason we are to pray for the State, for kings, according to Timothy (I Tim. 2:1-4), is that God desires that all men should be brought to the knowledge of the truth—but not that the State is going to bring men to the knowledge of the truth. It is because the State is keeping things peaceable that the Church has the chance to bring men to the knowledge of the truth. There is always this distinction between these two areas, or orders, and the duality is defined in that one is redemptive and the other conservative.

V. The final general question is: "What do we say to the State?" Indeed, this paper was written because people tell pacifists they have nothing concrete to say to the State. But if it is true that we have criteria for determining the point at which the State stands on the continuum of relative tolerability (relative "fallenness," or relative Christianization), then we have a message to the State on an objective basis. What is this message?

First of all, if we realize that the State is not an abstraction, but certain people doing certain things, as Lasserre has told us, and if we believe that the meaning of history is in the Church, not in the State, then we will insist, in spite of anything people may think about the faults of separatism or pietism, that an evangelistic call is addressed to every individual. We will not always find a way to say it to a specific man at a specific time. But the first thing we say to every man, including the States-man, is: "You ought to be a Christian." And being a Christian means being a disciple. And being a disciple means full *agape,* nonresistance. Many people try to tell us that the responsibility of the statesman defines what love is for him. It is just the contrary; we have to tell the statesman that his responsibility is defined by non-resistance and by love, and not vice versa. Perhaps he will come to a point where his responsibility will mean leaving his State function. If we want to be realistic about what occurs in State life now, we are forced to recognize that this break with functions of the State will probably come soon. But whether the Christian statesman leaves his job right away, whether he gets thrown out, or whether he is at a post where he can work for a long time, depends on what his job is. We cannot make abstractions. But the important thing we say to any man is: "You ought to say 'yes' to God."

But if he does not say "yes" to God, what do we say? Then we tell him: "Even in spite of your 'no' to God, you, as a statesman, are under the 'yes' of God; you are under the Lordship of Christ. This means that, even in God's respect for your 'no' to Him, even in His letting you be World and letting you be disobedient, God continues to have claims upon you." These claims are the norm which Lasserre sees in the Decalogue (whether we can say precisely that it is in the Decalogue itself or not does not matter for the moment); the claims are the basic demands of God within the Lordship of Christ, and they are different from what God demands of those who say "yes" to Him. For those who say "yes" to Him, God demands bearing the Cross; for those who say "no" to Him, he demands *justitia.*

We conclude with a specific question that exemplifies what we have been saying. At the meeting of the Continuation Committee of the Historic Peace Churches with several WCC leaders in Geneva last March, we were asked whether the introduction of atomic weapons changed the meaning of war, that is, whether war could have been right before and become wrong now. In a certain sense, we can always say that. Every time a worse weapon is introduced, the State sinks one rung on the continuum of fallenness and war is still more forbidden than it was before. The concept of the "just war," which may have had some value as an approximation in the classic eighteenth-century scene portrayed by Butterfield, has less and less value the farther down the continuum the State falls. This applies to the trespassing of the Geneva Conventions on the treatment of prisoners, for example, as well as to the atom-bomb case; indeed, on the level of what one does with what one has promised to do, the former is in many ways more serious than the latter.

We can formally conclude, then, that we can speak to every choice between two possibilities at different levels of this continuum. We can know what we need to know to say "That's getting worse" or "That's getting better—or less bad"; such is precisely the content of the prophetic message of the Church to the State which says "no," to man who says "no." Thus we can always ask the State to be more just. We will not begin by asking the State to be perfectly just, but that is not a possibility within its way of thinking, but we ask it to be more just. And as it becomes more just, we continue by asking it to be still more just. The interesting aspect of this is that in asking it to be more just, we appeal, not to *agape,* but to the State's concept of *justitia.* In France, for example, what we have to say to the French government for the moment is: "Take seriously your talk about 'liberty, equality, and fraternity.' If you have done that, then we will ask a little more." Because the State is already committed to order, our message to the State is an appeal asking it to live up to its own principles.

Resumé of the Conference

With thankfulness and rejoicing we report that we have discovered again in a concrete way that the unity of the Church of our Lord Jesus Christ takes form, as we listen together to Scripture, in a fresh realization of our common responsibility for faithful witness to our Lord and for service in His name in the world.

I.

1. From the witness of Scripture we learn that Christ is really Lord over both the Church and the world. The goal toward which God is working through the Kingdom of His Son is the building up of the Body of Christ; the meaning of history is in the redemptive work of the Church.

2. The Church's witness to and in the world is the proclamation of the

Lordship of Christ as Saviour, Servant, and Judge. This proclamation is embodied in the call to reconciliation, in works of love, and in the expression of God's claim upon the world.

3. Since God respects the "no" with which sinful man may respond to His work of reconciliation, the Church as the obedient Body of Christ is the community of those whose "yes" to God's work distinguishes them from the world. Their unity is a precursory sign of God's eschatological victory over the world and, therefore of the provisional character of the State.

II.

1. The Lordship of Christ signifies for Christian ethics that the "good" is one; there are not two separate and unrelated realms or criteria in the Church and in the world.

2. In the common confrontation with Scripture, we receive directions whose authority is not that of a legal prescription but that of a reliable exposition of the meaning of obedience.

3. The relevance of these directions for the world and thus for the State is conditioned by the "no" of the world to God and also by the "yes" of the Kingship of Christ to both the world and the Church. The tension existing between the Church and the world is thus the duality of human freedom and not a static dualism; it cannot mean that God's command is irrelevant, but only that its relevance is mediate.

III.

1. War is always sin. It can never be considered as an instrument of order and thus it cannot be justified even as a mediate expression of the Lordship of Christ over the world.

2. When the State wages war in spite of the witness of the Church against its use, the Church does not become silent, but rather continues to testify as to the way in which this violence is used. In its criticism of political events the Church will guide itself by criteria which translate into political terms the directives of the World of God. These criteria ("middle axioms"), such as concepts of retributive and distributive justice, are valid measures for relative judgments, even though they fall short of the righteousness of God and therefore may not be determinative for Christian discipleship.

3. The Church's responsibility for peace and justice consists in her incarnation of God's reconciling initiative, in her own fellowship, in works of

sacrificial service, in the promotion of understanding, in efforts to transform peacefully unjust social structures, and in the refusal of her members to participate in war.

****

With humility and repentance we recognize our past failure to obey our Lord faithfully; we seek to further study our responsibility for peace and to commit ourselves to the witness and life of unmixed love.

The Church and Peace

With thankfulness and rejoicing we report that we have discovered again in a concrete way that the unity of the Church of our Lord Jesus Christ takes form, as we listen to Scripture, in a fresh realization of our common responsibility for faithful witness to our Lord and for service in His name in the world.

In spite of the variety of our ecclesiastical traditions and theological conceptions, we have found ourselves unanimous in affirming that our Lord expects from us today an obedience to His Gospel which expresses itself through a self-sacrificing love for all men.

This love constrains us to action for justice and peace among men with all our strength, by every means compatible with the Gospel, and therefore without recourse to war.

We believe that the Church, as it accepts the constraint of this love, will be inspired and enabled to commend the Gospel by manifesting the neighbourliness which transcends differences of race and class, and by carrying out across all national boundaries the work of compassionate service and of Christian evangelism of which our world stands in such need.

We shall be glad to share the resumé of our discussions with any who are interested. We intend to continue our study of the theological problems which have engaged us at this conference, and we cordially welcome the cooperation of our fellow Christians.

10. The Lordship of Christ Over Church and State, II. (Iserlohn, Germany, July 29-August 1, 1957)

It was agreed at the first Puidoux conference that another meeting was necessary. This took place two years later at the invitation of the Landeskirche *of Westphalia, with the meeting site an Evangelical Academy. Nearly seventy representatives from Germany, The Netherlands, France, Italy, the United States, Japan, and England came together; some were official representatives, some were private. From the German churches came persons from Westphalia, Rhineland Hesse and Nassau, Hannover, Berlin-Brandenburg, Saxony, Anhalt, Wittenberg, and Oldenburg.*

The two main themes of the conference were: discipleship as a witness of unity in Christ, and the basis of human justice in the righteousness of God. "Whereas the first Puidoux Conference emphasized the unity of Christ's Lordship—that God's will for both Church and State is one—the Iserlohn Conference called for a definition of the content and implication of this witness, both in terms of discipleship (for the Church) and the human justice (for the State)."

The format was more formal and theological than the early meeting, partly because of the sponsors and partly because of the large number of those gathered. Despite the highly structured nature of the meeting, it seemed to be the case that real encounter took place. A British participant reported how important it was that members of the Landeskirchen *could come so closely together with representatives of the "sects," in the face of several centuries of a deep gulf between the two: "This background must be fully grasped before it is possible to understand the immense joy and thankfulness which seized both 'churchmen' and 'sectarians' when . . . they discovered that the gulf can be bridged, in fact had been bridged by them then and there, in free discussion and the loving exchange of arguments and mutual explanations."*

A closing statement to the Landeskirchen *summed up the extent of common agreement emerging from the intensive sessions. Among other points, it agreed that "the Christian cannot stand in the service of killing but instead will have to serve life in simple obedience for the sake of Him who became man, died for us, and is living again."* The conference urged a continuation of the discussion.

Discipleship as Witness to the Unity in Christ as Seen by the Reformers

Ernst Wolf

Discipleship, according to the New Testament, is the name for the Christian way of life in the world, specifically (a) as life in an alien environment, for those called to discipleship are called out from the world; (b) as readiness to suffer for the sake of the name [of Christian]—as the New Testament repeatedly states; and (c) as humble service for the world and to the world, as service in love out of freedom.

In all, this discipleship is bound to Jesus Christ. From this there result essentially three problem areas for theological ethics. First, the problem of the ethical authority of Jesus Christ. Secondly, the problem of making possible the decision for discipleship and that of practicing discipleship or, put in a different way, the question of the rules and norms for discipleship. Thirdly, the problem of the meaning of discipleship.

In recent Protestant ethics, especially in Germany but also generally on the Continent, discipleship has scarcely been dealt with. One can refer to any number of works: the Luthardt *Compendium of Theological Ethics* contains, for example, the entry "dueling," but not the entry "discipleship." There are but few exceptions. Bonhoeffer is the one great exception. There is also a paragraph in the Lutheran ethics by Söe on "The Discipleship of Christ and His Example"; that paragraph is one of the positive features of this ethic. Finally, Paul Althaus in his *Basic Outline [of Ethics]* has also a section about "The Ethical Authority of Jesus."

The reason for this is probably that the question of discipleship, especially in the Lutheran Reformation, very soon lost importance; in the Lutheran camp it was generally looked upon as a matter of "enthusiastic" or "Reformed" legalism. In addition, there were only certain individual attempts at ethical realization of discipleship in later years. This occurred, for one, in Pietism with a pronounced tendency toward denial of the world or a withdrawal from the world for the sake of individual sanctifying perfection, in other words, along the lines of a more or less sentimental *imitatio Jesus.* Next, we find a discipleship idea in rationalism, in which Jesus is set before us as the ethical ideal of perfect humanity.

We also encounter "discipleship" with one of the great German theologians of the nineteenth century, Albrecht Ritschl, although here it is in the form of an ethic of intent *(Gesinnungsethik)* within one's own secular vocation, which one was to pursue with a Christian, that is to say, with "discipleship" intent. Finally, discipleship was unearthed again in a very peculiar way by Kierkegaard in the sense of contemporaneousness and especially with emphasis upon the communion with the sufferings of Christ.

We shall not pursue these attempts in detail; there is really no need for doing so. We shall merely state quite summarily this: By and large, it was the fear of so-called legalism which led to the weakening of the directness *(Unmittelbarkeit)* of the call to discipleship within Protestant ethics. Here is just one example for this weakening of the directness from *Outline of Ethics* (1953) by P[aul] Althaus. In the section on "The Ethical Authority of Jesus" it reads:

> In Jesus Christ the will of God has become reality in the life of one man. As image of the nature of God (Col. 1:15), Jesus Christ is at the same time the prototype of the man of God which we are created to be, to which we are to be renewed. Thus all Christian life can be nothing but *discipleship* of Jesus, life in his *image,* obedience to his commandments.

So far, so good. But now it goes on:

> Yet Jesus is prototype and prefiguration of the man of God in the uniqueness of a special mission, in the concreteness and limitation of his historical place and his individuality which cannot be repeated. Thus he would not be understood as a legalistic model, thus discipleship must not be understood as imitatio Christi. By the same token his commandments—specifically and concretely—are not meant as universally binding laws. Therefore obedience must not be understood as blind, outward fulfillment of and limitation to his instructions. Rather, he wants to free his own from laws and legalism and lead them into the *freedom of the children of God.* . . . In many respects we have other things to do than he did, and we must deal with areas of life for which he has shown us no specific way either through his actions or in his instructions. But even all of this we must and can do in the name of the Lord Jesus (Col. 3:17). We are Christ's, but Christ is God's (1 Cor. 3:23). That means: Jesus

binds us to himself *only* for that and *only* in such a way as to bind us to God, the living spirit. Thus our ethical bond to Jesus and his commandments is one in the *Holy Spirit* (p. 38).

This direct relationship to Jesus is not very clear in other writings either, not even with Calvin, neither in his *Ethics* which he developed in the second and third books of his *Institutes* (especially in volume III, 6-10), nor in connection with a specific exegesis. If one, for example, looks up the exposition of Philemon 2:5 ("Have this mind among yourselves, which you have in Christ Jesus. . . . ") as a statement about the humiliation of him who finds himself in the presence of God, one is astonished that Calvin has actually very little to say about it; only something along the line that here the greater one, that is Jesus the Christ, and the lesser one, the Christian, are compared with each other; and that perhaps the glory of Jesus is confronted with false presumption on our part. In short, the exposition makes scarcely any clear reference to the problem of discipleship. Nevertheless, Calvin's ethic is an ethic of discipleship, in that it is a rule for the life of rebirth. The object of rebirth is "that in the life of the believers symmetry and harmony be manifested between the righteousness of God and their (the believers') obedience, that they might thus confirm the adoption, 'being taken on as sons,' through which they are accepted by God as children" (III, 6:1). This goal, it is true, will be attained only in the eschatological perfection, but eschatology must not be misused as dispensation from the demands of the present.

The norm of action is, on the one hand, God's universally valid law, which with Calvin is not narrowed by biblicism. God is and remains himself the content of the law and his honor is the object of obedience. More important, however, than the law is the providential situation, that is, the idea of God's guidance in the sense of God's precedence, the idea, therefore, that God himself leads the way in every concrete historical situation. Where with the Lutherans the creation order takes prominence later on, there is with Calvin this providential situation. Both, the law of God and his precedence are summarized for the Christian in the *vocatio Dei,* in the call from God. Thus Calvin arrives at the central axiom that the *vocatio Dei* shapes our life. I cite again literally, from the exposition on Jonah: "The entire condition of our life will be confused, if God does not precede, guide, and so to speak, raise his standard" (CR 43:208).

Thus the life of the Christian stands under the motto *sequi Deum vocantem,* the following of that God who calls people. This motto [is] proven [by] the transformation of the whole life of him who knows that he is placed under God's demand; [it is] not identical with the mandate to transform the world. Rather, Calvin understands the transformation of life primarily as *abnegatio nostri* that is, as self-denial, as a receding of all of our personal desires and wishes behind that which we owe to God and neighbor: all of the gifts which we have received are to be placed gratefully and humbly into the service of mankind. It is important that from this emphasis upon self-denial there is derived at the same time and in a positive way the duty not only toward the honor of God but also toward the service to man *per se*.

These essentially quite simple thoughts determine the ethic of Calvin throughout and one comes to understand that among these thoughts manifold individual applications are possible. The main tenor is crucial: we do not belong to ourselves but we belong to God (III, 7:1), that is to say, we are not to seek our own interests but God's. Calvin once summarized this very beautifully in the sentence: "This, then, is that denial of self which Christ enjoins with such great earnestness upon his disciples at the outset of their service" (III, 7:2). In this sense the discipleship concept is found with Calvin in a very central place indeed.

With this I shall now turn to Luther. It must be stressed that Luther, prior to 1523, developed a decided ethic of discipleship in his treatise "On the Freedom of a Christian," and this from the beginning as a social ethic. The Latin title of this treatise—*De libertate Christiana*—should more appropriately be translated as "On Christian Social Ethics." Here he rejected the mystical-moralistic preaching of the imitation of Christ usual at his time: *Non esse satis nec christianum* (this is insufficient and it is not even Christian). He then proceeded in the crucial passage to interpret the statements in the hymnus to Christ (Phil. 2:5ff.) differently than tradition had done. As we know, the churchly tradition had related the words of *morphe theou* and *morphe doulou,* of *forma Dei* and *forma serve,* of the nature of God and the nature of the servant, to the two natures of Christ, the divine and the human. Luther applied them directly and, as we would probably have to say today, exegetically correctly to the nature *(Daseinsweise)* of a ruler and the nature of a servant. Consequently, he applied them from this perspective not only to Christ but also with their whole severity to the Christian.

Accordingly, he demands from the Christian who is justified by faith a humiliation in and because of his newly given freedom. This humiliation for service is the necessary working of faith. In this Luther arrives at bold conclusions: "I will therefore give myself as a Christ to my neighbor" —that is to say, just as Christ, yes as a Christ—" just as Christ offered himself to me. I will do nothing in this life except what I see as necessary, profitable, and salutary to my neighbor, since through faith I have an abundance of all good things in Christ."

What does this mean? It has been said that in Lutheran thinking *Christus exemplum* had as its presupposition *Christus sacramentum*. Those are traditional formulae; they say: Christ as example presupposes that Christ has been bestowed on me as *sacramentum,* that is, as a gift of grace. But what Luther says in this passage is more than that. For when I take *Christus sacramentum* only as prerequisite for *Christus exemplum*—justification only as prerequisite for discipleship—I shall always be in danger of separating the two and, if necessary, of being satisfied with the prerequisite.

Certainly, discipleship is the witness or testimony to free grace but in such a way that it shows this grace so to speak not as presupposition but as a self-manifesting reality. In other words, I cannot speak of justification or free grace as presupposition, before I practice the reality of discipleship. I cannot, so to speak, place myself in a third position, rather, I can speak legitimately of the gift of grace only if I know myself to be actually drawn into the process of discipleship.

Specifically, this means: justification gives no dispensation from deed, rather, justification focuses the call to discipleship beyond the playfulness of *imitatio*. Secondly, discipleship is realized as an act of solidarity with the needs of the world, that is, quite specifically, as *quod proximo necessarium (et) commodum*—that which is necessary and beneficial for the neighbor. It also includes the protest against the world, for the third word in that quotation is *et salutare,* that which is wholesome for the neighbor. It has to do with eternal salvation, which no longer belongs with the world. At the same time and thirdly, acting in discipleship is, however, secular activity, secular calling, which, as a matter of fact, when practiced in discipleship receives new justification from the *gospel*. This third sentence needs further clarification.

The concluding statement reads: "secular calling, which when practiced in discipleship receives new justification from the gospel." I should like to illustrate this by way of an example. . . . According to Luther, the Christian, as a co-worker with God in the reconciliation of the world to God, is also responsible for the life of this world and, thus, for example, for the state, too. But the concern of the Christian for the state is of a different kind than the concern which the state has for itself. If one understands "state" as the concentration of self-assertion, then the Christian in his concern for the state is not interested in this self-assertive character of the state, but merely that it be an instrument for the preservation of this world from chaos—put more sharply, that it remains an instrument of God for the purpose of preserving the world from chaos. From this perspective, the secular calling of the care for the state receives, for example, from the gospel a new justification, indeed, its sole justification, insofar as all justification is based upon the righteousness of God.

At the same time, the other side must also be emphasized: "new justification in discipleship, practiced from the perspective of the gospel"; from the gospel, and that is because the fulfilling of discipleship results from faith, and faith on its part is the answer to the word of promise, namely, the gospel. Let me stress here that Luther at least in this passage and at least up to this time did not consider this question so much from the perspective of the law as from that of the gospel. From the perspective of the gospel this new acting in discipleship is done at the same time on the basis of the freedom of self-denial. This freedom of self-denial is at the same time the expression for the tension in which man finds himself in relation to a world of self-assertion. As long as man desires himself and his wishes, he himself belongs to the world of self-assertion, too. Through faith he is freed from this. Out of this self-denial he has won the new freedom from the gospel and under the mandate of God, as an extension of the actions of Jesus Christ himself, to interact with the world in a new way.

Thus we find here the same as in the New Testament: discipleship is the name for Christian life in the world. "In the world" always means at the same time "for the world as creation of God" and "against the world as power of self-assertion." From this viewpoint the problems are now posed anew. If, for example, war is the symbol of the power of self-assertion, every attempt at a Christian glorification of war is impossible. This attempt could be made as long as one thought it possible to interpret in a very general way the Christian life in the world through a law of God, or one of God's "orders." All of us know how much in Christendom the great and the idols of the world have been glorified in numerous Christian and religious variations. The gospel prevents this. Discipleship, which at the same time proclaims the exclusive normative validity of the gospel for the life and conduct of the Christian in the world, underlines this impediment.

This concept of discipleship, in which alone the lordship of Christ over church and world is realized in a hidden and mysterious way within Christendom, was very soon abandoned during the Reformation era. On this point Luther himself until 1521 and those whom he later persecuted as "enthusiasts" *(Schwärmer)* had been very close. This position was abandoned at that moment when in Lutheran thought the concept of vocation—the *vocatio* which we found with Calvin—was linked with the doctrine of the two kingdoms. The result of this development was that the equal responsibility of the Christian before God for church *and* world was replaced by the question of competence. This question has divided the responsibility, that is to say, has absolved the Christian entirely or in part of the responsibility for the world.

To this was added the interest in the *Landeskirchen* or *Staatskirchen,* that is to say, that the statement that the church was responsible to God for the world, was reinterpreted in such a way as to mean that the church cared more and more for her own cause and not for the cause of God's interest in the world, so that she did not carry out the cause of God with his people as a servant. Both the dissolution of the uniformity of the responsibility and this growing interest even of the Reformation churches in their own existence had a great deal to do with the dissolution of the unity in Christ and with that which, with the Reformers, was consistently linked with discipleship in the light of preparedness for suffering. Luther himself had again and again called this preparedness to suffer and the suffering the mark of the one church. More and more this preparedness to suffer was *de facto* attributed to the "enthusiasts." As early as during the Reformation they were living examples of this attribute of the discipleship of Christ in a very peculiar way. Today, we realize more than a short time ago, that all seems to depend upon Christendom's regaining and actually living an ethic of discipleship. Both belong together, because an ethic of discipleship simply cannot be attained by theory. In the preceding I wanted to examine the question whether and to what extent on the basis of the necessary *reflections* about an ethic of discipleship, noteworthy beginnings could be found with the Reformers. I believe that they are there, and I should maintain this even at the risk of Brother Yoder's declaring at the conclusion that I, too, made Luther a modern "situation ethicist."

Discipleship as Witness to the Unity in Christ as Seen by the Dissenters

Paul Peachey

If we really wish to make progress in the question of peace, then it is no longer a matter of individual pacifist inroads against, perhaps, the atomic experiments—although it would be high time to hear a clear Christian voice on this—but a matter of the Christian ethos and the Christian church generally. The fact that we in Christianity, including the so-called peace churches, are still confused about the war question, leads to the conclusion that we are dealing not with an isolated borderline question but with the very essence of what it is to be a Christian. This insight offers us a double benefit. First, it has a sobering effect on pacifists, because the inadequacy of some claims and argumentations of pacifist theses is brought to light. Secondly, a dialog of pacifists with non-pacifists is made possible.

In recent years it has been repeatedly stated that war was contrary to the will of God, that it was entirely incompatible with Christ and the gospel. In actuality, however, we not only leave participation in war to the individual conscience, but the great majority of Christians, in spite of everything, is reconciled to our war-oriented civilization. Accordingly, conscientious objection to war today is largely considered an exception which, according to our attitude toward human rights, etc., is to be respected, protected, and even appreciated, but not to be made general. If, however, we agree insofar as to say that war is contrary to the will of God, to the teaching, spirit, and the life of Christ, then one cannot help but think: might it perhaps be even true non-resistance is in fact normative for all Christians? Could it also be true therefore that precisely through this the concept of "being a Christian" would become distinctive, that there would suddenly be a separation of the spirits, a visible dividing line between Christians and non-Christians, a clearly defined church over against the world?

Now all of you were aware that you were going to be among the enthusiasts *(Schwärmer)* here, but do not be alarmed, I shall not answer these questions on my authority alone, nor presume to be the judge of other opinions. Furthermore, it is our task here merely to clarify a historical and therefore tentative, question. However, we must be sure to keep in mind also in this that possibly neither enthusiasts nor church [men] will be satisfied with my answer.

We know that the Reformers denied our question whether a Christian ethic could be formulated in such a way as to lead to a visible church separated from the world. We also know that certain so-called enthusiasts answered this question in the affirmative and that it never came to a compromise between these different opinions. Since the mayor of Iserlohn does not preside over us in his chair and there is no placard (or so I assume) posted to the city hall decreeing the banishment of enthusiasts, this dialog can—and in view of the current world situation—must be resumed, a process which was already started by Puidoux.

First of all, it must be stated that the image of the church as it is conveyed by Acts and the letters of Paul is not that "perfect church" so often imagined by sects and revival movements. We never encounter ethical perfectionism in the sense of sinlessness in the New Testament. On the other hand, neither do we find a sacramental system nor the appropriate clergy, which makes the church a visible entity. And yet, the early church is a tangible, somehow clearly circumscribed entity. Of what, then, does this visibility consist? The presence and effect of Christ were probably so real in the church that the concept of an "invisible church" would have been completely unintelligible. The question about the "how" of the presence of Christ or the "where" of the church had not yet arisen simply because the reality was there. As this fullness of faith gradually diminished it became desirable or necessary to make the presence of Christ concrete through the cultic. That is to say, this attempt at making the presence of Christ tangible in the sacramental system did not initially develop as a heresy but out of the psychological needs of man. Church could only be thought of as a cultic community. From there, the path led directly to Rome. Spiritual abstractions are no sufficient substitute for the living congregation; where there is no true church, there remains only an objective institution of salvation *(Heilsanstalt)*.

Despite this critical observation it cannot be denied that canon, creed, and bishop did transmit the Christian faith. But when the Catholic principle reached its full development in the Middle Ages and then—as is well known—led to general decline in morals and church life, the error of this attempt to portray the visibility of the church by a social institution became fully obvious. According to the *Catholic Encyclopedia,* the church is so fully embodied by its priestly-sacramental form that the lay person can be considered as belonging to the church only insofar as he or she is admitted to membership by the clergy. This means that the encounter of the individual with Christ is no longer constitutive to the church. The church continues in history even if no believer is present.

It seems to me that from this perspective the greatness, but also the tragedy, of Luther becomes visible. In Worms he stood before this visible church which understood itself as complete and perfected even without a believing and obedient congregation. And then he actually dared in that very instant to cast this entire church into the scales of his personal encounter with Christ, and just as earlier a hand had begun to write on the wall for Belshazzar, he found this same church to be "wanting" [Dan. 5:27]. Thus Luther dared at that moment to begin again from the very beginning and to call that the church which results from a living encounter with a living lord. However, we said not only greatness but also tragedy— although this word is perhaps no longer appropriate. There is no need for us to recapitulate the story. For two special reasons Luther (and Zwingli likewise) was unable to use and apply the conclusion from this understanding of the church. First—and this is partly to be valued positively— because the church of that time still constituted an unquestioned unity. The dissolution had already begun, but I believe that at least theologically the image of the unity of the church was still dominant. There was, therefore, no question of creating another church *(Nebenkirche)* which would be pure. Still more important was the historical situation of the sixteenth century. Rightly or wrongly, the church was the spiritual basis of society. It was a society in which several value systems existed concurrently and alongside of one another—what we today call "cultural pluralism" was inconceivable. Christendom, therefore, had to be retained for the sake of order despite Luther's insights of faith.

How this question was posed may be clearly seen in the example of Zwingli, who came more closely into contact with the Anabaptists and whom I therefore know better. Although his orientation was much more humanistic and his experience of faith much more a matter of the intellect than was the case with Luther, it is nevertheless a fact that Zwingli originally trusted the word of God so much that he believed that the mere proclamation of the word of God would make its own way. Therefore the first stage of his reformation activity directed itself quite simply to the freedom of proclamation. When the answer to this question received an affirmative answer from the Zürich city government and the people were consequently stirred up, the question about the next step presented itself: How was this renewal to take place?

Thus in the year 1523 a second disputation on faith was held in Zürich. Zwingli's opponents, however, raised an embarrassing issue. How could an assembly that was not called by the church but by the city government deal with matters of the church? As a response, Zwingli preached a forceful sermon on this subject. He showed that the Bible spoke of the church only in a twofold way. First, in the Bible the concept of church refers to the entire mass of the faithful. Secondly, in the Bible the concept of church refers to the local congregation. However, Zwingli continued, since all the assemblies and synods of the clergy were neither universal nor local congregations, they could not be considered churches at all. Indeed, the small churches of the neighboring villages of Hönigg and Küssnacht were certainly more the church than all the rabble of bishops and popes.

Thus the power of the pope was denied in principle and the autonomous task of the congregation clearly stated. Yet within two days Zwingli had to make a different decision for the historical facts were different. If Zürich was ready to separate from the pope, that was consistent with the increasing nationalism. But it was quite a different matter to do away in like manner with one blow with that which the *corpus christianum* signified. As a matter of fact, the congregation of Zürich had neither the power to reshape all of society nor the power to carry out the necessary reforms in the church. Zwingli was left with only one option—to appeal to the city government. Actually, the decision had already been made despite Zwingli's sermon when the city government called the meeting.

On this point, however, theologically and historically a separation took place. As different as Luther and Zwingli were in their basic positions on this point, they seemed to have had exactly the same experience. At first, when the appeal to the church authorities for reform met without success, both men started to act according to their own experience and conviction. However, when things began to happen and seemed to threaten the unity of the people, both were left with no other choice than to appeal to their respective secular governments.

However, those in Zwingli's camp who nevertheless insisted that the church included only that which developed from faith and obedience and that church existed only insofar as it was a matter of a living community in Christ, were now facing a dilemma. To turn church reform over to the city government, especially when that meant a delay in a matter which had already been decided by the spirit of God, could only mean compromise. However, to take the consequences of opposing Zwingli and the city government was also dangerous.

We all know that Zwingli (and Luther) was victorious on the surface. When the dissenters chose the second option they embarked on a fateful historical destiny. First came the persecution, which we need not discuss here in detail. Secondly, and more important for us here, the struggle for the justification or the authority of their actions ensued. Let us look at two examples. In 1532, about twenty Anabaptist leaders gathered in Zofingen to hold a dialogue with the churchly theologians on the Anabaptist question and to clarify the questions caused by their differences. Although the external power rested with the church, there was willingness to hear both sides, and to keep and later publish the records jointly. In this dialogue, the Anabaptists were pressed very seriously, especially on one point: in whose authority did they take the liberty of acting in churchly matters? Certainly, the theologians were themselves at a loss, for the separation from the pope had not yet resulted in the installation of a satisfactory new authority; simply to appeal to the city government was hardly an option for the theologians at this point. What is important for us is the answer which the Anabaptists gave. They said that the church came about through grace and obedience, through repentance and conversion. Wherever that took place there was indeed the church, and in this event, in this community, the authority to act as a church was given; that is to say, it was part of its nature.

The second example is Menno Simons. As you know, he was baptized by Obbe Phillips and ordained to service. Obbe Phillips, however, had received his baptism and his office from Jan Matthys, a member of the Münsterites. Added to this was the fact that several years later Obbe resigned from his office, supposedly because his call to it had been a false one. This left Menno and many others in the same dilemma. In fact, not only Menno's office was called in question but the Dutch Anabaptist movement itself. If the original preaching had been done without a genuine calling, then the question arose whether or not the entire Anabaptist movement was wrong. Of course we do not know to what extent the Anabaptist circles were alarmed by this crisis. Fortunately, Menno himself investigated the problem more thoroughly. His inner experience and the fruits of his activity convinced him in that very moment that his calling was genuine, that the presence of the church as a gathering in obedience to Christ, in the renewal of life, bore within itself its justification. In a later controversy with a Reformed pastor he accused the latter of claiming that the church was the church despite the absence of true fruits, as if the church could be inherited from generation to generation outwardly or by ritual, instead of arising from and existing in faith, spirit, and power.

Since it was not possible for Luther and the other reformers to take the Anabaptist way they had to find a different solution. They did adhere, in some form, [to the concept] that the church was a concrete entity as well as the fact that it was made up of people reconciled by God. However, from a human point of view, the believers could never be distinguished from the unbelievers. Therefore the reality of the church had to be brought about by other means. That meant, however, that what was specifically of the church remained but a platonic ideal, which was, of course, repeatedly alluded to by word and sacrament, but never historically experienced. Thus the historical church simply became a cultic body or a part of the social order. It is true that attempts were made to induce the congregation which gathered under the word to live by it also. However, given the above attitude, this question of "an improvement of life" remained an open question. This meant that largely improvement of life did not occur.

The Anabaptists, as we have seen, could not go this way. Although they did hold to the belief of the universal church as the "entire mass of the faithful" and even admitted that in the historical realization of the church perfection could not be postulated, they nevertheless insisted, in good Hebrew fashion, that the church could only be experienced as a visible entity and that this entity *(Gemeinde)* as, for example, Menno said, existed through faith, spirit, and power. In other words, that the church of Christ realized itself visibly through the common submission into the obedience of

Christ. The later development showed that this new perspective of the Anabaptists had not been thought through completely. One indication of this was that these Anabaptists, these "dissenters" prepared the way for a never-ending division of the church on the continent and later in England and America on the basis of the autonomy of the church which was given by the Holy Spirit. As another instance it was found—and that especially in Quakerism, but also in part among the other Historic Peace Churches as well as later in Pietism and in American Fundamentalism—that the emphasis especially on the spiritual substance of faith was likely to dissolve into a subjective individualism. (Naturally, this second development had its roots partially also in the Protestant concept of the invisible church, which we cannot further develop here.)

Two conclusions result from these reflections which seem to be important for our considerations here. First we ought to agree that obedience to the will of God, for example in the question of war but also in ethics generally, is laid upon every Christian conscience in equal measure. The fact that this is what makes the church visible as a community of obedience sheds new light on the ecumenical question. The decisive question would then not be primarily that of the constitution or of the sacraments, for example, but rather the question whether we place ourselves together and concretely under the living lordship of Christ. This is where the various concerns of the two great Christian confessions meet. The Catholic Church, for whom nothing matters but making the event of salvation visible, will be told that this concern is justified but that this visibility cannot be abstracted from a life of faith and obedience into symbolism: It is realized and found only in the living effect of the lordship of Christ. The church can therefore never continue its earthly existence as a sacramental system divorced from that community which lives in continuous, active obedience. The Protestant churches, on the other hand, will be told that the knowledge of the invisibility of the church points to the fact that the constitutive power rests with the Holy Spirit and not with any human acts of foundation or human institutions, but that this invisibility of the inner nature must never be interpreted without discipleship of Christ.

The second conclusion concerns ethics. Already in what was said above, the questions of legalism and literalism arose immediately. Curiously, however, the same sects that are accused of legalism had also been accused of antinomianism, or enthusiasm. One must admit, of course, from the outset that among these groups both extremes do indeed occur and will always threaten to occur. But the fact that it was possible to accuse the same group of two such opposing extremes seems to point to a deeper significance. For in fact, both elements of a legalism are present, that is to say, an ethic of principles or "ethic of ends," as it is occasionally called, as well as a lack of principles, i.e., a situational ethic or "ethic of inspiration." This means: The never-changing will of God which is rooted in God's very nature is a fact which can, in certain cases, be described and demonstrated from the outside as a doctrine of principles. This means two things: First, that the will of God confronts us through Jesus Christ, never changing it itself and consistent. And secondly, as especially George Fox emphasized, [that the will of God] always says the same about the spirit of Christ. In this sense it is possible to speak of a "doctrine of principles." The experience of the Historic Peace Churches shows how easily this can turn into a false legalism.

On the other hand, however, if one emphasizes the community of obedience of the church which continuously renews itself, one applies—up to a certain point—that which is meant today by "situational ethics." For the ethical norms of the gospel are not to be understood as abstract absolute principles which are to be applied automatically without regard to the specific situation, or which supersede the personal decision of the individual involved. Yet the Lord is always the same. He does not contradict himself, not even in his demands of people who live under extremely different conditions. Where these two, that which is never changing in the will of God and that which is situational in human life of man, separate, we are bound for one of the two opposite extremes, either legalism or illuminationism (existentialism). What was characteristic of the peace churches—although they often stray far from it in practice—was this fact that both elements were combined in a higher synthesis. But this is only possible where the church is a living community of faith and obedience.

Conversely, must it not be admitted that one can really speak of church only where people are gathered in living obedience under Christ? That is where the church is and that is where, correctly understood, the unity of the church is revealed. However important sacraments or orthodoxy may be, we are still confronted by the question: Can the question of the unity of the church ever be resolved on this basis?

Protestant Preaching on Peace

Hans-Werner Bartsch

We continually experience in our Protestant church that the task of preaching is perverted. This happens, for example, when the ethos of the soldier is dealt with in army worship services. But it has also happened through the agreement on army chaplaincies insofar as this does imply a justification of the military profession. And this is what signifies perversion of preaching: When in it a justification is given. The task of preaching is the call to repentance and the proclamation of the free gift of salvation, of grace, but never the transmission of the justification of a certain action. This [latter] only illustrates the cause of this faulty development which lies in the fact that we hardly know any longer what preaching really means. In the case of the agreement on army chaplaincies, for example, it means that we no longer know how far the area of preaching extends—that even those topics are part of the proclamation of the church and therefore must be examined to determine whether they are a legitimate part of such a proclamation. There are two questions involved: the content of preaching and the scope of its applicability.

Research on the New Testament, it seems to me, has given the possibility of an answer to these two questions, which I do not wish to separate for that reason. It has been discovered that the gospels, or their elements, the individual pericopes, have their *Sitz im Leben*—as Martin Dibelius said—in preaching. This means that in the gospels, we have, basically, the first collection of early Christian sermons. Thus it is not necessary for us to develop systematically what preaching is, but rather we have in the gospels the starting point for our understanding of preaching. For this reason our task in preaching is nothing but the interpretation of the early Christian sermon for the people of our time and for our current situation. I do not mean to say, of course, that all we have to do is to seek analogies between our situation and possibly existing situations which we encounter in the gospels. Rather, given our time, situation, and problems, we must do for our fellow human beings what the early Christian witnesses did given their time, situation, and problems for theirs. . . . I shall try to develop how we are to understand the gospels as early Christian preaching.

The focal point of early Christian preaching is the proclamation of the fact that the kingdom of God has come in Jesus Christ. The first witnesses proclaimed this by drawing the consequences of the kingdom's having come in Christ for their own lives, their own existence, in their records of the life of Jesus and their life with him. They show us how their understanding of their own lives, their being, is different because of the fact that Jesus Christ has come. Let me make this clear with an example. In the story about the storm at sea the miracle of the stilling of the storm is certainly recorded as a sign that the man who was in the boat with the others was the Christ. At the same time it is recorded that for that very reason the panic of the disciples with which they approached Christ was foolish. The witness confesses by this his own lack of understanding at that time, but does so from the vantage point that, through the revelation of Christ at Easter he recognizes his own fear, his own panic at that time, as foolish. Knowing that Christ has come, he now understands his life differently, namely, freed from fear. This he proclaims with the challenge [to others] to effect this same change of understanding in their existence.

If we attempt then to determine the content of our preaching from this perspective we shall likewise have to testify to our understanding of our own existence given to us by Christ, as it was done in Treysa with respect to our conduct during the last war [i.e., World War II] namely, that we had not believed enough, hoped enough, loved enough. In the same way we shall have to testify to the understanding of our existence under the lordship of Jesus Christ as freed from that fear which inhibited us then in speaking and acting. Thus we shall have to call for the same kind of trusting understanding of one's own existence and to draw the certain consequences for our existence today. With this I have now focused on that point where our preaching of peace originates, the preaching of that peace which God has given through the sending of his son. Just as the justification is reality only in obedience, then this preaching of the peace which God has given is received only in obedience to the commandment of love, specifically to the commandment: Thou shalt not kill. As Professor Wolf said yesterday, the same indissoluble relationship exists between the proclamation of that peace, which God has given in Jesus Christ and the obedience to the commandment (on the one hand) and the proclamation of grace and discipleship (on the other). Just as I can speak of grace only when practicing discipleship, so can I speak of peace only in obedience to the commandment: Thou shalt not kill. Moreover, it seems to me that this commandment has special weight within the Decalog because unlike the other commandments in the second tablet it cannot be subordinated under the great commandment of love of neighbor.

The first objection which is always raised against this concrete preaching of peace is that we must annul the sixth commandment here and there for the sake of the commandment of the love of neighbor. However, the sixth commandment, "Thou shalt not kill" cannot cede to this commandment because it is older than the Decalog, because we find it already in Genesis 9 where it is justified with this statement: "For God made man in his own image." Thus the obedience to this commandment is not primarily a matter of practicing the love of neighbor, but rather of humbly honoring God the creator, who in Jesus Christ has become man. When Jesus summarizes all of the commandments in "You shall love the lord your God and your neighbor as yourself," the sixth commandment belongs first of all under the first: "You shall love the lord your God." Reverence for the creator forbids killing; love of neighbor is only secondary.

Man enjoys the protection of the commandment because he is made in the image of God. Applying this according to the New Testament means that in the incarnation of Jesus Christ the dignity of man is founded. Therefore I can kill no human being because I encounter Jesus Christ in that person: not in the least of *my* brethren, as we understand it, but in the least of *his* brethren, who must also be seen in the very ones whom we believe we may deliver up to the sword. It seems to me impossible to draw a line here by saying that there are people in whom Jesus Christ does not meet us. Thus, this commandment is first of all a call to trust in God's love and power because of his coming to us in Jesus Christ, a call to a recognition of his authority as the authority of the creator, who meets me in Jesus Christ as a loving father. I acknowledge this authority by leaving to him the care for my life and by honoring his image in my neighbor.

With this understanding, the call of preaching [of peace] is freed from a certain pragmatism as if it involved only the specific case of killing. It is brought in its larger context into the total commandment of love of God and neighbor. The sixth commandment marks only the radical borderline case in which the obedience to this commandment is being tested. This commandment asks me first of all whether I am ready to acknowledge myself in my total existence as a creation of God and God as the creator and sustainer of my life. You will have noticed that I have been attempting with this to counter the objections against this preaching, which have been levied again and again especially by Lutherans. The second objection raises the accusation that such a radical proclamation of this commandment causes legalism. They have that sort of pacifist posture in mind which holds that by refusing to participate [in killing] one can keep oneself clean. The fact that this is largely a caricature shall not even be taken into account here.

By understanding this proclamation of the commandment from the perspective of the proclamation of the gospel and as a consequence of it, we have actually already repudiated this objection. Beyond this, however, it is quite possible to turn the tables on it. Where does really legalistic misunderstanding or legalistic misuse of the law occur? The prototype of such a legalistic misuse of the law occurs in the New Testament, for example, in the answer of the rich young ruler: "I have performed all of these things from my youth." It is the posture which believes itself to have acted in compliance with the law and which is therefore not in need of forgiveness. Now we must ask, however, what kind of proclamation is the most vulnerable to this sort of misuse. Jesus deals especially with this kind of legalistic misuse of the law in his speech against the Pharisees and the scribes (Matt. 23). He demonstrates the meaninglessness of one of the expositions of the law with an example: "You say, 'If anyone swears by the temple, it is nothing; but if anyone swears by the gold of the temple, he is bound by his oath.'" His criticism is directed especially against this differentiation of the demand. We can see here already that the legalistic misuse is coupled precisely with a certain differentiation of the demand into certain individual demands. Against this, Jesus says: "But I say to you, you shall not swear at all, you should radically say the truth." Therefore, it is precisely the consistent and radical proclamation of the demand which permits no exceptions and differentiations, that protects from legalistic misuse, whereas the legalistic misuse occurs wherever one tries to limit the validity of the commandment. This limitation is, after all, always done in order to make fulfillment of the commandment possible.

Let me cite an example here, which comes down from my teacher Martin Dibelius. He used to tell of the time when he showed a visitor through the Heidelberg university where they saw the ominous sign, "No smoking in lecture halls." The visitor noticed the sign and reacted immediately with: "Aha, then it is all right for me to smoke here in the corridor." This is that type of legalistic misunderstanding or misuse in which one immediately narrows the commandment to its specific area and then looks for that sphere which it does not cover, where the commandment does not apply. Now the question must be asked of those Lutherans who keep referring to the legalistic misuse of the commandment "Thou shalt not kill" as to who is really misusing it. Is it the one who tries radically to submit to the commandment and, in spite of all the need to confess our transgressions against this commandment as it is expounded by Jesus in the Sermon on the Mount, is determined to cling to its validity. Or, is it the person who says, "Yes, it is valid here, but not there." This legalistic misuse of the commandment has a long history in the church. Since the time of Constantine the Christian church has again and again narrowed the validity of this commandment. Thus, Eusebius of Caesarea celebrated Constantine as the ambassador of God and his (i.e., Constantine's) supreme rule as a manifestation of the monarchy of God with the express purpose that

Constantine was permitted to do what God was permitted to do, namely, to kill. It was from this perspective that Athanasius was able to write: "Murder is not permitted. However, in war it is not only legal but worthy of love to kill the enemy." Then the concept of the just war is found with Augustine: "We fight wars so that peace may be secured." All of this is well known so that I need not repeat it here. But from this perspective Luther, too, may be understood. He carried out this narrowing of the commandment the most obviously in the exposition of the sixth commandment in the Large Catechism. As pastor of a Lutheran church I make myself vulnerable to disciplinary action if I feel compelled to declare part of our confessional writings heresy. When Luther says in the Large Catechism about the sixth commandment: "Accordingly in this commandment neither God nor the magistrates are referred to, nor is the power to put to death, which they possess, taken from them. For God has delegated His right to punish malefactors to the magistrates in place of parents, who formerly, as we read in the books of Moses (Deut. 21:18-20) were themselves obliged to bring their children to judgment and condemn them to death. Therefore, what is forbidden here is forbidden to private judgment, and not to magistrates" *(Bekenntnis-Schriften der Evangelischen Kirche,* p. 606, par. 181). I do not believe that we can rationalize this by saying that it was valid then but not today; rather, I believe that our era shows not only that this is wrong today but also that it was wrong at the time of Luther. This is a similar question to that raised by atomic warfare: Are we up against something radically new which makes war impossible, or does not atomic warfare cause us to see what was already wrong before. The same seems to be the case here as well.

I shall not pursue these specific problems of exceptions that will repeatedly be raised by Lutherans. Instead, I shall deal with one other question in this connection, one which is more basic, namely, whether there can be any exceptions to the applicability of the commandment at all. The practical question, whether an exception may be made for this or that case, can be posed only after we have first answered the question in principle whether an exception is possible. I am fully aware of the fact that with this question I run the risk of belaboring a point which is no problem for you; however, my excuse for this is that I am presenting here a point on which I seek your criticism for the dialogue with our opponents in our church, our Lutheran brethren. It is important for us that we do not simply conduct this dialogue unilaterally by simply presenting a draft, but rather that we here in this circle of those who follow the same line in their theological thinking correct and complement one another.

I shall attempt to show what the consequences of exceptions would be.

If I assume that exceptions to the commandment of God may be made in some form, it would indeed mean that there exists a form of action for which I do not need the forgiveness and justification through the grace of God, because I have already been justified in the act itself. It would also mean that with regard to the security of my life or the lives of my neighbors who are entrusted to me, I am not allowed to trust to the grace of God in a certain area but must act myself. This would mean that for a certain area [of life] at least this is true: If you help yourself, then God will help you. It would also mean that there exists a sphere for which the fact of Christ's having come to this earth has no meaning. It would at least mean that God is in need of my help, my own actions, in order to serve me, to protect me, and to protect my neighbor. It would mean that we could stake off an area which God has excluded from his sphere of authority, an area where his will does not rule, a place, above all, in which I as a Christian know that I am not under his lordship. If it were true, as Luther says in his exposition of the sixth commandment, that the magistrates are excluded from this area where this commandment is valid, it would mean that these men in their official functions no longer belong under the lordship of God. Precisely when the fallen character of the world is given as the reason for this exception, it would mean that the magistrates are subordinate in their realms not to God but to the prince of this world. For only through a limitation of that area in which God's commandment and his lordship are valid is it possible to justify the action of the magistrates, which would otherwise mean a transgression of the commandment. Now the assumption of such exceptions has another further-reaching significance. We must not think that this involves only the sixth commandment; rather, when I make exceptions for the magistrates and for war, this affects practically all of the commandments. In war—to speak only from our own experience—indeed for much of political life itself, it is not only the sixth commandment which is annulled but above all the ninth commandment. Not only in psychological warfare, but also in the manipulation of the masses through the newspapers, the ninth commandment is generally invalidated. In the same way the eighth commandment—what I mean is that official [requisitioning] certificates issued in wartime by the occupation authorities only gloss over the fact that theft is committed. I do not intend with this to speak against the requisitioning by the authorities in their own land. That is a completely different matter because such requisitioning is done for the welfare of the total populace, to which also belongs that person whose property is taken. For example, when the state wishes to construct a railroad line and needs land, it is in principle different from wartime requisitioning by a warring power in an occupied country. Even the seventh commandment, "Thou shalt not commit adultery," which, strangely enough, still seems to be founded the most firmly within the moral code, at least in its outward form, also came under the exceptions during the war through the special law of modern warfare. The seizing of houses of prostitution by the warmaking powers and their availability to the troops signifies in fact at least a sanctioning of the transgression [of the commandment] by the authorities, even when the frequenting of the houses remained largely under moral condemnation. The fact that just on this point the military chaplaincy, for instance, becomes questionable for the preaching of the church, was brought home to me when I received a report from the aide of the military commandant of the German medical corps in France, according to which even the preaching of the validity of this commandment in respect to prostitutes, for instance, would have been considered sabotage and subject to a court martial. The church never realized this fact because it never occurred to any of the military chaplains to proclaim the gospel to the prostitutes who were in the service of the German army.

As long as the conduct of war involved only a certain area of life and seemingly protected others, the issue seemed to involve only the sixth commandment. The more the conduct of war intrudes into other areas of life, the more it encompasses all aspects of life in total war, the more obvious it becomes that the acknowledgement of exceptions to the validity of the commandments of God cannot be limited to certain specific commandments, but rather that it *de facto* means that in principle the authorities stand outside of the sphere in which the total law of God is valid. The fact that this becomes obvious is related to the broadening of war to total war; it is, however, always true that the question about the possibility of exceptions to the validity of the law of God never involves a single commandment only but always the entire law. Thus the question is really, whether there is any area in this world which is radically and completely exempted from the sphere of God's will, from his power and his grace. We must answer this question in the negative if we hold the belief that the mission of Jesus Christ was to the whole world.

From yet another angle this question must be posed in principle as relating to the totality of life. Luther exempts the magistrates from the sphere of validity of the commandment. He has that ruler in mind (or at least certain persons) who feels himself bound in his responsibility to God and his commandments. Not only modern warfare with its tendencies to involve the entire populace in it, but also the modern understanding of the state, break through this understanding of the magistrate. The modern interpretation of the state—as it is established in all democratic constitutions—names the people as the bearers of the legislative power. This corresponds to the modern conduct of war from which no one can exclude himself. Indeed, this fact is widely acknowledged in the Lutheran camp. My right reverend bishop used this very fact as an argument against conscientious objection to war. He stated that it was, after all, impossible to separate oneself from war and its events and it was therefore useless to say that one would not take up arms to fight. One would be involved in the war in one way or another. This shows that our opponents foist upon us their own rationale, namely, that the real reason for the refusal of participation in war was the attempt to keep oneself clean. Precisely this fact shows us that war today is no longer the responsibility of the government alone but rather that the entire nation is co-responsible for the war. If we place war activities under exceptional laws which are different from the commandment of God, then the entire nation is placed under such exceptional legislation. This began in 1793 when in France first compulsory military service was announced and then universal conscription was proclaimed. By virtue of this it was the people who became responsible for war instead of a government that faces the people and takes the responsibility for the war upon itself. Thus Luther's concept of the magistrate is fundamentally called into question at least in relation to the issue of war. The question of the possibility of exceptions can no longer be posed for a magistrate, but rather it must be posed in principle for the totality of war in respect to each individual.

This fact is obscured again and again by the fact that the magistrate is interpreted as the government, because the restructuring of the state proceeds only step by step and because the total structure of the state still has not been changed to a true democracy. Instead, at least here in the Federal Republic of Germany, only the head of the monarchy has been sawed off but the structure of the state from top to bottom has been left standing despite the statement which was contained already in the Weimar constitution, that all power of the state issues from the people. The question is, then, whether the church is to be reactionary and hark back to a past understanding of the state, which we are now in the process of overcoming, or whether she ought to call for the responsibility of the individual for the totality of events, and strengthen this change toward true responsibility for the totality of events in each individual.

During the innumerable trials of war crimes it became evident that every individual claims the exceptional law of war for himself. Although in these trials attempts were made again and again to relegate the responsibility to some anonymous entity (or a dead entity!) in reality—and this is clear to anyone who has given pastoral care to people whose consciences were burdened by such matters—each person knows that he is responsible for it. He did it in war knowing that he now stood under an exceptional law. This awareness, however, does not last but breaks down as soon as he reflects on these things calmly and when, removed from the frenzy of war and confronted by his God, he finds himself again. For this very reason it is a matter of mercy not to proclaim an exceptional law which already in this life proves faulty for him who dares to place himself under it. The preaching of the church must therefore take into account this modern understanding of the state. It is not its task to reinstate that government which is only the functionary of the people, to a position which the government had at one time. Rather, it is its task to call the actual bearer of the power of the state within the people to his responsibility. Thus we come to the point where on the one hand the assumption of exceptions affects the entire law and on the other hand even the limitation to a government and to the magistrate is impossible.

There seems to be yet another limit for the expansion of the exceptions and that is war. But even this limitation to war is undergoing today an expansion in that the line between war and peace can no longer be clearly drawn. The point of time after which we find ourselves involved in war can no longer be defined. It has already been established regarding the ninth commandment, that this commandment is suspended not only in war but in politics generally, and other commandments could easily be named which are quite cold-bloodedly broken even in times of peace, for example, through espionage related both to commerce as well as defense industry.

If it seems that all of this became important only in modern times, a theological reflection will lead to the realization that in our modern time things only become visible which have always been true. Not only [the apostle] James says that the transgressor of one commandment is guilty of breaking the entire law but this was already the Jewish perspective; Paul presents it in Galatians 5:3 in the same way. The expansion of the exceptions from one commandment to the entire law is due to the nature of the law and not the result of the expansion of war into all areas of life. The question of whether the magistrate as an office ordained by God is excluded from the validity [of the commandment] is nothing but the fundamental theological question of whether the possibility exists that a person at some time can place himself under a different law. One must ask whether Christianity can turn away from the statement of Tertullian:

> The Christian will nowhere be a different person from the one he is; he is everywhere the same. There is only one gospel, and Jesus is one and the same. He denies every one who denies God and he confesses every

one who confesses God. He will save him who was lost for his name's sake and he will destroy him who was saved [by being] against his name. He who believes cannot appeal to the necessities that claim validity outside of the faith.

This is a statement which seems so modern because it addresses the entire debate about natural theology. The necessities of this life must not turn into a theological argument. The crux of the question about the exceptions is precisely whether this is to be recognized. And basically, this question is identical with the question about natural law. I feel therefore that the Catholic Church is justified in pursuing this argumentation because she recognizes natural law. If one speaks about necessities, on the basis of which the actions of the state are carried out, then such necessity results from the natural law, for example, self-defense. If this is the basis for assuming an exception, then that would mean that this natural law contradicts the gospel and that in such a case natural law has priority. Already in our rejection of natural law we were unable to acknowledge this. Christian preaching can therefore never derive its proclamation from it and it can therefore never justify—in the sense as that chaplain does it and in the way in which Bishop Dibelius does it with the recognition of the agreement on military chaplaincies. It would no longer be preaching which has something to say to the people, at best it might recall to memory what people have already known for a long time and what they have only forgotten. This is true although the state, the political system, however it may be fashioned, is an institution of divine providence. Here I fully agree with Karl Barth in his *Christengemeinde und Bürgergemeinde [Christian Community and Civic Community]*.

One might even have to join him in saying that in this matter we are dealing with the state not as a product of sin but rather with one of the constant factors of divine providence and lordship over the world in its reaction to human sin which benefits man and thus with an instrument of divine grace. But with this the question of the justification of him who acts in the service of the state has not even been posed. As regards the matter itself, i.e., the practical outcome, we are dealing with an instrument of divine grace, but not as regards the representatives of this political system. That, however, does not mean that they are people who are placed outside of the law of God, who have special privileges. One could perhaps cite Nebuchadnezzar who was indeed an instrument of God, which, however, did not save him from his punishment. The same is true for the state in Romans 13. Nothing is said there that the representatives of the state, the government officials, are justified because the state is instituted by the grace of God; rather, the Christian makes a Christian witness out of his knowledge of the grace of God, which meets us everywhere, that we encounter this grace even in the political system. The state is divine ordinance in the same way as the physicians and medical knowledge which are given us for the preservation of our lives. We must understand this as a Christian confession, but not as an insight which is outside and somehow grows up alongside and then has its own theological significance. The state and its system simply provide the occasion to witness to the working of God in the total context of world events as a merciful work for us, on this quite specific point.

It probably would not have been placed in Romans 13 at all without a special reason for it. The reason was that the Christians believed it necessary to draw the consequence to the proclamation of the gospel by rebelling against the political system because it was a non-Christian government and, according to our modern concepts, even an authoritarian power which opposed the proclamation of the gospel. Against this opinion that one ought to incite revolution on Christ's behalf, Paul confesses the effectiveness of divine grace even through the heathen, anti-Christian, satanic authority. [Sentence unclear in original.] That is the reason why Paul emphasizes so strongly that God's grace is present here as much as everywhere else. This is further documented by the fact that Romans 13 is placed within the Pauline paranese. This paranese does take a part of its substance from the true words of Jesus, but it also applies some quite secular rules of conduct. These say that the Christian ought to guide his civil conduct in accordance with that which is ordinarily expected from a decent citizen. This becomes most apparent later in the pastoral letters and in the church orders, whose substance can be traced to secular rules of conduct. The same is true for Romans 13.

All of this, however, is placed within the eschatological framework which begins at the end of Romans 13: "Besides this you know what hour it is, how it is full time now for you to wake from sleep." And this is the only point of Christian theology in Romans 13, no more. If we really understand Romans 13 from this point of view, then the much discussed contrast to the thirteenth chapter of the Revelation of John is not due to a perversion of the power of the state; rather, the contrast is caused by the different aspects of the state. A contrast between the state as Paul envisioned it and that of the Apocalypse cannot be assumed for the simple reason that the Christians in Rome to whom Paul wrote envisioned the same state as that of Revelation 13, which from the beginning had been the persecutor of the church. [Sentence unclear in original.] Both [scriptures] speak about the same state but under different aspects. Romans 13 interprets the political system in its factual success as ordained by God, in order to enable and preserve human coexistence in [the face of] sin. Revelation 13 sees the same political system in its illegal demand of total obedience. Nothing is evil about the beast from the pit but the fact that it is worshipped, and that it blasphemes God by claiming his power. Even in this action the state does not fall from the order into which God has placed it. Even in this it fulfills God's will; for this beast from the pit can rage only as long as it is allowed to, as God has given it leave to. The Christian church, however, resists this demand of the beast and is called upon to profess. In the face of the beast she proclaims the name of the Lord. This opposition must arise—and that is again the link between our considerations about the understanding of the state in the New Testament and the Christian preaching for peace—where the state claims special exceptional laws for itself, where it forbids the church's proclamation to place the state's actions under the judgment of the word of God. By claiming a special authority to which the Christian owes obedience for the sake of the will of God, even where the breaking of the commandment is demanded of him, the state has already fallen into the role of the beast from the pit.

Here also a necessary distinction must be made. The resistance of the Christian against the state does not arise from the fact that it breaks God's commandment in its very actions, not even from the fact that it causes the citizens to do the same themselves—there we only need refuse—rather, active resistance arises first of all where such transgression takes place upon the state's authority and therefore occurs and is proclaimed outside of the divine law and its realm of validity. Therefore resistance is first directed against our church which legalizes this, and not against the state which does not know better. We must turn first, not against the transgression of the commandment itself—although we are called to a clear and unmistakable witness to the state about it—but rather against the fact that such a transgression is no longer acknowledged as such, against the fact that the state expects from the church justification of its actions.

Christian preaching will therefore direct its admonishing and promising word to all people, just as it intercedes in prayer for all people. It cannot acknowledge an exception for certain people, times, or situations.

Justice and Love

Richard Ullmann

To approach the problem of love and justice in a practical way, allow me first of all to begin from the theological aspect and that from the book of Job. Actually, I do not intend to investigate it from a theological but from a human point of view. We have here after all the story of a man who is just, that is, righteous, who has lived a life of charity and goodness, who not only did not oppress anyone but, on the contrary, actively loved people. And now he is punished by God. And he cannot understand it. From his human perspective he experiences the injustice of God. Finally, however, he gains the insight that his redeemer lives, even though he does not know why God has punished him so. He never really understands it, he cannot grasp why. He simply accepts it. And because he accepts it, there comes the "happy end." Everything is restored. But it is a curious and almost a somewhat primitive conception of the problem in which man somehow cannot understand God's will and for that reason does not know how, in deep faith, he can reconcile God's justice with the obvious injustice going on in the world.

The problem is then perceived in a much more profound way in Deutero-Isaiah in the wonderful figure of the suffering servant of God. Here the connection between justice and reward or punishment is clearly broken down. Here it is precisely the righteous—and precisely *because* he is righteous and precisely *because* he is good—who is prepared to take punishment upon himself, which he does not really deserve, which, according to all laws, all feelings of justice and fairness, are not meant for him at all. You may object that this is only a human understanding of justice, not the divine one. But when we recall . . . that it is God's will to help the very one to his right who is oppressed and unjustly treated in this world, then we see something quite different in the suffering servant of God. Then we see that it is the very one who lives righteously, who has even more injustice placed upon him from God himself, so to speak, because he is able, because he has the strength, to believe in the ultimate justice and love of God in spite of everything. In this way he clearly steps out of the circle of justice into the circle of love. This is not merely so because in doing this he, as it were, takes a punishment upon himself which in reality others should take upon themselves—as is often emphasized by theologians . . . but especially because through his suffering he introduces to the world a demonstration of the love of God, and thus becomes a challenge to others. To me, this seems to be the essence of the concept of the suffering servant of God. It is not that God is so pedantically just, in the old-fashioned, Jewish sense as we used to be taught by old-fashioned theology, that he must needs have someone to punish because he does not want to punish his beloved ones, but something quite different: This human being is enabled to become a challenge by virtue of the fact that the love of God is demonstrated in him, that God is treating him unjustly and love thus becomes visible in him.

This is the story of Jesus Christ as the suffering servant of God. This is precisely the point in which all of God's injustice, in this sense, is revealed. God punishes himself in Jesus Christ. He is unjust to himself. In my view, this point—that love means injustice to oneself—has never been made sufficiently clear. That is the nature of love that it is unjust, that with it, merit does not count, but that love breaks through the circle of merit, reward, and punishment, so that in its innermost nature it must be unjust. The justice of the kingdom of God is proclaimed accordingly neither as social justice, nor as a world without war—that is to say, not as some kind of utopia on this earth, but as love which sacrifices itself and thus tries to keep the social question from becoming crucial, tries to keep any social question from emerging at all, and tries to prevent the emerging of these conflicts, tries even to prevent the cause for wars at all. War is after all already the end of a tension which ought to have been resolved by love before.

Now it is true that we as human beings probably do not have the power to prevent even the arising of social problems and international tensions, precisely because of our sinfulness, so that we are therefore not in a position to prevent all such tensions, that we even actually contribute to them by our own conduct. But this is not the decisive answer for the Christian to give to it. A Christian, who knows that he has been forgiven, can but attempt himself—as far as he is able—to overcome these difficulties by breaking through the circle of justice by the sacrifice of love. I consider it not so much my task this morning to demonstrate in how far love always seeks to be *also* just (naturally, love is *also* just) or even how there, where no love is found, justice can under certain circumstances help things along. . . . This does not seem unimportant to me. But it is much more important, it seems to me, to point to that area in which they conflict, where justice and love seemingly oppose eath other, because it is here that the true Christian task lies.

As I said before, love is in its nature no more than *also* just, but in its innermost being it is always unjust, first of all by becoming unjust against itself and taking upon itself burdens which legally are not required of it at all. This happens in human circumstances and relationships of pure human love. What would the nature of love be if not to overlook the mistakes of the beloved being, to emphasize his or her good qualities, to give him or her all kinds of things which that person really would not have merited according to his or her true personal worth. Is not that precisely the nature of love that it does not calculate?

The same is true for God. Precisely because God loves, he is unjust and unjust precisely towards the ones who love him and who still feel and recognize his love in spite of this injustice. I wish that last night . . . the parable of the workers in the vineyard had been treated more fully, for there it becomes quite clear that some are treated with love in the same measure as others feel themselves treated unjustly. That is the other side of the injustice of God. It is not only an act of injustice towards himself. It is also an injustice towards those who are indeed deserving, who truly have every right, I repeat, every right.

Let us take the parable of the prodigal son. As we all know, the parable of the prodigal son has been misnamed. It is not quite clear what one should call it. It could be called the parable of the love of God or that of the loving father; it could perhaps also be called the parable of the elder brother. I believe that modern exegesis says that the elder brother actually represents the Pharisees, that Jesus is speaking here to the Pharisees and scribes. I believe that Jesus was saying: "Why can you not see that I have come to the poor sinners and not to you, the righteous"? Be that as it may, let us take it here as a simple human situation, which happens again and again; that person who has been truly good, decent, and also loving suddenly realizes that for some reason the sinner is more beloved than he, perhaps just *because* he was a sinner. And that has become a tremendous problem for people. That is the real difficulty which we have before us; that with us, justice and love somehow do not seem to be in harmony with each other.

If I am to try to relate this back to God, then we must understand the entire work of salvation in such a way that God was unjust even in sending his son to us when we did not merit it. Is this not the meaning of that passage in Paul, that God loved us and Christ died for us when we were still sinners? That is precisely the decisive point: the fact of not having merited, which more or less precludes justice and permits love to take its place. When Jesus, for example, speaks of the sun shining on the just *and* the unjust and the rain falling on the righteous *and* the unrighteous, the same point is made again. It is that injustice which is based on the fact that before God we cannot be distinguished from one another by our merits. We often conclude from this that we are all sinners and that therefore none of us has any merit of his own. But the case is not as simple as that. There is no doubt that Job was more righteous than, let us say, King David, and certainly much more righteous than Ahab. There is certainly no doubt that this appears to God just as it appears to us, namely, that despite our sinfulness we are not all equally sinful. Now Jesus applies this injustice of God ... which is contained in love, to man and says: "You must be exactly like this. You must not insist on your own right, but on the contrary, you must decrease your own right through love and relinquish it."

Is not this the meaning of the Sermon on the Mount: We are to love precisely not only the one who loves us, but we ought to love the one who hates us. We are indeed not to strike back or turn and walk away when we are struck on the right cheek but we ought to allow ourselves to be struck on the left cheek as well. We are not to go just one mile, when a Roman legionary makes us do our duty in carrying his baggage, but we ought to go the second mile also. We are, therefore, to overcome all of these injustices, these unjust claims on us by taking on even greater injustices, by diminishing our own right even more.

To a great extent, justice consists, after all, of weighing. But the nature of love is the opposite. Love not only has no sword—this has, after all, always been our main pacifist emphasis—but love has no scales either, it does not put anything in the balance. Love is therefore unjust against itself. It is also seemingly unjust toward those who seem to have deserved better according to all moral, practical, human viewpoints, than others. Love comes into its own precisely when the loved one has sinned. It is then that it seeks to serve him, to help him out of his difficulty and to make him realize his wrong by meeting him with forgiveness and love.

I believe that we too often hold to the Decalog when we talk about sin and commandments. I believe that none of us here will have murdered anyone (we shall leave killing in general, as in warfare, etc., out of this discussion). I believe that none of us here steal (even if the concept were enlarged to mean that stealing love, for example, is already stealing). The sin, however, which I believe all of us commit again and again is that we insist upon our well-deserved rights, that our sense of justice is hurt, and that we therefore lose our love because of this hurt feeling of justice. That is the great difficulty, that is the point where justice and love come into conflict. We insist on our rights and we contend that it concerns not only us as individuals. We insist on the rights of our families. We insist on the rights of our class, our race, our nation. ... And this is the curious thing about it: Again and again we find in Christian history the emphasis on the fact that justice is, so to speak, the outer courtyard of the temple of love. But that is an incorrect statement. Justice very often—but certainly not always—becomes the stumbling block on the path to love. If I insist on my rights then

I keep myself from practicing brotherly love and can no longer understand the rights of my neighbor. I then no longer try to help him gain his rights but rather seek to secure my own. Most difficulties, most conflicts—personal, group-related, international—arise because both sides have clear rights, and because no justice and no rights whatever—however good—can be established in the abstract to resolve this conflict which stems from the rights on both sides. Naturally, there is always wrong on both sides, but usually there is also in fact right on both sides, and precisely this causes the conflict. This conflict can be resolved only when something totally new is introduced: When love breaks through the vicious circle of insisting on one's own rights and especially when it finds the courage and strength to say to the other, "You, too, do not insist on your own rights, for that does not get us anywhere, we shall keep pitching right against right. I shall love you and trust you if only you love and learn to trust me."

Let me illustrate this with quite concrete examples, first of all one which I used once in an article: the strike of the railroad workers which we had in England two years ago. The strike was triggered by the fact that the railroad workers demanded to have their pay upgraded in relation to that of the locomotive engineers. They did not say that the locomotive engineers were too well off. Neither did they say that they themselves earned too little. They said that the gap between the incomes of the two groups was too great. They also said, "Why should our work be considered less responsible than that of a locomotive engineer? If we do not maintain the tracks properly, for example, if the ties are not tightly screwed down, then accidents happen, too." Above all, they could also say, "Why should it be less easy for my wife to buy and use a washing machine and a television set than for the wife of a locomotive engineer?" In all of this there is much logic or apparent logic, or whatever we want to call it. Naturally, the locomotive engineers will then immediately want to have a yet higher pay because of their own responsibility. This then was no strike between labor and management. That relationship is but one side of the social problem. It was a conflict between two different groups of workers. But in both cases the concept of justice is used.

One always hears it said that something is not fair. And everyone finds good arguments in order to present his really good and defense-worthy rights. There is no way out of this vicious circle until someone says, "I would rather that you are right than that I should be right." The very same is true for international questions. For the time being I shall not use the example of Germany—I may need to do this later. I shall use another example: Palestine, Israel. What is the right and the wrong of the Israeli? What is the right and the wrong of the Arabs? There is much right on both sides, and on both sides there is much wrong. One of the most important arguments is always the historical one (just as with the Oder-Neisse Line): We were here first. The Jews have gone back two thousand years in history. In A.D. 70 Jerusalem was destroyed and the last free Jewish state was established under the Maccabees. This is the basis for their present-day claim. In addition, they can base a moral claim on the fact that they have really used and developed the land which had not been used and developed under the Arabs. That is a right which they have only now earned. But the whole problem is not a question of what they had and what they earned: They drove the Arabs out. It is also quite impossible for them to take them all back even if they wanted to. Above all, they have deeply wounded the Arab's feelings of justice. What diplomat can now develop a wonderful universal justice between the two, a justice which is truly just for all sides?

The same is true for all other problems of border lines, wherever we look. This is not the way to solve them, for in spite of all justice, it is not enough to do it, even if there were such an abstract justice. It is, after all, necessary that both sides believe that justice has been done. An old English axiom says, "It is not sufficient that justice be done but that it is seen by all to have been done." It is not enough that justice is carried out, but that all recognize that it has been carried out. This is so important for all sides, and yet is not possible like this; the vicious circle must be broken through again.

Here we must again make every effort that all who are involved hear the challenge that they, if necessary, relinquish their just rights, so that love can occupy the place where justice only heightens the problems or seems to heighten them. Applying this to the large international East-West problem: We always demand that the other side give us securities and take on all of the risks. It never occurs to us to take on the risk and give the other side securities. We are not willing to do this. It is because of a lack of trust, which is an essential part of love.

To summarize briefly: In very few conflict situations all of the right is on one side and all of the wrong is on the other. The decisive problem which we as Christians must attack is not that we or most other persons consciously want to commit wrong, rather, that we consider as our right something that may be wrong. But even this is not quite enough. For the Christian it is perfectly clear—even that which is a just right becomes a wrong by our placing it above love, by refusing to do injustice to ourselves, our own side, our own friends, by thinking first of ourselves and our friends and their rights instead of the rights of the enemy, the so-called enemy or, as I should prefer to say, the unreconciled brother.

Now comes Reinhold Niebuhr and tells us that whatever I do, may do, or can do against myself, out of love to my neighbor, my first responsibility is still toward my own group. Two years ago he told me personally the following: He saw the division not so much between justice and love—the division was rather contained within love itself. We were not meant to decide whether we were to love the enemy more than ourselves because he, after all, was also our neighbor; the real problem was rather, whom we were to love more, the enemy or the friend. This was the real problem; this was "a division of love itself," as he called it. Does one have the right before God to sacrifice not oneself (that is not the question at all), but one's friend, wife, children, the nation, etc., or to see them sacrificed for the sake of the enemy? I answered at that time that I should certainly prefer to see my enemy sacrificed than my friend, but that the early Christian martyrs and the early Quakers experienced their closest community precisely because they needed not to consider the friends; because the friend, the fellow Christian, thought and felt exactly as they did themselves. One was truly a member of the other and could therefore count on the other just as he counted on himself. Thus they did not sacrifice one another, but sacrificed themselves together.

We present-day Christians must admit that we can no longer do this. Before God it seems essential, however, that I reconcile myself first of all not with my friend because, after all, he is not my enemy, but that I must look for my enemy and that I must reconcile myself with him. Therefore I must be unjust to my friends whether I want to or not, but first of all, to myself. This is part of the injustice of love. Possibly, as a result, I shall turn some of my friends into enemies. This is a very serious problem and I do not intend to minimize it. It is the decisive test of conscience for the pacifist. Let me state it quite clearly. We did not come to the aid of the Hungarians [at the time of the revolt in 1956]: the Western powers, for political considerations; we Christians, because we were unable to do so, could not have done it under any circumstances. When we think about our East German friends: We simply do *not* wish to liberate them with all politically useful means. Politically useful means are, after all, also war and arms. Nevertheless, we can by no means ignore their cry for help. The English word for this . . . is appeasement: the immoral use of the sacrifices of others so that the rest of us can live in peace. My friends, I have no answer for this problem but we must look it squarely in the eye.

By no means do I treat the cries for help from the East with detachment. It is here where I must seemingly be heartless because of my faith—where I seem to purchase peace not through my own sacrifice but through the sacrifice of others. And here is the point where I experience most deeply my own entanglement with the sin of the world, where I know most clearly that my hands are soiled precisely because I try to keep them clean. That is the great difficulty for the pacifist. But when the demand comes that I should therefore make them even dirtier than they are already, I cannot do it. There is still the prayer to God left for me. Above all I have the duty to keep reminding myself of what I am really doing, and not hide it under a sentimental love of peace. And I have the task not only not to do evil in order to bring forth good (which is naturally quite impossible) but, as far as I am able, to try to repair in my sphere some of the wrong in which I am entangled by admitting, for example, the lack of freedom in East Germany or the oppression of the Negroes in South Africa. Niebuhr still attacks us pacifists as if we wished to build the kingdom of God on earth with our own hands, as if we believed we could will our own perfection and bring it about ourselves. This may have been the mistake of pacifists several decades ago. I do not believe that it is still true today. We know as well as all other Christians that the kingdom of God comes from God and in his own time. But it is equally true that God wants us to be ready at any moment to receive it when it does come. And I can only be ready if I do not take entanglement and sin as motivation to sin even more, to heap yet greater sins upon myself, by, let us say, participating in war in order to liberate people. Instead, by attempting with God's help to do reparations in a small way for some things which I have done wrong through my entanglement and for which I receive the strength as absolved sinner. Here is where I must apply myself, in the discipleship of Jesus. . . .

Work for peace is therefore much more than opposition to war or reflection about the point on which I must oppose the state. The state and the magistrate are not abstractions . . . . They consist of men and women in certain offices and functions, people who by virtue of these functions are less capable than we of thinking in terms of individual beings and human souls, but who think in terms of groups and numbers and figures and not of human beings, [they are people] who must think in terms of sociological problems. And the worst that we can do is to treat them as such, instead of realizing that in this enormously difficult task they are still human beings to whom God has spoken in the same way in which he has spoken to us, and that we must help them precisely in their offices and government so that they can at least occasionally listen to God's voice, so that they cease at least occasionally to be officials and become human beings. This does not come about only by praying for them. We must empathize with them, especially when we oppose them for conscience' sake, when we protest against them. For here is where we often sin in practice: at the moment when we begin to protest we begin to condemn them; that is the great mistake.

One of the greatest difficulties in this life is to speak the truth in love. Let me give an example from Quaker history. The greatest saint among the Quakers is John Woolman, an American, who began in the middle of the eighteenth century to fight among the ranks of the Society of Friends against slavery. It was not that the Friends treated their slaves so badly; on the contrary, in most cases they were very kind and helped them greatly. But the fact that they were slaves at all was felt by John Woolman to be the great wrong. Therefore he went to the Friends and told them—by no means in the *form* of protest but in the inward *posture* of protest—to free their slaves. He said to them, "You are wronging yourselves because you are doing wrong to your slaves. You are sinning before God; you are educating your children in an environment of false, unchristian values which make one human being, one creation of God, the master of another creation of God." He did not say this in long talks and conversations. He said it clearly and succinctly whenever he first arrived. He stayed but a short time with these Friends as a guest, but did not accept any services from the slaves without paying them and said, "If I am not allowed to pay, then I will leave." Here we see the ability to unite love and protest. I could give other examples, especially from the life of Woolman. It is true, that it was relatively easy for him, because his protest was done within his own religious society. He tried to make the light shine more brightly in his fellow Quakers by telling them that he had a charge from God here.

It is more difficult to go to Krushchev or Adenauer, or whoever it might be. And yet, that is the right method, this is how it should be done. We must challenge these men, or to keep within Quaker terminology, we must challenge the divine, the divine spark in each of them. If this spark is not very bright, it is our task to make it shine brightly. And if we irritate them by our harsh protest, by resistance alone, instead of approaching and talking to them in a loving way, we achieve the exact opposite of that which we want to achieve. Then we come and demand "our right" against "their right." Naturally, according to the letter of the law I have the right on my side against a warmonger, don't I? But that is not the point. It is not a matter of my rights but that I muster the necessary love for this warmonger to speak the truth to him in love. And I should like to say that this is what we want to do in our Quaker work—not in the Service Committee which is probably well enough known here— ... but I am not certain whether you are as familiar with the work of reconciliation which we are attempting to do. I could cite a large number of examples. You may remember that several years ago we sent a mission to Moscow at the time when the Cold War was at its height. You may perhaps know that we also sent a mission to China. You may perhaps know that there is a Quaker

House at the United Nations where the diplomatic representatives of the various countries may meet inconspicuously.

We do not consider it our task to counsel in the areas of politics and diplomacy. These people are themselves the experts; we are not the experts, even though we familiarize ourselves as much as possible with these matters. These people are invited to the Quaker House and talk there with our representatives. There are European and American Friends there. They talk with these people so that they may have a moment for once when that which is of God within them is challenged and when they may be human beings again and not functionaries. That is the decisive thing. We have, first of all, international seminars, begun by American Friends, where students come together from various nations—all non-Quakers, most of them not even Christians but Moslems and others. But that is not so important as the fact that we have similar seminars for young diplomats. You will not believe this, but now even the East European countries send their young diplomats to these seminars. There they gather—Russian and Polish and Yugoslavian diplomats with Western and neutral diplomats—young people, most of them in their late twenties. There, completely free and human communication is achieved. They talk in an atmosphere which they would never find in their official functions. They like to remember these seminars and even attempt to continue them by calling together former participants in London, Paris, Vienna, etc.

This year the same thing is being started by American Friends for politicians, political representatives, etc. We do not enter the political arena ourselves. We do not advise. We show that we understand them in their dilemma, and we try to help them to become humanly free from their function, because we count on their function being carried out differently in the future for that. And that does happen. Opportunities are provided which do not otherwise exist. As I see this work of reconciliation, it is an approach to the very persons whom we distrust so deeply, whom we so often blame for the many entanglements. It is they with whom we must speak in truth and love and understanding.

This work of reconciliation belongs, in my view, very basically to our theme today, because we have always considered it crucial not to weigh the rights of the one side and the other and then perhaps find the best right between them; we have not tried to find just solutions, but simply attempted to communicate to both parties that we are truly concerned about both sides, that we feel love and friendship for them. We try to tell them that we are like them entangled in the problems and that this entanglement must under no circumstances lead us to fight each other. The reconciler will suffer most deeply precisely when he realizes that both sides are basically right in their opinions, that we are much more in the right than we can resolve. Therefore he does not know how he is to help them, that is, out of dilemma into the just right and into the circle of love.

I realized this especially, and I shall close with this, in an experience in the year 1947. At that time the English Friends invited a young German girl along with a large number of other young Germans. She then spent four weeks with young English Friends and in English homes in the year 1947, a time when conditions were still very, very bad here in West Germany. And then she returned to this Germany. She was here less than four weeks when she wrote us a letter and said, "Now I am again in the environment of dismantling—now I meet again families whose men are still prisoners of war in England. While when in England I felt the friendship so deeply which I received, especially as a German, I now suddenly believe that all of it was perhaps not worth the trouble." Then she said—and hear this, brethren—"The worst is that I can understand both sides so well." That was the worst, that was the cross; there reconciliation began in her own heart. She did not know what to do, but she was filled with an understanding of both sides. And surely in that moment she grew strong enough to work as a reconciler.

Report to the Landeskirchen

I. From July 28 to August 1, 1957, delegates and individual members of German and foreign state churches met at Iserlohn for a dialogue ("Puidoux II") with representatives of the Historic Peace Churches (Quakers, Brethren, Mennonites, Society of Brothers). We express our thanks to the state churches who sent representatives, for having taken responsibly part in this discussion. In this way it was possible to continue the dialogue begun in Puidoux in August 1955 on a broader basis.

The concern which brought us together was that a future atomic war might plunge the entire world in unspeakable misery, perhaps even into total annihilation. This danger, which confronts us on a scale never known before, forces us to rethink anew what the church has said up to now about war and peace, about use of arms and nonresistance. It has become very clear to us in discussion with representatives from the Historic Peace Churches that we can gain great help particularly from their sufferings and insights for our own path. This has led us to this conclusion: In the way in which Christians since about the time of Constantine have treated one another as regards this question and in what the church has said about it in doctrine and preaching, very little is to be discerned of the obedience which the Lord can expect from his church.

II. We have tried first of all to grasp the scope of what must be done here. Later conferences will have much work left to do. Yet we have found in our common labors that in the testimonies of the Historic Peace Churches, whom we have been accustomed to label with the name "enthusiasts" *(Schwärmer)* since the Reformation, we can hear something of the voice of the Good Shepherd even for us. We did not find it [i.e., this voice] in that theological place to which we usually relegate it.

III. In several points we have been able to establish clear agreement:

1. Jesus Christ, the incarnated, crucified and living one, is the Lord over church *and* state.

2. Christ calls us into discipleship as active and suffering participation in him. Discipleship is therefore not to be understood as imitation *(imitatio)* but as participation *(participatio),* that is, in it justification and sanctification exist side by side. Thus, legalism as well as arbitrariness are eliminated.

3. For the sake of him who became man, who died for us and is living, the Christian cannot remain in the service of killing, but will have to serve life in simple obedience.

IV. We consider it promising to remain in dialogue, and appeal also to the various churches to keep it open by their participation.

Iserlohn, August 1, 1957   The Theologican Conference
                                       of Puidoux.

11. Christians and the Prevention of War in an Atomic Age—A Theological Discussion
(Nyborg, Denmark, August 27, 1958)

In 1955 the Central Committee of the WCC named a commission of specialists to study the problem of preventing war in an atomic age. The group was made up of scientists, ethicists, and military experts. Over a period of three years discussions were held which resulted in the preparation of a document presented to the Central Committee in August 1958.

Its reception was controversial. The two recommendations which drew most fire were: first, the proposal that in case of all-out war the Christians should urge a cease-fire, if need be, on the terms of the enemy; second, that a nation is not permitted to be the first to use a megaton weapon. Although staff members of the CCIA had served as consultants for the commission, they raised a series of questions about the report, referring also to the two points mentioned above. They said:

> We believe that both these proposals need to be studied from the standpoint of the ethical requirements from which they are derived, and the political risks involved . . . . Insofar as the balance of deterrence does in fact today inhibit war-making, is it not a threat, at least psychologically and politically, to that balance to state in advance that there are limits without specifying what they are—beyond which the enemy can go without disaster to himself?

The Central Committee permitted distribution of the report only with the most careful designation that this was to be seen as a provisional study document addressed to the churches for reflection and discussion. The title page had to bear the notation: "No point expressed here is to be understood as an official view of the World Council of Churches. This document is in no sense a statement of World Council policy." Although the notation emphasized that the document marked but a first step in a "continuing study process," the work of the commission was not continued.

*The comment in the report of the WCC prior to the third assembly—*Evanston to New Delhi—*remarked rather blandly:*

The document caused vigorous debate in the Central Committee and evoked both support and criticism. It was decided to offer the document to the churches for their reflection and discussion, as a contribution to Christian research and enquiry on this vital issue of our time.

The Division of Studies revised the paper after receiving reactions from member churches and interested parties and published its results in 1961.

Christians and the Prevention of War in an Atomic Age

A Theological Discussion

1. The ensuing statement has been prepared by a Commission appointed by the Central Committee of the World Council to consider the problem of *war in an atomic age*. The Commission has understood its task literally, and has not engaged in discussions of the problem of the Christian attitude to war in general. It has felt that, whatever view one may take of war as a phenomenon in the life of the human race, the concrete issue of today is atomic war. This means war in which nuclear weapons and the means of their delivery are the dominant military factors. The development of these weapons, and their means of delivery, has so altered the character of war that, whether the weapons are used or merely threatened, they are of decisive importance.

2. The Commission has been asked to consider the *prevention* of war in an atomic age. This has caused its discussions to turn around two basic poles. The first involves the attitude which Christians should take to nuclear war. The Commission recognizes clearly that war will not be prevented by people merely taking an attitude of approval or disapproval toward it, but it has also recognized that "war" is a relative term. How should Christians analyse and evaluate the various meanings and degrees of the term "war"? Should, for instance, war be regarded as a means of preventing war? Should a hot war in any sense be used to alleviate the injustices involved in a cold war? One can scarcely speak of the prevention of war in an atomic age without coming to some conclusion concerning a Christian attitude to nuclear war itself. Secondly, there is the whole range of problems which must be faced in any effort to prevent war from breaking out, regardless of one's attitude toward it if it does break out. So fun-

damental is this point, that the greater part of the Commission's statement is put in terms of the measures which, in its judgment, are the most important and urgent.

3. The Commission has been asked to engage in a *theological discussion*. The Commission has understood this to mean that its starting point should be the Christian revelation of the Divine will, rather than the necessities of power politics or the desirability of saving civilization or even the defence of freedom and order. The essential task for all Christians, is to start from the revelation of the nature of God's will for man, and to see what that revelation means for the prevention of war in an atomic age.

4. A theological discussion cannot be true to itself without dealing, to a certain degree, with immediate problems and realities, even though these may involve highly technical problems. One of the perplexities of our present situation is that very complex technical matters contain within themselves moral and ethical problems of the highest moment. No approach which attempts to be based upon the revelation of God's will can fail to deal with such problems. Yet there are of course specific technical answers to technical problems that cannot be derived from this approach to the matter. What can be provided is a framework within which we may face and seek to solve the moral issues to which technical problems give rise.

5. The Commission has felt that its deepest and most important work concerns the direction of spirit and mind and will which must be taken, and within which Christians must think through and make up their minds concerning immediate practical issues. In essence, the Commission believes that nothing will help us short of the development of a new spiritual climate and discipline among Christians and men of earnest and good will everywhere, and it is with this and its relation to some of our most urgent problems that the Commission has been concerned.

I. The Present Situation

6. The present situation in regard to war in an atomic age is dominated by two facts.

7. The first is the possession by specific nations of the H-bomb, the megaton weapon, together with lesser, kiloton weapons, and the means of the delivery of these by these nations anywhere in the world in quantity. We shall shortly indicate something of the explosive power of these weapons. Suffice it to say here that the production of arsenals of nuclear weapons is one of the two dominating facts of the international situation of

our time. Nor can we forget the possibility of biological and chemical warfare and other means of mass destruction.

8. The second is the hostility between the Communist and the non-Communist world. This is the overriding fact which guides the conduct of international affairs and military preparations. Nearly all other conflict in the world of nations is judged, whether immediately or ultimately, in terms of this great division. This in turn may conceal the tension and conflict in other parts of the world.

9. In considering the prevention of war in an atomic age, it is essential to recognize a fundamental element in this present situation. This consists in the fact that all of the ideological, economic, political, historical, and cultural elements that go into human conflict, and human conflict itself, are qualified, intensified, and made more dangerous by the threat of atomic war. Mankind permanently possesses the capacity of nuclear destructiveness, and human conflict therefore has a newly dangerous and formidable character. The parties to the human conflict may change as indeed they have in the past. Yesterday the conflict was with Hitler and the Nazis; today it is a conflict between Communists and the non-Communists; tomorrow it may be between others. This conflict—these wars and rumours of wars—are always a matter of profound challenge to conscience and ethical conduct. The crucial element, however, in the present and the future generations of mankind, is the combination of human conflict and nuclear destructiveness.

10. This nuclear destructiveness opens the possibility of destruction which is uncontrollable and wholly indiscriminate. For this reason, the use of nuclear weapons in an all-out war poses a more serious problem than the use of any other weapons. In this paper, the term "all-out war" means a war in which the most destructive weapons are used to the full. Nuclear weapons are a more radical technological development than any hitherto known in the history of war. This development is so important as to require analysis and description:

11. First, this scale of destructiveness means that all physical objectives in that part of the world which is involved in war are destroyed indiscriminately. It is not possible to use nuclear weapons all out and to select and destroy physical objectives with discrimination. In all-out nuclear war one cannot "get" merely the armed forces and the war making class, or the centres of production, or military installations. Everything is subject to destruction.

12. Second, all-out war involves the indiscriminate destruction of political objectives. Such war escapes all dictates of policy, except one, namely indiscriminate destruction. What does the extension of order or

freedom or justice mean in the wasteland resulting from a nuclear holocaust?

13. Third, all-out war is uncontrollable. It is uncontrollable in space and in time as well. There is little reason to believe that in an all-out struggle the dirtiest of dirty bombs would not be used. They may be better weapons. To argue at this point that clean bombs might be used because of the fear of retaliation if dirty bombs were used, is not relevant at this point. That is an argument to limit war by the use of clean bombs. Dirty bombs, however, exist and they kill more people. It is possible that they may be used and the full implications of their use in all-out war must be faced. Such use of dirty bombs means uncontrollable destruction in space because fallout goes initially in large measure with the wind, and is in the longer term dispersed throughout the atmosphere; and in time, because the genetic effects of radiation go down through the generations. Thus dirty bombs permit no discrimination between belligerents and neutrals. There is, moreover, a further element of uncontrollability in the means of the delivery of these weapons. These means are increasingly rapid and difficult to defend against. Delivery of nuclear weapons by rocket will mean that everyone will be subject to virtually surprise attack: massive destruction without warning, or nearly so. Added to this is the fact that defence on the ground even if a population is warned, is virtually impossible of achievement. Can the population and key industry of either the United States or Russia be put underground? Technical and economic reasons make it highly doubtful. All-out nuclear war is uncontrollable, save by its end result, mutual exhaustion.

14. Thus mankind is now faced with the fact that human conflict, whatever its forms and motivations, may erupt into a destruction which in the full sense of the word is indiscriminate, with an overall effect utterly disproportionate to any issue or claim for which fighting can be justified. In our time, a profound and bitter conflict contains within it the very real possibility that this may happen. It is in a situation dominated by these factors that we must try to see our way.

15. As we do, we must take note of other factors. One is the element of deep and awestruck fear, of awakened conscience, of a sensitive anxiety on the part of many. Scientists and men of political responsibility are perhaps in the forefront of this awakening, doubtless because they are closest, day by day, to these dark and terrible realities. Yet this mood, unfortunately, is not the dominant mood among our peoples. Perhaps the most prevalent feeling is that of fear and helplessness. To most average people, the problems seem so big and complicated and removed that there appears little that they can do, even if they knew what to do. Perhaps it is this feeling

upon the part of the multitudes which is potentially the most dangerous of all the aspects of our present scene.

II. The Christian Affirmation

16. Our faith requires us to announce to the world that it is God in Jesus Christ who controls the destiny of history. He is a Holy God whose purpose is love and whose ways are righteousness and mercy. He will accomplish his purpose and no man need fear that God will be mocked. In mankind's great longing for peace at this time we are bound to say—

17. That righteousness and peace are God's will, but a peace in which we enjoy the fruits of unrighteousness, or in which we abandon our neighbours to injustice, is no peace. Our desire for peace must be founded in penitence for the evil things we do or tolerate and which are an offence to God's love. The elevation of the state to the authority due to God alone and with which He alone can be entrusted, the desires in the privileged West to preserve its privileges for itself, pride of race and unwillingness to share the burdens of mankind create conditions in which true peace is not possible. Not only present sin but the legacy of past injustice stand in our way. Therefore peace and a spirit of humble penitence belong together. The power of the lie which seeks to incriminate all others except ourselves and to excuse our failings as due to our external circumstances is a sign of our fallen state. The power of God, however, answers the contrite heart and compels us to seek new obedience in the conflict of our time.

18. That we cannot foretell the shape of future events in history but that we know by faith that they cannot remove men out of the hands of God or turn aside His victory. This is the assurance that gives meaning to life and that can give steadiness in danger or historical disaster. But it is to be remembered that it is an assurance offered to all mankind for it is mankind for whom God cares. His victory is not our victory, and comes both in judgment and mercy upon us. It is part of our Christian hope that all men may experience God's victory as mercy as well as judgment, and we may therefore never consent to the prospect of terminating human history by human act.

19. The causes and conflicts of men are those of sinful men and societies. They contain real elements of principle, and the confrontation of real differences of right and wrong, justice and injustice, but never in dissociation from self-interest and pride. No group of men may therefore identify their cause with the cause of God, nor say that their defeat is His.

20. In the Kingdom of the Lord Jesus Christ the conflicts of distracted men are overcome and the power of evil has been met not by force

but in the Cross of our Saviour and there defeated. Those who follow Him already have the first fruits of the Spirit and should show forth to the world the signs of this reconciliation and this sacrifice. To the extent that the Church fails to do this in its own life, the world is deprived most terribly of its hope.

21. But Christians live in the world. When they are faithful, they are a preposterous community in the world's eyes. They belong to human communities, but they must disrupt these communities by anticipating the coming Kingdom in the power of the Spirit. Their primary task, however, is to be used by the Risen Lord as he loves the world, including those disrupted communities. So it is a first duty of Christians to be by the side of all men, loving them in the Name of the Lord, and submitting to our need of their love which we accept also in His name; to identify themselves with the human situation and accept involvement in the world's life and thought and not withdraw too soon from men's predicament. We have the role not only of the Good Samaritan, but also of the man whom he rescued. When as now human societies so badly need active and responsible citizens, this is a Christian duty even when it leads Christians to opposite sides. Then the Holy Spirit as the only source of love remains as a bond between them and reminds them also of other human communities and of the men in them besides their own. Their life will be difficult always, since Evil is still at work in the world. The existence of the State and of violence will occasion some of their most difficult problems. Christians will therefore do well to remember that the obedience which they owe to the State is not absolute and unconditional; there will be times when an absolute refusal to cooperate becomes their Christian duty, even at the cost of martyrdom. This refusal, even if it creates disorder, is first and foremost a witness to God's love and command. We trust God may use it as a means of promoting a higher order in society, although this is not its justification.

22. In their involvement in the world Christians have to recognize the fact of governments which exercise coercive power as inescapable factors in the life of men. Most Christians hold them to be a part of God's providential ordering of human affairs in the present dispensation, having a duty to use this power in the service of justice and order. They cannot be obeyed when in unrighteousness or pride they use their power for other ends. But in international affairs there is anarchy in the sense that sovereign states and power blocs face each other without a superior authority to regulate their relations. Here Christians have long sought, with others, ways to regulate the clash of power so that man's life might be preserved and safeguarded. The exertion of power internationally by military means or the threat of them has been the main way of settling disputes when agreement

failed, and as yet this situation has not been transcended by a system of international government by consent. If Christians concern themselves with the business of war, they do so knowing that it is evil. Moreover, the only warrant Christians may have for resorting to war is the preservation of order and justice; and in any case destruction must be kept to a minimum, and in proportion to the end of upholding justice.

23. This has led Christians in the past to formulate guiding rules regarding their participation in war. Not every means of warfare was deemed legitimate. A means and scale of warfare which were destructive of the end in view, e.g., the maintenance of order and justice, could not be justified. This insight has particular relevance to the present situation and in our view has fresh importance and validity. We call attention to the fact that the use of nuclear weapons can certainly more than ever before cause such a scale of devastation and consequences so incalculable that they cannot be balanced by any conceivable advantage to mankind.

24. We wish to comment on the use of the word "justice" in earlier sections. The Christian knows only one command, the command of love. This command compels us to seek ways of action in the international order deriving from a truly Christian and unsentimental conception of love, and not founded on formal legalistic and traditional conceptions of justice. We do not deny the use of this word "justice" and the value of much that it has implied in traditional Christian thought, but we wish to insist that it must always be subordinated to the idea of love and be interpreted accordingly. For instance the *status quo* cannot necessarily be preserved by appeals to formal justice if in fact true care for mankind dictates changes in it.

25. We further call attention to a danger built into the structures of modern technological society. It is the inherent tendency to use without limit or discrimination, one after another whatever new powers and devices scientific discovery places in our hands. That the use of these powers and devices is given us by God for the protection and enlargement of all that is truly human is too readily neglected. There is an undiscriminating and impersonal factor in the modern world, as it affects war making, which greatly increases the danger that nations will embark on destructiveness for no recognizable human ends.

26. All of this lays upon Christians, not a set of rules to determine their action but a discipline under God in the highly dangerous situation in which mankind finds itself. It is:

27. A discipline of penitence which in the conflicts of our day concerns itself with the sins of our own nations more than with the faults of others.

28. A discipline of hope that refuses to give up the struggle for a more ordered and just life for mankind.

29. A discipline of faith which when men are afraid, empowers them and guides their judgment in the knowledge that God is victorious.

30. A discipline of wisdom which would discriminate amidst the clash of propaganda and the pressure of our technological society, and which keeps man as person in view as the object of God's love.

31. A discipline of obedience that seeks to fulfill our duty in the state in the light of our final duty to God.

32. A discipline of love that acknowledges an unlimited responsibility to all men, both friends and enemies, the oppressor and oppressed, however bitter the conflict may be.

33. What follows is an attempt by a group of Christians to work out for themselves what that discipline involves in practical terms in the preventing of war in the nuclear age.

III. THE PREVENTION OF WAR

34. *If war is to be prevented, there must be developed within technological civilization as a whole a spiritual discipline which is capable of using technological achievements in responsible and ethical fashion.* . . .

45. *If war is to be prevented, a first and foremost need is for a special discipline in the conduct of political affairs.* . . .

64. A. *A first requirement is for a discipline which is capable of possessing nuclear weapons and the means of their delivery, but of never using them in all out warfare.* . . .

69. It is now time for Christians to make a fundamental decision and seek to persuade their fellow men to make the same decision. The development of megaton weapons and their means of delivery represents an unparalleled crisis in the history of mankind. The megaton weapon includes a fusion reaction and its size is limited only by the adequacy of the means of delivery. Technologically it has an "open end," that is, there is no limit to the power of the explosions which are possible, and this open end in the production of explosive power has been reached for the first time in the development of the fusion bomb. And as it can be made bigger and bigger, so its delivery can be made "dirtier" and "dirtier." To follow the policy of using weapons to the full is to fail to set any limit upon destructiveness. *Since this limit is not now set by the limits of technological knowledge, it must be set by a decision of mind and will.* The decision not to resort to these weapons in all-out war is therefore a relevant decision. It is irresponsible to rely merely upon the mutually deterrent effect which the possession of these weapons exercises upon nations now in opposition to one another. From an ethical viewpoint, the mere reliance upon this deterrence simply

evades the issue. It is necessary to make the basic decision to which we have referred, and from that decision to work into other and broader disciplines which will give more meaning and content to the fundamental limit which we set for our actions.

Reservation by Certain Members of the Commission

69a. Without denying the necessity of seeking to limit an evil if it cannot be entirely abolished, some members of the Commission hold that it is not permissible to sanction or support the use in any circumstances of the H-bomb, the terrible nature of which is recognized by all of us.

69b. These members apprehend that the destructive power of this weapon is so prodigious that it is certain, or at least very probable, that it could not be used without causing suffering and death to immense numbers of human beings, both combatants and non-combatants. In its very nature it is a weapon of indiscriminate destruction. This makes its use an atrocity. It cannot be justified on the ground that on a lesser scale the same kind of destruction has already occurred at Hiroshima and Nagasaki and in the aerial bombardment of open cities which both sides suffered and inflicted during the last war. All these things would have stood condemned by the laws of war as they were understood and observed before 1914, and indeed before 1939. They ought not to be condoned now.

69c. On this view the use of the H-bomb constitutes an atrocity not to be justified in a belligerent even if the enemy is guilty of it, and not allowable on any ground of reprisal or retaliation, actual or threatened. We are confronted with the question whether there can be any weapon at all the use of which, while the decision is still open to us in time of peace, we will brand and renounce as an atrocity. Some of our members feel bound to answer that question in the affirmative. They consider that certain weapons are forbidden to a belligerent, even in an extremity, because they involve a scale of indiscriminate devastation necessarily destructive of the very objects the securing of which has hitherto been deemed to justify war on rational grounds. They hold that the H-bomb is in this category. It is the limiting case, and at this point they must say No.

69d. This is a conclusion which many who are not Christians have already reached on prudential or humanitarian grounds which have no direct relation to the Christian Faith. But those who are Christians are under a more compelling obedience. They are conscious that the development of modern warfare has brought out more starkly than ever before the contradiction between war and the Divine Commandment of Love. In the case of the H-bomb this contradiction is so great and palpable that it raises serious doubts of the validity of any line of reasoning which may be invoked to sanction the use of such weapons even if it has a thousand years of ecclesiastical history behind it. Christian men must ask whether the time has not come for them to take some decisive step to break the terrible circle of armament and counterarmament in which the world is locked. Some of our members think that the point has now been reached at which the Gospel which enjoins upon us the love even of our enemies calls for new modes of action and sacrifice for the sake of saving the world. And to this call they believe that men are ready to respond.

70. B. *The discipline of possessing nuclear armaments but of not using them in all out war must be a part of, and grow out of, a second and broader discipline, namely that discipline which is capable of using armaments whether conventional or nuclear, if at all, in a radically limited way only.* . . .

VI. Conclusion

84. We conclude with the same thought with which we began. The most profound need of our time in regard to the problem of the prevention of war in an atomic age is not a programme or a set of programmes. We need rather a new and widespread discipline of mind and spirit and action. The power for it must centre in the ultimate power behind all things, which is God. The direction of it must come from the ultimate truth and light of the Gospel. The content of it must be formed according to the spirit of the revelation of God in Jesus Christ. It must be a discipline which is lived amid the constant tension between the high demands of the Gospel and the difficult choices of this troubled world. It must be guided by careful and repeated analyses of the world situation in order that it may be relevant to the central issues of our time. In such a discipline, we believe, lies the key to the prevention of war in our atomic age.

85. The Commission [members] are acutely aware that the whole subject of their remit is one of baffling complexity and difficulty. Time and again they have asked themselves, "Who is sufficient for these things?" They have sought to approach their task with humility and with a due sense of responsibility knowing that it is only too simple for those who are exempt from the responsibilities of government to gain an easy credit by proposing heroic remedies in the knowledge that there is no chance of their being adopted. Great and terrible as is our danger, it may be that in the Providence of God the very magnitude of the peril presents mankind with an unparalleled opportunity. There is now set before us as a stark matter of life and death the choice to end war or be ended by it. May it not be that in the tremendous events of our time we should hear God saying once again to his creatures made in his own image, "Behold I set before you this day life and death. Therefore choose life."

12. The Lordship of Christ Over Church and State, III. (Bièvres, France, August 2-7, 1960)

A French retreat center near Paris was the site of the third in the series of "Puidoux" conferences planned jointly by representatives of the peace churches and European churchmen led by by Heinz Kloppenburg of Germany. Although the discussion was continued on the relationship of church and state, it received a different emphasis in Bièvres by the presence of church leaders from Eastern Europe. In all, over eighty participants came from fifteen different countries.

The narrower work of the conference focused on four presentations: Joachim Beckmann gave a paper on "The Political Responsibility of the Church"; Ernst Wolf on "Observations on Romans 13"; Warren Groff on "The Meaning of the Sixth Commandment for the Christian and the Statesman"; and John Howard Yoder on "Divine and Human Justice." These were all subsequently published in different scholarly journals but there was no unified publication of the Bièvres materials such as had been the case at Puidoux and at Iserlohn. The impact of the Bièvres conference was assessed in an article by Karl Herbert (published in English, French, and German) under the title, "Encounter in Bièvres."

According to senior Quaker spokesman, Douglas Steere, the papers which invoked the most discussion were by Groff, Yoder, and Wolf.

> They were all focused more or less on Romans 13, verses 1-7, in an attempt to see whether the traditional Pauline injunction to obey the authorities that God has placed over us is really definitive in the matter of Christians therefore being obliged to kill when ordered to do so by the state. . . . Both Wolf and Yoder were from very different standpoints trying to "de-ontologize" the state and its authority over the Christian and to make its claim always relative. Wolf was equally devastating in trying to remove any rule or law or code from having more than a relative or assisting status in the confrontation with Christ in the Gospel. . . . Groff . . . sought to build a structural constancy in what is required out of a tracing of the covenant relation between God and man, the Sixth Commandment . . . into its interiorization but continuation in Jesus and in the Holy Spirit. He was

at one with the others in denying that this gave to men any pre-formulated pattern in the alternatives which they are compelled to find if they will not kill.

An assessment of the three conferences held thus far commented on their overall impact, emphasizing:

(1) renewal of the debates broken off three and a half centuries ago between the free and the established churches of Europe; (2) placing the Christian pacifist witness within the context of the respectable theological encounters going on in Europe today; (3) providing the Christian church with a growing peace literature seriously undertaken by first-rate scholars with reasonable involvements in both church and society.

On Divine and Human Justice

John H. Yoder

I

Zwingli's small publication, a sermon preached in June 1523, from which we take the formulation of our topic, presents in an exemplary way the question with which we are dealing. Zwingli's rediscovery of the pure gospel brought with it the rejection not only of the mercenary system and the foreign pension, the mass and the "idols," but also that of the entire system of benefices, from reasons which were grounded in the letter of the Bible as well as on a broad theological perception. Are the benefices to be done away with?

Anyone who has some knowledge of the problematics of social ethics immediately thinks of two solutions between which the great Zürich reformer had to choose. The problem is, after all, a classic example of the basic problematic of Protestant social ethics: how can a moral order for society be derived from the gospel?

On the one hand there would be the way which might be called the "utopian" or "christocratic"; one sets out to develop a formula for the renewal of society out of the "principles" of the gospel and then implements it with the available means—those of church, pedagogy, and police. In the case of Zwingli this would have meant the introduction of legislation according to the gospel without asking whether this was possible. The word, after all, can work anything; away with considerations of political possibility!

If Zwingli could not assume—despite all of his readiness to take the leap of faith—that the Zürich city councilors were ready to convert the Zürich church members into a Jerusalem-like community after the pattern of Acts, then he had to choose the other path. This we shall call provisionally the "dualistic" path because it utilizes other guidelines than the gospel to order the societal relationships, or the "positivistic" path because as a rule these "other guidelines" presuppose and defend the existing order. The "other guidelines" could be read out of the existing conditions in a fully positivistic manner or purely rationalistically taken from an "order of creation" created by reason; that does not concern us here. Of importance is only the fact that they are not immediately contained in the commandment of love itself or that they have been deduced from the word of God.

This problem was especially pressing because of the special form of the Zwinglian message. His "reformation" was no purely religious matter. From its beginning in his early writings, which were pacifist, from its spiritual background in Erasmian humanism, and from its spiritual roots in the image of the blessed and purified covenant people, the Protestant message in Zürich was always also a social ethic. To replace its demands by the introduction of other norms would have meant to replace the word of God itself. Yet Zwingli could not do without the friendly protection of the city council. The above cited sermon was to solve the problem by making the refusal of the Zürich council to remove the benefices of the prebendary *(Chorherren)* understandable and acceptable.

Zwingli's actual solution is of no special interest to us here. The question he faced is to serve us merely as a paradigm or symbolization of those questions which we are addressing on these pages. For even today, the alternatives of principles or compromise, *utopian theocracy of love or dualistic affirmation of the status quo* are still forced upon us. These two logically possible paths serve to shed light both on history (compare Walther Köhler's analysis of the Zürich reformation) as well as on the present (think, for example, of the framework of ethical thinking with Reinhold Niebuhr). And if neither of these extremes is chosen, then the solution is not some *tertium quod,* but rather a tension-filled mixture of these two elements in various dosages.

One might visualize this entire process of thought as a scale of values. At the bottom, the ladder is grounded in that which has become. "There, where God has placed you," you will find your divine task. That which is, is good. Self-assertion is a sacred duty for man or nation. At the top, so high that it is invisible in the clouds, lies the perfect love, nonresistant surrender after the example of Christ. Between these "poles" of this field of tension everyone must then make his tolerable but never satisfying compromises in order to be neither unrealistic nor completely unbelieving.

II

Today this scheme which is generally accepted as self-evident is no longer adequate to deal with the problematic of social ethics. The "dualism" amounts to an uncritical approval of any kind of regime and the "inner laws of the departments of knowledge" end in the demonic. If the churches have become unable to give binding directions which would be more than good pagan wisdom, or to speak a word of comfort which would be more than worldly optimism, then even the theologians notice that things cannot go on like this. Since the struggle of the Confessing Church, even the strictest Neo-Lutherans can no longer claim without exactly qualifying their claim, that the office of the statesman represents a last instance ordained by creation and divine institution, and is recognizable by human reason.

However, instead of really starting from the very beginning and questioning the customary questions, one prefers to change the dosages of utopia and dualism within the old framework, to salt the doctrine of the two kingdoms with a tiny spoonful of Christocracy. The various attempts at drafting an ethical order since the renewal of the rearmament question have been in this direction—that is to say with a shifting of the emphasis within the polarity of utopia and dualism. Some examples:

(a) In order to dissipate the accusation of positivism and to avoid the danger of demonizing the state, one can refine the casuistic treatment of the ethic of the "kingdom on the left." The best example of such attempts is the concept of the just war *(bellum iustum)*, that is, that war which may be held to be commanded by God because it meets certain previously established conditions. The significance of this concept does not lie in the fact that it actually provides a guideline to an ethical decision; it has never done this. There is no test case of a war which the church rejected and in which Christians refused to participate. And yet the thought of the "just war" does represent the concession that not every war which a state may wish to fight is commanded unconditionally. However, once modern warfare has gone beyond all the limits of the previously defined *bellum iustum*, no respectable theologian will dream of calling "Stop!" (That would mean taking theology seriously!) Rather, according to this opinion, the doctrine of *bellum iustum* must be redesigned with an extension of the limits of the permissible in order to be still able to say *pro forma* that not everything is permitted. The reshaping of the *bellum iustum* doctrine takes place today not only among Roman Catholic moral theologians but also in CDU theology [Christian Democratic Union Party of the Federal Republic of Germany] and among the so-called "nuclear pacifists." (Note: For the CDU see H. Thielicke, *Die Atomwaffe als Frage an die christliche Ethik* (Tübingen, 1958). Thielicke does in fact reject the concept of "casuistry," namely in the specific sense (which misinterprets the intention of the actual casuistry) of a general solution specified in advance for as yet unknown problems; yet, the series of fine nuances which, according to his analysis of the problem, must be followed on the path to a valid solution is in the customary, respectable sense nothing but genuine casuistry. With the "nuclear pacifists" there are very fine distinctions between "tactical" atomic weapons and "conventional" warfare, or between armament for war and armament for the purpose of disarmament.)

Some thinkers discard these attempts on principle and out of formal considerations; (they say that) casuistry is suspicious by its very nature. This kind of nonchalant rejection of casuistry is sometimes helpful in pastoral counseling, but theologically it is a fallacy. It can be proven that in developing criticism of casuistry its opponent always develops a counter casuistry. What is suspicious about the newly formulated doctrine of the *bellum iustum* (always taken only as paradigm) is, however, not its casuistic nature, but its secret positivism. Outwardly it confesses that not every armament and not every war can be commanded. The test of the intellectual honesty of this admission will be, as already indicated, the finding of a case where a definite war or a definite armament scheme in one's own land would be designated as forbidden and where Christians would be called—not from pacifism but because of the sake of the state and of the *bellum iustrum*—to rejection of military service and to political resistance. This proof of honesty has not yet been given. In a case when, according to what has been said earlier, the call to resistance should have been sounded, the moral theologian has instead served up a further refinement of distinctions.

(b) As the simplest means to limit the positivism of the two-kingdom doctrine, the customary way of thinking has been provided with a "threshold." "Threshold," in the mathematical sciences is that point where quantitative difference becomes qualitative difference; it therefore designates a fixed point between that which is relative. Somewhere at the lower end of the scale of values on which the love content of various acts is indicated in degrees, such a threshold is determined. Above this line, all human acts are obviously tainted by sin; such acts, however, can be called for according to one's good judgment. Below this line there is another sort of sin, sin *per se,* which no good judgment or inner law may lead the Christian to commit. Thus the "Inquiry" *(Anfrage)* of the Brotherhoods *(Bruderschaften)* of March 1958 speaks of the preparation for atomic warfare as a "sin against God and the neighbor," in the act of which no church, no Christian must become an accessory. This kind of language presupposes:

(1) That certain actions may be recognized in general as "sin" regardless of the situation and of the intent of the perpetrators;

(2) that such "sin" can and must be completely avoided;

(3) that other possible decisions in this situation are not sinful in the same way.

Critics of the "Inquiry" quickly branded at this point a concept of sin contrary to the spirit of the Reformation. Either the general sinfulness of mankind or the message of the justification precisely of the sinner, or the subjection of the earlier Lutheran ethics of the office *(Amtsethik)* to the state as the decisive instance, or the more recent Lutheran situation ethics with its freedom from solid principles, is said to have been ignored. This may well be; indeed, each person decides for himself what is in the spirit of the Reformation. At any rate, one finds exactly the same "massive concept of sin" in the Augsburg Confession, article 16, where three times actions are mentioned which are "without sin." The second time the phrase clearly presupposes, and in the last sentence clearly states that the area of that which "may be done without sin" has a lower threshold which, when crossed by the command of the magistrate, the Christian is no longer to obey. Here is the same conceptual structure as in the "Inquiry"; formally, the seventh article of the inquiry is nothing but an interpretation and application of the last sentence of article 16 of the Augsburg Confession for the place and the time where the "command of the magistrate cannot be obeyed without sin." Whoever is of another opinion about the means of mass annihilation than the Brotherhoods does not think in a basically different way; he only puts the threshold lower. (Note: The train of thought with W. Künneth ("Berufung auf das Gewissen?" *Evang.—Lutherische Kirchenzeitung,* 11 June, 1956) is the same. He cannot honestly state the general claim that the civil authority "bears a representative responsibility which relieves the individual citizen of the great political decisions" without modifying it by the clause, "insofar as these very state measures do not clearly emerge as 'contrary to God.'" The German theologians do not agree as to where the threshold lies; for the Brotherhood, it lies between the conventional weapons (which would need to be discussed yet) and the nuclear weapons which are to be rejected in all instances; for Künneth it lies much "lower." However, the theologians are agreed in their trusting in *a way of thinking in which it is more important to avoid what is forbidden than to do what is commanded.* On both sides the question is: "Atomic weapons are forbidden: yes or no?" No one doubts the question. Perhaps this agreement in the method explains the meager result of the dialogue so far, both in the achievement of a common witness as well as in the participation of the church *(Gemeinde)* in the entire effort. Whether the threshold lies below a modern situation ethics or below the older ethic of the office, is immaterial; the ethic of the office, is, from the formal viewpoint, nothing more than a special case of situation ethics.)

(c) It is possible to equate Christian pacifism—as it is generally understood—with the above mentioned utopian upper pole of the scale. One no longer wishes to carelessly ignore this idealism; yet it is not possible to agree with it without testing too much of one's own tradition. Consequently, one grants the pacifist that he is completely right, but that there should be exceptions. It is not the content but rather the generalizing form of the commandment of pacifism which is wrong. The exceptions will be recognized from case to case as the requirement of the hour and thus they will protect against too-rigid principles. What is to be criticized in this occasionalism of quasi-pacifist coloring is not the concrete socio-ethical directive which it gives—which one could have obtained also by another way—but the assumption that it is a new solution. It is merely an alignment of the utopian and the casuistic answers. Insofar as one uses pacifist language within this occasionalism and bases the demands, for example, for disarmament directly on the lordship of Christ, it is in fact not clear how the realities of politics are to be taken into account. (Note: By "realities of politics" we do not mean the necessity for the defense of a country, which is nothing more than a myth today, but rather the prevailing public opinion and the actual control of the military in the present-day state.) When, on the other hand, the other borderline case happens as, for example, in the approval of the maintaining of atomic armament exclusively for the purpose of disarmament, then the line of reasoning lies entirely within the realm of casuistry.

We see therefore that the attempts to soften the positivism of the two-kingdom doctrine within the inherited framework of thought are insufficient. They clarify neither factual nor basic questions and lead to no common witness. Thus, it is not the details of the various thought processes but the scheme itself which must be called into question; the question is not about the differences between these attempts but what they have in common and, specifically, two presuppositions.

First: In the ethical thinking of the Christian-Western world, with Catholics as well as Protestants, with humanists as well as faithful

Christians, there is no more deeply rooted axiom, no presupposition so generally recognized than the so-called Constantinian postulate. Using this concept which has become current during the past few years, we wish to speak neither of the relationship between church government and state government, nor of political bondage or of the political power of the Christians; neither do we want to make a statement about the personal interest of the first baptized emperor in the change of church and world. As the "Constantinian postulate" we simply designate the presupposition, usually not consciously stated, that for all practical purposes there is really no actual presence of non-Christians in the total society, that is to say, that the totality of Christians and the total society are to be seen as one *(Corpus Christianum).*

In the area of ethics, this postulate means among other things that the Christian ethic for the state and the ethic of the Christian under the state are identical. What the state must do as state cannot be distinguished from the duty of a Christian as a statesman. There is no seriously taking into account the presence of a person in a responsible position who is not determined by the Christian faith. The *distinction between an ethic of the state and Christian duty* is not just conceivable, but ethically wrong; it is inconceivable. With the exception of one of the "sixty theses" of Heinrich Vogel and several statements by Martin Niemöller, this presupposition dominates almost the entire German debate about war and peace, atomic weapons and military service, even today. That which the state is to do and that which the Christian is to be responsible for (whether as responsible voter or responsible statesman) must be equated.

This assumption is part of the fundamental spiritual inventory of the Western world. It has become so all-dominating and, consequently, so unconscious, that one has the greatest difficulty in truly comprehending the significance of the actual minority position of the churches (in the West as in the East, in the "old" as well as in the "younger" churches). One keeps talking of social ethic as if the Christians—and only Christians—could govern state and economy, indeed, had to, because there are no other honest people around.

As in the fable of the emperor's new clothes, everyone hesitates to be the first seriously to test the venerable, generally recognized presupposition. One is so afraid of being decried an enthusiast *(Schwärmer)* that no one dares to pose the question. And yet this postulate makes absolutely no sense for the Old as well as for the New Testament, for the early church as well as today for the "younger churches." Israel did well know of Jahweh's lordship over the nations; its prophets called King Nebuchadnezzar the "servant of Jahweh" and Kyros, "Messiah," but it never occurred to them to develop ethical guidelines from God's working through the nations for the people of the covenant. The apostles spoke clearly of "that which belongs to Caesar," but they were never of the opinion that the ethic for the Christian had to be adapted according to the needs of the Roman governor. (Note: Except in such few places as, for instance, Eastern Nigeria or on certain Pacific islands, the "younger churches" are still in a "pre-Constantinian" setting. The motto of "responsible society" by means of which certain ecumenical thinkers intend to be helpful to the younger churches by applying the ethical wisdom of the West, is, in fact, the worst possible service conceivable; it is the exporting of a Constantinian-type ethos into lands in which there has never been a Constantine and, it is to be hoped, never will be.)

The identity of the Christian ethic and the Christian ethic of the state is therefore the basic presupposition, the questioning of which we hope to make fruitful here. The crucial distinction is not a distinction between the individual and the group, not between the personal relationships in which one can love and the social structures in which one must be just. Here the distinction is between faith in Christ and non-faith, between Christians who are actually a minority of their society witnessing to their faith—Christians, then, who are meant to have an ethic based on repentance, forgiveness, gospel, and faith—and society at large which is not witnessing to any definite faith in Christ, whose state and other administrative agencies (in themselves to a large degree manifestations of non-faith) which—although under the lordship of Christ—cannot be approached on the presupposition of a confession of their own.

Our attempt to call the Constantinian postulate into question and even reject it does not mean that we wish to turn it upside down and deny everything which it affirms. In every dialogue it is a natural misunderstanding to assume that the other partner stands simply for the reversal of one's own position. This error has been committed for decades by the non-pacifists who criticize unjustly every kind of pacifism as an escapist purism. This kind of *abandonment of the state on principle is not advocated here.* Just as we do not wish to deny the fact that the duty of the state and the duty of the Christian in certain cases can be compatible, we likewise do not wish to affirm it as a matter of course. We want to see the question left open: *that which the state is to do and that which the Christian is to do, should be investigated independently of each other* without the one being substantially dependent on the other. What the Christian—be he a conscientious objector to war or a conscientious objector to nuclear war—has to say to the statesman concerning his duty must be made neither logically nor theologically dependent on whether the speaker is ready to assume the office of the one spoken to.

The second questionable presupposition of the customary system of thought concerns the *formulation of the above-mentioned polarity.* According to it one imagines a continuum, a ladder, whose legs rest on solid ground and whose top reaches into heaven. The solid ground is the positivism of law: that which exists is good, because God made it to be so. Heaven above, like all eschatology, does not even exist—as we all know—but simply stands there above in our worldview as a symbol for an orientation, as a hypothetical absolutizing of love and total relativization of the existing. The various socio-ethical systems are placed on different levels of the ladder, according to the dosage of utopia and positivism.

This image is wrong in two ways, for reasons which do not come from ethics but rather from the theory of cognition. Both fallacies which became apparent here, are in the final analysis denials of the fact that Jesus Christ is the only word of God. Let us first consider the upper "pole." In content this signifies agape as revealed through the cross of Christ and commanded of men by his word. To this is added that the fulfillment of this command is impossible, that it was only meant as a mirror for sinners, that it implies either an escape from the world or a denial of interpersonal relationships. Here we find the first absurdity. If Jesus Christ is true man *(vere homo),* as the Christians, say, "yet without sin," then it is not possible to put down *a priori* that *discipleship* in community with him *(in seiner Wesensgemeinschaft)* is impossible or superhuman. Jesus, a fully human being, indeed a very important political figure among his people, lived "yet without sin," not in utopia, but in Palestine. Whoever rejects on principle the ethical relevance of the man Jesus as withdrawal from life, denies, in the final analysis, incarnation.

The lower pole of this tension is equally poorly defined. So far, we have spoken in general terms of "dualism" or of "positivism." Now we must describe more closely what is the essence of this position. In order to be fair to the discussion thus far and to describe that which the positions expressed in it have in common, the following marks of "dualism" must be recognized:

(1) God's commandment is heard here. The commandment announces God's will for here and today and the Christian ought to obey it. Therefore, this is not casual advice; it is commanded.

(2) According to the form this commandment does not come through the incarnation. Whether that which is commanded comes through the office, through the decision of the magistrate by divine right, through the situation, through reason, through innate ideas of duty or is perceived in any other way—that is unimportant here. Whether it is the Father, the

Creator, the pre-existent Logos, the enthroned Christ or the Holy Spirit in the church *(Gemeinde)* or in the conscience, whom one considers the originator of the revelation—that also may vary. At any rate, it is not Jesus Christ, the incarnated one, who transmits this commandment. (Otherwise there would be no tension between this commandment and agape.)

(3) In content, this commandment is also different from discipleship. It is not commanded to give one's life for one's neighbor, but—if necessary—to kill the neighbor for the sake of order. In the face of this commandment, to act as Jesus did would be disobedient toward God. The hangman is not to forgive seventy times, the soldier is not to turn the other cheek, he who has is not to give his possessions to the poor. This does not only mean that one may legitimately fall short in love (as, for example, that one cannot feed all of the poor because there is not enough money) but, for the sake of the office (or the responsibility for the neighbor; or the demands of the hour; or the given situation) man is commanded to have a different goal than devoting himself to the neighbor.

These three marks are necessary if dualism, regardless of what type, is to fulfill that function which in the ethical reasoning it actually claims and exercises. When, however, all three are present, it becomes apparent that here is present a dual perception of revelation, the theological consequences of which are difficult to overcome. If there are two different sources and contents of revelation then, in the final analysis, neither is revelation.

If by "revelation" an oracle were meant, then there could exist several channels through which individual truths could be communicated. If, however, in the Christian understanding "revelation" is an intervention of God in history and a criterion of all other claims to truth, if indeed, what is more, through the term "revelation" the Logos, the son of God in personal self-revelation is proclaimed and recognized, then there must not and cannot be two of the same. (Note: The formulation of "polarity" criticized in the above does not only distort the intellectual problematic but also history. Not every social ethic is placed on such a scale between an agape which is irrelevant for the world and an almost cynical dualism. Although the dualism has been played in all kinds of modes, the theocratic-utopian solution has never been seriously tried as a law for an entire society. It is merely a hypothetical construction. On the other hand, historically quite relevant solutions to the problem have been completely omitted from the mentioned model, among these are above all to be mentioned the temporary answer of the cited sermon of Zwingli's (which could be called "pre-Constantinian"; see J. Yoder's book review of H. Schmid, *Zwinglis Lehre von der göttlichen und menschlichen Gerechtigkeit, Mennonite Quarterly Review,* 25 (1961), 79-88) as well as the final solution of the later Zwingli (a theocracy according to Old Testament or Justinian pattern). Very seldom is it sufficiently recognized how far-reaching the confusing effect of such a falsified schema can be. Especially the first mentioned Zwinglian solution to the problem is not merely a point in the middle of a continuum between dualism and utopia; it is not even located on this line, because it brings in other dimensions. The image of "polarity" in describing the problem says in reality that one has already omitted the description and is engaged in apologetics for dualism, that is to say for the inner law of "human justice."

[Section III is devoted to a graphical analysis of the discussion.]

IV

The Concept of "Legitimacy" as Paradigm.

In order to make clear how concepts of the philosophy of law or ethics must first be exposed as fiction in order then to serve (or to be "assumed") as middle axioms, we take as an example the concept of legitimacy or rightfulness. Legitimacy not only applies to individual measures of administration, but the existence of the state itself is judged according to this standard. Some examples:

(a) During World War II Karl Barth was unable to acknowledge Hitler's Germany as a constitutional state, for when a state embodies injustice, then it no longer enjoys the protection of Romans 13. A war which removes this non-state renders the (true) state system a service.

(b) In a similar way, many have been moved by the difference in tone between Romans 13 and Revelation 13, to speak of two types of state. [They feel that] Romans 13 speaks of the legitimate state "which performs its duties" (v. 6); that of Revelation 13 has "become demonic," it has "temporarily torn itself away from the lordship of Christ." A given state may then appear in this or that form; whether we owe it obedience depends on which of the two forms it reflects.

(c) Some time ago Bishop Dibelius stated that a constitutional state was possible only on the basis of a theistically oriented confession of that state to morality. A state dedicated in principle to Marxism and thus to moral relativism will be rendered obedience for perhaps still other reasons, not for conscience' sake.

Similar, less clearly developed concepts are found elsewhere, for example when it was stated that it was the task of the church to see to it "that the state remained the state."

Despite (or because?) of the colorful mixture of those who presupposed the presence of such norms for the constitutional state, there is no clarity about where the norms for such legitimacy lie or how they are to be used. Does the legality lie in the practice of law itself, perhaps in such a way that a judicial murder or a pogrom of Jews disqualifies the state? If so, how great must the wrong be?

Or is it because of the ideology, with which a state or a people glorify themselves? Or is the approval of the subjects to be decisive? Or the economic system? Is a capitalist (or a Marxist) state *ipso facto* unjust? As is well known, today the legitimacy of a revolutionary regime is judged more according to its foreign policy between the blocs than to its origin or its inner practice of law.

The criterion of constitutional succession is somewhat clearer. This is what the "governments in exile" live on; but they live only as long as they find powerful friends abroad. Of all these suggestions, only the last is juridically clear, and that only in the sense that its consistent application would leave no state standing. Somewhere in its history, each state system is based on violent revolution or conquest.

Even if we had clear norms, good answers would not be assured by that. Between the daily, almost avoidable injustices and the extent of evil that disqualifies the state as state, there lies another threshold. Who determines the point and the hour of transgression? The theologian? The synod? The more one attempts to determine the legitimacy, the more it disappears in a confusion of differences in degree upon several intersecting scales.

A concept of legitimacy, upon the application of which an armed resistance or a war against a given state would be in order in favor of a constitutional state which is supposed to exist, has no place of origin in the New Testament. The supposition that yet another last revolution or yet another conquest could establish the true state is not only unrealistic in view of the definition of what is right and the feasibility of the undertaking; it is unbiblical. That is what the Maccabees and later the Zealots wanted. The state whose restoration they wanted to bring about through revolution could have claimed like no other to be the constitutional state. Jesus shared with the Zealots their sharp criticism of the existing conditions; however, he did not conclude from this that men should do away with them by violent means. Even the Messiah ought not to do that. Similarly, Romans 13 does precisely not command that one should resist the given state in the interest of a better state. Although there is a "threshold" of injustice, at which point the Christian becomes obedient as soon as the state transgresses it, the Christian in his resistance nevertheless remains subject and does not erect any counter state. (Note: It is curious to note how sweepingly one has reasoned here with the alternatives of "obedience—rebellion," as if "obeying" and "being subject" meant the same, which is by no means the case. See A. Rich, "Die Verantwortung des Christen für Staat und Politik," *Evangelische Theologie* (December 1960), 562ff; C. E. B. Cranfield, "Some Observations on Romans 13:1-7," *New Testament Studies* (April 1960, 241ff.) The state of Romans 13 is the state of Revelation 13. Both passages describe not two possible, mutually exclusive, alternating attitudes of the magistrate but the one ambivalent political reality. The duty of the Christian is the same under both perspectives: to be subject. (Revelation 13 deals in fact not with the non-state but with the non-church, which support the state ideologically.)

Although it is not possible to explain the nature of the state and especially to declare a state in need of rebellion through proof of its illegitimacy, *the concept of legitimacy does retain a function within the Christian ethic of the state.* This is because there seldom exists a single magistrate; there is competition between the state and the federation of states, between uprising and government, Mafia and police, legislator and supreme court, official and regulation. The question is not: "Magistrate: are you for or against it?" but rather: "Which magistrate?" Not only in those cases does the concept of legitimacy in its various forms (practice of law, constitutional succession, endorsement by the subjects, honesty) provide a very helpful guide—forms among which, when it comes to it, one does not need to choose after all. The various degrees remain useful but without ever being able to prove a basic illegitimacy, that is to say, a sanction of rebellion. The injustice of an existing regime does therefore not establish the legality of a rebellion. Neither the chances of success nor experience tells us that the new government will be essentially less dictatorial and oligarchic, that it will be a more successful defender of law and peace. An acceptable order—whether under capitalist, fascist or marxist rule—results, if it is attainable at all, much more likely through patient, continuous bit-by-bit change of the existing conditions than by a violent overthrow. The larger right of the oppressed exists as a relative critical criterion; however, it ceases to exist as soon as the violent methods of the oppressor and opponent are applied for the purpose of removing him.

The Myth of Civil Responsibility

It is one of the most widely accepted platitudes of this complex of problems that the creation of the democratic form of government has fundamentally changed the relationship between citizen and state, or even between Christian and state. "The state, it is I!"—this is what every citizen is supposed to be able to say now. This credo of the Age of Enlightenment is today as generally accepted as the conviction in the Middle Ages that the

Millennium had set in with Constantine. The fact that, despite repeated experience to the contrary, it is possible to maintain this conviction proves that modern man is no less capable of believing myths as man was in antiquity. In reality it is by no means true that the citizen is the state, or that he significantly governs the state through his vote. The powers that rule effectively are called Mammon, Mars, public opinion, the press, film—and, now and then, the witness of the Christians. The elections, the parliamentary apparatus, and all of the appurtenances are means of expression and safety valves of great value—just as in other times it was popular uprisings, interdict, general strike or the coup d'état—but they are not creative powers. The modern voting citizen has not much more hope left of truly and essentially influencing the state than did his counterpart under a benevolent tyrant.

Nevertheless, the democratic ideology presents a series of concepts which can serve the Christian social ethic. A greater or lesser degree of freedom in the expression of opinion, of recognition of a regime by the people, and of the constitutional objectivity of the government can be discerned and established; the mythical language remains useful even—and precisely—when it has been demythologized.

Summary

The lordship of Christ over the state means for the Christian not the founding of a constitutional state but the *aceptance of the given system of government although it is*—in its goals and means, especially when it resorts to the sword—*a form of non-faith and selfishness*. This structure is used as defense against an even worse disorder. The legal-philosophical principles of the state (regardless of the school of thought) can neither be reliably defined nor do they have actual theological value. To base their claim to be heard on metaphysical grounds would mean granting them an independent authority apart from Jesus Christ as a source of revelation, which is not permitted. Still, these concepts—as the state itself—may be "accepted" in order to serve as the vehicle of a Christian or Christologically grounded word to the state. The concrete content of the word to the state as well as its claim to be heard are based on the incarnated one and on no other logos.

The Sixth Commandment: Its Significance for the Christian as Citizen and for the Statesman

Warren F. Groff

The Christian lives in a state of dual citizenship. He is both a citizen in the kingdom of God in Christ through the Spirit and a citizen in the kingdom of this world. He must live in the world as "in a house sold for the breaking up" (Albert Schweitzer). He is called to surrender "to Christ and for the rest be uncommitted" (Herbert Butterfield). He must live in the world "as if not" in the world. "He who when he has the world is as one who does not have it, then he has the world, otherwise the world has him" (Sören Kierkegaard). He is called to live the kind of paradoxical existence expressed in the words of Jesus: "He who finds his life will lose it, and he who loses his life for my sake will find it" (Matt. 10:39).

There is the temptation prematurely to resolve the tension thrust upon the Christian by this twofold citizenship. But the activity of God in creation, in the incarnation, in the sending of his Spirit, prevents the Christian community from dissolving the polarity with an easy conscience. God's own affirmation of the world he has made blocks a Christian from complete withdrawal, although some form of Docetism and/or Gnosticism is a perennial tendency. Further, God's revelation of himself in Jesus Christ makes it specifically clear that the Christian's citizenship in the world is not the same as his citizenship in heaven. He is ever to be as a pilgrim and sojourner in the land.

The materials produced in connection with the Puidoux conferences (Note: For the most part the materials produced in connection with the Puidoux conferences are available only in unbound form.) amply document the centrality of this problem of a twofold citizenship. There seems to be extensive agreement that some type of "both-and" relationship is called for, but the consensus is less clear when an effort is made to set forth the precise nature and implications of this duality. Our theme raises once again this fundamental issue. In addressing ourselves to the more specific question of the significance of the sixth commandment (Note: The commandment is "You shall not kill." According to the Lutheran and Roman Catholic listing, this is regarded as the fifth commandment.) both for the Christian as a citizen and for the statesman we shall have to expose our own effort to avoid the Scylla of reducing the heavenly kingdom to an earthly one and the Charybdis of removing one's heavenly citizenship entirely out of the realm of this world.

I. The Commandment and the Ethic of the Old Covenant

The ethical requirements of the Old Covenant are rooted in God's being and act. The orientation is theocentric. Rights and duties are not determined abstractly, but in terms of who God is and what he has done. While there is a discernible humanitarian direction to the laws of the Israelites, their ethic clearly is theological rather than humanistic. Rather than some man-made norm, it is God in his activity who serves as the regulative center of man's personal and communal being.

A. *God's Covenant Activity*

God's electing-covenanting activity is fundamental to the ethic of the Israelites. The covenant at Sinai was the event that brought Israel into existence as a distinct political and religious community. We are in a position today to appreciate the significance of covenants in the ancient world as the means whereby new groupings were achieved. The following statement by Wellhausen now sounds out of date:

> The giving of the law at Sinai has only a formal, not to say dramatic significance. It is the product of the poetic necessity for such a representation of the manner in which the people were constituted Jehovah's people as should appeal directly and graphically to the imagination. . . . For the sake of producing a solemn and vivid impression, that is represented as having taken place in a single thrilling moment which in reality [is] slowly [observed] and almost unobserved. (Note: "Israel," *Encyclopedia Britannica,* 9th edition (1881), Vol. XIII, 396ff. Quoted by G. E. Mendenhall, *Law and Covenant in Israel and the Ancient Near East,* p. 6.)

Based upon research into the place of covenants in cultures that surrounded Israel, G. E. Mendenhall takes issue with the point of view which was given impetus by Wellhausen. Mendenhall reflects the contemporary shift of scholarly judgment when he argues that the emergence of Israel as a religious and political community is concretely connected with the Sinaitic covenant. (Note: Mendenhall, *op. cit.,* p. 5.) Therefore, Israelite law is first and foremost covenant law. Because of its significance as the frame of reference for the Decalogue, it will be useful here to define further the election-covenant faith of Israel.

The Israelites were convinced that God had particularly set them apart from the other nations. They were to live for God and for the world. "For you are a people holy to the Lord your God: the Lord your God has chosen you to be a people for his own possession, out of all the peoples that are on the face of the earth" (Deut. 7:6). Their election was to covenant mission! They were called to participate in the universal purpose of God in establishing his redemptive sovereignty over all the earth. Still, the election of Israel was enshrouded in the mystery of God's love. They could not explain God's "choice" of them on the basis of their greater sensitivity, their religious genius, their responsiveness to God's mission. Nor was their faith in election the result of neutral speculation. It was awakened in connection with the experience of being delivered from bondage in Egypt. The Exodus deliverance was seen as evidence of God's outgoing and unconditional love. Thus election is the foundation of the covenant relationship. Stated otherwise, God's electing love *('ahabah)* is the presupposition of his covenanting love *(chesed)*. The covenant is the historical expression and structuring of Israel's election. Through covenant language, ceremonies, and laws the Israelites were reminded of God's loving and saving work on their behalf and of the obligations incumbent upon them as a result of the activity of the sovereign God.

Call and response, divine sovereignty and human response are involved in the covenant relationship. The one cannot be set over against the other with calculable positions on a continuum. They are not susceptible to a neat synergism. The initiative is of God. The response of the people is motivated by the awareness that God has already demonstrated his self-giving and steadfast love toward the Israelites in their weakness. We have been helped in our understanding at this point by contemporary research into the form of Hittite covenants. The primary classification now agreed upon is between "suzerainty" and "parity" covenants. (Note: The Hittite covenants have been carefully analyzed by V. Korosec, *Hethitische Staatsverträge,* Leipzig 1931. Quoted in Mendenhall, *op. cit.,* 29ff.) The latter entail a bilateral type of agreement in which both parties assume designated obligations. In a "suzerainty" type of covenant, however, the relationship is more unilateral. The suzerain "gives" a covenant, and within the covenant the vassal finds protection and security. The vassal is under obligation to obey the majestic and authoritative covenant author, for the sovereignty of the king remains. But this obedience is motivated more by gratitude and trust, as based on the sovereign's graciousness and steadfastness. The stipulations which represent the sovereign's interests and which the vassal fittingly accepts and upholds, are set in the context of a historical recital of the king's benevolent deeds.

The differences and exceptions notwithstanding, this type of covenant understanding helps to illuminate aspects of Israelite law. The Decalogue especially seems to fit this basic pattern. The stipulations are preceded by the reminder of God's grace: "I am the Lord your God, who brought you out of the land of Egypt, out of the house of bondage" (Ex. 20:2). Since the monograph of Albrecht Alt, it is customary to refer to the specific commands that follow as "apodictic" rather than "casuistic" in form. (Note: *Die Ursprünge des israelitischen Rechts,* 1934.) That is, they are categorical and unconditional. They designate basic guidelines for covenant man rather than offer specific case applications. As such, they provide the substructure of Israelite law. The Decalogue presents community policy, the definition of right and wrong, of the interests of God, to which the people are bound.

B. *God's Activity in Creation*

Covenant is not only the concrete setting for the determination of rights and duties. It is the presupposition of all life. As Karl Barth has put it, "covenant is the internal presupposition of creation, and creation is the external presupposition of covenant." The interrelationship between covenant and creation may be illustrated by a study of two key words, *mishpat* and *shalom.*

Johannes Pedersen has helped us to see that the Hebrews traced fundamental values back to their root in the soul of man. In this way, the covenant law is organically tied in with the created order of life.

> The laws and codes of mankind, no more than other laws, are something which has been enforced from without, something which infringes upon the soul. The law is in its very essence the free development of the soul, the maintenance of its peculiar essense. . . . The law consists in that every human being maintains his soul after its special kind. (Note: J. Pedersen, *Israel: Its Life and Culture,* I-II, 351.)

The further implication of this is that covenant man

> maintains the covenant and confirms the position of his brothers in it, for the covenant is part of the essence of his own soul, or rather, he is himself a link in the covenant. He who thus develops his own kind does what is the usual thing, what is done by good people, and thus he maintains the harmony of the covenant; his action is normal. (Note: *Ibid.,* 351.)

Stated otherwise, his action reflects *mishpat*. This refers to the fitting and normal behavior within the covenant. It is the law for the actions of covenant man, the established *(hok),* instruction *(tora),* tradition *(miswa).* It has its roots in the very essence of the soul. It implies the health of the soul, harmonious growth within the covenant, the direct union with other souls. "It is 'straight' as is the normal soul. To bend *mishpat* is the same as to disturb the relation, to dissolve the harmony which conditions the maintenance of the covenant." (Note: *Ibid.,* 351.)

Shalom implies both the untrammeled, free growth of the soul and harmonious community. Peace and covenant are two expressions of the common life of souls. "All life is common life, and so peace and covenant are really denominations of life itself." (Note: *Ibid.,* 308.) This adds a significant dimension to the word *peace* which is often lacking in contemporary usage. Peace is not simply the absence of conflict. It is profoundly a theological category. Very positively, it stands for the happy development of the soul as created, and for the full harmony with the souls with which it is connected by covenant. Taken together, these two represent peace, the totality of the soul. It is the blessing of God that enables man to maintain peace, and the kernel of blessing and peace is righteousness. In a word a healthy soul is one that is marked by peace.

We are now in a position to appreciate the Decalogue as a foundational statement of the rights and duties of covenant and creaturely man. The specific commandments not only set forth the obligations attendant upon the Israelites in view of God's gracious favor, but also offer guidance for the healthy soul and the harmonious community. In short, "The Ten Words" provide a blueprint for peace.

The sixth commandment states that covenant wholeness or peace involves respect for the neighbor, and in his totality. The commandment implies the prohibition of unlawful manslaughter as well as violence.

> He who takes the life of a man takes his soul; for it is the soul in its normal development which must be respected, thus also including his house. . . . The totality of the man is himself and his house, everything that belongs to him, including his property; it is to be respected as well as his life. . . . In three pithy words: . . . "thou committest not murder, thou committest not adultery, thou committest not theft" the law expresses the respect shown by normal individuals towards each other's integrity: life, house, property. (Note: *Ibid.,* 354.)

In this way the law establishes a basic condition of peace or covenant wholeness. Such behavior conserves *mishpat;* i.e., it is fitting and normal behavior within the covenant community.

C. *Interrelationships Between Creation, Covenant, and Redemption*

Covenant is oriented not only toward creation but also toward God's mercy and saving activity, in the present and the future as well as in the past. Here again the covenant response that is called for is conditioned by God's own being and act. Norman Snaith has traced the progression of Old Testament understanding in this regard. (Note: *The Distinctive Ideas of the Old Testament.*) In the Old Testament, God's holiness *(qodesh)* implies not only sacred otherness but increasingly connotes righteousness. It is in righteousness *(tsedeqah)* that God's holiness is shown. "But the Lord of hosts is exalted in justice, and the Holy God shows himself holy in righteousness" (Isa. 5:16; cf. Isa. 6: 1-5.). But God's righteousness is not a static attribute. Nor is it simply that which God establishes as the proper norm for covenant man, as the pattern for behavior that is firm, straight, and steady. It refers to God's saving activity especially in relation to the humble, the poor, the widows, the sojourners. The soteriological setting for the covenant response is particularly pronounced in Deutero-Isaiah. Here, as well as in certain of the psalms, God's righteousness and his salvation are basically parallel in meaning (Ps. 98:2).

God's saving activity came increasingly to be associated with the work of God's Spirit in forging a "new covenant." The *ruach-adonai* is God's life-giving, energy-giving power active in the lives of covenant men, enabling them to do what otherwise they are unable to do. This was particularly thought of in connection with the "latter days" or the Messianic Age. In "that day," the time of the *eschaton,* the Lord would put a new spirit in the hearts of men, would pour out his Spirit even for the transformation of nature, would share his Spriit with all flesh, causing Israel's sons and daughters to prophesy, her old men to dream dreams, and her young men to see visions (Joel 2:28).

God is holy creator, righteous covenanter, merciful redeemer. (Note: A trinitarian perspective would lead us to stress the "coincidence" of God's ways of being. God's outward works are indivisible, even if distinguishable, to cite the traditional rule. God is holy but his holiness is righteous and redemptive. God is redemptive but his redemptive work is an expression of holiness and righteousness. God is righteous but his righteous activity arises out of his nature as holy and issues in redemptive deeds.) This is the pattern for the behavior of covenant man, who is called to respond in reverence (Isaiah), in justice (Amos), and in mercy (Hosea). The prophetic summary of Micah 6:8 gathers these together: "He has showed you, O man, what is good; and what does the Lord require of you but to do justice, and to love kindness, and to walk humbly with your God." Justice and love are here organically interrelated, by virtue of their theocentric setting. Covenant man not only is to respect the rights and souls of others in terms of just actions, but he also is to be merciful even as God is merciful.

The expectations regarding *gerim* particularly illustrate how the covenant response is conditioned by God's saving activity. "You shall not wrong a stranger or oppress him, for you were strangers in the land of Egypt" (Ex. 22:21; cf. Lev. 19:9-10; Deut. 24:19-22; Ex. 23:9; Lev. 19:33).

The sixth commandment is part of the covenant law which is to be obeyed in a spirit not only of dutifulness, but of reverence and of dependence upon the working of God's Spirit. From within the context of the "old covenant," however, the relevance of the commandment is limited in scope. In spite of the tendencies in the direction of greater universality, especially as evidenced by the stipulations regarding *gerim* and by the prophetic emphasis upon covenant community. It reflects concern basically for the respect of human life in Israel. It apparently had no direct bearing on such issues as suicide, capital punishment, or the killing of enemies in war. Still, its significance is positive and important. It sets forth a basic prerequisite for covenant wholeness, or peace; i.e., respect for the well-being of the neighbor in his totality!

II. The Commandment and the Ethic of the New Covenant

The distinguishing feature of the New Testament is the fact that the orientation is not only theocentric and soteriological but also Christological. For the Christian community the significance of the sixth commandment for the citizen and statesman must be determined basically in light of the Christ-event.

A. *Jesus Christ and the New Covenant*

Jeremiah had prophesied the coming of a new covenant. "But this is the covenant which I will make with the house of Israel after those days, says the Lord: I will put my law within them, and I will write it upon their hearts; and I will be their God, and they shall be my people" (Jer. 31:33). It is the conviction of the New Testament that in and through Jesus Christ this new covenant has been accomplished by the act of God.

Here too the relationship is one of grace. God has taken the initiative. His love *(agape)* is free and unconditioned. The grace *(charis)* of our Lord Jesus Christ is the historical expression of that love, even as, in the Old Testament, God's outgoing love *('ahabah)* took historical form in terms of the specific covenant with Israel *(chesed)*. (Note: N. Snaith, *op. cit.*, 173ff.) The fact of grace is prior to, and of an order different from, the call for a covenant response. This is the work of God and not of man. Still, from within this grace setting, a response is called for. We may recall here our discussion of the "suzerainty" in contrast to the "parity" form of the covenant. What is expected and fitting, in view of God's gracious activity in Jesus Christ, is a grateful response of unreserved discipleship.

B. *The Law and the Created Order*

It seems clear that Jesus, in the sayings included in the collection called the Sermon on the Mount, had the Ten Commandments in mind. He stands in the place of Moses as the lawgiver for the new covenant community. The commandments sketch the pattern for the creaturely fulfillment through covenant wholeness. Therefore, Jesus came not to destroy but to fulfill the law. Fulfill it he did. He probed its inward meaning and extended its scope.

> You have heard that it was said to the men of old, "You shall not kill; and whoever kills shall be liable to judgment." But I say to you that every one who is angry with his brother shall be liable to judgment (Matt. 5:21-22a). . . . You have heard that it was said, "You shall not commit adultery." But I say to you that every one who looks at a woman lustfully has already committed adultery with her in his heart (Matt. 5:27-28).

The old covenant ethic taught: "You shall not steal" (Ex. 20:15). Jesus phrases it positively: "Give to him who begs from you, and do not refuse him who would borrow from you" (Matt. 5:42). Thus Jesus upholds the Old Testament pattern for peace, or covenant wholeness. The normal behavior *(mishpat)* of those within the new covenant community includes basic respect for each other's integrity: life, house, material needs. Indeed, by pressing to the inward state behind the outward act, by extending the scope of what it means to be a neighbor, by giving impetus through word and example to the worldwide mission of the community, and by focusing attention once again upon the foundational *mishpat* pattern for life in the created order rather than upon the multitudinous *mishpatim,* or case applications, of normative Judaism, Jesus deepened and universalized these covenant expectations.

C. *The Age of the Spirit*

In view of their intensity and scope, it is quite understandable that Christians occasionally have insisted that the relevance of such teachings is to drive us to despair. Who of us can meet such exalted demands? They do indeed drive us to repentance. But the expectation of obedience is quite clear. Windisch (Note: *The Meaning of the Sermon on the Mount.)* has helpfully cautioned us against dismissing too quickly the obligatory character of the laws in the Sermon on the Mount. The Sermon, argues Windisch, reflects a positive orientation toward law. Granted, there is the awareness that divine grace is prior and necessary. But there is also present the expectation that such commandments will be obeyed.

Still, it is necessary to read the Sermon on the Mount in the light of the larger event of Christ. Somehow, the revelation through the Sermon and the witness of the Apostle Paul need to be kept in relation to each other. Paul crystallizes one of the clear convictions of the New Testament. In Jesus Christ the Age of the Spirit has come. The Messianic Age has dawned with the glorified Christ as the living Lord. The Spirit of God, now closely identified with the Spirit of the incarnate, crucified, and risen Christ is a work in and through his "people" in a new and decisive way.

Thus, the covenant response that is fitting includes not only obedience and repentance but also dependence upon the working of God's Spirit. To stress obedience apart from repentance is to fall into legalism and possible Phariseeism. To emphasize obedience apart from dependence upon God's Spirit is to be vulnerable to a naive and shallow perfectionism. But it also needs to be said, especially in the light of the contemporary theological mood, that to stress repentance apart from obedience and dependence is to fall into quietism and the likely acceptance of the status quo. It is also to reflect a deficient doctrine of the incarnation and of the Holy Spirit. The new covenant ethic is an ethic not only of law but also of gospel and of *eschaton:* It is an ethic not only of demand but also of grace and promise.

There is here presupposed a trinitarian orientation. We know God from within the Christian community not only as the one who is sovereign creator, but also as the one who is powerfully present in the life, ministry, death, and resurrection of Jesus Christ, and as the one whose work as indwelling and enabling Spirit is inseparably linked with the work of the glorified and ruling Christ. God is one, and yet exists and acts as Father, Son, and Spirit, and all three come at every point into the full Christian experience of God.

Karl Barth, D. M. Baillie, and others have stressed that the doctrine of the Trinity is immediately implicated in God's revelation of himself in Jesus Christ. (Note: Karl Barth, *Dogmatik,* I/1; D. M. Baillie, *God Was in Christ;* see also C. Welch, *In This Name.*) It is an essential summary of the distinctive understanding of God involved in the ethic of the new covenant. The God and Father of our Lord Jesus Christ is one who not only creates but also enters into history concretely in his word and works in and through history to the end that, by the power of his own Spirit, the demands placed upon man may be fulfilled. D. M. Baillie refers to this as the "paradox of grace"; i.e., the awareness that God's covenant demands in

Christ call for man's response and yet in the setting of dependence upon God's own strength that these demands may be fulfilled.

III. THE COMMANDMENT AND ITS SIGNIFICANCE

The sixth commandment is relevant for the Christian as covenant man. To be sure, he lives by grace and not simply by law, but law has been and is being redeemed rather than abrogated. Obedience is due to the law because it is grounded in the order of creation and the order of redemption. Covenant law both instructs the Christian regarding the way to creaturely fulfillment and peace and is dependent upon the redemption wrought by Christ through the cross, redemption which is being worked out in the present by the power of the Spirit and which will be consummated at the *parousia*.

The Christian's duties as citizen may be distinguished but not separated from his duties as covenant man. He is a covenant man being redeemed by God's working, but he is also a participant in the order of creation. This would caution us against any version of "dualism" which would bifurcate law and grace, state and church.

At places in the New Testament, it must be granted, a fairly sharp distinction is drawn between, say, state and church. For example, Paul's Corinthians and Romans correspondence sets up nearly a dualism in this regard. Here Paul is apparently convinced that the spiritual powers behind the state belong to the present age, and will pass away. But this is not the whole picture. There are other indications in Paul's imprisonment letters of a hope that the powers that now reign may be brought within the scope of God's redemption. Even these heavenly powers are among those who must come to acknowledge the Lordship of Christ, for it was to this end that they were created (Phil. 2:10 ff; Col. 1:16, 20). As G. B. Caird reminds us, this redemption of the heavenly principalities and authorities, which stand behind the law no less than the state, must not

> be confused with Cullmann's idea that through the Cross the state has, without knowing it, been brought within the kingdom of Christ. For Paul declares that the powers must confess that Christ is Lord, and that, through the mediation of the church, they must come to understand the wisdom of God's redemptive purpose. (Note: G. B. Caird, *Principalities and Powers,* p. 29.)

Nor is it clear that the Apostle Paul conceived these powers behind law and state to have their authority and claim to obedience by virtue of the order of redemption rather than the order of creation. Cullmann would have it so. Cullmann insists that Paul instructs the church in Rome to obey the powers of the state on the basis that they have been made subject to the Lordship of Christ even though, in distinction to the church, they do not know or acknowledge it. Caird's criticism of Cullmann at this point is sound:

> It is no service to the apostle Paul to father upon him a deficient doctrine of creation. . . . The powers of state are to be obeyed not because they have been made subject to Christ but simply because they exist, and no authority can exist apart from God's decree. Their authority belongs not to the order of redemption but to the order of creation. Paul achieves the universal centrality of Christ not by making the authority of the powers depend on the Cross but by declaring that Christ is God's agent in creation. (Note: *Ibid.,* p. 25.)

Caird seems to err in the opposite direction from Cullmann. He likewise breaks up the organized interrelationship between creation and redemption. The spiritual powers behind state and law have their authority by virtue both of the order of creation and of redemption. They exist and function in view of God's creative power even as they have been brought under the Lordship of Christ through the cross.

The sixth commandment, thus, has positive significance for the Christian as citizen and for the statesman. It is part of the pattern for creaturely fulfillment and covenant wholeness. As deepened and universalized by Jesus Christ, this offers guidance for personal and communal life. To be sure, the covenant man who knows and acknowledges the lordship of Christ, and therefore is in the church, will be the first to acknowledge its authority. He will be conscious both of the created authority of the law and of its limitations in view of sin. He will confess the law's claim to obedience even as he is driven to repentance and dependence upon the working of God's Spirit.

But there is no warrant, from the standpoint of this paper, for restricting the relevance of this commandment to life in the church while the state is run by prudential or other nonbiblical norms. This commandment, as we have seen, is part of the pattern for created as well as covenant life. Insofar as the Christian citizen or statesman makes decisions on the basis of standards that go counter to such a commandment, the judging norm must remain clear. (Note: Cf. J. Lasserre, *La Guerre et l'Evangile,* Paris, 1953.) Nor is it adequate to make rigid the status quo by insisting that the state in distinction from the church is forever doomed to some lesser level.

The response of the Christian entails obedience and repentance, but also hope. Caird states it well:

> The Christian's loyalty to society and the state, which are derivative authorities, must always be subordinated to his loyalty to the absolute authority of God in Christ; and . . . by the continued influence of Christ, working through his loyal followers in the church, the state itself may be brought progressively more and more within the Christian dispensation, and the affairs of state directed not merely by the ethics of law but by the ethics of the Gospel. (Note: Caird, *op. cit.*, 29f.)

SUMMARY

We have been reminded that the Christian has a twofold citizenship. On the one hand, he is a new covenant man. He participates in Christ through the Spirit, and therein finds his covenant wholeness—his peace, his blessing, his righteousness. On the other hand, he is a citizen of the world. His being as creature, his being as covenant man, and his being as reconciled son coinhere in Jesus Christ.

As citizen in the world, the Christian acknowledges the claim to obedience that accompanies the commandment "Thou shalt not kill," or, in its New Testament form, "Thou shalt not hate." He is driven to repentance as he confesses his own finitude and sin in relation to the law. But he lives and acts in hope and dependence, witnessing thereby to the faith that the principalities and powers behind the law are among those over whom Christ is now reigning as Lord. He realizes, further, that the redemptive work of Christ not only frees him *from* the law but also *for* a life of obedient discipleship. And this obedience includes respect for the life, family, and property of the neighbor.

The Christian recognizes the bindingness of the commandment for the statesman. He is not unmindful of the complexities and tensions involved. Indeed, he may find certain functions of the state (i.e., preparation for and execution of total war) in which he cannot participate. But insofar as it is his Christian calling to serve in a specific governmental office, the normativeness of the sixth commandment remains. Throughout, there may be the dynamic faith that the victory has been won. Christ's lordship extends over law and state no less than the church. Thus, in the confidence that the victory is Christ's, the disciple awaits and himself works toward the time when "at the name of Jesus every knee shall bow, in heaven and on earth and under the earth, and every tongue confess that Jesus Christ is Lord, to the glory of God the Father."

13. The Third Assembly of the World Council of Churches (New Delhi, India, November 19—December 3, 1961)

The third assembly of the WCC was momentous in many ways—the merging with the International Missionary Council, the adoption of an expanded doctrinal basis, and the entry of several numerically powerful Orthodox Churches including the Russian Orthodox Church—but the issue of peace was not as central as many pacifists had hoped. The message emerging from the assembly was characterized as "bloodless and fireless" and had only general reference to peace: "There is no more urgent task for Christians than to work together for community within nations and for peace with justice and freedom among them, so that the causes of much contemporary misery may be rooted out."

However, the assembly did issue an appeal to governments and peoples which spoke to the problem of war. A scholar of the WCC and peace has called this "the high-water mark in what the official mind of the ecumenical movement has said about war and peace . . . ." It is here printed in its entirety.

The sectional report on service contains a passage on disarmament, which was the subject of some behind-the-scene struggles. Several of the delegates wanted a much stronger statement condemning "production, stockpiling, and perfecting of nuclear weapons." Some adroit management by WCC staff prevailed to ensure language more acceptable to Western political circles in the final text.

Although the pacifists at New Delhi felt some frustration in the result of the assembly, they took comfort that the assembly, upon the initiative of the Division of Studies, authorized the convening of a consultation under the title "The Christian's Witness to Peace." It was recommended that the consultation be of about one week's duration and center in on the biblical and theological bases for such witness.

The New Delhi Report

SELECTIONS FROM THE REPORT OF THE SECTION ON SERVICE

International Institutions
62. Peace is dependent not only on goodwill and reconciliation, but in the first place upon the emerging of effective international institutions under the rule of law. Therefore, churches in their desire for peace must recognize the importance of the responsible use and development of international institutions, both in the United Nations and in regional affairs. The aim must be to establish a just system of world order, which provides security through the means to enforce its decisions, but the absence of a commonly agreed interpretation of law and justice, especially among the great powers, challenges the churches to explore such common ground as exists with a view to bringing them together under effective international control.

63. With respect to the policy of new and uncommitted nations in the present world struggles the churches should welcome the constructive possibilities of their mediation in the conflicts of the powers. The dangers of non-alignment may lie in the temptation to refuse responsible choice.

Disarmament
64. The recent violations of the moratorium on nuclear bomb testing have shocked the nations into a new realization of the acute danger and horror of modern warfare. Churches must protest against the accelerating arms race and the mounting terror which it portends. The First Assembly of the World Council of Churches in 1948 clearly recognized that war is contrary to the will of God. War in its newer forms is understood not only by Christians but by the general conscience of the nations as an offence against both the world of nature and the race of man, threatening annihilation and laying on mankind an unbearable burden of cost and terror. The use of indiscriminate weapons must now be condemned by the churches as an affront to the Creator and a denial of the very purpose of the Creation. Christians must refuse to place their ultimate trust in war and nuclear weapons. In this situation the churches must never cease warning governments of the dangers, and they must repudiate absolutely the growing conviction in some quarters that the use of mass destruction weapons has become inevitable. Christians must press most urgently upon their governments as a first step towards the elimination of nuclear weapons, never to get themselves into a position in which they contemplate the first use of nuclear weapons. Christians must also maintain that the use of

nuclear weapons, or other forms of major violence, against centres of population is in no circumstances reconcilable with the demands of the Christian Gospel.

65. Total disarmament is the goal, but it is a complex and long-term process in which the churches must not underestimate the importance of first steps. There may be possibilities of experimenting with limited geographical areas of controlled and inspected disarmament, of neutralizing certain zones, of devising security against surprise attack which would reduce tension, of controlling the use of outer space. The approach to disarmament needs to be both global and localized. Experts must debate techniques, but the churches should constantly stimulate governments to make real advances.

The Service of the Church in a Divided World

66. The bond of unity of the Church was vividly experienced as a fact during and after the last world war when political opponents found each other again in the fellowship of Christ. So now the very being of the ecumenical movement is a fact of incalculable value, overarching as it does in a divine fellowship all the bitter international conflicts of today. The entry of the Orthodox Church of Russia into membership of the World Council of Churches is a dramatic confirmation of our faith that God is holding his family together in spite of our human sin and perplexity and as a sign of hope to the world. The visible unity of the Church would be a service to world peace, certainly not because of any aggrandisement of ecclesiastical power, but as a testimony to mankind that in Christ the barriers are broken down.

67. Already the churches can save brethren estranged by political conflict from the neurosis and false judgments of isolation by seeking every opportunity of renewing their fellowship with them. The churches can commend and encourage further human and cultural encounters across political barriers whereby understanding is increased and the common interests of men recognized. And Christians should strive for a removal of obstacles to communication, the jamming of radio and restrictions on printed matter, which leave men deceived about one another.

68. Where possible the members of the churches should lead public opinion (and should certainly avoid merely reflecting it) in the direction of the objectives of peace and disarmament, and should as local churches and denominations organize themselves to do so effectively. Where the churches do not have power to influence events directly, they can often serve to release a body of opinion in a country, or crystallize it, which

would otherwise remain unheard because it believed itself friendless. Everywhere churches should call upon all Christians unceasingly to pray for peace, and to engage in those ministries of reconciliation and mercy which constitute creative peacemaking.

69. To fulfil these functions the churches need to ask seriously whether some of their frustration is not due to past failure to care for the public affairs of the world. There is need of a much deeper understanding of the structural aspect of political life. Christians have to transcend in a new way the ideological positions of the communities in which they live. They are in a unique position to do so.

70. Specifically Christians in all the countries of the world are called by God:

—to hold each other in brotherly concern and prayer,
—to sustain each other in witness under all circumstances,
—to affirm their fellowship, with Christians of all races and nationalities through worship, suffering, joy and service "in the unity of the Spirit."
—to show, as real brothers in Christ, their experience, convictions and all they have learned under any given political, social or economic situation. . . .

III. AN APPEAL TO ALL GOVERMENTS AND PEOPLES

The Assembly in Business Session adopted the following Appeal:

1. The Third Assembly of the World Council of Churches, at which are gathered Christians from all parts of the world, addresses this Appeal to the government and people of every nation.

2. Today, war itself is a common enemy. War is an offence to the nature of man. The future of many generations and the heritage of ages past hang in the balance. They are now easy to destroy, since the actions or miscalculations of a few can bring about a holocaust. They are harder to safeguard and advance, for that requires the dedicated action of all. Let there be restraint and self-denial in the things which make for war, patience and persistence in seeking to resolve the things which divide, and boldness and courage in grasping the things which make for peace.

3. To turn back from the road towards war into the paths of peace, all must renounce the threat of force. This calls for an end to the war of nerves, to pressures on small countries, to the rattling of bombs. It is not possible to follow at the same time policies of menace and of mutual disarmament.

4. To halt the race in arms is imperative. Complete and general disarmament is the accepted goal, and concrete steps must be taken to reach it. Meanwhile, the search for a decisive first step, such as the verified cessation of nuclear tests, should be pressed forward despite all obstacles and setbacks.

5. To substitute reason for force and undergird the will to disarm, institutions of peace and orderly methods to effect change and to settle disputes are essential. This imposes a duty to strengthen the United Nations within the framework and spirit of the Charter. All countries share this duty, whether aligned with the major power blocs or independent of them. The non-aligned can contribute through their impartiality; with others they can be champions of the principles of the Charter.

6. To build peace with justice, barriers of mutual distrust must be attacked at every level. Mutual confidence is the most precious resource in the world today: None should be wasted, more must be found. The fundamentals of an open society are essential that contacts may freely develop, person to person and people to people. Barriers to communication must go, not least where they divide peoples, churches, even families. Freedom of human contact, information, and cultural exchange is essential for the building of peace.

7. To enhance mutual trust, nations should be willing to run reasonable risks for peace. For example, an equitable basis for disarmament involves, on the one hand, an acceptance of risks in an inspection and control which cannot be foolproof, and, on the other, the danger that inspection may exceed its stated duties. Those who would break through the vicious circle of suspicion must dare to pioneer.

8. There is a great opportunity for constructive action in the struggle for world development. To share the benefits of civilization with the whole of humanity is a noble and attainable objective. To press the war against poverty, disease, exploitation, and ignorance calls for greater sacrifice and for a far greater commitment of scientific, educational, and material resources than hitherto. In this common task, let the peoples find a positive programme for peace, a moral equivalent for war.

9. A creative strategy for peace with justice requires universal recognition of the claims of humanity—of all people, whatever their status, race, sex, or creed. Lest man's new powers be used to degrade his human freedom and dignity, governments must remember that they are the servants of their citizens and respect the worth of each individual human being. The supreme achievement for a government is to enhance the dignity of man, and free him for the creative exercise of his higher powers.

10. In making this Appeal to all governments and peoples, we are con-

strained by obedience to Jesus Christ, the Lord of history, who demands righteousness and mercy and is a light unto the nations and the hearts of men. For the achievement of peace with justice, we pledge our unremitting efforts and call upon the Churches for their support in action and in prayer.

14. The Lordship of Christ Over Church and State, IV. (Oud Poelgeest, The Netherlands, July 9-14, 1962)

The last large conference in the Puidoux series was held in the summer of 1962. The theme chosen was "The Sources of Christian Social Ethics." Unlike the third conference, the format was much less heavy, with only one major lecture per day (with response) allowing more extensive discussion by the forty-two participants from ten countries present at the retreat center.

Major conference papers were published in the series Background Information for Church and Society, *issued by the Division of Studies of the WCC. In addition, excerpts from the papers and from the taped discussions were released in a thirty-four-page booklet. By conference design, "the platform was given mostly to non-pacifists, with the idea that the pacifists would then press them on what they had presented."*

An example of this occurred when John Howard Yoder, American Mennonite theologian, responded to Professor van Oyen's paper:

> I could perhaps ask Professor van Oyen what reason there would be for not requiring of every Christian in the church the rejection of war for which the Gospel calls. I can understand when you say we cannot require it of the state; but for what reason need we not require it of those who testify to the Christian faith? May we say with resignation, "This is utopia," or must we not say, "This is our task for today," to preach that the entire church today must reject war?

The response of van Oyen was:

> Yes the Church should preach that war is sin and do so more radically than she has done before. But it still belongs to the individual who is caught in the dialectic relationship between his civil citizenship and the demands of the gospel to decide what he will do. The church cannot impose her demands in the worldly way upon all her members. I would ask Yoder the counter-question, what does he mean by requir-

ing of her members that they refuse to participate in war? The church can preach this, but beyond that what can she do?

Yoder:

This question is a very good demonstration of the fact that we get back to general problems of ecclesiology which have nothing to do with war. ... In a worldly way we cannot demand anything of anyone, but the structure of Christian fellowship calls for prior commitment of individuals to whom we speak as brethren.

Following this meeting, the emphasis of the Puidoux conferences shifted to smaller meetings with a basically stable membership in the hope that the theological discussion could be strengthened and deepened.

Fundamental Problems of Evangelical Social Ethics

Hendrik van Oyen

The term "social ethics" seems to me to be not entirely acceptable, as it is not free from objection. The term presupposes a distinction between personal and social ethics. It is based on the sharp division in Lutheran doctrine between the two Kingdoms. The Gospel, however, does not seem to justify the distinction between personal and social ethics. Man, particularly when committed to Christ, is thus from the outset involved in truth and in community with his neighbour. No action of his can be excluded from this and none could be responsibly taken if it led to the detriment of man's relation to his neighbour. We realise that the task of introducing this subject today involves raising a number of fundamental problems arising from the present situation in social and political life, viewed in a Protestant perspective. But these questions must not be regarded *a priori* as involving a *petitio principii* of ideological thought, for it would not otherwise be possible to specify the assumptions underlying the distinction to which objection is raised.

I want first to survey the present debate on fundamentals regarding ethics as they refer specially to the problems of state and society, and I shall begin with the so-called "theology of society," briefly indicate its background, and then turn to the various lines of thought which nowadays are tending to take its place: (a) one tendency towards a personalising of the present era; and (b) another towards tackling the problems on the basis of the concrete worldliness of the history of Jesus Christ. This expository part is followed by a brief *apercu* of how I see the encounter between the message of Jesus Christ and the social situation which I want to illustrate with a number of examples, concerning property and the state.

Ecumenical Ethic of the Responsible Society

It has been rightly pointed out that the W.C.C. theology of the "responsible society" has evolved out of the theory of natural law which subsequently developed along Christian lines. It has been observed that Oldham's formula had great significance as a Christian battlecry after the terrible destruction of all values by the Second World War, and that his programme (as in the case of the great ideologies) seemed to presuppose a quite specific and clearly defined theory, the very programme of the Christian Church and of Christianity itself. At the same time it carefully kept in view the elements of such a programme that was shared with the non-Christian world. At Amsterdam the concept of the "responsible society" was defined as follows: "A responsible society is one where freedom is the freedom of men who acknowledge responsibility to justice and public order, and where those who hold political authority or economic power are responsible for its exercise to God and the people whose welfare is affected by it."

It should be observed that the formula "responsibility in Christian freedom" is entirely composed of the concepts of freedom, public order and responsibility which spring from the natural law. The ideological nature of this structure was attenuated at Evanston, where first it was pointed out that the "responsible society" was not an alternative social or political system. It was more cautiously described as a criterion "for the assessment of all existing social orders," and then in the same breath this criterion was termed a "guiding principle" indicating the "specific decisions which we have to take." Then was added: "Christians are called upon to lead a responsible life, as God's redeeming act in Christ demands, and *that* under any order of society, even when the social structure is utterly unfavourable."

The difference between these formulae and the Amsterdam definition is certainly remarkable. There has been a flight away from an ideology, in which society is given a special churchly basis towards a whole series of criteria for testing the social structure, in which Christians must set a good example because of the responsibility placed upon them as a result of the redemption brought about in Christ. Nevertheless, the main ideas are still as follows: freedom, responsibility, criterion, *ordo* (both in the form of society and state). They form the coordinates of a Christian humanism which diverges from the Catholic Thomist doctrine of natural law to the extent that "the responsible society" still takes account of historical form and the fact that its realisation has been corrupted through sin. In the theory of natural law as conceived by the Thomists, there is available an intact, organic world order *(ordo)* which constitutes the valid system of human society at all times, and which merely needs to be slightly modified from time to time in order to meet all the relevant demands of history. However, one of the leading collaborators of the World Council of Churches, Professor Wendland, expresses the following view:

> Protestant social doctrine can only apply a very critical and realistic concept of natural law, on the one hand discerning and recognising the demand of man in society for order, justice, freedom and for mutual rights and responsibilities, and his efforts to attain them; on the other hand ruthlessly showing up the social dimension of his enmity with God, his "social sin," i.e., injustice, harshness, lust for power and possessions, because these defects poison and destroy the mutual interdependence of mankind as originally created by God. (H. D. Wendland, *Botschaft an die soziale Welt,* 1959, p.169)

Here, then, is where the dividing line would in the first instance be drawn between the Thomists and "Christian natural law." Instead of speaking of natural law, we should therefore speak of the law of God, because Christian social ethics are concerned with the maintenance of the eschatological orientation of the divine order. Here too it is assumed that there are specific institutions established by God, such as marriage, the state, work, and so on. These constitute the basis for God's maintenance of this world, and the cornerstones of the social edifice (*Ibid.,* p. 135.) for which the eschatological and "heilsgeschichtliche" finality of these divine ordinances is "of decisive importance." The *telos* of the institutions (according to this view) is to be distinguished from their historical realisation and perversion thus becoming "daemonic" within their own autonomous realms, by a listening to the Word of God, the word which creates and orders their existence—a listening which stems from Christ and draws its life from him, and which is called (as critical love in thought and action) to assess what forms institutions should be given if they are to serve and preserve man in his shared humanity.

Christian natural law, therefore, is concerned with the critical scrutiny and modification of the constitutions of any particular institutions, so that man is not subjugated and deformed by them.

These remarks give an outline of the theology of society which has gradually grown up round the slogan of "the responsible society." This theology is not derived from the Lutheran basis of such German theology, for there, apart from a number of major social impulses which have their roots in pietism (Wichern, Fliedner, Bodelschwingh, Naumann), a scepticism regarding a Christian-social theory was especially marked (Troeltsch, Naumann, and now Dombois). Social questions, in Germany, are regarded as a matter for home missions and for charitable institutions. In the Anglo-Saxon countries, on the other hand, the Social Gospel Movement, the Christian Social Union and the Conference on Christian Politics, Economics and Citizenship (COPEC) were the significant precursors not only of Stockholm and Edinburgh but of all the recent trends in Germany and other countries, as regards the basic problems of Christian social teachings, right up to the Assembly at New Delhi.

In this Anglo-Saxon Christian trend, two basic currents converged. On the one hand there was the Calvinistic ideal of the rule of the Kingdom of God over the whole creation, and on the other the claim of natural law (derived from antiquity) as a cosmic order of life, in other words, the ideal of reason. In the Anglo-Saxon countries it was possible for a Christian social movement to evolve which derived the idea of natural progress from a materialistic belief in salvation ("We must criticise and modify the orders which have become diseased") (*Ibid.,* p. 136.) and also the idea of a Christian-humanist shaping of society, of human rights, self-government, loyalty and adjustment, and the growth of faith through freedom and responsibility exercised in concrete action. As Peabody puts it: "Religion is the way which leads from decision to insight, from duty to vision, from obedience to faith." (F. G. Peabody, *The Approach to the Social Question,* 1912, p. 177.) The personality does not discover faith except in taking decisions and acting. Faith is developed *ex opere operando,* i.e., in the act itself. And this faith is Christian because it is common to all mankind and is universally valid. What is Christian is also truly human and where the individual attains religious maturity through action genuine community is created at the same time. Maladjustment is a depersonalised form of society; that is sin. It can be overcome by the correct integration of man into all the institutions of society, once he has become aware of his responsibility. As is well known, in the Social Gospel opinions differed as regards the extent of this sin. Is it merely the apathy of the individual or is there a supernatural daemonic kingdom of evil incarnate in the capitalist-imperialist system? We do not think we are exaggerating when we say that the tensions in this sphere in the Anglo-Saxon world at the turn of the century are now, via the World Council of Churches and the theology of society, emerging on similar lines in the latest German theology, although it cannot be assumed that the writers in question have a thorough knowledge of the earlier discussions.

If we ask what social aim is in view here, it is clearly summed up in the formula "worldly Christianity." This means that institutions such as the family, the home, the authorities and the schools should form nuclei of orders which serve the world. "Christianity in the world is both the starting point and the path of the proclamation of the Gospel evangelism in to the world." (Wendland, *op cit.,* p. 32.) The Church has at its disposal a whole series of advanced strong points such as Evangelical Academies, workers' groups, men's groups, rural and youth work, a whole series of charitable institutions which can be the spearhead of missionary influence and thus break up and modify the arbitrariness and autonomy of the secular spheres. The categories of world, society and institution offer opportunities of fundamental importance for missionary work. The Kingdom of God includes them both protologically and eschatologically. What God has preordained in creation is action which will one day bring about the universal End in the eschatological consummation of the dominion of Christ over all things, and *this* despite sin which has split up and daemonised the world in the face of God. During the time between its creation and its final salvation, the world is open to the impact of preaching and action based on the Christian message. The world is neither utterly corrupt nor utterly sound and intact. It lies in a twilight area, and therefore constitutes material, varying according to the historical situation, which is capable of being shaped and transformed. Although perverted, daemonised and distorted, God's commands nevertheless contain the elements which (in accordance with the three mandates of polis, marriage and work) can be restored by worldly Christianity, by Christian humanism.

It will be observed that here too the perspective (already noted in the Social Gospel) of the inner capacity for change inherent in the various spheres of society depends on right action being undertaken by men. The given situation can be interpreted as the God-given chance which is there waiting for the Christian, or the Church, to seize it and to direct it eschatologically towards the Rule of Christ.

Influence of Existentialist Theology on Social Ethics

In this connection recent ethical discussions are tending strongly to stress the fact that institutions are capable of being reformed. I should like to mention very briefly a few of the stages of this trend.

The Christian way of life is conceived, on the basis of the Sermon on the Mount, as springing entirely from personal effort and personal responsibility (in the works of Dietrich von Oppen, *Das personale Zeitalter,* 1960). As opposed to the marked emphasis on institutional, legal and sacral elements in earlier times, the modern world is characterised by a high degree of mobility and elasticity between persons and institutions. The personal orientation of society owes its origin to the influence of the Gospel:

(a) the Christian Church freed the orders existing at the time of its origin from their magic and sacral status;

(b) it directed their gaze towards the future, and away from the past;

(c) it insisted, in secular life, on the equality of all its members before God (the Communion);

(d) in its awareness of its mission, it set the world before an open horizon, the world which had originally been dominated by awareness of limitation, immobility and cohesion (i.e., institutionalism);

(e) it gave the world a glimmering of a base which lay outside the traditional class structure; as a result, society was torn apart, and everyone stood before God as an individual. (D. von Oppen, "Strukturfragen der christlichen Gemeinde in der mobilen Welt," *ZEE,* 1961, p.293 ff.)

These five are symptoms of the present realities of the social structure but also secularised elements of the Christian community. We cannot speak of a new world as being primarily an industrialised world, but as a personal society implying a personal revolution. For this reason the traditional forms of institutions give way to personal forms of organised collective life—the firm, the cooperative, the association,—all these depend on their remaining open and flexible. (D. von Oppen, *Das personale Zeitalter,* 1960, p. 53.) It is a person who is responsible for running and directing the organisation, and partnership develops from the mutual responsibility of the various people involved. The nucleus of this partnership is to be found in the first place in the family, which is no longer regarded as an unchangeable institution, but as an extremely mobile and flexible group, i.e., an "organized partnership." It will be observed that von Oppen tries to break down the autonomy of institutions into personal action. The category of *person* is of central importance, and is the key factor in the whole, since it is demonstrably a genuinely biblical category, as is clear from the Sermon on the Mount. For the basis of this analysis is the assumption that in the person of Christ man appeared as a person in all his purity, and as men imitate and follow him the traditional, autonomous institutions are transformed into personal forms of organised partnership. The "orders" are planned so as to encourage this personal development. As von Oppen says: "The historical effects are such that the world has assumed forms which constantly point towards the pure *person,* not only as a distant impetus centuries back, but at the present time. (*Ibid.*, p. 214.)What we thus have is a personalistic existentialist orientation of instutionalism coexisting in time with Christ, as a pattern of pure partnership. The historical element in this form has become irrelevant. Demythologisation develops the Christian concept of a reality which is visibly growing towards the realisation of the real Person. The reality in which we live, precisely because it is free and has broken away from accepted and traditional values, is moving towards the shape of the Future.

Behind von Oppen lies a whole row of names centering round Eberhard Grisebach, Rudolf Bultmann and Friedrich Gogarten. Behind them all stands the philosophical influence of Martin Heidegger. An explicit ethical system was provided by Knud Lögstrup. I would like to summarise the position here too very briefly. As far back as Grisebach, an attempt was made (in his ethics) to unmask all institutions, all autonomous forces of an ideological and traditional nature, in order to clear the way to freedom for man as a genuine, acting being. This liberation consists in the transcending of one's self in one's neighbour. Only through the real impact of debate can the institutional element arrive at an understanding of social values. This line of thought is taken a stage further by Friedrich Gogarten in his talk of "the sonship of man." Here lies the secret of how to deal with secular factors, for thanks to our sonship we no longer stand helpless like an immature child when confronted with the powers and principalities of the institutional, but—through irreproachable and sound secularisation— man (now "of age" and acting on his own responsibility) has assumed responsibility for the world and for its transformation into the future that God provides.

Thus man, as he attains his authentic being through action, overcomes inauthenticity of the historical and of secularism by loving his neighbour and by rediscovering his faith in the justification of the sinner.

This tendency, to define the Christian ethos in wholly worldly terms, becomes the existence of living-with-and-for-one's neighbour in Ebeling and Lögstrup, both under the influence of the philosophy of Heidegger. Ebeling denounces as cowardice and self-deception the belief that we have to think in terms of divine commands. He quotes a saying of Hermann's: "Morality is poisoned at the root as soon as an idea (one, admittedly, which is sacred to all pious men) is made the basis of moral conviction, i.e., the idea that the moral imperative is the command of God." (G. Ebeling, "Die Evidenz des Ethischen und die Theologie," *ZThK,* 1960, p.318 ff.) This is characteristic of the anthropological-ontological basing of ethics in the person, an attitude which is markedly stronger in Lögstrup, who dissolves Christian ethics as such into a general ethic of trust and self-surrender to other men, and taking care of them. The so-called social norms of institutions, on the contrary, are constantly changing, and are subject to assessment according to each particular situation, their validity being questioned at every point in history. Opposed to this is the silent but radical demand for self-surrender to others; which the whole social range of moral, legal and conventional obligations tries to obscure and avoid. On the one hand we have received the divine gift of life, with its radical demand; on the other we are constantly in revolt in our social practices against this demand. Our nature demands that we should take care of our neighbour, but at the same time we are constantly revolting against this obligation.

Social Ethics in the Theology of Barth

With the above remarks we have come in touch with a developing discussion that threatens to dissolve the whole social problem into the existential interpretation of the Person as an anthropological factor of creation (the "gift of life"). In this we have arrived at the subjective pole of the tensions referred to above, where can be no further question of a Christian or a Protestant ethic with its own answers. Existence finds in the interpretation of its own being the imperativies profoundly concealed in Being itself.

A procedure which is similar in structure to that of Lögstrup, but which has a completely opposite starting point, is to be found in the ethics of Karl Barth and his disciples. According to Barth, there radiate into reality from the centre of God's Word in Jesus Christ, in concentric circles round this Word, the pointers of the Church's proclamation. However little Lögstrup might have been concerned about the reality of the social structure involved in this, Karl Barth is equally reserved; he conceives of the Word as having a bearing on a concrete situation (thereby avoiding generalisations based on natural law), but does not allow the social facts to decide how the Word is to be directed. For him there is only one reality—the Word of God, which includes God who commands and man who acts. "If we have listened to the Word of God, it must be clear to us that the reality in which the ethical event takes place (as revealed in the Word of God) is no other than its own reality which we do not have to seek and to find, but only to discern it as it is vouchsafed to us in and with this event itself." (K. Barth, *Kirchliche Dogmatik,* III/4, 1951, p. 29.) The history of the Word of God in creation, atonement and redemption is the basic reality, which assumes concrete form in Jesus Christ, and from which every ethical event derives its shape. Barth completely rejects the idea that man can independently discover, construct or define reality. He asks both Brunner and Bonhoeffer how they imagine they know anything about mandates and "orders"—and why Bonhoeffer specifically refers to *four;* why these four and no others? (W. Schweitzer, "Die menschliche Wirklichkeit in soziologischer und sozialethisch theologischer Sicht," *ZEE,* 1959, p. 193 ff.) Of course Barth must sooner or later deal with these "orders" or relationships, but for him they do not represent a reality to be seen alongside the reality of the Word of God. Barth regards reality not from the point of view of protology (the existential method) but from the point of view of the *Eschaton*—the fulfilment of Time. This too means that the institutions, with their autonomous values, are as it were, dissolved. W. D. Marsch speaks of a profound hostility towards institutions on the part of Barth, in his eschatological ethics. "His ethics threaten to exhaust themselves in critical references, in an ecstatic dissolution of standards and in breathless hostility to tradition." (W. D. Marsch, "Christologische Begründung des Rechts?" *Ev. Th.,* 1957, p. 145 ff.) In Barth the concept of the *analogia fidei* constitutes the method which integrates everything; the Word of God in Jesus Christ constitutes the *concretissimum* of history which, by analogy, supports human existence through grace. All the social structures are to be understood in relation to the existence of Jesus Christ. They are rooted in that, and can only be conceived as the result of that grace. The different fields of social life are related to the divine Event. They only achieve significance if they are regarded from the perspective of *Heilsgeschichte,* of God's Covenant with man.

We have now reached the point where a completely different discussion is opened up by the objectivity of the Word of God, which once became flesh in Christ and which will ultimately be consummated as the true Reality—carried over into the material realms of human life which are only "real" if they are integrated into the *Heilsgeschichte* of which Christ is the focal-point. Otherwise they are only "phenomena" whose significance is undeniable but which are theologically irrelevant. Admittedly, any talk about "phenomena" arouses suspicion. It shows that the reins of the system have been too tightly drawn. The basic problems of social ethics cannot be solved apart from God's concrete act of salvation in Christ. As Marsch observes:

> It is not possible for a neutral observer to determine what constitutes the continuity or binding force of such institutions. It is not the task of theology to catalogue the characteristics of institutions." (*Ibid.,* p. 169.)

True, Barth then tackles specific continuous forms of mutual responsibility such as marriage, work and so on which take on varying institutional characters, as expressions of the divine command of partnership; these need not be confined to traditional forms (such as monogamy). In particular, it is in the category of law that Barth feels that mutual responsibility becomes institutionalized, through the law of God which in justification shows itself as bringing order and shape into human life. What is real is grace, but it is also rational. Even more markedly than in the case of Wendland, God's law (Christian natural law) is conceived of by Barth as action which constantly becomes Event through belief in Christ.

In this connection we have specially in mind Karl Barth's semi-Christological analysis of the basis of the State, in which, to be sure, authority is again fully integrated as *ordinatio Dei* into the particular situation at any given time, but where Barth emphatically asserts that the fact of "authority" is a law of God's grace, because it is a principle bringing order into reality.

Hans Dombois' great work *Das Recht der Gnade* ("*The Law of Grace,*" 1961) is closely related to Barth's theory of the Word of God, but also strongly influenced by the sacramentalist theology of van der Leeuws. Dombois takes a further step in the dissolution of the ethical problem of institutionalism. If I am not mistaken, Dombois is evolving in a direction which ascribes to the sacramental aspect of justification everything which Barth accepts as ethical guidance, as a divine command to act rightly. Dombois strips institutions of their ethical content, by integrating the different fields of actual life into the *Heilsgeschichte;* he does this even more consistently than Barth does. Dombois has distinguished himself by the pains he has taken to ascertain the contents and the definition of institutions *in status* and *actus,* and has shown their non-adoptedness by bringing out the integrationist structure of their basic motives. (An institution is like a house; it must be occupied, otherwise it will decay). He points out the nature of law as a form of faithfulness on the one hand, and of grace on the other, deliberately rejecting a positivist interpretation of institutionalism, as well as a metaphysical-idealistic one. Yet we cannot help feeling that, through a complete sacramentalisation of institutions based on the concept of grace, the missionary message and its appeal to the world are impoverished. The existential factor in Dombois' case is no longer to be found in language as with Ebeling and Løgstrup, but in the law of God's grace, which explains and shapes reality and the world from this preexistent datum. The relation between the Gospel and the world would thus be the geometrical figure advocated by Barth: the concentric circles of the different spheres of reality centred in the Word of God. On the other hand, it seems to us that the figure of an *elipse* would be more appropriate if we try to translate into geometrical terms the tension between the Gospel and concrete reality, as Dombois has already suggested.

Social Ethics in the Bible

André Dumas

I will begin by making three preliminary observations:

(1) This conference brings together the traditional and contemporary thinking of two rather different types of church: (a) churches which, within the Reformation, inherited the notion of Christendom and adapted themselves to it in their attempt to be a national Church. This global vision of a society established under the rule of God made them inclined to draw inspiration from the ethico-social regime of the Old Testament, particularly in Calvinism; (b) the Church which was a minority church from the outset, as much from historical situation as from religious conviction. These minority communities tended to emphasize the new regime set up by the New Testament, where the invisible ecclesia no longer coincides with the visible dimensions of the nation amidst which Christians "camp" as strangers and sojourners. From the beginning, what were later known as the right and left wings of the Reformation thus leant upon the diversely interpreted authorities of the Old and the New Testament for examples for the life of the contemporary Church. (The presence with us here of Russian Orthodox and Baptists should enable us to find certain analogies with this double current in the Western Reformation, in Eastern religious history.)

(2) Our meeting forms part of a continuing research into the importance attributed by exegesis and by ecclesiastical practice to certain classic passages of Biblical ethics, for example the understanding of the state in Romans 13 as revived by the work of Strobel, Käsemann, Wolf, Lasserre, etc. The Bible, in Dodd's phrase, is a "pluralist universe." Why then have certain texts been privileged in their ethical application? Has this privilege been favourable to true understanding or has it instead congealed or warped it? Why, for example, do we traditionally rely more on Ephesians 5 than on Corinthians 7 in connection with the doctrine of marriage? Here is the second type of question centred on the history of exegesis as a concentrated reflection of the history of Christian ethics, which I should like to follow up.

(3) An ethic implies concrete choices, or more exactly it thematizes intellectually the contest of events which have already happened and of which it is more true to say that they give birth to it than that it ideally shapes them. Just as Jesus Christ was the Word in his being, in his doing and not only in his speaking, so the Christian ethic makes explicit analytically the engagement of life in faith and obedience. In describing the meaning of the forms of the social ethic in the Bible I seek not so much to establish the abstract norms, as could an idealist philosophy which holds out an absolute as the purpose of life, as to bring out the meaning, already lived and still to be better lived, of successive and constant incarnations of the presence of Jesus Christ in the life of his Church.

My research is thus directed by the historical existence of ethical traditions, by the relevance of certain biblical passages, and by an exhortation born of an analysis which nourishes it.

I. *Difficulties of the transition from the Bible to an ethical system*

There is difficulty in proceeding from Biblical pointers to a social ethic related to the modern world. This difficulty appears sometimes so great that an outside observer may think it impossible to surmount. Thus the leftist Italian writer Elio Vittorini has written, "One can see how it is possible to work out a patriarchal moral system suited to the Middle Ages starting from the Bible, or even an individualistic moral code corresponding to the bourgeois and protestant Renaissance. But it is on the other hand rather difficult to see how the Bible could be the source of a new moral system for our time, that would be neither feudal nor bourgeois."

And indeed sometimes we are in danger of repeating, although using more profane and contemporary language, such typically biblical ideas as substitution, covenant, justification, but in this case it is often an exposition of biblical theology rather than a search for an ethic for today. At other times, even when we use a Christian vocabulary we are in danger of adopting a purely humanistic view of society: for example, is the idea of a "responsible society" familiar to ecumenical ears, an alternative based upon God's exhortation to social disorder or is it the expression of a balance of power between capitalist *laisser-faire* and socialist planning, a sort of "balanced economy" seeking to conciliate individual initiative and the security of the social organism?

In the former case we are reproducing a biblical perspective which remains in opposition to our society, that is alien to its development. In the second case we make the most intelligent possible reading of our situation. We live it from within, but in this case it is the witness of the Bible which seems to be an addition made when all the elements of appreciation have already been given. One can look to it for confirmation or even correction but not for guiding inspiration.

To escape from this rapidly outlined alternative of extrinsic repetition or unessential addition, I think we need to look in the Bible itself for the transition from God's exhortation to social expression which causes difficulty for us today; in other words to understand that it is impossible for us to formulate our question as "from the Bible to the modern world" (which was the title of the conference in London and at Bossey in 1946 and 1947 in preparation for Amsterdam), but as "the relationship between God and society in the Bible and the possible modern form of that relationship."

The Bible comprises both the setting in motion of the world by God, the constituent revelation, the initial kernel of the Creeds (for example, the exodus from Egypt for the Old Testament, according to von Rad, the Lordship of Jesus Christ the vanquisher of death and of powers for the New Testament according to Cullman) and the response, inclusive or erroneous, obedient or rebellious, of man to this challenge from God. The "foundation" is laid and everyone builds his "work" on this foundation as St. Paul says in 1 Cor. 3:11-19. The Bible contains not only the divine attestation of the foundation, the self-revelation of God, but also the account of the works of the people of God in response to this initiative. It would then in many respects be more accurate and enlightening to say not: "the Bible is the word of God" but "the Bible is the story of God's covenant with man, including the reactions and interpretations of this man." The Bible is God's command with its human echo. It must at once be added that this formulation entails no differences of value, for God makes use both of events which he directs and of interpretations which he causes in order to reveal himself. But such a definition of the Bible has the great advantage of firmly including the human subject in witness to the Word of God, which is not only Word to man but Word with man. In this connection one might say that the error of fundamentalism is not its search for immediacy between the Bible and ourselves, but its misunderstanding of the non-fundamentalist character of the Bible itself from the very start. The Bible is not like an egg, smooth, impenetrable, the egg of total revelation, but much more like an onion, the responses of man constituting the successive skins engendered by the initial seed of God's interventions. The interaction of these constituent events and of the human interpretations constitutes the movement in the Bible from God to man and from man to God.

Four quick biblical examples will make these affirmations more concrete:

(1) The priestly account of creation in Genesis 1 insists upon the

creative initiative of God, the covenant, the "diatheke" which he establishes towards man. According to this priestly tradition God speaks and acts without man explicitly responding to the great foundation acts of God, whether it be the creation, or the covenants with Noah, Abraham or later Moses. As Zimmerli points out, in this source we have to wait until Genesis 17:17 to hear of a human reaction, (Abraham's inward laughter at the announcement of his future paternity). On the other hand, the Jehovist story of the creation in Genesis 2 stresses the consultation, the questioning, the approval and the exclamation of the human partner of the covenant, of the "syntheke" established with man. For this reason in this story the man is in the first place created alone, before the woman and without her, in order that he shall be obliged to express an opinion himself upon the merit of the creation of humanity in two sexes as affirmed in Genesis 1. From Genesis 2:23 the man reacts to the divine initiative with his cry of wonder: "This at last is bone of my bones and flesh of my flesh."

(2) The whole of prophecy between 760 and 530 consists of the double interpretation, anterior, full of judgment, and concomitant or consecutive, full of promises, which the prophets make of the central divine event: God leads back his captive people. As Amos 3:7 says, God acts and God reveals the secret of this action to his servants the prophets. Here also then is divine foundation and human consultation, interpretation and reaction.

(3) The New Testament is no different in composition, deliberately including as it does the event of Jesus Christ and the understanding, the realization which followed. Therefrom on the part of the first community until the Gospel having been proved in its universalism, from Jerusalem to Rome, the book of the Acts stops abruptly without even telling us what finally became of St. Paul.

(4) In a general way the historic discontinuity of the Bible, which comprises at least the two great silent periods of the exile in Egypt and the centuries which preceded the coming of the Messiah, makes one attend to the interpretive existence of man at the heart of the biblical whole. Witnesses live the Word of God in between the founding Words of God. The Bible is made up of the combination of these acts of God, of the human reactions to them, and I shall add, paradoxically, of the silences which separate them.

Our question is thus to be found in the Bible itself, (far from following the setting up of a canon) formulated around a purely divine given: How are we to pass from the order of God to the constitution of a social ethic? We have an ethic engendered through the call of God in the Bible and not an ultimately insurmountable opposition between a Bible, the Word of God only, and an ethic, a later attempt on the part of man to make the world conform to him. The Bible is not only the source but the current, too. The Bible is not externally normative for the church, as though the church were absent from the inside of the Bible. On the contrary, the church in the sense of a people seeking to listen and to obey is engendered with and through the Bible just as the Bible only comes into being for this people and through them. The Bible is thus both foundation and norm of the Church in as much as this Bible already contains the Church which it brings into existence. Barth, who does not always seem to me to have insisted sufficiently upon the intrabiblical presence of the human response, well expresses this inclusive relationship when he writes: "The relationship which effectively exists between the Bible and the Church is founded within itself. It can easily be described, but no argument can demonstrate it. For this relationship is comparable with that which exists between a mother and her child. It has no other foundation than the fact that a certain mother is the mother of a certain child." If the transition from God's order to human realization is thus established and sought in the Bible itself and not later, then two big questions still remain: (1) How can we characterize this transition or these transitions within the Biblical evidence? How can we analytically pick out their meaning starting from the synthetic whole which is available to us? (2) How can we relay this movement in a manner appropriate for our time? How can we rediscover by analogy with the Biblical currents flowing from God to man and from man to God, a perceptible and persuasive pronouncement for contemporary society, which is also invited to live the reality of the covenent between God and the world, but which must ever return for guidance on this point to the times in history when this covenant had prophets and apostles to expound it in a visible Word?

These two questions will dictate the two parts which follow:

(1) The discoverable direction of the move towards social ethics in biblical Testimony.

(2) The bearing of this upon our situation.

II. *The sense of the double Old and New Testament form of social ethics in the Bible*

If certain churches have found an easy kinship with the terrestrial extent of society established by God in the Old Testament, if other churches on the other hand have found easy relationship with the supreme moment of the rupture foretold by the New Testament, it is important that, when these different traditions meet, they should make clear to each other the importance of their almost instinctive kinship with this or that part of the biblical testimony. It is all the more important if we believe that these two forms, in many respects very different, have a significance which for us is permanent, in a word, if we believe, also ethically, that the church is built upon the foundation of the apostles and prophets, Christ Jesus himself being the chief cornerstone (Eph. 2:20). (Note: I take prophets here in the Old Testament sense in spite of Eph. 3:5 which speaks of "apostles and prophets" in the New Testament sense; Kittel, K. L. Schmidt, Rengstorf believe in the Old Testament meaning in Eph. 2:20.)

I set out then from the hypothesis of a constant relevance of these two forms of an act of God and a response from his people for the Christian moral system, of (no?) radical advance by the New Testament upon the status of the Old Testament such as would make it simply the story of an abolished stage, even a condemned example. But I must specify the exact field in which I believe this significance to be permanent so as not to lead to confusion at the outset.

I am not thinking of the actual content of the ethic. The two covenants are often contrasted at this point: The Old Testament would be the evidence of the law, of human obedience faced with the radical alternative, the yes or the no of works which will expose man without redress to blessing or cursing: "You are witnesses against yourselves that you have chosen the Lord to serve him" (Josh. 24:22 or Deut. 30). In this sense the chosen people is a nation of people separated from sin, etymologically Pharisees. The New Testament on the contrary would be the witness of grace, of the yes of God's forgiveness responding to the no of man's sin, of the non-alternative but irreversible way which leads always from the cross to the Resurrection. In this sense the holy people is a nation of forgiven sinners. There is thus a radical opposition between the two acts of God and the two responses of man.

I do not believe in the permanent significance of that duality, for a major reason: this duality itself is not biblically founded. According to the Old Testament it is the whole of Israel that is a sinful people, chosen by the pure grace of the love of God, as one sees in the oldest creeds on the meaning of the provocation of Israel to existence by God: "Your Father was an Amosite and your Mother a Hittite" (Deut. 25:5, 7:7, Ezek. 16:3, 45). Israel was raised up by grace and not by works. St. Paul recalls this when he underlines the fact that Abraham preceded Moses by 430 years (Gal. 3:17). At the heart of the Old Testament as of the New is to be found the love of God and the love of one's neighbour: Leviticus 19:18 teaches long before the Sermon on the Mount "you shall love your neighbour as yourself."

Conversely, the New Testament in its turn contains calls to obedience accompanied by threats, if God's command is mocked. The story of Ananias in Acts 5 is not so different from that of Achan in Joshua 7. Certainly, there are differences of emphasis between the two covenants but not a radical duality of content which could have any permanent significance for us, since the content of grace is everywhere primary and the consequence of disobedience is equally serious everywhere.

Having relativized this first possibility of significant duality I should equally like to relativize a second which is just as frequently mentioned. According to this opinion the Old Testament had an ethic of visibility. Circumcision, a sacrament inscribed in the flesh, was considered to constitute the nation-church whose apogee upon earth was manifested by the territorial and temporal Kingdom of David. This governmental theocracy concentrated on the King, upheld by the prophet, would be the Old Testament ideal. On the other hand, the New Testament would be held to proclaim the Kingdom of the Son of David which does not come from this world and does not establish itself in this world in a way which is clearly visible. The supreme day of the coming of this Kingdom is not the entry into Jerusalem, David's capital, on Palm Sunday, but the nailing to the cross outside the city gates of the King veiled from glory. Baptism, the invisible sacrament of water and of the spirit, is the sign of the Church, a mystery hidden with Christ in God and only accessible to faith.

Of course, here also the distinctions between the two Testaments are important, but not to the extent of providing a convincing permanent and above all significant duality for our present-day Christian ethics. Indeed the whole of the Old Testament is a struggle against the confusion between the assurance and the visibility of election. David is not the King of established power that these caricatures of Messianic Kingship who preceded and followed him, Saul, Absalom and Solomon, wanted to be. David is already, like Jesus later, the King of grace in weakness of self-effacement. Not all the sons of Abraham in the flesh are automatically so in the Spirit. And conversely the New Testament also aims at the visibility of the Church, when the secret charismata given by God are established in public ministries, when the Church bears in the world or earth the external marks of her calling. In this sense the Old Testament is not only the book of institutions and the New Testament only the testimony of the heart.

It is in a third place that I shall find a permanent and significant duality between the ethics of the Old and the New Testament: This is in their respective stages, on condition that attention is paid to the inherent movement of the ethics which correspond with each.

I will explain: the Old Testament speaks in duration (time). It is the book of genealogical inheritance, or, as Bonhoeffer writes, of the terrestrial and penultimate realities. It is the account of the history of life here below without either resurrection for life beyond where the real encounter with

God could take place. It offers no afterlife wherein man can live out his redemption since upon this earth, in its duration, its memory and its expectations blessing and cursing are fully unfolded. For this reason the ethical system of the Old Testament is related to the importance of its institutions: family descent, the ownership of the land, the regime of power, the priestly organization of religion, in a word, incarnation in history.

In complete contrast the New Testament speaks in the instant of fulfilment. It is the book of the last days and the ultimate realities of eschatology without genealogies. It carries history to the end of its judgement, always accomplished and always imminent. Also the New Testament culminates in this irruption of the beyond into the here and now which is the Resurrection. It is thus logical that New Testament ethics should at first approach appear so detached from and indifferent to the provisional which still subsists and is so full of passion for the end which is coming soon.

This third opposition between the two covenants is radical and substantial and, as we shall see, carries a permanent significance. Indeed, if dogmatically we cannot know the Jesus proclaimed by the New Testament if we leave out the Christ awaited by the Old Testament, so ethically we cannot listen to the eschatological New Testament appeal without living through the historical incarnation of the Old Testament.

But let us be attentive to the major movements, at first sight paradoxical, which these two widely different periods set in motion from the ethical point of view. We are here at the often misunderstood centre of the significant duality of the two Old and New Testament social ethics.

In fact the Old Testament, since it is the time of historical duration, contains an ethic of disestablishment, of itineracy, of defensiveness against all the temptations of majority christendom. Israel is the people born of the *Passover* of the Paschal feast, in covenant with God in the Sinai wilderness, warned of the deadening effect of Canaan, brought in captivity to Babylon. As soon as it establishes itself in a Kingdom which is autonomous and in proportion to its duration, God overthrows it and reminds it of its vocation as a Hebrew *(ivri)* or wanderer. The institutions of the whole Old Testament aim at correcting acumulations which are a source of temptation, whether of power, of land, of priority of birth, or of national or religious pride. Their profound effect is not to establish but to keep on the move a society which aspires to transform Canaan into a new Egypt, tranquillizing and enslaving. Israel does not live in his own home, in the land of his personal conquest, but with God in the land given through the grace of the liberator. "You are strangers and sojourners with me" (Lev. 25:23). This is why the Old Testament theocracy always has revolutionary tones. It attacks slavery as only those do who still remember that they have been slaves themselves. It is not necessary to resort to the later prophetic traditions to find this tone. The ancient historic traditions equally contain it, those which describe the wanderings of the patriarchs: Abraham dispossessed by Lot, Isaac coming late after Israel, Jacob despoiled by Laban, fearful in the presence of Esau, astonished at the deliverance from the Red Sea and celebrating David rescued in his troubles. It is the whole Old Testament, its historic side turned towards the memory of Exodus and its prophetic side turned towards the Messianic expectations of the New Creation, which uproots society from all sacralized conservatism.

The New Testament in fact presents us with a precisely opposite social ethic. In the phase of imminent eschatology it upholds adherence to and respect for the already established authorities. It warns against the temptations of a minority pietism. It turns man towards daily work, to tolerance towards his neighbour, towards the acceptance of institutions and to intercession on their behalf. It secures the believer who is always tempted to project himself into the beyond. In this sense it is conservative, but in the name of this ethical paradox which from eschatology deduces insertion into the human universal. Examples would abound to attest that this perspective is that of the whole New Testament and not only of some Pauline exhortations to citizens, slaves, women, or children. It is even true that it is on this essential point that primitive Christianity is neither an ascetic nor an idealistic stoicism, nor as Nietzsche affirmed the "platonism of the people." Since final salvation is even approaching, as Romans 13:11-12 says, "It is full time now for you to wake from sleep. For salvation is nearer to us now than when we first believed." We must attach ourselves to the specialist ministries of the Church (Rom. 12:3-8)), to the diversified love of our neighbour (12:9-21), to the characteristic multiple functions of the impersonality of political power (13:1-7). Hence the constant reminder of human universality in the midst of which, with which, and for which the Christian community exists (the "all men" of 1 Tim. 2:1, 4; Titus 3:4; 1 Peter 2:17, etc.). The New Testament distinction between the sect and the Church is not of the minority-majority order, nor institution-charisma, but rather thought of, or neglect of, human universality on the double, soteriological and political plane. We must attach ourselves to the present stay in the situation (1 Cor. 7:6), adhere to the institutional, to the universal, indeed to the social "conventions," simply because they are the present reality in which to live and bear witness to eschatological faith. The New Testament as a whole is an ethical exhortation to memberships of, or, we might even say, insertion into, social conservatism.

If this is a true view, the Bible contains two types of social ethic opposed neither in their content of grace nor in the invisibility of faith, but in respect of the characteristic stage of the church-world relationship. The Old Testament is revolutionary within an established Christendom. Its prophecy is especially that of opposition. In contrast the New Testament exhorts a separated and suspected minority to insert itself into the universality of the world. Its apostolicity is mainly of submission.

I think that these two types of relationship have a permanent value for the Christian social ethic, since the discernment of circumstances, that is the reality of the relationships between the Christian community and the world which surrounds it, is essential to proclaim not a moral system of untemporal principles but an exhortation suited to concrete existence.

III. *The possible importance for our time of this duality of the social ethic in the Bible*

It is certain that every attempt to discern the politico-social phase, as prior to the choice of the corresponding biblical ethic, is singularly hazardous. Do we not hereby run the risk of making the authority of scripture depend upon an evaluation which is cultural and subjective? I shall not diminish the risks of this attempt if I confess the name of the man who has incited me to these researches and who could hardly expect to pass as a Father of the Church (even if this evangelical academy of Oud Poelgeest was in former times one of his places of refuge!): Spinoza. In his "Treatise on theological and political authorities" at the beginning of chapter VII entitled "Of the interpretation of Scripture" he writes a propos of the nonviolence recommended by Jesus Christ in the Sermon on the Mount: "It appears very clearly that following only the principles of Scripture itself this teaching given by Christ and Jeremiah, that is the acceptance of injustice and non-resistance to impiety, applies only when justice is despised and in times of oppression, not in a healthy state; the exact opposite holds in a healthy state where justice is safeguarded and everyone is bound, if he wishes to show himself to be just to ask the judge for punishment of the injustice suffered by him (Lev. 5:1) and that not from vengeance (Lev. 19:17-18) but from the desire to defend justice and the law of the land and so that the wicked may not gain an advantage from evil. All this is in entire agreement with natural reason." (p. 775, French Pleiade edition.)

A harmonization like this of the Bible contradictions purely by the light of reason cannot be upheld. It lacks the christological and spiritual motivations. On the other hand, what is right is the consideration of the moment of the exhortation and the why of it. To the churches of the majority and established type the Old Testament must bring the revolutionary ferment, whereas on the contrary it has traditionally sanctioned their conservatism, whether theocratic, patriarchal, feudal, bourgeois or technical. It must teach them a morality of conviction, such as Max Weber contrasts with the morality of responsibility, a morality which entails the necessary and realisable revolutions in proportion as the holders of the established power are or say they are led by the Christian norm.

On the other hand, to the churches of the minority type, suspected and sometimes persecuted, the New Testament must teach social insertion, whereas usually it has encouraged them in their pietistic and individualist evasion, in their aloofness from the world whether for eschatological or ascetic reasons. It must teach them a morality of responsibility, where they would be tempted by a morality of conviction, harmless insofar as it has no grip upon social reality, since the powers that be are not in the least concerned for the word of the Church.

We know that history usually offers us a very different picture: the regimes of Christendom are strengthened in their conservatism by the Old Testament and the minority regimes are confirmed in their piety by the New. In this it seems to me that both truly observe a duality of social ethic in the Bible but miss the deep significance, the exhortation which is only apparently paradoxical, whereas fundamentally it meets every man's true need. The established churches are stifled by confusing the social order with the will of God and the churches of professing Christians are stifled by deserting the social order in favour of a disincarnate order of God. That a powerful Christendom (Christian community) should be conservative, and that only when it becomes a minority it should become revolutionary, is neither interesting nor biblical. It is in both cases the opposite paradox, lived in the name of faith, which would be meaningful for the world. André Gide declared that "one must follow this current but upstream." Let the majority groups then live out their conviction but the minority groups hold to responsibility. Perhaps the greatest difficulty for the world to believe through the Church is to be found not in the disunion of the churches nor in the necessity for certain violations, but in this all too human spectacle of a church which is conservative in the good days and pietistic in the bad, whereas the force of prophetic witness was that it cried out against injustice in the days of opulence and the power of the apostolic witness is that it calls men to patient conformity in the world in the time of persecution.

These two ethics seem to me to have permanent value, for our churches know no identical situations either in time or in space. Now we must hear the particular exhortation which everyone needs, in its time and in its place. Social ethic means an ethic for *my* Church and *my* society.

The Significance of Historical Events for Ethical Decisions

J. M. Lochmann

The question of the importance of historical events for our ethical and political decisions is one of the most urgent and most discussed problems of theology today. For all of us world history has become an almost inevitable destiny. Of course it is true that in the past also people were bound by the conditions of their time and conditioned by history. That is one of the conditions of human life at any time: no one chooses the time and place in which his life will be passed. He enters a situation which is already to a large extent already ordered. We are members of a certain race, a certain nation, a certain class, a certain Church. We inherit the rich heritage of our forefathers—but also their sin and their guilt.

Today, however, this general situation has become far more acute. Never before has human life been woven into such an intricate web of world events. In former times people could live within the comparatively narrow limits of their tribe, their town, their country, which were only seldom directly affected by the events of world history. Today this is no longer possible. During the second half of the 20th century it has become absolutely clear that "everything is connected with everything else." An explosion on the other side of the globe which would not have concerned us at all fifty years ago now has direct repercussions on our own lives. This is particularly clear in relation to the question of peace and war: On this planet we are all in the same boat. It may even be said: For thousands of years the first problem facing mankind has been how to control Nature. Today our first problem is history, and how to control the future history of mankind. The question of the significance of historical events for our decisions is therefore extremely *urgent*.

And theologians today *disagree* about this problem. Let us try to indicate the field of discussion, pointing out two typical possibilities.

I

1. A realisation of the decisive power of history over our lives may at first stimulate attempts to formulate *philosophy of history* or a *theology of history*. That may be the classic opportunity for theological thinking about history. It was the Bible (especially the prophets of the Old Testament) which first showed mankind that the stage of world history is the decisive scene where our decisions have to be taken. Nearly all the religions of antiquity were directed towards nature-mythology; the philosophy of antiquity was strongly metaphysical and transcendental in its orientation, seeking

truth, meaning and reality *beyond* time and history. But the prophets and the Apostles emphatically draw attention to this world and its history as the sphere in which God deals with His people, in which He brings forth Jesus Christ as His ultimate act of salvation, and in which He will maintain His loyalty until the end of history.

Of course, the Bible does not work out an abstract, general philosophy of history. It has little interest in the course of world history as such. Its whole attention is concentrated upon the history of the Covenant—the history of salvation. But the light of this history—which takes place within world history and which ultimately means the salvation of the nations, of the human race—falls also upon the whole history of the world and of the nations. They too are in the hand of the One God; the Cross stands above them too; God's ultimate purpose is also their purpose. So the message of the Bible always provides a stimulus to examine the course and the meaning of history—including those aspects where the strict concentration upon the *Heilsgeschichte* has become generalised and secularised. The biblical background can be clearly traced in all the past philosophies of history—including those which are deliberately non-Christian.

The great time for philosophy of history, both in the Church and in the world, was probably the 19th century. Schleiermacher, the great father of 19th century Protestant theology, already called theology and the Church to do so: "History is . . . the loftiest object of religion; religion begins with history and ends with history" (*Addresses on Religion,* 2nd Address). History is "the profoundest, most universal revelation" of [that] which is deepest and holiest. And the greatest thinkers of the 19th century, Hegel and Marx, were also the greatest philosophers of history. Hegel regarded it as sheer lack of faith if the Church did not venture upon a philosophy of history, for "Christians are initiated into God's mysteries, and this gives us also the key to world history" *(Vernunft in der Geschichte,* ed. Hoffmeister, p.46). So these attempts were ventured upon, both in the Church and in the world. Many people, who lost their faith in the Christian *Heilsgeschichte,* retained their faith in history as the ultimate religion. (Note: E. G. Burckhardt, Dilthey, Croce and Troeltsch. See K. Löwith: p. 176f.: "The modern over-appreciation of history, and of 'the world' as 'history,' is the outcome of our estrangement from the natural theology of antiquity, and from the supernatural theology of Christianity." "Faith in the absolute relevance of history, which has made the books of Spengler and Toynbee best-sellers, has been brought about by the emancipation of the modern view of history from its original limitation by classical cosmology and by Christian theology.")

Through the terrible catastrophes of the two world wars this faith was shattered during the 20th century—and so were other types of philosophy of history such as the American Social Gospel with its faith in the progressive attainment of the Kingdom of God through the democratic ordering of modern society. Nevertheless, despite all those blows, the philosophy of history is far from dead. In Germany, theology is usually hypersensitive about any trace (real or suspected) of an idea of a philosophy of history—a fact which is a weakness rather than a strength in its theology. But even in Germany, some of the younger theologians have recently been trying to revive the 19th century traditions of a philosophy of history, and to carry it further—even as far as the somewhat ambiguous slogans about "the Revelation as history" (Wolfhart Pannenberg and his friends).

2. In opposition to the old and the new philosophy of history and theology of history, the 20th century has produced an increasingly strong tendency to *mistrust history*. This mistrust does not spring only from the destruction of faith in the great philosophies of history, owing to the shattering events of our time. It springs also (and that is its strength) from a protest against the "wearier" forms of "confidence in history," especially against relativistic historicism, which regarded the truth merely as a predicate of changing history. It sprang also from despair, and that is perhaps its weakness; despair about the course of contemporary history. This type of theological view of the events of history assumes many different forms. It would be worthwhile, for instance, to describe the ideas of Danek, an outstanding Old Testament theologian in Czechoslovakia, against the background of Czech theology. But I will confine myself to the form (of despair) which has had the most influence: the theology of Rudolf Bultmann.

Bultmann's philosophy of history is based on the work of Martin Heidegger. According to him, the nature of history is *Geschichtlichkeit*. The whole attention of this philosophy is concentrated upon this "nature" of history, i.e., upon my *"Geschichtlichkeit"* as *"Wesensverfassung"* of existence—not upon history as a process of personal and collective events. Finally Heidegger pronounces this history to be "the commonplaces of external history," and our involvement with it as a failure to perceive its real nature, forgetting what we really are and concentrating our attention on "the commonplaces of Mr. Everyman." The question of the events of world history is a false flight from death. The history of philosophy is therefore the arch-lie: "All history calculates what the future will be like, on the basis of certain views of the past. History is the constant destruction of the future and of the relation of history to the impact of destiny" *(Holzwege,* p.301).

The ideas of Rudolf Bultmann follow the same lines, He too starts with the nature of history, which he finds in the *Geschichtlichkeit* of human nature—human temporality. Man always lives in the future; his real life is always before him; he is "always on the way to what he wants to be." The essential thing is always to attain the real nature of that future, and not to miss it. That is the meaning of human history, and the meaning of history altogether. For ultimately there is no real history beyond this *Geschichtlichkeit* of mine. Our thought and our action must therefore be concentrated upon that—solely upon that. "The man who complains that he cannot see any meaning in history, and that his own life therefore has no meaning either because it is interwoven with history" must be roused. He must be told: "Don't look around you at the history of the world; look into your own personal history. The meaning of history is always present with you; you cannot look at it as a spectator; you can only see it by taking responsible decisions. Every moment contains the dormant possibility of being the eschatological moment. You must awaken it" *(Geschichte und Eschatologie,* p. 181).

Bultmann argues as a theologian, and his view of history is expressed as a Christian, eschatological view. He must therefore work the biblical motives into his own concept—especially the prophetic view which regards the events of history also as signs of God's judgment and of His mercy. How can he do this? Bultmann takes his stand on the thesis that a sublimation of the prophets' theology of history into existential *Geschichtlichkeit* corresponds to the message of the Bible itself, on all essential points. It is true, the prophets regarded history as the scene of God's concrete action. But this belief was soon sublimated (in apocalyptic thought) into mythology and metaphysics; apocalypticism was then still further removed from this world; and this opened up a way for us—the way to the existential interpretation. Bultmann insists on this existentialisation. My own existence is the only point to which our decisions in history are related: "In the decision of faith I decide not for a responsible action, but for a new understanding of myself as a man freed from himself by God's grace and given back to himself anew, in order to live by the grace of God" (*Geschichte und Eschatologie,* p. 191). The history of the world does not concern the Christian at all—at any rate, not directly. This applies already to the work of Christ: "The coming of Christ is an event in the Kingdom of Eternity, which is incommensurable in relation to historical time." It applies also to our own life and action: "In his faith the Christian is a contemporary of Christ; time and world-history are superseded" (*Geschichte und Eschatologie,* p. 182).

If we try to apply the results of our comparison between the two different Christian concepts of history to our question ("The significance of historical events for ethical decisions"), we arrive at two different answers. In fact they are diametrically opposed. The "philosophy of history" concept regards the events of history as supremely important in relation to ethical decisions. This applies especially to the *heilsgeschichtlich* form of this philosophy: if history is really *Heilsgeschichte* then it is absolutely crucial to recognise the KAIROS of history and to seize it—for a genuine decision can be taken only in relation to this KAIROS, recognising truly the "logic of history" and actively adapting itself to the necessity of history. *"Volentem fata ducunt, nolentem trahunt"—tertium non datur.*" ("The fates carry us along, whether we will or not; there is no third course." For our own action, therefore, it is essential to decipher the signs of the times. It is they which decide even what is "good" and what is "bad"—for what is good is what corresponds with the course of history. But the historical situation is also ethically decisive for the "tireder" forms of philosophy of history: If truth is a predicate of history, and if history is the beginning and the end, then the course of history is our final hope and our final point of relation: We must act in accordance with history. So the philosophy of history takes the events of history very seriously.

It is quite different when history is existentially transformed into *Geschichtlichkeit*. This regards the events of history as quite unimportant. They are a sea of chaos, and it really is not worthwhile to take too much interest in them. The only thing which may therefore be profitable for our ethical decisions may be an attempt to perceive a new meaning in the processes of history, "as long as the pressure and the conflicts continue, under which the Christian has to purify his soul." So it is quite logical if Bultmann regards it as one of the two main temptations of the Protestant Church today, that it is clearly and concretely taking political action in contemporary history. It is true, the Christian has a political responsibility—but it concerns not so much his faith as his reason and his personal judgment. "It is the duty of theology and of the Church to point out his responsibility in its preaching. But it is not the task of theology and of the Church "to draw up political rules and thus relieve the individual of responsibility for his own decisions" (*Glauben und Verstehen,* III, p. 196). Our decisions of faith have nothing to do directly with the events of history. It is characteristic of Bultmann that he regards the course of world history as somewhat disastrous and catastrophic. Faced by the events of contemporary history "men and women realise not only their dependence on those events, but also their own helplessness. They feel that they are not only involved in the history of the world, but that they are at its mercy. There is particular bitterness in this feeling today. . . . " Our actions are obstacles to our lives, just as much as our sufferings are" (*Geschichte und Eschatologie,* p. 2f.). There is a certain nostalgia in this concept of history.

Both views of history are put forward as "Christian." The second view is a warning, not to base our ethical decision on *one* of these views alone. They are a Scylla and Charybdis between which we must steer our course; both fall short of the biblical view.

We realise their shortcomings if we compare them with the main emphases of the Bible's message. The biblical view of history seems to me to be marked by two perceptions, which may be summed up in the pregnant phrase: *"hominum confusione et Dei providentia historia regitur"* ("History is governed by human confusion and by divine providence"). (For the biblical-theological basis for this view of world history I should like to draw attention especially to what Karl Barth writes in *Kirchliche Dogmatik* (IV. 3, pp. 784-825). Both must be taken seriously: The Bible is well acquainted with "human confusion," with history as the sphere of human freedom and human guilt. But in defiance of all this confusion the Bible attests its firm faith in the omnipotence of God—even in history. God has not abandoned history. This is a statement of faith—not a principle of one's own philosophy of history. But as a statement of faith it is the power of the Christian life. So the Christian lives in history. He regards human confusion quite soberly. He believes quite soberly in God's providence. "We are living just before the Last Days—we believe in the Ultimate"—this phrase taken from Bonhoeffer's *Ethik* applies also to our decisions in face of history.

Both the views of history mentioned fall short of this biblical view. The philosophy of history certainly understands something about human confusion; but is it not in danger of underestimating it, and thus impairing the boundary between the Ultimate and the Time-just-before-the-Last-Days? The existential view of history certainly understands about God's providence; but is it not in danger of separating it (as "the Ultimate") completely from our human history, thus leaving us in despair? The two things are inseparable. In my own view, it is only against this background that the question of the significance of historical events for our ethical and political decisions can be given a proper theological basis. How can we now answer this question, concretely and positively?

II

Our view of history as one of the spheres "ruled by divine providence and by human confusion" seems to me to lead to important consequences for our theme—consequences which are of central importance for our basic ethical attitude in face of history. (In my opinion this view of history is also of importance for other questions, e.g., are these decisions concerned with matters of faith, or are they merely questions of judgment? As is well known, this question is one of those most debated by theologians today. If one bears in mind the two different concepts of history, it is fairly clear what the answer will be in this case also. A philosophy of history regards decision in face of history as a matter of faith; if history is a divine revelation (direct or indirect) it calls for a corresponding attitude—an attitude of faith. According to the existential concept, however, history is a factor which is irrelevant to theology, and our attitude to the events of history is a question of judgment. Ultimately faith has nothing to do with history. In the secular sphere of history faith can at most emphasise our responsibility in principle, but it cannot give concrete guidance. That is only in the power of reason and judgment. According to the concept of history indicated, both answers seem to me inadequate. If history is a sphere of "human confusion," then the events of history must really be considered with extreme soberness. We must not be too hasty in proclaiming "judgments of faith" in the confusion of human quarrels; we must not be too ready to "preach," where the immediate need is to have a clear grasp of the facts. Most important of all, we must not claim that our own limited view is "the Christian view" and make our political differences into religious or metaphysical fronts. Our views must not assume the character of a "last judgment"; our quarrels must not be carried on as if they were crusades. There is constant justification here for Bultmann's concern in emphasising the sober, logical, reflective aspect of our views of history. But in my opinion this concern is made into an absolute, and this is not justifiable. Of course, we are living in the Days-before-the-End and should think and argue accordingly (i.e., logically). But we believe in the Ultimate; amid all the relativities of historical events, amid all logical considerations, our faith is not dumb. It is also concerned in all soberness with problems of faith and with decisions of faith. Wherever we encounter man, there faith must speak. This does not mean that logic is simply excluded. In this respect it is not a choice of "either faith or logic"; nor is it a question of choosing between "human confusion" and "divine providence." On the contrary: Faith calls for *logical thought;* but it is *faith* which calls. Faith is not neutral, it is "partial"; following in the steps of Jesus, faith takes sides with man, and appeals to reason to seek in this direction. So our ethical decisions in face of history must not be understood "enthusiastically" as bare decisions of faith, nor dualistically as bare questions of judgment; they must be understood in the unity of the obedient life which tries to act in faith and in the light of reason—without separating them.)

If history stands under God's providence—or to express it in clearer theological terms, if history is the place where Jesus Christ accepted our human lot in complete solidarity, in which he became our contemporary in history, and "dwelt among us" (John 1: 14)—then it must be taken *with great seriousness* also because it is *our* place.

Our place in history is not a matter of chance, it is not an *Adiaforon*, it is not a side-stage imposing no responsibility upon us, and which we can change at will. It is our "unique opportunity" entrusted to us here and now. We have no other. And it is also the scene of our vocation—the actual scene of our concrete responsibility, the only one we have, in which we must either prove our mettle—or fail. All that sounds rather commonplace, but it is by no means a truism. For it is so easy to miss that opportunity, and so many people do so! Some people are always behind, they come limping after, they are always longing for the past. And others are impatient with the present time; they are already living in the dreams of their future. Both these types of people are in danger of missing the opportunities of the present—their concrete tasks, the people around them, their actual occupation. And how easy it is for people to miss the concrete opportunities of their calling; discontented with their lot, they long for a different one, and dream of other opportunities; or else they withdraw into themselves and become embittered and defiant. All that is humanly understandable in certain situations. But from the Christian point of view it is not justifiable. "It is here, and not in any other place, that God's call must be perceived and His commandment fulfilled. Loyalty to Him requires loyalty also to one's place in life" (Karl Barth, *Kirchliche Dogmatik,* III. 4, p. 710).

All this applies especially to our ethical decisions. From the biblical point of view, ethics cannot exist at all apart from their historical setting, ethics cannot be divorced from time. In this respect the eschatological orientation of the New Testament should be taken very seriously, and the consequences which the Apostles deduce from it in their ethical commandments. The New Testament is not concerned with abstract principles, nor with dogmatic laws divorced from time and space; it is concerned with recognising time soberly, seizing it, "redeeming" it—and acting accordingly in the place and time appointed to us. We need only recall the eschatological Paranese of Romans 13:11ff.; 1 Thess. 5:1ff., etc.; also the "house-tables" mentioned in Eph. 5:22ff.; Col. 3:18ff., etc. This eschatological orientation of the ethics of the New Testament—and the ethical orientation of the eschatology of the New Testament—applies also to our decisions when faced by the events of history. Of course, eschatology is not simply history, and history is not simply eschatology. But the light of eschatology illumines faith in history and compels us to shape it accordingly—to decipher the signs of the time, and to do what is necessary here and now. Thus the Christian ethic, because it is eschatological, is definitely related to history. It can never be sufficient simply to repeat what was demanded of people "in past times and in different places"—however well they may have responded to the challenge of that time. It is here and now that we have to fulfil the commandments of the Living God. Faith takes that commandment seriously; and for that very reason it strives to fulfil that commandment here and now.

I should like to give an example to illustrate this importance of the historical situation for our ethical decisions: the question of *war* (the central theme before the Puidoux Conference). We all know the theory of the "just war," and we know that for centuries it has been the classical teaching of the Christian Church about war. But many of us have always been opposed to this teaching, which seems to us to be a distortion of God's will. There are other people, however, who have no objection to warfare in principle as applied in the past, but who clearly feel that the old categories are no longer applicable to our present historical situation, because in the atomic age the danger of atomic warfare is a complete negation of every form of justice, and because it constitutes a radical menace to the very existence of mankind. It is becoming increasingly clear that today we can no longer simply hand on the traditional, classical formulations and decisions relating to war. They are an absurd anachronism in our present situation. We must seek new ways and new formulations. And that is where the astonishing thing happens for many of us; the clear message of Jesus is illumined for us afresh—because we take the new situation seriously. It is not the historical events themselves which give his message this additional force. Nothing in history could ever do that. But Jesus' commandment, which had been watered down into abstract terms, becomes strong and powerful when we obediently apply the Gospel to actual life. This is another reason why the historical situation must be taken seriously.

(It is one of the important points in the theology of J. L. Hromadka that he stresses this fact. The slogan "take the historical situation seriously" has become a real *"ceterum autem"* of his message. especially during the last decades. In the ecumenical movement today we find hardly a single important theologian who has devoted so much thought to our position in history, and to the meaning of the tremendous changes in church and society. He is therefore criticised on account of having a boundless preference for philosophising about history, and theologising about history. When reading Hromadka one constantly comes across phrases which indicate a tendency to philosophise about history, such as "we are confronted today by a completely new era in the history of mankind," contemporary events "reflect the deep change, the turning point which has taken place in the structure of history," "the challenge of the hour," we must examine "the dimensions-of-depth in the course of history," and so on. And if, in addition, one takes account of the fact that Hromadka is a pupil of Troeltsch, and that he is clearly influenced by his teacher in spite of being a theologian, the conclusion seems to be clear: Hromadka is a philosopher of history cloaked as a theologian.

(In spite of all the apparent evidence for this, however, this conclusion seems to me to be an example of rushing to a conclusion, which is not justified. A clear distinction must be drawn. The theological fatality of a philosophy of history breaks out where one transforms history, consciously or unconsciously, into a religious or secular "doctrine of salvation," when one ascribes the nature of a Revelation to historical events, and then turns one's own views of history into an absolute—into religious judgments. But this is just what Hromadka does *not* do. He angrily rejects any attempt to interpret history as *Heilsgeschichte* or as Revelation: "It is not legitimate to regard history and its events as a source of Revelation; I will waste no words on this point" (Letter to Karl Barth, *Antwort,* p. 4). And he is sincere in this. His whole lifework is a protest against everything which tries to restrict the Gospel within the limits of natural factors. The Gospel is free—and it liberates. This great certainty shines out of all Hromadka's writings—and not only out of them but out of his whole life. So it frees us too from history—and of course from all forms of philosophy about history, which are always tempted to weave the Christian Gospel into their theories. But the Gospel, the Message of Jesus of Nazareth, the Word incarnate of God, "liberates us from history *within* history, just as it liberates us from death and the grave" ("Kirchliche Existenz in der heutigen Situation," symposium *Kirche und Verkündigung,* p. 15).

(The fact that the Christian Gospel is free from history, but at the same time within history and for history, is perhaps the very heart of Hromadka's theology. It is clearly rooted in Christology, in "the Message of the way to man" (as he has called his *"kleine Dogmatik"*). Hromadka says that we must obediently occupy the place which the Son of God has occupied for us. He entered earthly history to the full; he therefore cannot be related only to our religious life beyond history, its purification and spiritualisation; he must be sought in the middle and in the depth of the reality of history. That is the ultimate meaning of Hromadka's concept of history: the *reality* (actuality) of following Christ. "My concern is to show that the Church of Jesus Christ and its theologians must face history courageously, and must grapple with contemporary realities in all their naked pitilessness. And the purpose of this is not to adapt oneself to history and its changes, for any reason whatever, or to mould theological thought in accordance with history; its purpose is to attain real theological control of any historical situation" (*Antwort*, p. 4). And this concern—to take history seriously for the sake of the way of Jesus Christ—must be whole-heartedly approved. So Hromadka is not a philosopher of history in the cloak of a theologian; he is a genuine theologian—though he perhaps sometimes dons the cloak of a philosopher of history.)

Although faith takes the events of history seriously, it does not take them *"with deadly seriousness."* For history is also the sphere of "human confusion," and should not on any account be taken with deadly seriousness. Both facts are stressed in our slogan: History is a *human* activity, not the work of daemons; the power of history is not the power of God nor the power of the devil. It must not be regarded either as divine or as devilish. And history is the outcome of human *confusions;* it is not entirely sublime, venerable or holy. We need not be bewitched or dazzled by the course of history. Of course, it does bewitch and dazzle us, filling us either with "enthusiastic" optimism or with sceptical defeatism. (Both the concepts of history that we have mentioned may perhaps bear some traces of this). But there is no biblical justification for this attitude. The events of history must be evaluated soberly and realistically.

In concrete terms this means: that no historical position must be raised to *an absolute.* This is true already of our own lives. We are not the prisoners of history, and we must not live as if we were. Our situation in history is the base from which we act. We cannot take action from any other position; but we do take *action* from it, i.e., we are not simply dominated by it. Karl Barth has expressed this in a very apt way; he says, "We must not regard our position in history as our grave, but as our cradle" (see Karl Barth, *Kirchliche Dogmatik* IV, 3, p. 714). Our position is not equivalent to our completed vocation; it is a preparation for that vocation. This vocation (the call of the Christian Gospel) illumines our history—not vice versa. In this light we recognise our "cradle" as a gift and gratefully accept it—but at the same time we realise that it is a task, a point of departure for a life of faith. So the eschatological call first shows us our concrete place in history, and then calls us to move forward from that place—not in order to leave it empty (in the general-abstract, cosmopolitan sense) but in order to fill it with the Message of Christ. It is the place where we prove ourselves, the place where we make our witness; it is not to be accepted passively, but to be moulded actively. So the Gospel teaches us to take a positive attitude to our position in history (but not "positivistically"), in Christian solidarity, not in *"vergesetzlichter Selbstidentifizierung"* (legalistic self-identification).

Our position in history must not be turned into an Absolute in its relation to our own lives, and even less in relation to the lives of others. This is a constant temptation: to judge others by one's own standards. In a certain sense it is "natural"; we cannot help thinking and acting from our own point of view. This "bias" is inevitable when thinking about history, and acting in it. But this situation must be soberly realised; we must not *hypostasieren;* we must be ready for genuine encounter and conversation with people in different situations. Otherwise our own view becomes a norm, if we do not remember our own "human confusion"; history becomes dehumanised; the sphere of human decisions develops into a battleground for daemons; for whenever I turn my personal view into an absolute norm, the other person will do the same.

It is of particular practical importance to recognise this today; it is a particularly acute point of our ethical responsibility in the contemporary world. We are living in the age of the *Cold War* in a world in which every conceivable means is enlisted (except nuclear warfare which would mean universal suicide) to fight our opponents. It is an age full of divisions and tensions. In this situation even the Christian Church is tempted to adopt the strategy of the Cold War. Especially in view of the fact that one of the two blocs is deliberately and openly based on a non-Christian ideology, the other side is in danger of identifying its own policy with Christianity itself (it is not by chance that many of the leading parties in Western Europe call themselves "Christian") and of regarding its political struggle as a Christian crusade against anti-Christians. This intensifies the spirit of the Cold War, for it is precisely in the religious categories that one's opponent is easily stamped as an adversary of God (i.e., daemonised). This is clearly a danger to the spirit of understanding; one cannot negotiate with daemons. The difficult, but hopeful, way of negotiation and effort is defamed from the outset as an illusion. Christians must try to counter this tendency. In the world of "human confusion" the struggles are not between angels and daemons; they are human tensions. That does not mean that they are innocuous; they go very deep. But they certainly must not be regarded as insuperable. For they are just human tensions. The task of Christian theology is soberly to develop this view of history, and the Christian churches have the special task of expressing this view in their ecumenical contacts and in their efforts for peace in the divided world. By being clear and concrete in our thinking, without concealing the differences between us (realising the human relativity of our views, in the light of the Gospel) we shall not only prove that our ecumenical contacts are genuine; we shall also set up a sign of hope for our fellowmen. This is a very practical way in which to express our theological reflections concerning the significance of historical events for ethical decisions.

The Social Aspect of the Teaching of the Early Church

Hans-Werner Bartsch

We are accustomed to speak of *Paränese* [exhortation], and hence of ethical guidance, only when the Christian Church has consolidated itself within society, and is endeavouring to maintain its existence as a factor in the world. We therefore regard *Paränese* as a collection of ethical instructions given with the purpose of making the Christian Church a respectable body in society. For the Gospels we usually take the preaching of the Early Church as our point of departure; but this is not the same in the case of the *Paränese* which is rather regarded as something supplementary, something secondary. Its *Sitz im Leben* is not preaching, but the instruction of the congregation. Within the Gospels, however, there is a criterion which may destroy this view. We regard as "instruction of the congregation" all those sayings of Jesus which were addressed to his disciples; whereas we find missionary preaching in Jesus' preaching to the people.

This distinction has proved very apt. It shows that the Sermon on the Mount is "instruction of the congregation," catechism for the first Christians; but does the same apply to Jesus' "teaching in the plain" recorded in Luke 6:20-49? It seems at first sight as if Luke were describing the same situation as Matthew. Luke 6:20 begins: "And he lifted up his eyes on his disciples . . . " But this is only a brief introductory sentence, which relates solely to the Beatitudes. In 6:27 a new element is introduced: "But I say unto you . . . " is addressed to an audience. And 6:39 opens with a similar introductory sentence. The actual situation in which the "teaching in the plain" was given is therefore not shown by 6:20, which merely refers to the situation described before, and introduces nothing new. The scene of the "teaching in the plain" is described in 6:17-19. Contrary to Matthew 5:1f., Luke draws a clear distinction between the "teaching in the plain," and Jesus' going up into a mountain with his disciples. According to Luke, Jesus "came down with them and stood in the plain"—the place for a missionary sermon.

The "situation" of the "teaching in the plain" gives us a collection of maxims (as we know them within the *Paränese*), in the form of missionary teaching. And as missionary teaching is in any case the starting point of the Early Christian tradition, we may legitimately take for the *"Paränese"* the same point of departure as for the other tradition of the Gospels. However, we shall have to try out this working hypothesis to see whether it is true, by an interpretation of the teaching given by Jesus "in the plain."

1.

The Beatitudes included in the teaching "on the plain" have been interpreted as secondary, on account of the direct form of address not otherwise found in Beatitudes, and different from the account given by Matthew. Within the setting of a missionary sermon, however, these Beatitudes are revealed as the original, pre-literary form of the Beatitudes recounted by Matthew. They promise the listener salvation, without restriction, just because he is a poor man with nothing on which he can build his life, and is therefore open to the salvation offered to him in Jesus. Originally there may have been only three of them; the fourth may be an addition based on the position of the Church. These three Beatitudes speak of the lack of any basis for life, whereby man could understand himself. In the affirmations of the Sermon on the Mount, through extension, the direct promise of salvation has been developed into a statement of the conditions for that salvation.

The cries of "Woe unto you!" are given by way of contrast, on analogy with the Beatitudes, each being placed in direct opposition to one of the Beatitudes. But it would be a mistake to assume that they were *added* by Luke, or by his source. We find the same contrast in the Gospels, especially in the other material of the Gospels. Jesus' power to perform miracles is contrasted with the power of the devils; faith is contrasted with the disciples' failure to understand. By this the audience are told to rejoice because they need not fear the power of the devils, and they need not be like the disciples who could not understand. The cries of "Woe unto you!" say the same thing: Rejoice! you need not understand yourself in terms of what you possess, and perish with it; for you now receive the promise of salvation which forms the basis of your life here on earth, and of your eternal salvation; for this basis is not part of the transience of this life: It is the Lord who holds your life in His hand.

If the beginning of the "teaching in the plain" may be understood in this way as "preaching," we may go on to ask whether the admonitions which follow maintain the same situation, and especially what social implications spring from the fact that the admonitions are rooted in this particular sermon.

2.

The first of the admonitions—the development of the commandment to love one's enemies (Luke 6:27-35)—is broader than the parallel passage in Matthew (5:39-48). But in Luke no reference is made to the Law, whereas Matthew brings out the distinction between the old Law and the new one. This omission of any reference to the Law seems to be characteristic of the whole "sermon in the plain" which is not concerned with the better fulfilment of the Law (Matt. 5:20). Whereas Matthew stresses that Jesus came in order to fulfil the Law (Matt. 5:17), Luke does not refer to this at all. The admonitions of the "sermon in the plain" are therefore not to be understood primarily as the fulfilment of the Law—not even as the *better* fulfilment of it. The question then arises, how are they then to be understood?

The commandment to love one's enemies is developed in two parallel series of axioms, between which is interposed the Golden Rule. The first series is older than Matthew, as is proved by the fact that there is no reference to the position of the Church ("pray for them which despitefully use you, and persecute you," Matt. 5:44). The admonitions are expressed more broadly, with no special antithesis in mind which could determine the understanding of the listener. But the admonitions are also sharper. Luke makes no reference to a lawsuit about a coat (Matt. 6:40) but speaks about *taking* the coat. And the tone is sharper in Luke's version: "Give to every man that asketh of thee!" Again, there is no mention of borrowing; Christians are admonished not to ask for anything back which is *taken away* from them!

The second series of admonitions demand conduct which transcends the normal conduct required by the Law. This is most clearly expressed in connection with treatment of one's neighbour: Lend, and don't expect to get any of your goods returned! This same admonition is found in another form in Matt. 5:42: "from him that would borrow of thee turn not thou away!" Thus the Sermon on the Mount is set in relation to the demands of the Law, it calls for the highest fulfilment of the Law, extolled by the Rabbinic teaching based on Psalm 15:5: "he does not put out his money at interest, and does not take a bribe against the innocent." In the Sermon on the Mount these admonitions are all summed up in the words: "Be ye perfect, as your heavenly Father is perfect."

On the other hand in the "sermon on the plain" the second series of admonitions are contrasted with the piety that is based on the Law. The purpose of such conduct is not to be perfect like God, but to prove oneself to be children of the Highest in His mercy to "the unthankful and the evil"

(Luke 6:35). Here we have the real motive of Luke's admonitions: We are to prove that we are children of God, as exhorted by Jesus. If man treats his neighbour as God will treat him on the Day of Judgment (as Jesus said), he proves that he has accepted Jesus' message; at the same time he is passing that message on. God's mercy in judgment (of which Jesus assures his hearers) is the norm for the admonitions.

The difference between this and the Sermon on the Mount is shown in the second parallel to the closing words in Matt. 5:45: "That ye may be the children of your Father which is in heaven; for He maketh His sun to rise on the evil and on the good, and sendeth rain on the just and on the unjust." God's behaviour in the world is the norm for Christian behaviour. So in this world Christians must prove that they are children of God. On the other hand, the "sermon on the plain" (reported by Luke) is not interested in proving anything in the world, but in bearing witness of salvation to one's neighbour.

In this connection the "Golden Rule" presents a problem. It is inserted between the two series of admonitions, clearly in order to sum up the first series and bring them to a close. Thus a *logion* is given as a summary of the commandment which was widely known, both in its negative and its positive form, and which (corresponding to the Rabbinic version in Matt. 7:12) appears as the summing up of "the Law and the prophets."

Its insertion can be explained by the analogous construction, and in view of such considerations of form this may in fact be regarded as the first step towards expanding the admonitions into the "Sermon on the Mount." One is struck, however, by the inadequacy of the "Golden Rule" as a norm for behaviour: "Love, that ye may be loved in return. Lend, that ye may borrow!" So in this context the "Golden Rule" is really a foreign element; its original purpose can only have been to form a line of demarcation. "Ye have heard that it was said by them of old time: All things whatsoever ye would that men should do to you, do ye even so to them! But I say unto you: Love without expecting to be loved in return! Lend, without expecting others to lend to you!"

This is followed by the injunction not to judge others, but to forgive them, as God forgives us. It is implemented by familiar comparisons resembling proverbs, and culminates with the injunction not to assume that salvation is obtained merely by calling "Lord, Lord!" but to carry out the commandment to love and forgive in actual practice. Here again the passage differs from the Sermon on the Mount.

We will now examine the social aspect of these admonitions, which are all instructions to pass on the message of salvation through action which is in itself a form of preaching: The message of salvation is to be passed on to our neighbour by showing him forgiving love. What relation has this concept of concrete action to the position of the Christian in a non-Christian society? The point is not that the Christian should "prove his mettle" in society by fulfilling the Law better. Nor is it a question of a *nova lex* being given to the Christian to guide his conduct. The situation is rather that by accepting the message of salvation the Christian has the possibility for a devotion which is not envisaged in the Law at all, because unlimited devotion is impossible from the point of view of this world.

We cannot help interpreting this from the angle of the generally-accepted concept of life, which is also the angle on which the Law is based, because it is only from this angle that the *impossibility* of such conduct, and the new *possibility,* become comprehensible. Within this world—also under the Law—man understands his own existence from the angle of his own possibilities. He has nothing else upon which he can base his existence or understand it. This fact is not altered in any way by faith in the God who created him, insofar as that faith is based on what man sees and understands: that God makes the sun to shine, and the rain to fall, upon the just and the unjust alike. Man has at his disposal what this action of God's brings to him. He also has at his disposal the action of his neighbour, insofar as he can determine it—as the Golden Rule says, both in its negative and in its positive form. For the Coming Judgment he has "at his disposal" his own blameless conduct as contrasted with the conduct of his neighbour, which is to be judged. And just because man knows that his own conduct is far from blameless he is bound to contrast it with that of his neighbour, which is far worse. Ordinary love which expects to be loved in return, and ordinary justice, are therefore merely conduct based on one's understanding of one's own life, in the light of the means "at one's disposal." In regard to man's behaviour in society, such conduct reflects that it is ultimately based on the Ego, even when the conduct is blameless.

The "sermon in the plain" is a message of unrestricted salvation, irrespective of what man has "at his disposal." The Christian Church has received this message through its encounter with the Risen Christ; for this encounter was a testimony that God came to save those who were lost. The Church now passed on this message in its own preaching. But because this message was given not only through Jesus' words, but also through his death and resurrection, the only way in which the Church can effectively pass on this message in history is through *action.* Transmitting the news of salvation is not merely an additional commitment (taking second place after the *receiving* of salvation); salvation is received only by passing on the message through action. If the Church is really the Church of Jesus Christ, therefore, it has a duty to its neighbour. Its relation to society springs from its responsibility to bear testimony, because this responsibility is bound to include action in relation to the neighbour.

For the Christian his neighbour is not merely an object whom he uses to demonstrate a new form of conduct derived from his faith, thus fulfilling a *nova lex*. His neighbour is the person to whom he passes on the message of salvation through action—in order that he himself may thereby receive salvation. Christian conduct therefore consists in *carrying out* the salvation received. The gift of salvation opens up a new understanding of life, based on God's act in Jesus Christ. By his way of life, by his devotion to his neighbour, the Christian bears witness that he has accepted this message for himself. The "sermon in the plain" explains this devotion as loving one's enemies in this world, and not passing judgment on their life hereafter.

My attitude to my neighbour in society must therefore always be: Am I bearing witness of my new understanding of my own life, in my relation to him? It is through expressing (or failing to express) this new understanding that I show whether I have accepted salvation or not. My conduct within the community (my social behaviour) therefore always reflects my concept of life—whether I think my life is my own to dispose of, or whether it is determined by the salvation bestowed upon me, and which I can accept only by passing it on to my neighbour.

When deciding what the exhortations say about social conduct, the norm will always be: Does my conduct transmit the salvation bestowed upon me? Thus an attitude based on the Law, which misinterprets these admonitions, must be condemned, because such an attitude is based on "what one possesses."

It is true, my attempt at an explanation overemphasises certain aspects of the Sermon on the Mount (the first product of the Early Church's attempts at exhortation) in a way which might appear deprecatory. My intention was, however, to show that if these exhortations are interpreted in the light of the Church's consolidation in the world, this means reverting to the Law, thus missing the true approach to a new concept of life. The Sermon on the Mount must rather be understood in terms of the exhortation practised in the Early Church, and this gives it social relevance. My neighbour, who lives side by side with me in society, is not only the person to whom I must pass on the message; he thereby enables me to accept salvation myself.

The gift of salvation becomes a reality in history when its acceptance is reflected in my new attitude to my neighbour—but never in a personal act of faith resulting in new behaviour (as a by-product), which would be quite independent of my acceptance of salvation. Since my new attitude reflects my acceptance of salvation, and since preaching is indissolubly bound up with action, preaching itself is relevent to social conduct. This is a basically different concept from the view that social conduct is merely the outcome of personal faith.

War and the Christian Ethic
Theses and Questions

Jean Lasserre

In the New Testament there is no clear border between individual and collective, between private and political ethic. The New Testament challenges the Christian consistently to a coherent and homogeneous kind of behavior without duplicity or contradiction.

1. The obedience of the Christian is founded in gratitude; sanctification is the answer to justification. The response to the salvation given in Christ is grateful praise. This means that gratitude is not only the foundation and the motive but also the content and criterion of Christian obedience.

My question: Can the action of a soldier be understood as grateful praise? Interiorly can the attitude of a soldier be compatible with an attitude of grateful praise and does it call forth in those toward whom he acts an attitude of grateful praise—or rather of blasphemy?

2. The Christian ethic is an ethic of communion. The branch can only live as part of the vine; if the branch does not bear fruit it is cut off and dries up and is destroyed. This communion, though, is not only with the Father vertically but also with the neighbor horizontally. This right angle is unbreakable; the one relationship is only present with the other, which is the reason for Jesus' introducing in the Lord's Prayer the pedagogical condition, "as we forgive those who have trespassed against us."

Is the position of a soldier not incompatible with this total communion with the neighbor? Is not the soldier's commitment by definition a breach of communion with the enemy? But it is central to the Gospel message that when my neighbor refuses communion with me I remain nevertheless in communion with him. This is the sense of the instructions, for instance, concerning the right and the left cheek and the second mile.

3. The Christian ethic is an ethic of witness. The Christian's commission is to pass on the message of forgiveness which he has received.

Does not the position of the soldier and the function he has to carry out render impossible by definition his witnessing to this grace?

4. The Christian ethic is an ethic founded on the word, the living word which Christ speaks to His disciple. This means that any kind of legalism or moralism or system-building is a ridiculous caricature of the Christian ethic.

But the counter-question must still be examined: Is not any other system—situation ethics, an ethic of history, an ethic of responsibility— equally in danger of padlocking the mouth of the living Lord? There is only one way ethic can validly proceed and this is, growing out of the constant dialogue between disciple and Lord, between child and Father.

5. The Christian ethic is an ethic of victory. Its basis is the victory of the Resurrection of Christ; and there is no Christian ethic which is not a testimony to and a building upon this victory.

The army seeks a kind of victory which has nothing to do with the Resurrection of Christ. Its presuppositions are pagan and fatalistic. Is not a Christian who inserts himself within this framework of the army placing himself in a position which by the assumptions of its organization denies the Resurrection or does not count on it as a victory?

6. The Christian ethic is an ethic of hope. It lives from the expectation of the return of Christ. An ethic is only Christian if its actions presuppose, illuminate, call forth, suggest expectation. In this light all human values and kingdoms and institutions are relativized. The Christian can only look at them with a kind of humor, a kind of detachment, which refuses to absolutize them. To take life whether in the form of the death penalty or on the battlefield is not compatible with this relativizing of human values and human institutions. It assumes that the state in whose commission this action is carried out has made itself an absolute, that it is the kingdom which is ultimate.

Does not the Christian's acceptance of killing therefore actually mean, through an absolutizing of the state in its claims over the life of the criminal or the enemy, the proclamation that Jesus Christ will not come?

7. I needn't argue that the Christian ethic is an ethic of love answering the love of God toward us. But I do want to make in this context the point that our love is addressed to man with a small "m." Jesus concerned Himself with the woman at the well, He concerned Himself with Zacchaeus in spite of the fact that he was a collaborator, He concerned Himself with the servant of the centurion in spite of the fact that this man was a part of the occupation force. He looks at a man as a human creature whom we are to love without measuring him in terms of his place in the social and political situation or his worthiness.

Can the church support a war ethic contrary in each aspect to the Christian ethic and still be proclaiming the Gospel of Christ? Is there really any hope of avoiding the guilt and horror of nuclear war except in the possibility that the church may even yet repent—turn?

15. The Authority of Government and the Lordship of Christ (Bethany Theological Seminary, Chicago, Illinois, Spring 1962)

Several of the members of the faculty of Bethany Theological Seminary, the graduate school of theological education of the Church of the Brethren, had participated in the early sessions of the Puidoux conferences. This stimulated total faculty interest in developing a statement on the relationship of the church and the state in Christian perspective. In a series of meetings, these understandings were put into written form.

Although the statement was a corporate effort by the faculty, the document has no formal or official status. It was never passed on by the Annual Conference of the Church of the Brethren, the denomination's highest forum of decision on matters of polity, program, and doctrine.

The Authority of Government and the Lordship of Christ

A Theological Statement Concerning the Relation of Church to State by the Faculty of Bethany Theological Seminary, 1962

A. *Prologue.* The purpose of this statement is not to set forth binding rules but to penetrate into the reality of life in such a way that is possible only in and through the Christian faith. Our task is to discern the way in which God in Christ has already entered into our present situation. In these terms we may better assess and determine our response to the problems raised by modern warfare. This reality to which Jesus Christ points is considered in the gracious activity of God in relation to man, the nature of man's response, the role of the church and her relationship to the governing authority.

B. *Creation, Fall, and Redemption.* "In the beginning was the Word, and the Word was with God, and the Word was God" (John 1:1). God in and through his Word created and continues to create man and the cosmos (Gen. 1; Isa. 40:12-31). The same Word who was from the beginning humbled himself and walked within his own creation as Jesus of Nazareth, even to the point of death on a cross. In the beginning the world and man in it were pronounced by God to be good (Gen. 1:31), i.e., sound and whole. Man, moreover, is created in God's image and is a real self when properly related to God and his brother, both of whom are fully visible in Jesus Christ.

Within the freedom of the image of God, man is tempted to place his own wisdom above the direct commandment of God; he rebels (Gen. 3:1-4), disobeys, and shatters the pristine relationship of wholeness with God and his world (Gen. 3:5-10); he falls under the principalities, powers, and rulers of this age; self-willed and in bondage, he goes forth to create his history and civilization after a pattern that reflects both his original goodness and his anthropocentric brokenness in a world that is itself now fallen. Man finds himself estranged from God, fearful, anxious, and obsessed with guilt and the need to deceive (Gen. 3:10-13). He is also alienated from and at enmity with his brother whom he learns to murder (Gen. 4:1-10). Moreover, he is torn and shattered in his inmost self, a fugitive and a wanderer, at odds with all of God's creation and cursed within himself (Gen. 4:11-16; Rom. 7:14-25), marked out for an endless chain of blood revenge (Gen. 4:15; 24.) Since all meaningful existence is based upon the Word of God, man's varied attempts to create God and the world in his own image invariably end in disaster and the return to chaos (Gen. 6:1-8; 11:1-9; Rom. 1:18-32).

With the same faithfulness to and love for man that is evident in creation, and incarnate in Jesus Christ, God seeks the restoration of man through a chosen line (Gen. 5:1-32; 6:8-10; 32) an elect people bound to him by covenant (Gen. 12:1-3) and chosen to be his servants in the task of reconciliation. In the context of this covenant he reveals through his Word the true life of faith (Gal. 3:6-9; Rom. 4). At the same time, and with the same love as seen in all his creation, he establishes such authority as is necessary for the preservation of mankind. The power of government is such an authority, and it shows both the creative and redemptive mercy of God as well as the fallenness of creation. So within even this fallen history of man, God reveals himself to and through his people, and by one redemptive act after another, calls man back unto himself (Ex. 3:1-12; Ps. 105—107; Rom. 9-11).

C. *The Nature of Man's Response to God's Action.* The character and quality of response expected of man in light of God's action is described variously in the Bible. The Old Testament speaks of covenant participation, trustful loyalty, dutiful obedience, humble openness to God's Spirit, and the transformation of life that may come through personal relationship with the living Lord. It is always God, his Person, and his activity, who sets the norm for life. "You shall be holy, for I the Lord your God am holy" (Lev. 19:2). While the holiness of God connotes his otherness, nevertheless, because of its righteousness (Isa. 5:16) it has a profoundly ethical quality. It manifests itself in that which is proper, firm, straight, and just—in keeping with the requirements for peace. The Israelites were repeatedly challenged to open their lives to God in repentance and humility so as to manifest His own character. In their teaching they were urged to remember the nature of God's righteousness and mercy toward them as they considered their behavior toward others (Deut. 24:17f.). In their cultic life, they recounted the gracious acts of God in living memory (Ex. 12:17). In their preaching, the prophets challenged the Israelites to imitate God's own character and actions (Micah 6:8).

D. *The Church and the Grace of the Lord Jesus Christ.* The history of Israel, and the nations, is the history of man's failure to live according to God's purpose either by political theocracy or by religious legalism. Man could not live according to the former things (the *proton,* Isa. 48:3), but in the fulfillment of time (Gal. 4:4) God sent his Son, Jesus Christ, in whom and by whom God's final purpose was realized (the *eschaton*).

The Church affirms in faith that Christ has gained the victory over the powers that enslave the world and man. In his death and resurrection Christ's victory over sin, death, law, and Satan is conclusive and final. In this victory God initiates the age of the new creation in Christ. In the resurrecting power of this new age man also, by faith, dies to the old aeon of chaos and self-centeredness and is raised a new creation (Gal. 2:20; Rom. 6:1-11; 2 Cor. 5:17). He is once more restored to fellowship with God, to harmony and peace with his fellowmen and to wholeness within his now purified self (Rom. 5:10f.; 6:17f.; 22f.; 8:1-17), presaging the restoration of all fallen creation along with the sons of God (Rom. 8:19-23). Christ is Lord over Church and world, the power of governing, and all other powers of creation.

The Church herself is the community of those who are inseparably linked to the life, death, and resurrection of Jesus Christ through historical memory, church proclamation, sacramental participation and sacrificial discipleship. It is the Messianic "flock" or true "remnant" of Israel that is called to manifest the quality of covenant obedience and wholeness of peace which represents the fulfillment of creation's *telos* and which typifies the coming of the "new age." Still, we are living "between the times." The work of Christ and His Spirit is conclusive, but not concluded. The Church witnesses to the faith that the powers of chaos, disintegration and evil have been broken through the work of God in Christ, and yet is called to marshall its resources to do battle with such forces wherever met in life. The individual Christian is simultaneously justified and sinful. He participates both in the "new age" of Christ and the Spirit and the "old age" of sin and death. And yet it is anachronistic to live as though Christ's victory had not been realized, as though the fulness of time had not come, as though there were a symmetrical relationship between grace and sin, between the new and the old. To be sure, sin persists but it no longer reigns. Without declaring it illusory, sin has been "relativized" through the "triumph of grace."

The Christian community then is called to a life of mercy and humility, which may issue in or be accompanied by humiliation and suffering. Jesus explicitly summoned his followers to be imitators of God. "You, therefore, shall be perfect as your heavenly Father is perfect" (Matt. 5:48), or "Be merciful, even as your Father is merciful" (Luke 3:36). The way of Christian discipleship is set forth by Jesus in the challenge to sacrificial service (Mark. 10:42ff). The Apostle Paul portrays the character and quality of the Christian response when he writes: "Have this mind among yourselves which was also in Christ Jesus, who though he was in the form of God, did not count equality with God a thing to be grasped, but emptied himself, taking the form of a servant, being born in the likeness of men" (Phil. 2:5-7).

E. *Christ and the Governing Authority.* The power to govern is created by the Word of God in the same love and mercy as all his creation (Rom. 13:1), but also has fallen with that creation (Rev. 13:4-7). In his redeeming act Jesus Christ has become victorious over the power of governing along with all other powers. This was done by subjecting himself to the governing authority rather than by violently usurping it (1 Cor. 2:8; John 19:11). On the cross the right relationship between governing powers and God was restored. Meanwhile, although the powers of chaos that so often characterize governing authority have been defeated, they are not fully subdued. The potential for acting both within the gracious nature of creation and the chaotic despotism of fallen nature still resides within the governing authority. Though Jesus Christ is Lord, his Lordship has not yet been evident in all its reality.

When the state does use violence, it displays the fallenness of the governing authorities and their disposition towards self-will and chaos, and it reveals its own dissolution under the judgment of God. In contrast to the Church, the state cannot fully understand that the powers of evil have already been overcome. Consequently, in pessimism it frequently finds no other possibility than to meet evil with violence. On the other hand, when it overcomes the power of evil by the proper administration of justice, the governing authority most nearly approximates its divine mandate to maintain order. But when it resists chaos and destruction, or even the threat of them, with similar means, the governing authority rebels against its Creator, uses a chaotic power that is alien to it and endangers its own authority.

As an instrument of God within the historical and sociological context of the "old age," the Church is called to responsible action in relation to government for the latter also is an expression of God's gracious and redemptive activity among men. Since the state is oriented toward the "old age," there remains the ever present possibility that its actions might lead to a completely chaotic condition. The Church knows the reality of the power of her Lord and the imminence of his return, and she constantly stands in judgment of, even as she shares in, the failure of the state to realize justice—the fulfillment of which the church knows to be love, mercy, and righteousness. Failing to perceive the victory of the Lord, the state may never quite understand the witness of the Church, and therefore the Church can expect to be misunderstood. Nevertheless the Church cannot abandon either her support or her judgment of the governing authority. Especially when the state resorts to violence in order to meet the reality of evil and chaos must the Church recognize the ambiguity of the situation. While the church must realize the demonic nature of evil, it must also be aware that if the state opposes violence with violence, then the state succumbs to the same demonic power it opposes.

In this nuclear age, as in any other age, the Church has a twofold function in relation to the state. First, and positively, the Church must witness theologically to the true nature of life redeemed in Christ, sociologically to the nature of corporate living upon which true peace is based, and politically to the redemptive nature of reconciliation whereby true peace may be realized. Secondly, and more negatively, the Church must remind the governing authority of its origin in God's creative purpose, its present role under the Lordship of Christ and its ultimate dispensation in God's history. In short, the Church today, by its life and its witness, must speak, as the servant of God, to the governing authority, as the order of God, concerning the Lordship of Christ in the nuclear age.

16. God's Reconciling Work Among the Nations Today (Bossey, Switzerland, June 28—July 3, 1965)

As part of the program of discussions and conferences sponsored by the Ecumenical Institute—a branch of the WCC—at Bossey, near Céligny, Switzerland, a conference was sponsored which centered on peace. Some of the planning was done by the participants in the Puidoux conferences. (Interestingly, the topic suggested by the Puidoux planners was "God's Reconciling Word among the Nations Today"; in the Bossey conference the phrase "reconciling word" became "reconciling work.") According to the director of the Institute, Professor N. A. Nissiotis, the conference was one in a series planned "to promote better understanding between East and West in cultural, political, and religious sphere." Noting that other groups were working in the same area, Professor Nissiotis commented that there was no intent to compete nor to correct. Rather,

> We want to add something to the whole effort, especially in studying the biblical and theological foundations of the effort for peace of the different churches; we want also to avoid remaining in an academic discussion and to try to apply our thinking in one of the crucial political issues of our times. That is why we entitled the conference "God's reconciling work among the nations today," to make it clear from the beginning that our intention is first to see how the reconciliation of all men in Christ has to be interpreted by the churches today, and second how this interpretation can help in a given concrete political situation.

Nearly ninety persons from twenty-two countries participated; major speakers were: Hans-Werner Bartsch, Paul Verghese, Vitali Borovoy, John H. Yoder, Jan Lochmann, Paul Evdokimov, Ernst Wilkens, D. Micheli. The attempt was made to balance the speakers from Eastern and Western perspectives, in the areas of Bible, church-state relations, and the prophetic message of the word of God. By design, the debate between pacifists and non-pacifists was not to be featured in the conference. Notable was evidence coming from churchmen from the Eastern countries which documented the problematic of the "Constantinian" link of church and state.

The final report of the conference, drafted by its planner and director, summed up part of the emphasis:

> The service of the churches to the maintenance of peace is almost identical with their fidelity to the word of God and the share of man in the sacramental life of his community. It is on this basis that the churches, in both East and West, can share in all the reconciling activities of the secular world and offer to make their contribution and work together with them.

The Biblical Message of Peace: Summary

Hans-Werner Bartsch

1. The biblical word "peace" corresponds more closely to the Old Testament *shalom* than to the Greek *eirene*.

2. The biblical word "peace" refers therefore firstly to a relationship between two parties, and here again primarily between nations, and only secondarily between individuals. Unlike the Greek it is not primarily a description of a state.

3. The relationship described in this way is the foundation for man's well-being, salvation, which means that "peace" (in a more inclusive sense, salvation), refers to the nature of human existence as God intends it.

4. Salvation is God's gift, so that the intention expressed in "peace be with you" is essentially a desire for blessing. As a conventional greeting both in speech and in letters, despite its triteness, it still has this original meaning.

5. Therefore peace is in essence eschatological and unattainable by human endeavor. Since it is eschatological it remains a goal of man's desiring to which he cannot attain.

6. In his authoritative preaching of God's lordship Christ brought this eschatological promise. Those who believe in him already have this peace while waiting for the imminent coming of his kingdom. They already live as his own under God's rule which is not yet manifestly visible.

7. In faith Christians witness to their existence's being rooted in God's

salvation (= in peace) by allowing peace to enter into every relationship whether the other party understands the relationship in this way or not.

8. Therefore the exhortation to make and keep peace is not only and not primarily an ethical command but also, when understood in this way, a call to witness to one's faith.

9. Insofar as the Bible looks firstly at the nations and only subsequently at individuals, faith's witness to peace has immediate political significance.

10. However, since the people of God is not identical with any political unit (nation, class or ideological group), the people of God of the Christians and the Jews takes its responsibility for witnessing to its faith seriously by witnessing to the peace which God creates in political events to its various partners in the political communities in which it lives.

11. Christians witness to their faith in the knowledge that God himself is there at work. He creates a new foundation for men's relationships with one another. They are kept from the mistaken idea that these relationships can be rightly ordered by human endeavor. But, at the same time, they are preserved from the pessimism of thinking that nothing at all can be done for the right ordering of worldly relationships.

12. In Christians' witness the coming kingdom is made real by their faith. Therefore this witness is fed by an uninterrupted waiting for the Lord's coming.

Church and State According to a Free Church Tradition

John H. Yoder

A. *Definitions*

What is meant by the phrase in our title, "a Free Church Tradition," is in special need of definition. Recent usage has given to the term "Free Church" various too narrow definitions.

From the perspective of political science, the "Free Church" is any church which has no organic relationship to a government, whatever be its theology or polity. In this sense all the Churches in the USA are "Free Churches"—obviously a definition which does not help us.

From the perspective of contemporary interdenominational relationships, especially in Europe, the "Free Churches" are small, generally pietistic, communities set apart from the larger "mainstream" or "official" bodies. Yet this kind of status among larger church bodies, often not by choice, is not theologically constitutive. Just as Professor Nissiotis has encouraged us to strive toward not a special "ecumenical theology" but simply a true theology, which by definition should be properly ecumenical, so I ask not for a Free Church theology, as held by certain small groups, but for an adequate vision of the Freedom of the entire Church of Jesus Christ. Then I shall further ask what relationship to government best expresses this liberty.

Since our conference theme relates to the issues of government and of peace, it should not be inappropriate for me to speak from within the more radical wing of Free Churchdom, namely from the perspective of the "Historic Peace Churches" (Brethren, Friends, Mennonites). Yet in much of what I shall say I hope to speak as well for the common original vision of Baptists, Disciples, Methodists, and Pentecostals as well. Behind the superficial definitions (referred to above) and behind these issues where the Free Churches differ among themselves (war, age of baptism), the fundamental structural definition of the Free Church stance is its rejection of the Constantinian synthesis, the acceptance of which has been (classically, whatever recent changes they have accepted) common to all other traditions, Protestant and Catholic. By "Constantinian synthesis" we refer naturally not to the Emperor himself but to the radical reorganization of church-society relationships which took place in his century, so that henceforth the assumption became normative that sovereign and people were Christian.

If a genuine Free Church vision is to be encompassed in ecumenical discussion, a great degree of flexibility and imagination is necessary; more in some ways than in conversations between the other traditions. By the nature of the case, it is not possible to presuppose in such conversation any binding common historical tradition. Even the ancient so-called "ecumenical councils" already reflect a particular relationship of church and state, radically different from the New Testament picture, and a corresponding redefinition of the structures of the church. The proceedings of the first such council, that of Nicea, already represent a "sectarian" rejection of the Free Church concern.

This flexibility must include the readiness to challenge some axioms which have dominated "mainstream" ethical thought in East and West for centuries. It has been assumed that what a government should do and what the Christian as a member of the political community should do are identical. It has been assumed that the standards for Christian behavior in the political realm are to be derived from a vision of what the State should be or do. It has been assumed that the primary context of Christian concern for the State is the fact that Christians, by virtue of their franchise or their office, are responsible agents of State decision and action.

Most ethical debate has classically been a matter of applying these assumptions in varying ways. My suggestion is that the logic they represent must be called into question if the church's alliance with a particular state structure, and the Church's identity with a given society, which has prevailed generally since Constantine, is no longer to be taken for granted.

Thus before we are ready to base our discussion of the State on a description of the calling of the Christian statesman, and before we ask, "Where do we get our political standards: from natural law or from the Incarnation or from the secular order or from the Amsterdam definition of 'responsible society'?" we must reaffirm a broader, more Biblical, point of departure for the discussion.

Therefore, even though Biblical study is not my assignment (our common Bible study in this conference not being on the subject of the State), I must return to a Biblical starting point to lay the foundation for an understanding of the State in the present by ascertaining what vision of the State is at home in the New Testament situation, where Christians were a tiny minority under an outspokenly pagan government. Certainly no general dogmatic or systematic doctrine about the State and about the church's relation to it can be justified whose terms (like those of some Reformation creeds) forbid application to a pre- or a post-Constantinian situation.

B. *New Testament Orientation*

1. A synoptic statement: Matthew 20:25-28, cf. Luke 22:25f. Jesus does not say here what a State should be like, nor that it is good that there should be a State. He does not so define "State," as sword or as human community or otherwise, so as to allow for the possibility that a given government might by comparison with the norm be denounced as a non-state. Jesus simply affirms and accepts that the State exists. He implies some scepticism about whether the rulers of the world are truly the "benefactors" they pretend to be. The social revolution which Jesus calls for is not that His disciples will react to these rulers in their own terms (as Zealots) nor that they should flee the world. He calls disciples to be different from the world, in the world, and to be like the Son of Man in His servanthood. He comes to speak at all about the state only backhandedly not as an object of major interest in its own right.

2. A general apostolic view: 1 Peter 2:13-21, Romans 13:1-7, 1 Timothy 2:1-4. The Christian attitude toward government is not one of revolt, nor of demanding justice, but of acceptance and submission. This acceptance is based not empirically on the relatively good deal Caesar was

giving his subjects, but "dogmatically" on the meaning of Christ's Lordship.

3. A Pauline perspective: 2 Corinthians 10:4, cf. Revelation 5, Ephesians 6. (The comment here is on the apostolic vocabulary, not only on the substance of these texts): The way Paul takes the language of military combat and applies it to the spiritual battle of the building of the Church, against the opposition of the principalities and powers of the present evil age, is a symbolic affirmation of the claim that the primary political fact of history is the building of the Church. The church is nearer than the "nation" or the "state" to being a true *polis*. The distinct, nonconformist existence of the Free Church is not monastic withdrawal but the visible manifestation in history of a viable society. The contemporary State with its patterns of domination is a counterfeit community. The community which God chooses to build is not a progressively remodeled, total empirical society, but a new creation out of every tribe and tongue and people and nation. The church does not either withdraw geographically or by sublimation (to become the "inner" or "spiritual" dimension of the whole society): She must be authoritatively present, in her distinctness from other "societies," within the world of human relations.

If I were to find fault with our conference's Bible studies, it would not be for failure to seek (which would have been in vain) for a Biblical doctrine of the State. It would rather be for failure to observe that the language in which Old and New Testament speak of God's Work of reconciliation is sweepingly *political (qahal,* people of God, messiah-Christos, Lord, Kingdom, *politeuma).*

4. An Apocalyptic view: Revelation 13:1-10. It is often claimed that this vision of the self-glorifying, persecuting State is an alternative to the view of Romans 13 so that the two passages would represent two different possibilities for the State, one good and one bad, with specific governments oscillating between the two poles. Then the task of Christian discernment begins with classifying a given State so as to be "for" or "against" it. I see no grounds for this idea. It would seem rather that both statements apply at once. Every State makes religious pretentions (as we saw in Jesus' sarcastic reference to "benefactors"). Every State should call for the Christian's response to be one of the spiritual combat (as in Paul). Under every kind of Rule (also in Revelation 13) the Christian attitude is one of suffering submission rather than of violent rebellion.

C. *Systematic Implications of the New Testament Perspective*

The New Testament does not provide a "doctrine of the State," or even the materials for formulating such a doctrine, in a form comparable to what such a doctrine has performed within the Constantinian vision. A "doctrine of the State" has classically provided in one way or another for the following:

(1) a definition of what the State *essentially* is (in such a way as to be able to say as well what is not a State);

(2) an evaluation of the State as good in itself by divine institution, and of its place in the economy of salvation;

(3) goals and norms for its concrete guidance (concepts of legitimacy, *Rechtsstaat, bellum iustum*);

(4) a statement of the obligations of Christians to and for the State, as derived from the above;

(5) guidance about how to deal with the non-state or the enemy State (war, legitimate revolution).

Classically, all of this doctrine can be elaborated without any need to refer, in form or in substance, to the New Testament or to Jesus Christ, although of course the idea of divine institution, once formulated, can be found in Romans 13.

This entire body of thought is missing in the New Testament. Some would explain this as a reflection of the apocalyptic foreshortening of the New Testament's vision of history: the State is uninteresting because the interim before the end is to be so short. Others would explain the gap as reflecting the New Testament's concentration on "religious" or "existential," i.e., personal matters. My claim is rather that, as shown by the absence in New Testament vocabulary of any noun for "state," and by the political character of the language of Faith, the New Testament tells us that *no such doctrinal structure is needed.* Within New Testament thought on the State there is most markedly no room for two crucial characteristics of the "doctrine of the State":

—there is no derivation of Christian duties from the consideration of what a proper government should or must do. Christian duties are derived from the Servanthood of the Messiah and not from the demands of some other non-servant king.

—there is in the New Testament no non-state option; i.e., no consideration of just war, justified rebellion, or the Crusade. Revelation 13 and Romans 13 are simultaneously valid. This rejection of Maccabean rebellion is explained not by withdrawal, by quietism or apocalyptic expectancy, but by the concrete human character and career of the servant confessed as Messiah and Kyrios.

It therefore should not be said, as it has so often been said in the heritage of Ernst Troeltsch, that there exists a specific Free Church vision of what the State should be. This explains why I cannot fulfil my assigned task by describing Anglo-Saxon pluralism as a "proper" kind of Church-State relationship, or even by arguing, as do some, that in North America the Free church vision has triumphed. This would be a new kind of Constantinian synthesis. The point can at most be made negatively: that a vigilant, critical, independent church will tend to favor modesty, constitutionality, and decentralization in the State, by criticising the self-glorifying State. But all the Historic Peace Churches, like the New Testament church, came into being in societies which persecuted them. Their first concern was not to change the persecuting State into a better, juster one. They accepted government rather than prescribing for it. *Later,* by their moral independence and refusal to conform, they helped to change it.

D. *Changes in the State Since New Testament Times*

It is quite currently argued that the New Testament attitude toward the State has been rendered obsolete by changes in the nature of States, changes which are generally assumed to have been basic and all for the good.

To the extent that these changes are real, they must of course modify the relevance of New Testament precedent. It can, however, not be assumed that the meaning of these changes is unambiguous, nor that they are necessarily for the good. We cannot begin by assuming some contemporary or medieval pattern of State action or of Church-State relations to be logically more normal than, or preferable to, that of the New Testament. The developments of Church history can therefore be assimilated into our thought only as they can be tested by New Testament norms; they cannot themselves invalidate those norms.

(1) The change in the number of persons who nominally belong to Christian bodies, or in the willingness of prince and society to be the wards of the church, is no ground for a fundamental revision of Church-State relations unless it can be demonstrated that the greater numbers of "Christians" are genuinely and personally committed to Christian discipleship. To say, "between the first and the fourth centuries the situation of the Church was reversed because by the time of Augustine everyone was Christian" is not a meaningful statement if in making it we must (as Augustine did) admit that the meaning to the individual of being Christian had also changed radically.

(2) Beginning with Constantine the churches had the favour of political authorities; this change as well is ambivalent. The New Testament did not define the Church-State relationship as a reaction of the church to the antagonism of the civil authorities; a change in the rulers' attitude is thus no clear grounds for the church to change; especially if (as seems often

to have been the case) the church must "purchase" this new recognition by services to the state.

(3) Another change is the development of democratic institutions by virtue of which it can be claimed that "the people" share in government. But neither is this change fundamental. The concept of "government by the people" is a most useful ideal or myth; it is not a factual description of any viable form of human sovereignty above the village level, nor of the historical or metaphysical origins of government. Nor need it be assumed that the person who exercises his franchise is morally more "responsible" for the decisions of government than the subject in another age.

(4) It can more substantially be argued that the modern state's welfare and economic functions are truly a novelty. Yet this does not change the nature of the dominion which continues to be exercised by some over others. The welfare functions may very well be prostituted by demagogues into "bread and circuses" or into payment for votes. If so there is no change in the nature of government. If on the other extreme these public welfare services are exercized in a truly unselfish spirit of service, there will be every reason for Christians to be involved in such service, but this does not mean that they are thereby bearing the sword.

E. *The Meaningfulness of Sociopolitical History*

To state that the Church is central in the meaning of history is not a mere pious phrase. It is a concrete statement about where we find the key to genuine meaning in human events. It is in her thanksgiving, her proclamation, and her service that human history makes sense, whether the newspapers cover it or not.

This history, because it is genuine history, is not unilinear. If our vision of its movement is to be biblically and ecumenically complete, it cannot proceed without a concept of apostasy or of the Fall of the Church; whatever be the qualifications and limitations in the use of such terms in ecumenical etiquette. Ecumenical encounter does not grasp the full dimensions of its task if the reciprocal accusation of apostasy cannot also be dealt with. Beyond being a concern of general relevance for interchurch conversation, this point applies especially to church-state relationships in that apostasy is often state-related, from Revelation 13 to the *Kirchenkampf*.

The multilinear character of history makes it both impossible and illegitimate to ascribe to history one clear meaning, such as "progress" or "secularization." Progress is also decay; as the world gets better it also gets worse. Efforts therefore to discern "what God is doing in the world" as if it could be known in an ambiguous way, so that the Church could learn from it are therefore deceiving. Such an effort means the arbitrary selection of one line within history, or of one community (a nation, a class, a race), as bearer of that meaning. This identification suffers necessarily from provincialism and pride.

Neither can we therefore pretend effectively to guide history in the way it should rightly go, whether by the sword or some other kind of directive power. Such an effort is proud in the superior moral insight it claims, and will be self-destructive because of its ignorance. To claim to be able to determine in what direction the whole course of events must go, or be taken by the rulers of this world, is itself a denial that true divine sovereignty is to be discerned in the Cross and Resurrection alone. "Telling the rulers how to get peace" outside of the presuppositions of faith, or by commending actions inconsistent with the Incarnation (such as certain categories of "just wars") can also be such a pretentious misreading of history's possibilities.

This is not to disavow interest in, or proclamation concerning political events, or concern for what should or should not take place. But the Christian's proclamation in both judgment and promise to men in society is not to be qualified by his or his hearers' prior calculation of the changes of "bringing it off," and may not properly develop a rationale for another ethic than that of radical, suffering discipleship, or for saving at all costs any particular national order or social patterns.

F. *Ecumenical Social Theory: "Responsible Society"*

If the slogan "responsible society" is taken to refer to a secular translation of specific biblical insights about man and society, the concept can be used responsibly by Christians to guide their own social involvement. This interpretation is favored by statements in several of the "responsible society" documents about the centrality of Christian congregations as laboratories and as powerhouses for social creativity. In this framework it could then be assumed that what the New Testament says about those who bear the sword is still basically true, and that the Christian attitude toward them, whether in "young nations" or old, is that of the apostolic teaching; submission, service, suffering faithfulness. "Responsibility" is not a euphemism for a newfound justification for dominion over others.

If, on the other hand, by "responsible society" is meant the importation into Christian thought of moral standards derived from some other source than Jesus Christ, under some such heading as "incarnation" or "Christianizing a pagan legacy" or "natural law" or "holy worldliness" or "common ground with the nonbeliever" or "what we have found God doing" or "creation," then the promise that this concept will provide relevant, substantial Christian guidance where there is serious difference between Christians as to how to read "the truth of a given situation" is deceptive.

If the concept of "responsibility" is taken, as often in current use, to mean "it is up to us to save the situation by doing the right thing as strongly as possible," this makes normative a social situation which is actually quite rare. If through their numbers, their reputation, or their special gifts Christians are able to change the course of history, let them do so; but this is much less often the case than they think. Normally, i.e., in the missionary situation where Christians are a minority, this should not be expected. Nor does it matter much that it cannot be. The fulfilment of God's purposes in the world is not dependent on efforts of socially insightful and powerful Christians, seeking by the manipulation of the powers of history to make things come out right. The New Jerusalem is not produced by remodeling the Old in line with even the best contemporary insights. Our hope cannot be fully sublimated into affirmative expectations of the possibilities of the structures of society when properly used.

G. *The State and the Free Church*

The *institutional* separation of Church and State, though superficial as a definition, reflects the necessary priority of church over state as instrument of reconciliation. The Church may not content herself to serve as chaplain, blessing whatever situation she may be placed in, being grateful for a Constantine when he comes and grateful again when he is taken away. She must serve rather as prophet, bringing things to pass by her example in service and by her refusal of limited loyalties.

In this framework the "pacifist" stand of the radical Free Churches must be understood not as a moralistic insistence on a particularly simple interpretation of the Sermon on the Mount, but as reflecting the priority, as the context of Christian moral decision, of the community sharing in Christ's death and life (2 Cor. 4:10-11) over the counterfeit communities of this world, which not only proclaim their right to live at the cost of others but even would draft him into that self-preservation.

The superficial sociological character of the Free Church as a voluntary association, if emphasized unduly, would deny the objectivity and the universality of the Church. But this pattern is still preferable to all those, also superficial and sociological, where membership is compulsory and structures are dictated by the magistracy.

The superficial character of Free Churches (notably in Europe) as small is an accident, yet this superficial trait safeguards the awareness that the Church must not *expect* or *seek* size and power. It safeguards against delusions of grand responsibility, and against apostate alliances with race, class, or nation as a path to power. Ability to accept social impotence as the path of servanthood might be the touchstone of the ability of the "mainstream" Churches, now that they have been freed (often in spite of themselves) from the old Constantinian alliance, to accept this freedom as a gift rather than seeking a new concubinage with the new "secular" powers.

The testimony of the Free Churches is not to a particular, modern Western, pattern of social expression. It is to the "jealousy" of our Lord and the priority of covenant peoplehood over the claims of other communities and their lords to represent the ultimately valuable society. The call to all Churches, or to the whole Church, is to be freed by faith from dependence on and from ultimate loyalty to other given social structures.

The Tasks of the Church

Heinz Kloppenburg

Every discussion of the concrete tasks of the church must begin with a consideration of the actual condition of the churches. It is relatively simple to draft a program for the churches under the aspect of our theme in a theologically respectable way. However, the question of whether that which we call "the churches" is in a condition to hear and to act according to what it hears, is a different matter.

The following is to be considered: the condition of Christendom in the area of the so-called Christian West. The problematic of the existence of the "established" churches in a still-Christian area of the world is obvious to all of us. The majority of Christians does not yet realize how much the substance of the churches' proclamation, and hence the churches' power of authority, has been diluted by an accommodation to the thinking of a certain epoch in intellectual and cultural history. The institution (and thus to a large measure also the "claim" of the church) is in its present form supported by the mass of those who, in good faith and subjective honesty, consider the symbiosis of church/world (which has put its stamp on Western culture) as a possible form of church life. This is especially so because within this symbiosis subjective Christian piety is tolerated and, as long as it does not interfere with the historical transformation process of the world, encouraged by the Western world. Yet, in actuality, this symbiosis, which is equally dangerous for the church and the world, has taken the place of the church's claim on the world, of true dialogue, of confrontation. The renewal of thinking about and within the church, the so-called "rediscovery of the church," has by no means penetrated into the congregations. However, the concrete actions and words of the institutional churches are in large part determined by consideration for this "thinking of the church *(Gemeinde)"* which, at best, understands the gospel as a means for alleviating the needs of the Christian in the world, as solace and as eschatological hope, but not as a radical questioning of that type of thinking which starts with the needs of man rather than with the gospel of God. The service of the church then becomes an "injection" of good thoughts into a hopelessly ill body, but it does not call to a new life through the power of the resurrection.

The mandate of the church is often much more clearly recognized where the false symbiosis with society has either been terminated or is dying (a dying over which the minds of the church are divided: some see it as the end, others, as the great opportunity for a new beginning) and where this symbiosis has never existed. The renewal of the church and the understanding of its mandate to witness is therefore most likely to be expected from the "younger churches" or from the persecuted church *(ecclesia pressa)*—and from those churches that have resisted the Constantinian era from the beginning.

Yet these considerations are not meant to discourage us: The church does not live on its spiritual status but from the new creation and mission in the Holy Spirit promised and fulfilled daily through the word. There remains for the entire church even in her various captivities the mandate to proclaim the saving grace of God, which has appeared in Christ and calls us to a new life.

This means that the church has to proclaim the reconciliation between God and man, which places him who accepts it into the service of his fellowmen, because the peace created by God is commandment and free gift also for interpersonal relationships. The church of Jesus takes the risk of assuming peacemaking as part of its witness. Every individual congregation and every individual Christian is called to find out what that means in concrete terms.

The church *(Gemeinde)* will not misinterpret this witness idealistically, it will not ignore the guilty entanglement of the world, but confront the reality of sin with the reality of Christ. It will not ignore the fact that people give one another cause daily for hate and that enmity is one of the everlasting marks of the lost world. But, wherever there are Christians, there is more than enmity, for there reconciliation and peace must have a dwelling place—for otherwise everything which Christians proclaim loses credibility.

For society this means that enmity exists between different systems, but that the Christian will never contribute to absolutizing this enmity. He will attempt within society to help replace an unbearable situation by a somewhat less unbearable one. (Peace is not the cementing in of the status quo!) In his personal decision he will do what his conscience, which is bound to the Word, commands him to do. (Conscientious objection to war can be one of the marks of the Christian's awareness of his status in the world.) He will know that the church cannot prescribe decisions as laws, but he will unmask cheap evasions that use the realm of personal decision as excuse and call to that witness, which comes from personal encounter with the gospel as a voluntary but unalterable witness whose realization is not in our hands.

If that which we call the societal and political service of the church results from the witness of reconciliation, then it is its task to prepare the way for reconciliation among human beings. This means:

(a) within the church: the radical witness of reconciliation of the church in its own life;

(b) outside of the church: cooperation in bringing about reconciliation among the nations, whether they call themselves Christian or not.

(a) This implies that the symbiotic churches will not be frightened when some of their members take obedience in faith radically seriously, but they will place themselves protectively in front of these members and will not be ashamed of their witness but acknowledge it publicly and accept it as a call to examine each individual's position. Within the symbiotic churches the slowness of hearts is the greatest spiritual danger. The Puidoux conferences which deal with certain basic decisions of the churches, are a necessary theological support for the questions arising here; the churches really ought to give priority to this theological work.

(b) The task outside of the church implies an abundance of services in our present world:

(1) information about that which threatens peace between nations, as counteraction against all propagandistic and incomplete information;

(2) dissemination of this information down to the last congregations;

(3) the furthering and sponsoring of encounters between people from different nations, especially from those living in tension with one another; the promoting of cultural, scientific, and technical exchanges;

(4) affirmation of all attempts at creating centers of worldwide understanding, such as the United Nations, its suborganizations, and the protest against exclusion of any nations of groups from such organizations;

(5) active emergency aid in overcoming tensions through concrete suggestions in all areas, and taking the risk of swimming against the current of popular public opinion.

The work of the CCIA (Churches' Commission on International Affairs) and the CPC (Christian Peace Conference) should become much more widely known in and supported by the congregations, than has been the case. It is a bad sign that the churches do not distribute CCIA news and that the significance of such attempts as that of the CPC for the witness of Christendom are not considered at all out of symbiotic reasons.

Finally, the churches ought to encourage and support all of those projects where groups of Christians are preparing the ground for reconciliation. Such work is likely to become a symbol of reconciliation for many. International encounters and work camps for young people are of great significance. Institutions should not hesitate to use the voluntary organizations and agencies, advise them, assist them, and refrain from rushing into the institutionalizing of every vital movement.

It might be that in an age in which external peace has become the prerequisite for the survival of mankind, this survival is dependent on the readiness and ability of the churches to activate their members for the services of reconciliation among nations, and on the credibility of their proclamation of the merciful God, who wills life and not death.

17. World Conference on Church and Society: Christians in the Technical and Social Revolutions of Our Time (Geneva, Switzerland, July 12-26, 1966)

A landmark conference—this is an appropriate designation for the 1966 conference at Geneva which brought to the fore issues of development of Third World nations, the role of justice for liberation movements, and the appropriate response of Christians from advanced technological nations. A large conference, it brought together more than four hundred participants from eighty nations and one hundred sixty-four churches. Response to it was electric—ranging from enthusiastic approval to outright rejection. Several books were written by leading theologians to debate both its findings and its methods.

In terms of peace discussions, the newest development was the introduction into a wider circle of the concept of indirect or systemic violence which harms and oppresses the weak and the poor by the very framework of the society. In a section on the nature of the state and the issue of Christian participation in politics these statements were made:

> The clear Christian teaching regarding the respect for persons and love of one's enemy requires the Christian to seek all possible peaceful and responsible non-violent means of action in society.... Some Christians affirm that this commitment to non-violent means of witness is absolute, and their witness must be respected. But violence is very much a reality in our world, both the overt use of force to oppress and the invisible violence ... perpetrated on people who by the millions have been or still are the victims of repression and unjust social systems. Therefore the question often emerges today whether the violence which sheds blood in planned revolutions may not be a lesser evil than the violence, which though bloodless, condemns whole populations to perennial despair.... It cannot be said that the only possible position for the Christian is one of absolute non-violence. There are situations where Christians may become involved in

violence. Whenever it is used, however, it must be seen as an "ultimate recourse" which is justified only in extreme situations.

The larger treatment of peace came in the section on international cooperation and dealt with the problem of nuclear warfare and responses to its threat.

Listed among issues needing further study in the final report was: "A theological understanding of: (a) revolution and especially the ethics of violent action; (b) non-violence and the new experiences of non-violent revolution; (c) the rights of conscientious objectors to military service."

Report on Section III: Structures of International Cooperation. Living Together in Peace in a Pluralistic World Society

I. INTRODUCTION: GENERAL AFFIRMATIONS

1. God wills life, he gives life, he loves the life of men, and he will guide men to his kingdom. Although we reject him and incur guilt, although we are blinded by the enigmas and evils of this world, we know it is his purpose that men should have life and have it abundantly (John 10:11). That is the joyous message which we receive by God's coming into this world in Christ. The mission of the Church, and therefore our task, is to witness to this message in word and deed.

2. Jesus Christ died and rose again for all. In him all things are held together (Col. 1:17), the whole of mankind is a unity, and each person is entitled to the life God wills for all. The Gospel gives man the peace of God, and it is the God of peace who equips us with everything, that we may do his will (Heb. 13:21). His grace is made manifest through service to mankind.

3. We are called to serve God's peace among our fellowmen. Although God's peace and peace in the world of nations are not identical, he who serves because he has been given the peace of God will seek peace among men.

4. The cross of Christ rebukes our egotism, and delivers us from concern with our own life only. We have been taught that true life is found in a

new way, in a new nature, in which Christ is all and in all, and in which there are no conflicting divisions among men (Col. 3:10-11).

5. For these reasons, the churches have urged their members to participate responsibly in the life of the state and society. In spite of many differences, our ecclesiastical traditions agree that the function of the state in God's purpose is to provide, if necessary by lawful coercion, that order which enables men to live in peace and justice with one another. Human experience as well as Holy Scripture shows us that the power of law is required to compel man to respect the rights of others. While this remains true in our day, many circumstances in the modern world force men to revolution against an unjust established order. The right to revolt is recognized by Christians, but the problem which revolution poses for Christian ethics needs further study. In general, the churches have not condemned the use of force, when it has been according to accepted rules and to preserve or to create a just order in society.

II. INTERNATIONAL PEACE AND SECURITY

Nuclear Warfare

6. In all ages churches have been confronted by the problem of war. The majority has affirmed that Christians may participate in the defence of their country against attack, through military means if those become ultimately necessary; a significant minority has disagreed. However, the development of military technology, and especially of atomic, radiological, biological and chemical arms and the means to deliver them, marks a decisive turning point in the history of mankind, of states, and their wars. The frightful possibilities of indiscriminate war exterminating not only combatants but civilian populations as well, the impossibility of self-defence by smaller nations, the danger of annihilation of human cultures, the continuing danger of future generations from radiation—all this radically changes the situation of the states and their relations with one another.

7. This new and terrible situation forces Christians to reexamine their previous thinking concerning war and the function of the state in relation to it. In Amsterdam in 1948, the First Assembly of the World Council of Churches declared, "War is contrary to the will of God," and at the same time distinguished three possible attitudes towards the participation by Christians in the evil of war. Today the situation has changed. Christians still differ as to whether military means can be legitimately used to achieve objectives which are necessary to justice. But nuclear war goes beyond all bounds. Mutual nuclear annihilation can never establish justice because it destroys all that justice seeks to defend or to achieve. We now say to all

governments and peoples that nuclear war is against God's will and the greatest of evils. Therefore we affirm that it is the first duty of governments and their officials to prevent nuclear war.

8. Inasmuch as war between states results from the present disorganized and unjust political and economic conditions of international society, it is the duty of all men and governments to strive together to strengthen the existing structures and to create new instruments of a responsible international community. The task requires unprecedented political and moral effort. Of Christians, it demands the contribution of the preaching, teaching, and action of the Church, and the efforts of individuals. It requires new thought concerning Christian attitudes to the state and war, the relations among states, the demands of economic and social justice in and between states, the development of international ethos, law, and structures by which the international anarchy can be supplanted by justice and order. The rise of the new military technology creates a situation in which God's judgment challenges men to end the old history of the international jungle. The future of mankind depends upon this.

9. We recognize that, apart from these affirmations, we found no single, simple, general Christian insight regarding the threat to peace posed by the existence of nuclear weapons. . . .

Towards a Responsible International Community

28. The ultimate responsibility for the prevention of major war lies primarily on the great powers. No other nations carry that awful responsibility. War can start between smaller nations, and local conflicts can escalate when great powers are drawn in, sometimes against their will. Therefore the United Nations or regional organizations can render useful service through the settlement of local conflicts. But the fate of the world is largely in the hands of the great powers.

29. The churches should be under no illusions with regard to the state of the world. There is no world government nor can we foresee one. The nuclear nations exercise their power uncontrolled by any international agency, and at the same time the international ethos of the nuclear age is still highly ambiguous.

30. The churches must warn the nations that the balance of power requires ever-increasing defence budgets, keeps men in a condition of distrust and fear, and lessens the ability of the powers involved in it to act justly amidst the struggles for national liberation and social justice. Nevertheless, the nuclear powers have a great common interest in not letting their precarious balance escalate into nuclear war. They also have a common interest in preventing nuclear proliferation, and the escalation of local con-

flict. The churches should add that they have something more in common: the duty to preserve the life of the peoples of this world, and to work for a world order which will transcend the present uneasy peace of the equilibrium of power.

31. The crucial problem is how this supreme task—the avoidance of nuclear war—can be fulfilled. It is not enough for the Church to declare, as it has in the past, that war is contrary to the will of God, and for it to say "No!" to nuclear warfare. Too few churches have made positive statements and then sought to implement them. If war is to be prevented, it is the situation which could lead to war which must be changed. We must take the long way of changing a balance of power into a community with institutions which are responsible for the common interest and through their remedial action help to prevent the escalation of conflict between the main powers.

32. Neither international law, nor the existing rules against aggression, indiscriminate warfare or war itself, nor new international legal provisions will by themselves prevent the outbreak of hostilities: The history of this century is one long list of broken covenants and violations of legal commitments. But the discipline which the great powers will be forced to observe in order to prevent nuclear war could and should be embodied, step by step, in a code of conduct, concerning limitations on the use of force, leading to the development of a new international law controlling nuclear policies.

33. At the same time, the equilibrium of power should be subjected to joint controls in order to enhance the sense of security. International agencies should be established for the universal control and inspection of the different phases of disarmament in the nuclear, biological, chemical, and conventional fields. The peaceful use of atomic energy and all nuclear power programmes should be open to inspection by the International Atomic Energy Agency in Vienna.

34. A system to prevent the proliferation of nuclear weapons should also be established, in which all nations should cooperate. There must be a balance between the sacrifices required of non-nuclear weapon states and those required of states which are stockpiling increasingly effective nuclear weapons. But such a system should also be jointly controlled, open and set up on a legal basis in order to pave the way for a new legal order in which the peoples of this world can learn to live with the new power which has been put into their hands. One of the next steps should be the extension of the existing Test Ban Treaty to other fields of nuclear testing and the adherence of those states which have not yet signed. We condemn the continued polluting of the atmosphere by nuclear testing, especially when con-

ducted outside a country's national boundaries.

35. Peace is not the responsibility of the great powers alone. In the atomic stalemate which to a certain extent paralyses the nuclear powers, smaller nations enjoy greater liberty to act for good or evil than ever before. Accordingly, all nations should be aware that a new world order is impossible without their full cooperation, their willingness to renounce nuclear weapons, and their exercise of discipline to prevent the eruption of local conflicts.

36. The nuclear stalemate, while making outright war between large nations more unlikely, has enhanced the danger of the use of substitutes for open war, such as foreign intervention in internal revolutions or subversive activities from outside. The danger and cruelty of such activities, in which the population of the country concerned is the victim of a world situation, should be well understood. . . .

III. World Social, Economic, and Political Development

61. In the Christian understanding of society and human relations there is no place for discrimination against persons on the basis of race, religion, ideology, economic or social condition, since all men are equal before God, and all benefit from his love and his grace in Jesus Christ and all stand under his judgment.

62. Further, Christians are responsibly committed to all men, and their action should fully express this commitment. Yet we Christians confess our sins of racial prejudice and injustice, our failure to treat each other as brothers, the violence we do not only to the body but also to the mind and soul of our brothers and ourselves. We honour all those, whether Christian or not, who are working actively to redeem their societies to make them inclusive of all God's children, and would support them in the transformation of economic, social, and political structures to assure full participation and equality of opportunity and status. In every circumstance, the Christian is called actively to seek reconciliation where there is tension, justice where there is injustice, freedom where there is bondage, and opportunity where this is denied. We are aware that our failure to fulfil these missions promptly in our day is likely to lead to violence and war. . . .

IV. The Church's Involvement

91. In the midst of the complex, dangerous, and fearsome problems of contemporary international affairs, we have five things to say to our fellow Christians.

(a) We thank God that a nuclear holocaust has not occurred, that men have been inspired with patience, restraint, and courage, that new possibilities of communication and dialogue have emerged among the nations and peoples, and that in spite of our sin and guilt there is still time in which to strive for peace. We thank God for the men and women in many agencies and walks of life who labour tirelessly for peace.

(b) It is our belief and experience that in suffering God's grace abounds. We know—because sometimes it is present in our hearts too—that a sense of futility and hopelessness concerning peace and justice lies in the background of millions of lives. But even in the midst of fear and futility God's grace touches and opens the heart. In this lies our hope: No power of earth or man can ultimately defeat the power of God. It is to men who live in the valley of the shadow of death that God's power is manifest and the light of hope is given in Jesus Christ.

(c) We urge Christians and the churches, by every means at their disposal, to join those who seek to arouse the conscience of their fellowmen concerning peace and justice. The life of the Church itself is the principal means, but others will also be needed. These will vary: Patient political effort and impatient protest, advocacy of feasible measures and projection of long-range goals, the creation of greater order, and the transformation of existing orders will all be involved. Whatever the means, Christians must bear one another's burdens of loneliness and weakness, and support one another in their common witness. But the goal must always be to arouse the conscience of all men everywhere, that it may be made sensitive to the claims of justice and peace in our world.

(d) The witness of radical non-conformity has always been part of the Christian tradition. It may be an act of an individual or group, but all Christians should support the right of such individuals or groups to take such a stand. Such non-conformists do not, of course, any more than other Christians, escape responsibility for the disordered affairs of the world—they cannot do so. Their responsibility remains. However, a majority of Christians in working within the existing order believe themselves called to work for its transformation and to accept a role in its civil or military organization. They must never lose sight of its inherent imperfection which is obscured by the self-deceptions that come from within it, for then they will maintain a constant pressure for progress.

(e) We ask Christians to bear constant witness to their faith in the life of their nation in the world. Occasional action is not enough: Continual witness is required. It is not enough to speak and act in isolation. In our time, churches may pioneer in the development of world community by formulating their own witness as part of the ecumenical community. Thus they may transcend the nations, contribute to their search for peace, and in their worship uphold the world before God.

92. In order that the churches may make critical social and ethical judgments in a Christian perspective, the first essential is a knowledge of the facts. We therefore recommend that the World Council of Churches accept responsibility for the collection, critical evaluation, and dissemination of relevant facts to all the constituent churches, so that these churches may in turn pass them on to their parishes. The constituent churches should for their part collect clear information on situations of ecumenical importance for passing on to the appropriate department of the WCC.

93. As situations evolve they should be kept under constant review through periodic consultations, and suitable collective action can then be taken. The CCIA could be strengthened accordingly. In this way, and through contacts, consultation and cooperation at local and international levels with Roman Catholics and other interested Christians an ongoing worldwide dialogue can be maintained and a Christian community can be built and fortified by intercessory prayer.

18. The Quaker Peace Testimony (Guilford College, North Carolina, 1967)

During 1966 a series of meetings were held under the sponsorship of the Friends World Committee for Consultation, attempting to draw up a statement on the position of the Society of Friends toward war. It was hoped that it "may be of service to Friends in a number of countries who are endeavoring to express the Quaker testimony for peace in modern terms." The intent was to draw up something which would have validity across national and cultural lines. Quakers from The Netherlands, Norway, Sweden, Germany, Switzerland, Great Britain, Finland, Ireland, Japan, and the United States were involved at some point.

A process of writing and rewriting was followed which allowed a distillation of most of the points brought forward by the participants in the process. The statement was also presented to the Peace Section at the Fourth Friends World Conference held in North Carolina in 1967. Although it proved impossible for those Friends present "to examine, adjust, and agree to every detail" of the statement, it was agreed that this and another similar document would be circulated to all yearly meetings for study and reaction. Within these limitations, it may be held to be representative of recent Quaker viewpoints on peace and war.

The Quaker Peace Testimony
Notes Made Following Three Consultations in 1966

1. Friends have, throughout their history as a religious Society maintained a testimony for peace. War, we say, is contrary to the mind of Christ, and if we are to be true followers of Him it is laid upon us to do our utmost as George Fox wrote in 1651, "to live in the virtue of that life and power that takes away the occasion of all wars."

2. This testimony for peace has three aspects. In the first place, it leads

us to refuse to take part ourselves in acts of war. In the second place, it leads us to strive to remove the causes of war. In the third place, it leads us to use the way of love in any manner open to us to promote peace, to heal wounds and to promote human brotherhood.

3. Friends in Great Britain in the year 1661 made a declaration to King Charles expressing their testimony against war in clear terms, and this testimony has been quoted by generation after generation of Friends as expressing a deeply felt conviction. "We utterly deny all wars and strife and fightings with outward weapons, for any end or under any pretence whatsoever. And this is our testimony to the whole world. The spirit of Christ, by which we are guided, is not changeable, so as once to command us from a thing as evil and again to move unto it; and we do certainly know, and so testify to the world that the spirit of Christ, which leads us into all Truth will never move us to fight and war against any man with outward weapons, neither for the Kingdom of Christ, nor for the Kingdoms of this world."

4. In the twentieth century, while the purpose of war (to achieve by force an object which cannot be achieved by agreement) remains unchanged, its method of waging has changed radically. Right up to the war of 1914-1918, wars were fought hand to hand by individual soldiers, mounted on horses, or on foot. Local wars may still be so contended. But in greater wars the contestants may hardly see one another. Thousands of "the enemy" may be killed or maimed by high explosive or atomic weapons wielded from a distance, and in such cases there is no distinction between soldiers and civilians among those who suffer.

5. Thus the testimony that "the spirit of Christ . . . will never move us to fight and war against any man with outward weapons . . . " calls for a wider expression and interpretation today than it did in the seventeenth century.

6. The conviction that it is wrong to take arms against our fellow men remains with us and is our testimony today. It involves that we must take care in choosing our employment (for those of us who are fortunate enough to have such a choice) that we shall decline to involve ourselves in occupations which are concerned with war or preparation for war. It involves that in all our human relationships we shall strive to express the principles of human brotherhood and mutual service. It leads us to endeavour to devote our lives to the service of our fellow men and not to the harming of any among them, of any race or colour.

7. The fact that many of our fellow Christians find themselves able to serve in the armed forces, however much this may to them be a "regrettable necessity," makes it necessary for us to indicate that our testimony—arises

from a deep conviction of the true nature of the Christian gospel. Since we are a minority in the whole Christian Church we must express ourselves with humility as well as with boldness; but we say with deep conviction that Christ's way of life and the manner of His death reveal to us God as the loving father of all men, who are thus seen to be brothers. Therefore it is more Christlike to suffer wrong than to endeavour to oppose it by methods of violence which are themselves wrong in His sight.

8. In recent years many Friends in a number of countries (in common with all their fellow citizens) have known the experience of being invaded by a foreign power, or of living under the threat of invasion or of living under constant bombardment. For them the experience of war has been inescapable. We have learned with George Fox "to live in the virtue of that life and power . . . " which allows us to be in peace and tranquility of mind even in conditions of great stress and thus to be liberated to serve others in their time of need.

9. This conviction of non-violence does not stem from a reading of texts in the Bible, nor is it derived from the writings of those who have gone before us. It arises from an intuitive understanding of the true relationship between God and all his children, which leads us to speak of "that of God" in every man. Dependence on the spirit of Christ is an appeal to an instinctive or intuitive perception, fortified by demonstration in the life and character and teaching of Jesus Christ himself. It is our testimony that this same spirit still speaks to us in our inner conscience and when we hear its voice we feel ourselves under a compulsion which cannot be denied.

10. There will be some who will wish, in their minds, to go back still further behind the teachings of Christ, and who appreciate that there is an ultimate truth directing us in this matter, and that this ultimate truth was in the world from the beginning before Christ was, and that others beside Jesus Christ have perceived this and declared its truth. To us as Friends, however, He is the one who above all others has shown us the way of the Divine Spirit with His creation.

11. Many Friends have had the experience of living in a country under the dominance of an alien power. These have been confronted with the dilemma of divergent loyalties. The first loyalty is to Christ who calls us to love our enemy and this restrains us from exercising violence against him. The second loyalty calls us to endeavour to aid any persons who may be in trouble or sickness or pain whatever their race or nationality or status. The third loyalty calls us to love our own country, its people, and its way of life. This loyalty prevents us from being willing to aid an invader in his violation of it. In these situations of conflict no one can lay down rules of

conduct for others to follow. What we can do is to testify that in our experience the spirit of Christ leads us into all truth and gives us the needed guidance in every situation.

12. In a country threatened with invasion most citizens will flock to the colours because they feel that the evil of war is less than the evil of enemy occupation and foreign domination. In such a situation the understanding of Christ's way of life which we feel is that the Christian life of dependence on God, and of love towards all our fellow men may be lived and sustained even under outward circumstances of great privation, anxiety, and suffering. We believe in divine guidance and in dependence on God, and the life of the spirit does not depend on tranquillity, on affluence, or even on personal liberty, all of which have often been denied to the saints. Wherever we are, whether in affluent circumstances or in poverty, whether at home or in prison or in concentration camp, we are under the guiding hand of God, and He has a service for us to render in the circumstances in which He has placed us, whatever that may be.

13. Warlike operations are sometimes pursued by one nation or group against another without any declaration of war. Economic measures are often taken by one nation or group of nations against another. In time of peace preparations may be ordered which involve citizens in civil defence or in other operations which imply a spirit of animosity or of fear of vindictiveness all of which are alien to those who are trying to live their lives in the spirit of Christ. Against this background Friends will be concerned that as far as possible their thoughts and energies, their professional skill and daily occupations are directed to positive and constructive ends. Those engaged in industry or in scientific pursuits will wish to be on their guard lest their skill in research or in construction is prostituted for purposes which are destructive or which engender animosity or hatred, almost without their being aware of it.

14. In the political field there are occasions when, short of using armed force, two countries, or groups of countries, can become involved in hostilities under the name of "sanctions" the purpose of which, as in warfare, is to compel the other party to do unwillingly, something which cannot be brought about by persuasion. Sanctions may not involve the cruelty of destruction of life and property which war involves, but certainly they do bring hardship and suffering to many people who are innocent of any offence and powerless to defend themselves against the economic weapons directed against them.

15. The substitution of sanctions for the declaration of war may be seen as a movement of the public conscience of the world away from the horrors of war and may be welcomed as a movement in the right direction.

But even so, sanctions are seen to cause hardship and suffering such as hunger and mass unemployment. In such circumstances it has often been given to Friends to exercise a reconciling role and to take part in the relief of suffering in any way open to them. The task of reconciliation, of speaking truth in love to both sides is one which has often been entrusted to Friends, in common with other men of goodwill. There are many examples in the history of the Society of Friends, of action taken which involved personal sacrifice in the labour of bringing reconciling love into a situation of selfishness and hatred.

16. Love is a great power in the world. It is ultimately a power greater than that of evil. That is our fundamental faith in God and in His purpose for the world. It is our experience that there is something of God in every man and this innate goodness is always to be appealed to. In the short run the appeal may not always succeed, but in God's good time it will succeed because it is the divine way with men. The example of William Penn who founded the State of Pennsylvania on the basis of mutual trust with the Indians, demonstrates that trust and goodwill can build sound community relationships.

17. Since we renounce war as the ultimate means of settling disputes, it must follow that we must give every support we can to the peaceful means if war is to be renounced.

18. This is the second aspect of our testimony for peace. It leads us to support the work of the United Nations and its associated bodies. It leads us to work with any agencies which are seeking to promote better race relations and the promotion of movements which are designed to make the natural resources of the world open to satisfy the needs of all mankind. A world at peace is a world filled with Christian charity and a concern for the needs and the welfare of all.

19. It has always been a testimony of Friends that we should live simply so that we may share our means of living with others less fortunate than ourselves. This is part of our peace testimony. John Woolman challenged Friends to consider whether "the seeds of war have no nourishment in our possessions," and today when we compare the affluence of western civilization with the poverty of Africa and Asia it becomes clear that if men are to live at peace with one another, means must be found to secure a kinder and more brotherly distribution of the world's resources. Our testimony for peace sets this as the great task before us.

20. The third aspect of our peace testimony is that which calls us to be peacemakers, promoters of human brotherhood. We are called to use all the influence we can bring to bear in favour of disarmament and for the promotion of peace between nations. Peace is not a mere absence of war. It

is a state in which there is human contentment because injustice has been removed and opportunities for a full life have been opened to all.

21. It is considerations such as these which have led Friends everywhere to become engaged in service projects and in experiments in cooperation in industry and international affairs.

22. A great change needs to be brought about in the thinking of men and women across the world if the world is to become a community of people living under conditions of social and international contentment. All our effort should be directed towards achieving this goal. Our testimony for peace is thus seen to involve so much more than a mere negation of war. It involves the creation of a loving relationship in which the good life which God has provided for us is made available to all his children.

23. Therefore we feel called, in this day and generation, to renounce war as a means of settling disputes or of securing national objectives, to live ourselves at peace with all men, to love and to serve and to create.

24. The world is moving through a long creative process which we call evolution. In this process man, having developed from the lower animals is distinguished from them by his power to reason and to lay bare, step by step the divine providence by which the universe is fashioned. This process of evolution may now have developed into a *spiritual* evolution of man himself, bringing to birth a spiritual being worthy of creative partnership with God himself. It is allegiance to this objective of unity with the Divine creator who loves mankind and desires the well-being of all his creatures which is the ultimate justification of our pacifism.

19. Consultation on the Christian Witness to Peace (Bossey, Switzerland, May 28-June 1, 1968)

Although the New Delhi assembly had given specific direction to the WCC staff to hold a week-long consultation on peace, little was done to implement the directive until shortly before the fourth assembly in Uppsala. The official report of the Division of Studies contained in the Central Committee's publication, New Delhi to Uppsala, 1961-1968, *had this comment:*

> The New Delhi Assembly authorized the Division to organize a consultation on the biblical and theological bases for The Christian's Witness to Peace. . . . Possible ways of fulfilling this task have been annually reviewed, as the search has continued for the right formula by which a mere repetition of former debates may be avoided, and something worthwhile may be achieved.

After mentioning several possible ways of carrying out the mandate, the report stated:

> It was finally decided to hold a consultation in the early part of 1968, less with the hope of any spectacular "breakthrough" than in recognition that more faithful study "spadework" may yet lay the foundation for constructive ecumenical thought and action in this important field.

This consultation was a small-scale gathering, with few of the characteristics of the elaborate preparation and logistics of many WCC consultations. The fifteen participants were invited by the Division of Studies with some view to including representatives of various church traditions. Some of the Historic Peace Churches were present and also some who could be classed as "nuclear pacifists." Some supported the traditional attitude of the church on "just war." Others with little background in the problem were invited to attempt to provide a kind of objective analysis and interpretation of the process.

Although no preparatory documents were assigned or compiled, the participants were provided with ten documents varying from excerpts from letters to the booklet The Christian and War *(1958). They did not provide the focus for the actual deliberations of the group.*

A document was drafted to indicate areas of agreement, disagreement, and topics needing further study. This is included here. It was reprinted in a later edition of the booklet The Christian and War *(1970).*

The Christian Witness to Peace
A Pacifist/Non-Pacifist Discussion of Its Theological Bases

The New Delhi Assembly called for the convening of a consultation between pacifists and non-pacifists to examine together the biblical and theological bases for the Christian witness to peace. For some years this question was kept under review, while the general subject of the Christian concern for peace was on various occasions being taken up in different contexts. The specific mandate given at New Delhi was not the task of, and did not prove in fact to be fulfilled by, any of these conferences. In May 1968, therefore, a group of pacifist and non-pacifist Christians was convened at Bossey for the express purpose of discussing the biblical and theological bases of their respective positions. Their report on what they regarded as their most important agreed findings is as follows:

I. Biblical and Theological Affirmations

1. We agree on the validity and urgent necessity of the theological task in ethics. Ethical decisions must indeed be made in given situations, but Christian decision is responsible only if the attitudes and behaviour patterns which prepare for decision, and the presuppositions which underlie the values sought and the means adopted, are tested within the community of faith by the criterion of the whole of the Biblical witness.

2. Within the scope of our mandate to discuss the biblical bases of the Christian witness to peace, we have sought to learn from contemporary studies on biblical hermeneutics. We are agreed in rejecting any "naive" hermeneutic approach which would apply Scriptural statements too directly to our present situation. Theological reflection on the subject of peace should take account of the following principles:

(a) In order to ascertain their true meaning, the texts of holy Scripture should be considered within the context of their historical and cultural, as well as literary, situations.

(b) The variety of traditions within the Old and New Testaments should be respected, as preserved for us by the People of God, without prematurely reducing them to a unity.

(c) It is the Old Testament which gives to certain biblical concepts their basic structure, and which shows us the People of God living in time and space. We must give these Old Testament concepts serious study, both in their own right and as the indispensable basis for our understanding of the New Testament. We should especially seek the Old Testament understanding of such concepts as creation, sin, redemption, the People of God, the nations, and peace. Research should not neglect the testimony of the prophets, and traditional understandings of notions such as "the Lord of hosts" and a "holy war" require full reexamination.

(d) The biblical conception of peace should be related to other notions which give it its full meaning, in particular those of reconciliation, justice, and the Kingdom of God.

3. There are certain biblical concepts which should guide our thinking on war and peace, though we recognize that immediate conclusions cannot be drawn from them. Those which have the greatest bearing are:

(a) *Reconciliation,* i.e., the saving work accomplished by God on our behalf in His Son and within us by His Holy Spirit (cf. 2 Cor. 5, Eph. 2 and 4). Reconciliation has two aspects: redemption (the forgiveness of sin) and regeneration (the gift of new life). This is the foundation of our peace, and makes us witnesses to and makers of peace.

(b) *Peace.* We found that in the New Testament peace is the fruit of the whole work of Christ. Thus it signifies primarily peace between God and man, and this works itself out between man and his fellowmen, particularly in the Christian congregation. Here especially the testimony of the Old Testament should be heard as well, because there *shalom* takes on a political dimension. It implies much more than the absence of war: It is wholeness, prosperity, fullness—i.e., salvation present and future.

(c) *Justice, or righteousness.* In Scripture peace is closely linked to righteousness, of which it is the fruit, so that to seek peace implies the struggle for justice (a notion which is far richer than is commonly understood).

(d) *The Kingdom of God.* In Scripture this concept is closely related to the theocentric purposefulness of human history. By founding the realization of peace in the manifestation of the rule of God, it already shows us our place, and determines our behaviour, as heralds of the Kingdom.

Nevertheless, although we generally agree in seeing the Christian witness to peace as founded in these Biblical notions, we differ in our understanding of their precise meaning and their implications.

II. Differences Within Agreement

4. Although we agreed on the importance of the eschatological perspective for all Christian ethics, we differently understand its import for the present. One of the real issues dividing us is our understanding of the nature of the reality of the new life in Christ as available here and now.

5. We are agreed on the importance of responsible social involvement. We differ, however, as to the ways in which this can appropriately be practised by Christians:

(a) Some doubt that pacifists genuinely accept this involvement; others fear that non-pacifists are too conformist in their involvement.

(b) We differ in our perception of historical reality, and in our understanding of the applicability of Christian standards and goals to the structures of this reality.

6. We agree that Christians must find the path of faithfulness in the concrete givenness of each situation. But we are not agreed on the nature, clarity, and obligatoriness of the thought and common commitment through which Christians prepare for their decisions. Do pacifists illegitimately prejudge the future by ruling out war in all conceivable cases? Do non-pacifists prejudge the future by accepting preparation for war, or by refusing to set the limits of their collaboration?

7. Although we agree that the Christian witness must take into account careful interpretation of social and political facts as they are, we do not read these facts alike. Some believe that the nature of modern war has moved into a qualitatively new phase which reveals a "demonic" dimension of the whole military enterprise. For others, the differences are only quantitative, making it more difficult, though only in degree, to restrain the effects of war within fitting proportions.

III. Agreement Within the Differences

8. We have noted that the differences between pacifists and non-pacifists are at some points not what they might have been supposed to be:

(a) Pacifists and non-pacifists do not form two closed camps. Each of the positions is held in varied ways, some more radical than others.

(b) We agree that non-pacifists are not necessarily militarists, nor are pacifists necessarily naive idealists or individualists preoccupied with their own moral purity.

(c) We agree that it is improper to assume that the difference of views can be characterized in terms of legalism or perfectionism. For both pacifists and non-pacifists, Christian ethics are derived from grace, forgiveness, and freedom.

(d) We agree that the absence of overt violence is not peace. A stable social order may be intrinsically oppressive. A pacifist position may well go together with an understanding of social conflict as a positive phenomenon, within limits, to the extent that it contributes to the removal of oppression. We note that non-violent social techniques may be effectively coercive. Pacifists do not necessarily advocate passivism or the avoidance of all kinds of power.

9. We are agreed that change in social structures is a constant, and desirable, phenomenon. In line with the widespread current emphasis on the need for social ethical thought to be informed by empirical and pragmatic knowledge, we stress the need to study:

(a) the validity of the assumption that in the past violence has been necessary and/or useful in bringing about desirable change, and

(b) the comparison of non-violent and violent strategies of change.

Our concern for attention to the historical reality within which we live is not merely a concern about techniques; we must listen to the world's own hopes and despairs, the certainties and the questions of men outside the Church, as we seek to be open to the leading of the Spirit.

10. We agree that Christians are called actively to participate in the removal of the causes of war, in bringing about desirable changes in social structures, and in alleviating the sufferings caused by war and oppression. In these efforts they should cooperate as extensively as possible with non-Christians. It is neither the intention nor the practice of pacifists to concentrate their major concern on refusal to participate in war; nor, on the other hand, do non-pacifists consider military preparedness as the primary bulwark of peace.

IV. Conclusions

11. Despite our many agreements and the warding off of prejudiced interpretations, we have confirmed the existence of a deep and genuine cleavage which is both theological and practical. New developments in the nature of war, or in Christian thought about war, do not render this issue obsolete, but rather heighten its relevance. We have discovered that this issue is such as to bring to the surface almost the entire scope of the problems of the structure and method of Christian ethics. The further study obviously necessary must therefore be able to include the full breadth of ethical theory. Nevertheless, this will not justify the forgetting of the par-

ticular case, for formal discussion of ethics must always be tested by application. We have confirmed that the example of recourse to violence, in war or revolution, is a most appropriate paradigm for the ecumenical exploration of those fundamental ethical axioms which divide us: The issue is one where the disagreements are clear, and presents a vital contemporary challenge to all the Churches.

12. Although we are agreed that Christian ethics must be studied and Christian obedience be lived out within the realities of the Church and the world, yet we differ on the place of ethical concern and tension within the Church. For some, the pacifist/non-pacifist issue is of ethical but not ecclesiological significance, such as would justify separate existence; for others, the place of ethics, or even more precisely that of the rejection of war, is integral to the Church's self-understanding. Some fear that pacifists are too willing to perpetuate illegitimate dividedness over ethical differences alone; others fear that non-pacifists, in their readiness to serve their nation's military objectives, jeopardise true catholicity by placing other loyalties above that which binds all Churches to one another. In conversing about war, we are thus dealing with an ecclesiological problem, namely, the justification of the distinct existence of Churches on the basis of their particular ethical positions. Each Church asks to be accepted on its own definition of its churchly identity.

The Churches as Churches are committed to listening to one another, especially at points of major difference. They have not only mutually to clear away prejudices and misapprehensions. The Peace Churches need to hear the challenge to revitalize and clarify their traditional witness, and to be warned against the dangers of theological naiveté and self-righteousness. The other Churches need to face the challenge addressed to their continued too easy traditional acceptance of war as the *ultima ratio,* and to expound their own case in a brotherly way to the Peace Churches.

In this encounter it must be hoped and believed that the Holy Spirit can bring Christians not only to hear one another, but also together to arrive at insights new to all.

13. Some specific recommendations:

A. Our task within the 1961 mandate was the modest one of analysing, within the framework of our common biblically and theologically based witness, the depth, shape, and nature of a particular division among the Churches. For this purpose the form of our group was appropriate. For the further study which is needed, attention would have to be given:

(1) to continual biblical research as part of the process;

(2) to the representation of a broader variety of types of pacifism and non-pacifism;

(3) to a more critical evaluation of existing statements of the rationale for both positions; and

(4) to the interrelation of this study with the continuing common concern of the Churches for a more total commitment to servanthood in dealing with the world's needs.

B. We would suggest as particularly appropriate topics for further close attention:

(1) the biblical concepts listed in paragraphs 2(c) and (d) above;

(2) the issue of the nature of the reality of the regenerate life (para. 4);

(3) the interrelation of this issue with understanding of the nature of the Church (para. 12); and

(4) the findings of any empirical study (para. 9).

20. The Fourth Assembly of the World Council of Churches (Uppsala, Sweden, July 4—20, 1968.)

The path entered on in the 1966 conference on church and society was continued in the 1968 world assembly. Racism, poverty, and development were at the center of the assembly's deliberations. Whereas orthodoxy was once at the heart of ecumenical debate, now "orthopraxy"—right conduct—became the test. In the much quoted words of Dr. Visser 't Hooft, heresy became as much a matter of lack of attention to social needs as willful misinterpretations of doctrine had been earlier.

The sectional report dealing with peace issues had its controversial moments. Some of these were pointed out in the personal reactions of the Rev. Paul Oestreicher, of the Church of England, which was appended to the sectional statement:

> Its reassertion of the Amsterdam insight that war was incompatible with the teaching and example of Jesus was not a contentious issue; nor was the assertion that nuclear, chemical and bacteriological warfare are abhorrent. . . . The real questions that divided the section concerned the implication of these insights. Could these be spelled out by all in morally binding and politically effective ways? The majority thought not. A vocal minority, on the other hand, felt that perhaps it would be better to say nothing than to appear to say less than had, for instance, been said at the Conference on Church and Society. . . . Governments are admonished to put an end to much of their wickedness as best they can, to disarm when they feel able. . . . None of this divided the section. What divided it was the question whether Christians are not bound to go further. And it was not quite the old pacifist versus non-pacifist argument: In particular the youth wanted the churches to commit themselves to calling on Christians personally to opt out of direct involvement in the process of manufacturing and threatening to use nuclear or other weapons of mass destruction.

Dr. Martin Luther King, Jr., had been invited to address the opening session of the assembly. In his memory, a resolution was presented and accepted by standing vote. Some Quaker delegates had pressed the Policy Reference Committee to establish a program for studying non-violent methods of social change which had been so close to Dr. King's ministry.

Towards Justice and Peace in International Affairs

The Report as Adopted by the Assembly

INTRODUCTION

1. God's promise, "Behold, I make all things new" (Rev. 21:5), includes for us the hope that God will bring about salvation, justice, and peace. "Behold, all is made new" (2 Cor. 5:17). This word includes the certainty that in Christ the new reconciled creation has already dawned. The Church lives in this certainty and presses on towards this hope.

2. This pressing forward implies that we turn away from that which separates us from Christ, and slough off that which hinders our obedience to him. It changes also our political thinking and acting. We are directed away from anxiety, resignation, self-assertion, and oppression by guilt towards openness and solidarity with all men, towards the venture of trust and the readiness to sacrifice for constructive solutions. The aim of our political thinking and acting is to benefit and to help men.

3. This is also the aim of many non-Christians, and leads us to cooperation with them in concrete tasks. In so doing our particular contribution will be made not only in the sober realization that all we do remains inadequate and limited, but also in our unshakable hope in him who says, "Behold, I make all things new."

CHRISTIAN INSIGHTS

4. The Word of God testifies to the unity of creation, and to the unity of all men in Christ.

We Christians, who have often denied this unity, observe how through science and technology the world is being tied together in interdependence. The nations are thereby both threatened and made dependent on one another. This calls us to action oriented to the brotherhood of all men.

5. The Word of God bears witness to Christ who sacrificed himself for his brethren.

We Christians, who have often acted selfishly, hear today the demand for a more just society for the sake of which states and nations should give up a part of their power, prestige, and interests. By this we are challenged not only to ask sacrifices of others, but to make them ourselves.

6. The Word of God testifies that Christ takes the side of the poor and oppressed.

7. The Word of God testifies that in Jesus Christ God makes the world new.

We Christians, who have often resisted change and progress through our anxiety or indifference, now see the acceleration of social and political change. We are called at the same time to critical examination and to unhesitating involvement.

8. The Word of God testifies that in Christ God makes peace on earth.

We Christians, who have often lived in hostility toward one another, see how the nations, in order to avoid wars of inconceivable dimensions, seek the way to coexistence. This challenges us to creative "pro-existence," with the welfare of our neighbour in view.

9. The Word of God testifies that the reconciling work of God makes an end to all division and enmity.

We Christians, who have often been irreconcilable, hear the call for the end of racial divisions and political tensions. This drives us to seek to open and to keep open the lines of communication between races, age-groups, nations and blocs, in order to bring about reconciliation.

10. In the struggle for peace and justice, the Church must bear witness. This witness must not be cheap or verbose. Neither must the Church invalidate its witness by clinging to outdated structures and by wrong attitudes. But it must speak out where no one else dares to, or where truth is not respected, where human lives or human dignity are endangered, and where opportunities for a better future are neglected. In readiness to change their structures and attitudes wherever necessary, the churches must constantly endeavour to recognise the signs of the times. The ecumenical fellowship can help them to stand by their convictions and not simply to reflect the predominant opinions in their own country.

1. The Problem of Peace and War

11. The World Council of Churches reaffirms its declarations at the Amsterdam Assembly in 1948: "War as a method of settling disputes is incompatible with the teachings and example of our Lord Jesus Christ." Of

all forms of war, nuclear war presents the gravest affront to the conscience of man. The avoidance of atomic, biological, or chemical war has become a condition of human survival. This is true, not only because it would be suicidally destructive but because, unlike "conventional" war, nuclear war would inflict lasting genetic damage. The churches must insist that it is the first duty of governments to prevent such a war: to halt the present arms race, agree never to initiate the use of nuclear weapons, stop experiments concerned with, and the production of weapons of mass human destruction by chemical and biological means and move away from the balance of terror towards disarmament.

12. In no way can the present nuclear stalemate be accepted as a lasting solution or as a justification for maintaining nuclear armaments. The churches should welcome agreement among the great powers in the nonproliferation treaty as an important step towards averting nuclear disasters and all nations (including China and France) should be urged to sign it. Further steps will be needed, especially the extension of the test-ban to underground tests, and the prevention of the establishment of anti-ballistic missile systems by agreement between the USA and the USSR.

The concentration of nuclear weapons in the hands of a few nations presents the world with serious problems:

(a) how to guarantee the security of the non-nuclear nations;

(b) how to enable these nations to play their part in preventing war, and

(c) how to prevent the nuclear powers from freezing the existing order at the expense of changes needed for social and political justice.

13. Since smaller nations are expected to accept the discipline of nuclear abstinence, the nuclear powers should accept the discipline of phased disarmament in all categories of weapons. At the same time, the nuclear nations should accept the right and responsibility of the non-nuclear nations to their share in vital decisions regarding their own security and the peace of the world.

14. Non-nuclear wars with all their cruelty have the additional danger of escalating into uncontrolled violence. In a world that regrettably still resorts to the use of arms there are those who hold that absolute pacifism is the true Christian response. For them, and also for those who do not share this conviction, there is the old problem of limiting the use of force. Such limitation involves the attempt to preserve the social fabric of the enemy, to spare non-combatants, to lessen human suffering, and to recognize that military force alone never ensures the emergence of a new order and may even prevent it.

15. A special danger today is the encouragement of wars by proxy

through the competitive delivery of armaments, so aggravating the dangers in many explosive situations. This consitututes an international scandal which governments must no longer tolerate or permit.

16. The churches are urged to support contemporary work in the field of peace research. They should also encourage educational programmes in the service of peace. . . .

II. Protection of Individuals and Groups in the Political World

B. *Majorities and Minorities*

23. "All peoples have the right to self-determination." This is a basic essential of human dignity and of a genuine family of nations. But nations are seldom altogether one homogeneous people. Most nations have ethnic, cultural, or religious minorities. These minorities have the right to choose for themselves their own way of life insofar as this choice does not deny the same choice to other groups. Majorities can be insensitive and tyrannical, and minorities may need protection. This is a special responsibility for the Church of him who is the Champion of the oppressed.

24. But if pressed too far the rights of minorities can destroy justice and threaten the stability or the existence of the nations. The frustration of a majority by a minority is as incompatible with justice as the persecution of a minority by a majority.

25. There is no clear-cut or final solution for this tension. Countries practise various compromises. None of them is universally applicable or offers any secure guarantee of peace. The tension must be accepted and worked at constructively, but the churches should be ready to offer some criteria of human value by which to judge. But majorities must recognize that as well as rights, they have a responsibility for providing the widest possible freedom for their minorities; and minorities also must recognize that majorities also have rights.

26. The churches must defend minorities when they are oppressed or threatened. They must at times urge restraint upon minorities in the pursuit of their ambitions. But also they must help majorities to respond creatively to the impatience of minorities in their struggle for injustice. . . .

V. Conclusion

42. The growing dimensions of the ecumenical movement offer new possibilities for concerted contributions to international relations. There is an increasing demand for common action by all Christians in the international field, and new possibilities in many sectors of the international

situation for joint or parallel action by Christians. Even if differences in historical ecclesiastical structures, cultural backgrounds, political systems, and styles of action present substantial obstacles to cooperation, these possibilities must be fully explored. More serious efforts at dialogue with the adherents of other religions and all men of goodwill provide a potential resource on a wider scale. At the same time, responsive Christian witness to the world of nations should be expressed at the parish level. There is no parish so small or isolated that it should feel free of involvement in this common responsibility through prayer, education, consultation with Christians of the nations concerned and through ecumenical service and action at local level. . . .

THE MARTIN LUTHER KING RESOLUTION

90. *Martin Luther King*

On the recommendation of Policy Reference Committee II it was *resolved* by a standing vote—

that the Assembly of the World Council of Churches meeting at Uppsala, Sweden—

1. express its deep sense of the loss to the Church on earth brought about by the assassination of Martin Luther King, whose presence as preacher at the Opening Service had been so eagerly awaited;

2. thank God for the faithful and prophetic witness he bore to the New Testament commandment of love through his ministry and the relating of non-violence to social changes;

3. encourage the member-churches to continue to bring his example before their members with the aim of deepening their own Christian witness;

4. ask the Central Committee to explore means by which the World Council could promote studies on non-violent methods of achieving social change, bearing in mind that the issue of using violent or non-violent methods of social change has been raised in the Reports of Sections III, IV and VI.

21. Puidoux 1955—1969: Report of a Dialogue About the Theological Foundation of a Christian Peace Witness (Heinold Fast, 1969)

Although after 1962 no further large conferences were held in the Puidoux series as such, work did continue on a different basis. In 1965 the specific decision was made to concentrate on a smaller working group which could meet more frequently with a fairly constant membership. It was hoped that this would permit more intensive theological achievement.

In 1948 there was established in Heidelberg the Research Institute of the Protestant Study Fellowship *(FEST). It was sponsored by the Protestant church of Germany and worked closely with the seminar for ethics of the University of Heidelberg under the direction of Professor H. E. Tödt. After 1959 the work of the study commission intensified. An early concern of the discussion centered around the so-called Heidelberg Theses, concerning the impact of nuclear warfare.*

Beginning in 1967 there were three annual meetings between members of the study commission and some of the participants of the Puidoux conferences. The German Mennonite pastor Heinold Fast, of Emden, who had been asked to coordinate Puidoux concerns, has written an appraisal of these meetings, putting them into a context of the longer Puidoux series of discussion.

The study commission has taken the leadership among the German churches in research and publication in the area of conflict resolution and peace research. Its publication series Studien zur Friedensforschung *has many books to its credit, including two editions of a comprehensive bibliography of peace/war studies.*

Puidoux 1955—1969

Report about a Dialogue on the Theological Bases of the Christian Peace Witness

Heinold Fast

From August 15 to August 19, 1955, there met at Puidoux in the French section of Switzerland twenty-seven theologians and churchmen for the first in a series of conferences which have become known under the name of Puidoux even when they later met in other places. The first conference at Puidoux itself was planned as a meeting of the Continuation Committee of the three so-called Historic Peace Churches (Quakers, Church of the Brethren, and Mennonites) together with the International Fellowship of Reconciliation. Since European theologians of Protestant background had been invited to deliver addresses (for example, Hans-Werner Bartsch, Joachim Beckmann, Götz Harbsmeier, Ernst Wolf) there resulted an encounter between representatives of the Peace Churches and those of the tranditional *Volkskirchen*. Thus, for the first time since the Reformation, a dialogue took place between representatives of these churches on the theological questions raised by a Christian pacifism. They discussed problems of the relationship of church and world, especially that of church and state, for example, the relationship between the lordship of Christ and the church in the New Testament or the relationship of church and world as understood by Luther on the one hand, and the Anabaptists on the other. It became apparent that essential differences depended upon a different type of church concept, that the ethical questions could not be considered without a discussion of ecclesiology.

The second meeting under the name of Puidoux took place upon the invitation of some churchmen at the Evangelical Academy at Iserlohn, Westphalia, from July 28 to August 1, 1957. The number of participants had grown to sixty. The theme chosen was "Discipleship of Christ" as well as the question of the relationship between justice and love. Besides biblical and historical papers there were addresses on "The Body of Christ and Discipleship With Dietrich Bonhoeffer" and the Christian pacifism of Karl Barth. It is noteworthy that in a "Report to the *Landeskirchen*," "a clear agreement" could be noted on several points:

1. Jesus Christ, the incarnated, crucified and living one, is the Lord over church *and* state.

2. Christ calls us into discipleship as active and suffering participation in him. Discipleship is therefore not to be understood as imitation

(imitatio) but as participation *(participatio)*, that is, in it justification and sanctification exist side by side. Thus legalism as well as wilfulness are impossible.

3. For the sake of the one who became man, the one who died and is living, the Christian cannot remain in the service of killing but will have to serve life in simple obedience.

In addition it was felt that much theological work needed yet to be done in later conferences.

About eighty participants met for Puidoux III from August 2 to 7, 1960, at Bièvres near Paris. Once again the theme of "The Lordship of Christ Over Church and State" was chosen, this time with the specific question about the possibility of Christian influence on the state. The special event of the conference was the part-time participation of a group of theologians from nations under Communist rule, among them Professor Hromadka and Professor Lochmann, but also the Lutheran Archbishop Kiivit from Tallin, the Baptist Alexander Karev from Moscow and the Orthodox Professor Parijskij from Leningrad. The example of those churches that live in countries with overtly atheist governments was not without significance for the question of the lordship of Christ over the state.

The criticism by the Peace Churches of the Constantinian era and of the Constantinian relics in thought and structure of present-day churches found support through the experiences of churches in the Communist societies and this may have helped to make the effort of the Peace Churches to avoid the appearance of withdrawal from the world—despite all nonconformism—more convincing. Also after Bièvres there was agreement that the theological work would have to be continued even more thoroughly.

Puidoux IV, which took place from July 9 to 14, 1962, at Oud Poelgeest in The Netherlands, was planned with such a more thorough theological emphasis in mind. The theme did not ask specifically for the justification of a Christian pacifism but generally for the "Sources of Christian Social Ethics." The opportunity of thorough work was given also by the way the conference was organized. On the four full days the forty-two participants needed to deal with only one paper and response each day. Also, on the fourth day, three task groups were formed which were to work up tabled questions. In this way many important problems were actually discussed, the solution of which formed the prerequisite for a clarification of the traditional differences. As an example I shall mention the address by Professor Lochmann about the "Influence of Historical Events on Ethical Decisions," a classical topic for the discussion of the relationship between principle and situation. The response was given by Professor [John H.] Yoder in a paper on the same topic. There was agreement that the norm for the assessment of a historical situation could be derived for the Christian only from the gospel or, as was said, from the Incarnation of God; from this viewpoint the revolution of 1917, for example, was not to be understood as an event of salvation but only as an event through which people had been helped. Yet when Professor Kossen in applying this norm maintained that there could be no situation in which Christians were allowed to wage war, other participants immediately relativized the common theological or ethical conclusion and carried on the theological argument from the context of the situation. Such a course of dialogue, which is too typical that it should itself become the object of theological (and sociological) reflection, has been perhaps the greatest handicap of all the conferences thus far. That is the reason why, at the conclusion of Puidoux IV the question remained unanswered whether the basic difference had been isolated or whether and in which direction there were possibilities for further discussion or approach.

Because the direct continuation of the larger conferences did not seem to promise much progress in theological work, it was decided in July 1965 to transfer the dialogue to a smaller study commission for an interim period. This study commission was made up of twelve to fifteen members and met three times at Höchst/Odenwald, namely in January of 1967, 1968, and 1969. Between the meetings the attempt was made to continue the dialogue through exhange of position papers. The work of the study commission took on a special flavor by the fact that in addition to representatives of the Peace Churches and theologians from Czechoslovakia and The Netherlands, there were among the participants from the German Federal Republic as many as five representatives of the *Evangelische Studiengemeinschaft* in Heidelberg. As recently as 1966, they had begun work on a rather large peace research project under the topic "The Contribution of Theology and Church to Peace." These representatives were: Professor Heinz-Eduard Tödt, Frau Dr. Tödt, Frau Dr. Gerta Scharffenorth, Dr. Ulrich Duchrow, and Professor Günther Howe, who died in 1968. The chairman of the commision was Dr. Reinhard Köster from Essen.

The problem posed to the study commission was threefold. First, it was to investigate the Christological foundation of ethics. Secondly, the significance of the Lutheran doctrine of justification for ethics was to be studied. These two sides of the problem had emerged as the *desiderata* of the previous Puidoux conferences. The third side derives from the particular theme of the peace research project of the *Evangelische*

Studiengemeinschaft. The question was not merely in general for the Christological foundation of ethics and for the significance of the doctrine of justification for ethics, but for an "ethic in the technical-scientific world." Thus the problem was polarized around the question already discussed in the Puidoux conferences about the relationship of principle (Christology, doctrine of justification) on the one hand, and situation (technical-scientific world) on the other. The overall theme for the first meeting was therefore called "Principalism and Situational Ethics." The main papers were given by Professor Tödt and Dr. Duchrow. In this way the Heidelberg position moved very much into the center, whereas the position of the Peace Churches had to be deduced indirectly from the critical queries. Since this was felt as a disadvantage, Professor Yoder was asked to prepare the Peace Church position during 1967, albeit not directly but in the form of an analysis of the so-called Heidelberg Theses of 1959 on the question of war and peace in the atomic age; Professor Yoder was to select those elements of the theses which seemed to him useful for his own viewpoint. This analysis turned out to be so critical that the second session of the study commission (1968) was devoted almost exclusively to it. On the basis of lectures by Dr. Scharffenorth and Professor Howe the question about the importance of situational analysis for ethical decisions was again treated as was the question about the criteria for situational assessments and especially the question about the complementarity of opposite decisions within the church. The second session ended with the assignment that each member of the study commission present his or her view of the problem under particular consideration of the opposing position.

The position papers which were received served to facilitate a division of the problem into different groupings. These groupings of problems were again dealt with at the third session in January 1969 in dialogues between individual members and in conclusion in a general debate. Widespread agreements but also open differences resulted. Given the makeup of the study commission a continuation of the dialogue did not seem possible for the time being.

The question which emerged as central in the work of the study commission was that of "transition." It was first formulated by Professor Tödt as the question of the transition from Christology to ethics and from ethics to Christology, but soon it came up in completely different contexts. It became significant whenever in the contexts discussed a caesura became noticeable which could not be readily bridged. In the following I shall give a survey of these caesuras which seemed possible in the discussions, and through which the problem of transition was raised. In doing this I am reviewing the various groups of problems which have surfaced in the Puidoux conferences.

(1) The simplest form of caesura is found in the Lutheran protest against a pacifist ethic of imitation. A pacifist ethic of imitation would mean that one could conclude directly from Jesus to the situation:

$$\text{Jesus} \longrightarrow \text{situation}$$

The protest denies the directness of the process:

$$\text{Jesus}//\text{situation}$$

With this we have a caesura which was recognized by all participants of the study commission. The pacifists wanted no ethic of imitation as had already been apparent at Iserlohn, but an ethic of participation.

(2) Just as the first caesura was recognized by all participants, a second caesura was equally rejected by all of them. From the perspective of the pacifists the ethic of world responsibility of the Lutherans seemed at times to be a denial of the connection between Christology and ethics and the ethic of world responsibility itself seemed like a pure situational ethic.

$$\text{Jesus Christ}//\text{situation}$$

The pacifists had to learn that the Lutherans felt themselves misunderstood in this. The fact that Christology and ethics *do* belong together was a conviction held in common by all the participants. It was only on the question of *how* the two should belong together that they diverged.

(3) The first self-interpretation of the Lutheran understanding of the connection between Christology and ethics brought a third caesura into view which distinguished between Jesusology and Christology. According to it, not the earthly life of Jesus but cross and resurrection were of significance for ethics—the cross especially in the sense of its being an expression of the impotence of God in the world. The impotence of God, however, corresponded to the mandate of man to shape the world. If God removed himself from this world by suffering the cross, he entrusted man in the resurrection with the concrete responsibility for the world. Hence we are dealing with a caesura between Jesusology and Christology, and with an ethic which primarily relates to Christology:

$$\text{Jesus}//\text{Christ} \longrightarrow \text{situation}$$

The caesura which excludes the earthly life of Jesus and separates the cross of Christ as God's declaration of impotence from the investiture of man with full powers, is naturally of significance for the manner of transition from Christ to situation. The concepts which signalled this transition were "Holy Spirit, conscience, reason." They were to describe the transition as a transition not only from Christ to the situation but also from the situation to Christ. However, to what extent Christ could really become the norm in this, that is to say, to what extent he constituted the content of the transitional concepts, that was the crucial question.

(4) Now the Lutheran self-interpretation could also be read another way if one realized the danger of the caesura between Jesusology and Christology, if one formulated Christology in such a way that it included Jesusology and thus drew the entire gospel into the situation.

Jesus------>---Christ------>---situation

The caesura which is lacking in this line is reinstated by subdividing the situation in principle into "for me" and "for others" and by assigning these two situations to two types of Christian love, the *opus alienum* and the *opus proprium:*

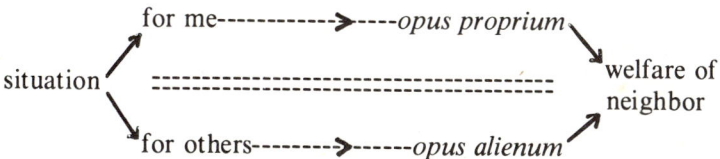

This caesura then will not allow any other norm, but will adapt one and the same gospel, one and the same love to two different situations. The unity of the two forms of love is made possible by the fact that the deed which appears to man as an *opus alienum,* is an *opus proprium* before God. Thus the caesura proves to be real only for man, not in the sight of God *(coram deo).*

An ethic which operates in this manner aims to distinguish itself in principle, for example, from the medieval Catholic ethic according to which from the very beginning two different norms resulted in a two-track thinking:

way of thinking:

On the other hand, the pacifist question arises of where the criterion is to be found for the differentiation between "for me" and "for others"; where the *opus alienum* could receive its content, and whether, from the goal of action—the good of the neighbor—which, for the time being, has been set in general terms, a differentiation between the good of the neighbor and that of the enemy must not be made after all.

In order to properly appreciate this frame of thinking, which introduces the caesura into the situation itself, it is necessary to note that with a changing situation a change from one form of love to another can occur easily. If, for example, by the invention of the atomic bomb the danger of the annihilation of the entire human race through war increases, then war could be forbidden as *opus alienum* and the *opus proprium* be commanded:

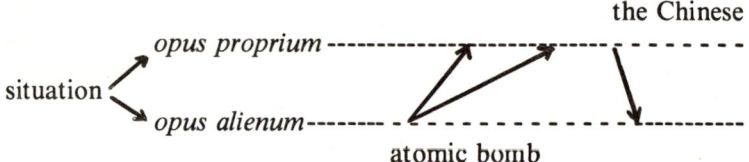

The *opus proprium,* which is *coram deo* hidden in the *opus alienum,* is forced into the openness of the *opus proprium coram mundo* (before the world) by the historical event of the atomic bomb. This, however, need not happen suddenly. One could also provide a longer period of transition for it. In that case, for the time being, that is, for a certain period of transition, intimidation, atomic bomb and, possibly, war would have the right of necessity.

But it is also possible, that historical events force the Christian responsibility into the opposite direction. If, for example, the Chinese prove to be too bellicose despite the suicidal danger of the atomic bomb, then the development of world history would be thrown back again, in other words, the time of transition would be considerably lengthened.

The decisive significance of the historical situation in such cases may seem necessary to some because Christian ethics seems realistic to them only in this way. For the pacifist the question immediately arises whether in this case the caesura of example 2 has not crept in after all:

Jesus Christ//situation

(5) Another possibility for a caesura surfaced with the Lutheran par-

ticipants by inclusion of eschatology. A Christologically oriented eschatology views the present situation under the goal of salvation for all as established through Christ:

Jesus Christ ⌒⟶ situation ⟵---------- eschaton

The present situation must, however, include the very planning for the future, in other words, those goals which are to be understood not as the last but still as determined by the eschaton:

Jesus Christ//situation ⟵------⟶ penultimate goals ⟵----- eschaton

Thus a possibility offered itself to found the goal of our action Christologically without the primitive fallacy of concluding from Jesus Christ to our situation. The caesura between Christ and today needed not interfere. This line of thought was so enticing that the representative of the Brethren was tempted to become the advocate for this approach. He did admit, however, that as a New Testament scholar, he did not feel competent to explain why it should be possible to view the present situation differently from the perspective of a Christologically interpreted eschaton than from the eschatologically understood Christ event. For other pacifists the "penultimate" goal of the survival of mankind, for example, could be founded just as much or just as little eschatologically as Christologically. That is to say, the goal of our planning, which ignores Jesus Christ, cannot lie in the direction of the eschaton revealed to us by Jesus Christ. Such goals tend as much toward isolation over against the eschaton inaugurated by Christ as the situation is separated from Christ:

Jesus Christ//situation ⟵------⟶ "penultimate" goals//eschaton

(6) There was a caesura even among the representatives of the Peace Churches, at least among the Mennonites. In order to make this more clear I must briefly address myself to the question of the subject of ethics. All of the possibilities discussed so far count primarily the individual Christian as the subject of ethics. It is the individual (albeit as member of world society) who, according to example 3 has been empowered to responsibility for the world. It is the church, if she consists of such individuals. Likewise in example 4, it is the individual who has to make the decision in the concrete situation whether he acts for himself or for others, whether an *opus proprium* or an *opus alienum* is called for. Even in medieval thought it was up to the individual to judge whether he was to be reckoned on the side of

those who pledged themselves to obey the counsels or those who decided to be obedient merely to the commandments. The church was involved in this to the extent that she legitimized various decisions either within the framework of the idea of a *corpus Christianum* or a Christianity which understood itself to be complementary.

In Anabaptist thought the significance of the congregation for the ethical decision is more direct. It is the theological place for ethical decision, whereby it is understood as antithesis to the world which is fed from other sources:

Jesus Christ----------➤congregation⬅----------➤ethic

==============   ===============

Paganism-----------------➤world⬅--------------➤ethic

If we ask what has happened to the situation which, after all, cannot be bypassed, then we must answer that the connection between Jesus Christ and congregation as the antithesis of the pagan world represents the situation. The situation therefore cannot be interpreted in any other way than Christologically and hence also ecclesiologically.

However, the caesura which is thus introduced contains the problem even here. The non-pacifist members of the commission could not understand how the congregation could be responsible *for* the world if the duality between church and world was emphasized so strongly. Easier to comprehend in this context was the Quaker perspective which placed the Holy Spirit in lieu of the congregation and thus obviously seemed to have a missionary and service antithesis in mind:

Jesus Christ-----------➤Holy Spirit⬅----------➤ethic

==============   - - -

Paganism-----------------➤world⬅--------------➤ethic

Quakers and Mennonites explained that in the final analysis they *meant* the same thing in different languages, but this was not obvious to every one.

I shall close my survey with this. It should have become clear that the question of Christian pacifism is not only a special question of ethics but in each case questions the entire theological framework.

22. Report on the Consultation on Violence, Nonviolence, and the Struggle for Social Justice (Cardiff, Wales, September 3-7, 1972)

An ad hoc group from the Historic Peace Churches worked with the WCC leadership in proposing ways in which the Martin Luther King, Jr., resolution passed at Uppsala could be implemented. The Central Committee meeting at Canterbury in 1969 agreed that the Department on Church and Society should be asked "to follow closely the discussion of the issue of violence and nonviolence in rapid social change" with a view to calling a consultation. Coinciding with this thrust was the burgeoning debate over the WCC program to combat racism. A consultation on this issue held in 1969 concluded that the churches should support "resistance movements, including revolutions" which were aimed at overthrowing unjust and oppressive regimes.

The Central Committee meeting in Addis Ababa, Ethiopia, in 1971, reflecting the debate over the racism program, asked the Department on Church and Society to develop further the program on violence and nonviolence, establishing a half-time staff position for a two-year term in carrying this out.

A group of consultants met in Nemi, Italy, in June 1971, to help block out the study program for the staffer, David Gill. The result of the 1971 meeting was the document on "Violence, Nonviolence, and the Struggle for Social Justice." To further this process, a major study consultation was held in Cardiff, Wales, in September 1972. This was preceded by extensive talks with representatives of peace churches, institutions, and others concerned with peace.

The Cardiff statement was not intended to be a final document, but a major step in the process. Reactions were requested from WCC constituencies. Fifty persons from five continents worked on the paper. According to the chairman, the intent was to "clarify the concepts 'violence' and 'nonviolence,' to spell out what is involved in nonviolent action and to identify some of the biblical and theological issues confronting the church." The Cardiff meeting was asked to speak "to the WCC and not for it." Another consultation on the specific issue of the biblical evidence regarding Jesus' attitude to power was held.

Report of the Consultation on "Violence, Nonviolence, and the Struggle for Social Justice"

I. *The Christian Vision of World Community*

1. If we begin our report with reference to the total Christian "vision" which sustains us it is not because we ignore our common experience with all humanity of the tensions and polarities of a violent world. The assassinations at the Munich Olympic games came in the middle of our meeting. We heard an analysis of the background to the violence in Northern Ireland. We visited Aberfan, many of whose children were killed in 1966 through a landslide from a pit top, the safety of which had not been sufficiently checked. Events such as these are the common experience of humanity of whatever continent, confession, or ideology. They lay behind our discussions of structural violence and subsequent call to the Churches. Nor do we intend to gloss over the ways in which the behaviour of Christians seems to contradict the faith they profess. But in preparing a document for the World Council of Churches we remind ourselves at the start of the Christian position from which we speak, and of the vision and commitment it embodies.

2. The Psalmist's declaration "The earth is the Lord's and the fullness thereof" more than ever needs our affirmation. That earth's fullness includes human beings in whatever state or condition. No man, group, sector, or nation lives or can live for himself or itself. All mankind is bound together in an inescapable web of community and responsibility one for another. Therefore even before the introduction of the religious dimension, we can say that no man is a master of himself. Here is where religion begins. Christian, or for that matter religious, endeavour, whether it be called nurture, mission, or evangelism, is an effort to release men and women from seeing themselves and their immediate group as living for self. It seeks to make them see themselves and others within the context of the human community, man-in-community.

3. That people are made for, and only realise their humanity in community is already accepted when that community is in the known forms of the family, the clan, tribe, class, or nation. It is salutary to note, however, that even these forms of community are not any person's own choice. This emphasises therefore the "God-givenness" of community. In the past thinking, teaching, preaching, and living have been conceived and conducted as if these accepted human communities were closed and cut off from one another. The result has been a parochialism in all thinking, and a sectarian

"over-againstness." Understanding of good or evil behaviour has developed these relative sectional connotations.

4. However the vision of God's will for the world, as it unfolds before us, is definitely contrary to this view. Christ came into the world so that "all men" might be saved. He suffered and died in total dedication and obedience to the Father's loving will for all mankind, in which he saw his own mission and message concerning the Kingdom of God to have a decisive part. He gathered together the nucleus of a new community as the first fruits of a new mankind. Reconstituted after his death and resurrection followers of Christ usually enter it by Baptism. It is set in the world with Christ's commission to his disciples to go into "all the world" as a visible sign of that community of mankind of which we have already written. It widens the understanding of community so that it transcends the family, clan tribe, nation and race, culture and the rich-poor condition, sex and even the community of believers. But in the past even the Church has been sectional in its views of itself as over-against the world. Theological reflection has often centred in "the People of God" as if the rest of mankind were not also God's people. This tendency in man, singly or in groups, to draw close the circle which describes community is rooted in his search for security for himself and his group. Its folly is exposed by the Lord's saying, "He that seeks to save his life shall lose it." But it also affects others negatively in that a denial of community is a denial of the humanity of the other. In other words it is an abrogation of the image of God in the other and therefore the denial of God. This refusal to extend love *(agape)*, i.e., recognition, consideration, and care to the other, is doing violence to him. Violence therefore can be understood as any breach of the community of mankind as we are led to understand it in the light of Christ.

5. It is from this standpoint and background that the debate about violence, nonviolence, and the churches must begin. We cannot speak in 1972 of anything less than the community of mankind. One enters that community not by race, sex, religion, class or nation, but by birth. Any action, premeditated or not, which excludes any human person from participation in this community of mankind or from sharing its blessings and responsibilities is doing violence to that person or groups of persons.

6. "Community" may be understood, more precisely, in terms of the covenant relationship which the Church proclaims. Man is not part of an eternal structure nor is he a self-universalizing power transcending all limits. He is person-in-relation to the God who has called him into being with his fellows, limited and at the same time liberated by this community, whose existence reflects God's purpose to redeem mankind. Violence, then, is not the breaking of a given order, the defiance of an established authori-

ty or the constraining of individual self-expression. It is that force used by man on man which breaks, destroys, or runs against the relationship of mutual affirmation, trust, sharing, in short the peace, of the covenant which God intends. The Church's calling is to be a sign and witness of this covenant, and a servant of God's intention to bring the world into this relationship with himself.

7. The Church must be seen as witness of Christ's victory, not just in individual life but also in society. It is in this context that its ministry belongs. The vision of the will of God for the world through the Church is that of a new community including all mankind in all its variety of colour and culture. The nature and character of the debate that confronts us is concerned with the sinful tendencies in the midst of mankind which persistently seek to violate this hope and goal. The point at which the Church the whole world over is called to repentance is where it has been sectarian, and has failed to see its fundamental role as the creation of that quality and understanding of community which includes all humanity in its love, recognition, care, and consideration. The fact that this community is not evident in our relationships in the world today is an indictment of the Church's preaching and teaching and congregational life.

8. Thus in our account of the vision in Christ of a world society we are not intending to gloss over the gulf between the vision and the actuality in the life of the Church. Neither the world nor the Church has known the community we speak of. We recognise how grievously the Churches have tended to avoid in specific instances a commitment to a community on the side of the poor and to take refuge in pious generalities without precise analysis. Awkward questions like an examination of class or of the mechanisms of repression have been avoided. Concepts like "reconciliation" and "love" have been cheapened, obscuring their summons to costly Christian partisanship with the forgotten and downtrodden of the earth. Yet we affirm that the Church can be her own most severe critic: She worships one whose sovereignty judges and relativizes all lesser allegiances; she calls Lord one whose self-giving love reaches out to all people; and she knows in her own experience what it means to be a "fellowship of Holy Spirit." Thus, despite her failures, she can be a source of strength, renewal, and reconciliation.

II. *The Concept of Structural Violence: Its Relevance and Utility*

9. Community and a reconciled humanity is achieved only when violence does not take place among its members. Violence represents a breach of community. Violence can also be defined, more precisely, as the cause of the difference between the potential and the actual in human self-

realisation as far as the structures of society are concerned. (There are many levels of self-realisation beyond this, including self-transcendence by serving causes we make our own). This definition needs some further clarification here.

10. Firstly, it is only the *avoidable* difference which should be considered relevant. When the resources and insights existing at any given time limit the self-realisation, this is outside the question of violence. Only that difference which is man-made (in its widest sense) should be examined here.

11. Secondly, there are two main forms—or manifestations—of violence. One is the *direct* or *personal* form, carried out by one person or group intentionally against some others. Most of this is physical violence (killing, torturing, wounding, imprisoning). It obviously reduces the self-realisation of the victim, and in many cases that of the perpetrator. The other manifestation is that of *structural* violence. This occurs when resources and power are unevenly distributed, concentrated in the hands of a few who do not use them to achieve the possible self-realisation of all members, but use part of them for self-satisfaction for the elite or for purposes of dominance, oppression, and control of other societies or of the underprivileged of that same society. Structural violence occurs also when the use of power and resources takes place without a continuous and reciprocal discussion between the members of the society on the purposes for which they should be used. Such discussion should, to avoid structural violence, give all members an equal influence on the decisions taken. Thus there are two characteristics of the occurrence of structural violence. One, that there is not an equal sharing of the fruits of the society, and two, that there is not an equal (and equally effective) participation in the making of decisions.

12. Over time, such structures of unequal distribution of resources and power come to embody violence—it is built into the structure—even though it will be impossible to identify individual persons as "responsible" for the violence thus existing. It will be possible, however, to identify those persons, groups, classes or nations which are responsible for particular acts carried out to maintain or extend the structures of dominance and control. Any effort to recreate community and reconciled humanity will require the transformation of such structures into others that do allow for the full self-realisation of all people as members of the community.

13. Thus the concept of structural violence also is helpful in pointing to its antithesis—those structures that have an even distribution of resources and power and where, therefore, the barriers are eliminated for a self-transcending participation by the person in the creative processes of the community.

14. The concept of structural violence is primarily useful, however, for clarifying the sources of violence even when there are no particular actors who can be held responsible for it; that is to say, when it is the very functioning of the society as it has grown and developed in the distribution of power and resources which is the source of violence. On the other hand the existing structural violence is frequently upheld by dominant classes or groups who consider their self-interests served by it. This applies to dominant states (or groups of states) in all parts of the world. It is not only a problem of the West and the East, or of superpowers; it occurs in many instances in the Third World too.

15. In the context of the very wide definition of structural violence that was frequently used in our group it was pointed out by some participants (but not discussed) that society is largely based on male values, and power is largely entrenched in male hands. The Church is a striking example of this. Women must be prepared to search and struggle for their own identity (not one imposed on them by men), and men should be prepared to help them do so.

16. Clearly the structures have to be analysed on all levels; local, national, and international. The concept of structural violence makes it possible, in many cases, to trace the sources of violence manifesting itself in one part of the world to processes originating in entirely different parts of the world. In developing areas, for example, alliances have grown up between indigenous elites and outside forces that entrench exploitative relationships. These alliances promote and protect political regimes, economic relationships and patterns of development compatible with their interests. They impose styles of modernization, sometimes in cooperation with new military elites, which lead to paternalism and dependency. Wide disparities of power and opportunity emerge, within nations and between them. The masses of people remain relatively passive, unable to participate effectively in basic decisions affecting their lives. Their world becomes fragmented. If they become aware of such basic rights as health care, education, or participation in community and political life, they feel unable to cope with the forces around them which seem alien and overwhelming. Those countries and groups that occupy a privileged position soon discover contradictions and conflicts within themselves. Social injustice and political oppression produce a harvest of alienation, not only in submerged or disadvantaged groups who are the first victims but also among those, in particular the youth, who are its supposed beneficiaries. In time, despite these formidable obstacles, groups rise up to protest and resist the social injustice which oppresses them. They strive to awaken and mobilize their people for the hard tasks of human liberation: national reconstruction, community

development, popular control, individual creative enrichment.

III. *Personal and Communal Violence*

17. Alongside of structural violence there is also another form of which we must take account: personal or communal violence. This has its roots in the rage, the fear, the despair, the hate, often self-hate, in the hearts of human beings, and these in turn are often the psychological result of social hopelessness of injustice, created by structurally violent conditions and powers, but the relation between the two is never simple. Personal and communal violence tends to erupt spontaneously in acts which are self-destructive; they may be directed at the wrong targets or perhaps be despairing gestures not linked to any strategy or long-range goal. We see it in the tragedy of physical crime perpetrated by the poor upon the poor. We find it in riots which vent the rage of an oppressed people on any target which is near. We find it in the conflict of one community with another, as in Northern Ireland today or in the Christian-Muslim conflicts in Mindanao in the Philippines, to mention only two examples where people bearing the name Christian are involved. We find it in the desperate hopeless extremism to which some revolutionaries resort, as instanced by the sense of powerless rage which led to the attack by a few Palestinian guerrillas on Israel's Olympic team during the days of our meeting. We find it in the consciously chosen strategies as well as the unplanned side-effects of some contemporary movements aimed at liberating social groups from intransigent structural violence. But we find it far more pervasively in the support by millions of fear-ridden defenders of an endangered status quo for acts of police brutality and military intervention, a support which often goes beyond the acts themselves to urging still stronger and more violent repression.

18. Violence of this kind interacts with the structural violence of social conditions both as cause and effect. It needs, however, to be understood and treated in its own right as well. Changes in the political power structure do not in themselves bring release from fear, hate, and prejudice. New social conditions do not automatically change human hearts. Better laws, if enforced, may bring a rough justice, but they cannot create a community of mutual responsibility and trust. Liberation of human beings from the grip of violence is both an internal and external task, both personal and sociopolitical. They may not be separated; neither may either task be absorbed in the other. Inner freedom from hate and fear is a preparation for the work of social liberation, never a substitute for it. The destruction of structures of injustice and violence in society prepares the way for covenants of peace among people, but these covenants must be sealed by individuals in-

wardly free of violence toward the neighbour.

19. How does this interaction work? We pose the question without offering answers which can only be sought in practice. Out of the social practice in which the members of our group are engaged, however, we offer two examples:

    a. Where a revolutionary movement is able to channel the bitterness and hatred of an oppressed people into strategies of disciplined resistance (violent or nonviolent) to the structures of power that rule them, to give them a realistic hope and a sense of their human worth in the covenant of their struggle, a powerful context is created even in the midst of violent conditions for release from personal violence.

    b. Where a reactionary citizenry is able to see in the violence of revolutionaries in its midst a challenge to correct the conditions of injustice which produce their revolt, a foundation is laid which is a powerful antidote to the violence which fear produces.

The problem in each case is to transmute the self-destructive violence which is rooted in personal spirits and attitudes, into action aimed at a creative goal in a community where human beings rediscover themselves as valued and accepted anew.

IV. *The Witness of the Church*

20. There are, then, three levels on which the problem of violence needs understanding: personal, structural, and strategic. The Church has a ministry on all three levels:

    a. There are countless examples in the Bible, especially in the New Testament, of personal violence being exorcised by the Spirit of God. Usually it is referred to as demon-possession. Sometimes it is the spirit of the law (as in the case of the apostle Paul) or of greedy exploitation (Zacchaeus) or of fear (1 John 4:18). The task of the Church has always been to make men free of the violent self-destruction that possesses them by bringing them into community with Jesus Christ, and into new life with him. Here is the power by which human beings are freed from themselves—and from all the distortions of their being which unjust and violent society has imposed on them—to be effective persons in the creative task of realizing in human society the justice and love of God's covenant for all men.

    b. There are also powers and principalities of the social sphere which can be demonic and hold men in subjection. In the New Testament Christians are told to put on the whole armour of God to resist them. (Eph. 6), and at the same time to bear witness to them of God's purpose for this world in Christ in which they, when redeemed, belong (Eph. 3:9-11).

The Church has this ministry to the structures and powers of politics and economics, which are often violent in their way of operating. As Christians we must resist the power of structured violence. We must share the experience of the poor and oppressed, and seek their justice as did God himself in Jesus Christ. We must do so as a ministry to these structures seeking their transformation into servants of the covenant relation into which God seeks to bring all people in freedom and mutual responsibility.

c. The Church belongs with the poor and oppressed as witness to Christ's victory, not just in individual life but also in society. In this context her ministry to resistance or liberation movements—violent or nonviolent—belongs. Christians who support the violence which occurs in this strategic context hold that it should be controlled and limited by its service to the end of changing social conditions and establishing justice for all. This goal is reconciliation in Christ of enemies through the judgment on structural violence which by God's providence the struggle may bring. Power is not an end in itself; it is the servant of human beings restructuring their relationships. Liberation is not an end in itself; it is the means to a new and more creative responsible interaction among people. The new covenant community, including all humanity, is the future for which we suffer and struggle and hope. It is to this goal and hope that Christians should be dedicated.

21. In dealing with the role of the Church and the Christian response to strategic violence we must take note of the ongoing discussion in the Church between those who think that life and teaching of Jesus rule out the use of physical violence "in principle" and those who think that it has a regrettable, some would say necessary, place in Christian obedience. The latest stage in this discussion concerns whether Jesus did in fact exemplify nonviolence or was in broad sympathy with the violent Jewish nationalist, patriotic resistance movement of the so-called Zealots. Most of us are persuaded that the assertion that Jesus had Zealot sympathies is very doubtful and that the traditional understanding of him is much more likely. According to this his understanding of God's kingdom and his devotion to it was so radical and apparently paradoxical that it brought him into conflict with all the religious and political groups he encountered. But in this he was not divorced from his Old Testament roots where God's special concern for the poor and oppressed is emphasised. But just to maintain that Jesus came into conflict with the Zealots does not solve our problem. Was he laying down "moral principles," some of which cover nonviolence? How does the radical ethic of the Kingdom of God bear upon the structures of human life, especially the State? Does "taking up one's Cross" mean solely nonviolent struggle or self-sacrifice however we struggle? What is the rela-

tion of the Old Testament ethical teaching (the penultimate) to that of the New Testament (the ultimate)? We had little time to examine these matters and made no progress in resolving them.

22. Theology in its justification of violence over the centuries has been strongly influenced by the near-permanent mutual and uncritical support of Church and State (a support which, by its nature, has tended to reinforce structural violence down to this day). Many of us believe the time has come to challenge and radically revise this theology in order to help Christians first to see their personal involvement in structural violence, and then to help them overcome it. This report touches on only one aspect of the vast rethinking of traditional attitudes and relationships now required of the Church as it moves beyond its "Constantinian era" towards a more prophetic role vis-a-vis the State.

V. *Challenging Structural Violence: Empowerment Strategies Which Include Violence*

23. We have recognised that power in society is frequently concentrated in the hands of a few, and that this unequal distribution of power is a major factor in perpetuating dominance and social injustice. Such structural violence may be challenged by forms of resistance which are nonviolent or violent, or some combination of both, depending partly on the social conditions under which the struggle takes place and partly on deliberate choices of strategy and approach.

24. The question of violent and nonviolent forms of struggle ought not be confused with the quite different and larger question of the degree to which a particular social order should be supported or opposed. Either or both forms of struggle may be used with a wide range of intents, from the revolutionary overthrow of a whole social system to relatively minor alterations within a social system (e.g., a coup d'etat may be violent yet alter nothing but the name of the head of State). Violence should not be equated with radicalism and revolution, nor nonviolence with gradualism and reform—nor vice versa. A tendency to confuse these two quite different issues is one of the less fortunate features of the present discussion within and beyond the churches.

25. Some groups, in assessing the political, social and economic realities of their system, have concluded that violence is necessary for the liberation of their people. Their reasons for making this choice vary, as do their strategies and the extent to which they succeed in keeping the violence limited and controlled. Generalization, therefore, is difficult and may lead to misrepresentation. However, probably many advocates and users of violence would argue along the following lines:

a. The first and continuing violence has been that of the oppressors. The imposition of their control brings not only beatings, imprisonment, torture, suppression and death to those who dare resist it but also cruelty even against the general population and a pervasive atmosphere of fear. Worse, the powers that be have sought to indoctrinate us with a sense of inferiority, to destroy our respect and self-confidence as human beings. All this is in addition to the general political oppression and economic exploitation of our people which has brought suffering and death to a multitude of men, women and children—and which will continue to do so unless effectively challenged.

b. Over many years we have sought redress, appealing and petitioning for justice, freedom, and the effective recognition of our human rights. Our pleas have been largely or entirely ignored. When we have tried peaceful protest or strikes, we have been beaten or killed. Our oppressors, including their religious leaders, have exhorted us to practise the virtues of nonviolence, but the violence they impose upon us and our children continues. Patience has served only to perpetuate and deepen our oppression.

c. We have learned that those who dominate us understand only their own language—that of the power which is supported by armed force. We do not want this violence, but we are being forced to resort to it by the brutalities and intransigence of the status quo. Nor can we have self-respect and feel ourselves to be full human beings, until we stand up to resist our oppressors. Our people have needed this call and example to rally together and to restore their hope for change. We shall use every means of resistance open to us including violence—and this not because we like the prospect of yet more suffering but because all other avenues for change have been foreclosed.

d. Hopefully our resort to armed struggle will weaken and eventually bring down those who at present dominate us, or at the very least will induce them to negotiate. In the interim, it will inhibit them from afflicting us with new brutalities. International attention attracted by our resistance may bring additional pressure to bear on them. We know that our use of revolutionary violence to counter oppressive violence will bring suffering, perhaps very great suffering, to our people who have already suffered too long. They do so every day now; at least we can look with hope to the day when that shall end and our people shall be free. Exactly how the course of the struggle will develop we cannot say. But two things are clear: We will never again submit and we will fight to the death—at least there is dignity and freedom there—and the enemy will pay a heavy price for every day he continues to oppress us. We will not relent, for we are impelled by a vision of a society of freedom, dignity, and justice which is more important to us even than life itself.

26. The history of conflict and struggle, however, reveals that noble motives do not necessarily ensure the satisfactory resolution of social, economic, and political problems, let alone moral and ethical problems. Therefore movements opting for strategies which include violence must confront questions such as the following:

    a. How can the struggle be kept from itself becoming an instrument of dehumanization?

    b. How can the means used be kept from engulfing the ends desired?

    c. How to prevent the emergence, in victory, of new systems of structural violence—how to break the old chains of oppression without forging new ones in the process?

    d. How to keep the power accountable in relation to avowed purposes?

    e. A successful military system requires centralization for efficiency, but how can it be democratic?

    f. How to repair the psychological damage that human beings suffer when they use violence?

    g. How to integrate former oppressors, whose families and friends may have been victims of violence, into the liberated society?

    h. How to prevent escalation of violence as a result?

    i. How to recognize when the battle has been won and to ensure the surrender of arms?

    j. Is it alienating public opinion rather than enlisting support?

    k. Have all other options and alternatives been explored and are they still being explored?

    l. Will the liberating forces lose their independence to the foreign power/powers supplying arms?

27. Christians confronting liberation struggles which include violence must ask themselves such questions as:

    a. What is this act of violence saying to us? What are the issues involved?

    b. What were the frustrations, lack of communication, forces and pressures which led to this violence and what can we do to alleviate and call attention to these?

    c. Is there a danger of romanticizing heroes of violent action because of their commitment, rhetoric and perhaps charisma?

    d. To what extent are we reacting because our own position is being threatened?

    e. How can the interacting needs for peace, justice, and freedom be tested in concrete situations when they conflict with each other?

VI. *Challenging Structural Violence: Empowerment Strategies Which Reject the Option of Violence*

28. Although violent action has been widely used in struggles against oppression, this has not been a uniform pattern. In other cases, forms of struggle without significant physical violence have been used in many cultures and historical periods, on issues of human dignity, economic and social injustice, political oppression and foreign domination, even against ruthless opponents. This history is still largely unknown. In our present need to destroy oppression, at a time when the tragic consequences of political violence are increasingly obvious even to its advocates and practitioners, this largely neglected type of struggle deserves reappraisal.

29. Theories of the "just war"—whether of the Christian St. Thomas Aquinas or of the Marxist Mao Tse-tung, whether for defense of one's homeland or for bringing in a new social order—state that a war can be just if among other conditions violence is the only effective means of fighting the political evil. The assumption that violence is the ultimate power in politics is now challenged. If that challenge is successful, it will have the widest implications for Christian theology, revolutionary theory, and human social action.

30. It is now clear that a nonviolent technique of struggle exists. What is it, and is it capable of dealing with the extremities of oppression of today and tomorrow? Looking at the struggles without violence which have occurred, we can say that they are not to be equated with the testimonies of the historic peace churches (although aspects of them are certainly concomitant with their beliefs and example). In these conflicts the emphasis has usually been on struggle, the means of pursuing the goals effectively, and on abstention from violence during the course of the particular conflict which was being waged by nonpacifists.

31. This nonviolent way of conducting struggles therefore requires consideration as a distinct phenomenon and cannot be brushed aside as part of the pacifist-non-pacifist arguments of the past, whether within the churches or among social revolutionaries.

Examples of the kind of cases included in nonviolent action are these:

a. the destruction of the dictatorships in El Salvador and Guatemala in 1944

b. the resistance of teachers and clergy in Norway during the Nazi occupation

c. the February Revolution of 1917 which destroyed the Russian tzarist system

d. farm workers' struggles in the United States since 1965

e. the Indian 1930-31 campaign for independence

f. the Montgomery, Alabama, Afro-American bus boycott of 1955-57

g. labor strikes and boycotts without violence in many countries

h. peasant land seizures and occupations in Latin America and elsewhere

i. African bus boycotts and the potato boycott in South Africa

j. some struggles against coups d'etat such as the Kapp Putsch in Germany in 1920

k. the 1963 Buddhist struggle in South Vietnam which undermined the Diem regime

l. struggles against foreign invasions, as in the Ruhr in 1923 and Czechoslovakia in 1968

There are many, many more. The degrees of success and failure in them have varied, as they have with violence. They nevertheless constitute a different type of struggle, undeveloped and unrefined, which may have great future potential, especially if efforts are deliberately made to understand it and to increase its effectiveness.

32. Nonviolent action is the name most commonly given to this alternative technique of struggle, waged without the use or threat of physical violence, even in retaliation to repression. Yet that is an abstention which derives not from submission but from defiance. It is a choice to fight with psychological, social, economic, and political weapons, rather than with military ones which the opponent is almost always best equipped to use. Also, this type of combat is not to be equated with voting and elections, important though they may be where available. Nonviolent action constitutes many forms by which people may directly apply pressures and forces in the absence of constitutional democratic procedures.

33. The range of this nonviolent technique is wide, and can be divided into methods of:

a. protest and persuasion (largely symbolic actions to express views, such as marches, vigils, and picketing)

b. noncooperation, including many forms of social, economic, and political acts which withdraw or withhold support and cooperation (such as social boycotts, strikes, economic boycotts, civil disobedience, administrative noncooperation, etc.)

c. intervention in which the usual behavior patterns or system are disrupted (as by sit-ins, alternative social institutions or parallel government).

These specific forms of nonviolent action are closely associated with the structure of society and political organizations, because in these methods people are either using their existing roles, or are creating new ones, in order to change society or to prevent an unwanted change (as by a military junta or occupier).

34. The classification of an act as nonviolent is not to say it is necessarily ethically appropriate. Difficult ethical problems remain after adoption of nonviolent struggle: some are inherent in any form of struggle, others are peculiar to nonviolent action.

35. The range of methods suggests that the technique does not operate only by persuasion. There are forces within it which may produce partial or full conversion of members of the opponent group to the goals of the actionists. On the opposite extreme the capacity to paralyze and destroy the system by withdrawal of support may prove coercive. More often, success when achieved has come as the result of mixed influences and accommodation.

36. This form of struggle has nothing to do with passivity or submission—it is their opposite. It is not a magic formula. It has requirements for effectiveness which if not met will lead to defeat. There will often be casualties, often many dead and wounded, although these appear generally to be much lower than in comparable violent conflicts. Nor in facing present and future conflicts can one expect great success if intuition and spontaneity alone are relied upon to initiate and guide the conduct of such struggles—preparations, planning and careful utilization of strategy and tactics are important for greater effectiveness. This is not an easy way. It requires discipline, sacrifice and courage, as well as skill and strategic judgment.

37. Since a critical problem in dealing with oppression is how to empower the powerless, how to gain control by the oppressed over their own lives and societies, nonviolent action merits the most careful attention. Effective military forms of struggle are dependent on supplies of weapons and ammunition, and on an ongoing command structure and organization. Dependence on such weapons and structures limits the power of the people as a whole. Those weapons and military organizations can be turned against the people, either by the old leaders or by a new group which has carried out a coup. Here nonviolent struggle may provide a distinct advantage, since in it people are not dependent on material weapons nor does it by its own internal dynamics create a centralized potentially repressive institution. Moreover, experienced people may resort to nonviolent action against new threats or repression, and in further efforts to improve society when milder alternatives are not available.

38. It can be argued that violence distracts attention and effort from the real issues, unites the opponents's camp against the resisters, alienates much opinion from people not involved in the conflict, and limits the

numbers of fighters from the oppressed group. In contrast, it is argued that nonviolent struggle enables attention and action to remain concentrated on the real issues, contributes to uncertainty and finally dissension in the opponent camp, encourages moral support from third parties sometimes expressed in positive actions, and unites the oppressed population behind the struggle with active participation of people of both sexes, and all ages and occupations.

39. Nonviolent social revolution may develop in several typical *stages:*

a. Cultural preparation—developing awareness among the general population of the need for fundamental changes, arousing hope for the possibility of change, and creating the awareness of the capacity in the people to bring about these changes.

b. Organization building—specific organizations of varying types are fashioned: local committees, radical caucuses, supportive groups, cooperatives, and the like. In highly repressive situations, this stage may instead follow direct action which may be spontaneous instead of planned.

c. Direct action—since the need for change presupposes that existing institutions and agencies are inadequate or corrupt, a direct action strategy needs to be developed. Specific tactics will be determined by such factors as long and short-term goals, existing resources, appropriateness, and careful evaluation of their effectiveness.

d. Political and economic noncooperation in a process of fundamental change—people withdraw their support of existing oppressive institutions (whether a government or local power).

e. Alternative institutions and in some cases parallel government—as people withdraw their support of existing institutions they need to develop allegiance to their own structures. Constructive programs which develop self-reliance among people often develop into these new institutions and in extreme situations a parallel government; therefore, new institutions and governing bodies with new structures, goals, and values need to be established and maintained.

These stages of nonviolent revolution (or fundamental social change) should be seen as roughly developmental. As organization building begins, cultural preparation should continue.

40. Engagement in a long, protracted struggle for radical social change generally requires *training*—whether for a protest demonstration or for years of difficult struggle. Cesar Chavez has written: "Soldiers must be trained in techniques of war, and fighters for social justice must be trained in nonviolence." For organization building, training in specific organizational and technical skills, as well as in group dynamics, is crucial.

41. Training for direct action can include preparation for specific ac-

tions, such as guerrilla theater, civil disobedience, marshalling, and specific anticipated difficulties. The more participants can anticipate what can happen, the more likely they will be to be able to control such events. Specific training manuals have been written for developing goals, elucidating strategies, and preparing for specific campaigns. Persistence is a major factor in any struggle for social justice. People not prepared are more likely to give up, crumble under repression from authorities, or fail to see successes when they occur. Training attempts to increase the chances for nonviolent social change campaigns to be successful.

42. Gandhi and others have emphasized constructive work as a complementary and valuable ingredient of the training process. The psychological milieu of resistance presents specific hazards that to some degree can be mitigated by involvement in constructive programs. A protracted campaign requires both aspects, sometimes together, sometimes in alternation as the intensity of the conflict increases or diminishes. Training can also be seen as organizing and speeding the movement, and the capacity for change, rather than simply preparing for a particular event. Evaluation of training effectiveness is a significant element in keeping training relevant, and preventing it from becoming an unnecessary step "we haven't time for."

43. Strategies, preparations and training for the use of non-violent action may also be developed for helping people defeat domestic or foreign-instigated coups d'etat or for defense against foreign occupations, as well as for the purposes of social change emphasized here. These other problems are also important for social change and for narrowing the gap in both policies and ethics between internal and international modes of conflict. We can only mention them here.

44. In examining the whole question of nonviolent action as a neglected alternative, the most crucial question, of course, is whether nonviolent action will "work" in the extreme situation. That question now requires the most careful thought, research, analysis, planning, and experimentation. If it should be the case that nonviolent action has at least as much possibility of success as does violence, this could constitute the key to continuing development of a humane revolution and a humane society, and the abolition of reliance on military defense. It would also facilitate the resolution of some of the most serious ethical problems which the presumed necessity to use violence has posed both for religious people, for nonreligious revolutionaries, and for all those caught up in the exigencies of conflict. In our judgment, it is the responsibility of churches to assist in all possible ways that thought, research, analysis. planning, and experimentation into the nature and potentialities of nonviolent struggles.

45. Movements opting for nonviolence are confronted by questions such as the following:

   a. What will nonviolent action do to (a) those who use it, (b) those against whom it is used, (c) the general community within which the struggle is waged, (d) the relationship between these three?

   b. What are the risks or dangers inherent in nonviolent action, as far as the goal sought is concerned?

   c. How to ensure that the masses which are not involved in the nonviolent struggle do not give active support to the opponent group? What would such support mean for the nonviolent struggle, and what response should it evoke?

   d. How important is a particular understanding of nonviolence for those who use it, those against whom it is used, and the general community within which the struggle is waged?

   e. How central to the success of a nonviolent strategy is direct and efficient communication with and between (a) those who use it, (b) those against whom it is used, (c) the general community within which the struggle is waged? Can such a struggle prevail without it?

   f. What attitudes or belief does nonviolent action require from the activist? How crucial are these attitudes? How can such attitudes be created within the individual activist without creating injustice to the individual?

   g. How are strategies for nonviolent action prepared and developed?

   h. How can activists adhere to a nonviolent strategy in the face of (a) repression by the opponent group, (b) threat or use of violence against them during and/or after the struggle, (c) out-maneuvering by the opponent group, and (d) apparent defeat?

   i. If a concession has been won, how to (a) consolidate that gain, and (b) avoid creating an attitude of entrenchment with the opponent group?

   j. How much and what kind of discipline should a nonviolent movement require of (a) members of the movement, (b) participants on the side of the movement, and (c) opponents of the movement?

   k. Does the attempt in a conflict situation to separate the nonviolent technique of action from a commitment to nonviolence as a religious or ethical principle constitute betrayal of nonviolence?

   l. How does the structure and quality of the leadership affect both the general and the unique aspects of a nonviolent movement?

   m. Does nonviolent action emasculate effective resistance at crucial points? Can it become an unwitting tool of neocolonialism?

VII. *Problems of Choice*

46. It was not possible for the consultation as a whole to reach a firm

conclusion about situations in which the course of the struggle for social justice entails both violent and nonviolent strategies. What effect the use or mixture of both has had in particular situations needs intense study, analysis, reflection. Some aspects of the problem can be tested only in light of a commitment that transcends strategic considerations. Most struggles for freedom have been as a matter of historical fact a mixture of nonviolent and violent action. Even in actions based on the strategy of nonviolence (civil rights struggle in the U.S., independence movement in India) there have often occurred violence and the advocacy of violence.

47. Violent and nonviolent action have impinged on each other in such ways as these:

a. a nonviolent struggle in which violence also appears but is clearly peripheral;

b. a nonviolent phase of a movement which is consciously a prelude to armed struggle;

c. a nonviolent phase that serves as a front for the real objectives, where the crucial decisions are made outside the formal decision-making structure of the public campaign;

d. an armed struggle where nonviolent actions appear but are peripheral; a struggle where both violence and nonviolent aspects contribute significantly to the outcome, either positively or negatively;

f. a movement where two groups offer and work for rival strategies, where a choice needs consciously to be made between the two, and the strategic implications charted accordingly.

48. We would reject two extreme positions:

a. that there are everywhere and forever two categories, violence and nonviolence, which move in separate worlds and remain only as rivals;

b. that there is no time or place where hard choices need to be made between those two courses of action and alternative strategies. Occasions arise when groups must consciously and deliberately choose a particular strategy because to use competing strategies may be self-defeating; for example, a small amount of violence can defeat an essentially nonviolent strategy of change.

49. In previous sections of this paper we have listed major arguments for and against violence, for and against nonviolent action. Some of these arguments can also be applied to situations where both forms of action, violent and nonviolent, are used in the same struggle for social justice. We pinpoint the following questions as most relevant to the discussion and further exploration:

a. What have been the consequences of violence used in an essentially nonviolent struggle (possible case studies—Hungary 1956, examples from labor history, May [1968] events in France)?

b. Why was violence used in these circumstances? What relevant nonviolent strategies could have been implemented to minimize use of violence?

c. Under what conditions might the introduction or the threat of violence serve to advance the struggle towards victory (possible case study: Zambian independence movement)?

d. Under what conditions might the introduction of nonviolence into an essentially violent struggle hinder the attainment of victory (case study: Bangladesh)?

e. Under what conditions might the introduction of nonviolence into an essentially violent conflict serve to advance the struggle?

f. Under what circumstances does the introduction of violence into an essentially nonviolent struggle, or vice versa, make no appreciable difference to the outcome?

g. Is it possible to answer the above questions in the form in which they are posed, or is there needed a prior examination and comparison of the mechanisms and requirements for effectiveness of types of nonviolent and violent action?

50. It is not within the power or competence of this consultation to recommend a priori or abstractly whether violent or nonviolent action should be used in particular situations. The range of conditions is too vast—from the direct action to throw off an oppressive regime to the struggle against inefficient and unresponsive governments and the hidden violence in the structures of society and institutions. No simple formula can be applied to all of them. Moreover, those who stand outside a particular conflict situation do well to be wary of handing out gratuitous advice for which others will be called upon to pay the price. That is not to say, however, that general evaluations of the efficacy and ethical significance of violent and nonviolent struggle, respectively, are not possible.

51. Faced with oppression, many people do not believe that choices are open. They simply do not see that there may be alternative possibilities for action. Those engaged in the struggle can be assisted by accurate information, new perceptions of the issues, and suggested alternatives and techniques for social change.

VIII. *Mobilizing the Churches*

52. We endorse the closing statement in the report from Church and Society to the WCC's Unit I Committee in Utrecht (August 1972):

Our greatest problem is not that some Christians are acting nonviolently for justice and peace while others are resorting to violence. The great problem is simply that most of our fellow Christians are not consciously acting on such matters at all. Thus we must ensure that this widespread concern about violence and nonviolence will highlight rather than obscure the larger challenge to which the ecumenical movement in recent years has given increasingly clear expression: the challenge to all Christians to become wiser and more courageous at translating the generalities of faith into the specifics of social and political engagement.

53. This challenge must include scrutiny of the *life-styles* of the churches. There is urgent need for systematic assessment of the role of Christians and ecclesiastical institutions in supporting wittingly or unwittingly, the violence which often masquerades as "order" in the contemporary world. Awareness must be matched by actions which befit repentance. As examples we propose:

a. The relationship between Churches and State authorities should be investigated and analysed, so that an erastian cooperation is avoided and a critical dialogue is begun. This also includes a continuing evaluation of the ease with which Church leadership mixes with powers that be and is cut off from emerging leadership and forces for change. The traditional alliance between Church and wealth is one instance of this problem. Another is the no less traditional alliance between the Church and the military (symbolised by military chaplaincies, regimental flags in Churches, ecclesiastical ambivalence towards conscientious objectors, scandalous misuse of the "just war" theory, etc.).

b. The Churches' educational role in many countries has been uncritical, often fortifying oppressive relationships in society at large and in educational systems themselves. This demands sharper evaluation, at the same time as the whole system of traditional institutions (schools, hospitals, etc.) needs to be looked at insofar as they may be as much monuments to power as services which encourage self-conscious sharing in power.

c. In the regular Sunday-by-Sunday pattern of church worship, traditional rituals and worship forms often tend to reinforce the existing system rather than constituting acts of hope and stimuli to prophetic criticism.

d. The style of theological work itself can be a support to alienating and oppressing systems. The power of the churches in this regard needs to be carefully examined—as manifest, for example, in their patterns of ministerial training.

e. The Church's evangelism and mission too often have served as vehicles for the penetration of a particular society by alien cultures and exploitative political and economic interests. Self-analysis is called for, to disentangle our proclamation of Jesus Christ from such service to idols.

54. The churches of the world represent tremendous concentrations of wealth—and hence *power*. Often this wealth is arrayed against the poor and oppressed of the world, aiding and abetting their impoverishment and oppression. The choice of where the churches spend their money and what securities go into their investment portfolios often involves them in a silent, albeit sometimes unconscious, partnership with forces inflicting misery and human suffering. Indeed, some of us believe that the Church would be more consistent with its own affirmations of faith, as well as healthier in its own life, if it were to convert wealth held in its current investment/endowment portfolios to the needs of ongoing programs and come to rely solely on the support of its members.

55. The Church's obligation in these times goes far beyond the need to avoid assiduously all uses of its wealth in ways injurious to mankind. It requires as well that the churches act, with respect to such wealth as they may possess, in ways that will help alleviate deprivation and enhance the realization of human possibility for all peoples. In particular, there is a special need for the Church to go beyond easy rhetoric about the virtues of nonviolence, to use its vast resources in support of efforts being made throughout the globe to bring about constructive social change through nonviolent direct action. To this end the churches should:

—Continuously evaluate their own investment policies;

—Withdraw investments from oppressing economic structures and seek alternative investment arrangements (such as the "non-contaminated" investment programs of the World Peace Fund);

—Investigate the use of Church land, especially trust land that is not being used for its intended purpose, where that purpose was to aid a deprived group (e.g., Maoris in New Zealand);

—Where national and/or local situations permit, use resources to encourage governmental authorities to explore and adopt nonviolent defense programs.

In addition, we considered proposals that the churches and related agencies might:

—Explore the idea of a Peace Brigade (nonviolent mobile force).

—Mobilize boycotts of international firms guilty of exposed exploitation—particularly violators of U.N. sanctions.

—Develop an "alarm system" to forewarn of possible violence and to mobilize nonviolent forces.

—Develop a communication network to launch a frontal attack on institutional violence.

—Establish a commission to study institutional violence within church systems (hierarchy, salary, housing, etc.)

56. As far as the World Council of Churches is concerned, fresh initiatives should be taken within and beyond existing WCC programs. The decision of the Central Committee (Utrecht, August 1972) concerning the Churches' investments in southern Africa was an exemplary way of participating in the struggle against structural violence. But precisely because the Utrecht decision was so exemplary it calls for others, directed against the vital power-centres of imperialism (wherever it occurs), especially inside the superpowers and rich nations. Many of us believe a new dramatic action should be undertaken by the World Council, similar to that of September 1970, in providing grants to groups of the racially oppressed, but this time for the benefit of those who because of their solidarity with liberation movements break the laws of the superpowers and rich nations and thus also become victims of repression (e.g., conscientious objectors, deserters). Regarding existing WCC programs, we propose:

—That the General Secretariat initiate more effective consultation and coordination among the churches at international, national, and regional levels for their participation in the kinds of nonviolent action we have outlined in this report.

—That the Commission of the Churches on International Affairs press for international recognition of the rights of freedom fighters (including nonviolent action people).

—That the Program to Combat Racism intensify its support for liberation movements including those which are developing nonviolent strategies in the struggle for racial justice; that it facilitate contact between liberation movement leaders and pastors (e.g., a two weeks' conference); and that it set up more dialogue situations on nonviolent action.

57. To help rescue the concept of nonviolence from being misconstrued as passivity and to show the positive possibilities of nonviolent action, much more work is required of the churches and the WCC in the realm of *training and education*. It is a forlorn hope for nonviolence if the churches merely prefer it without making extraordinary efforts to expose more and more people to an experience of its possibilities and to train more and more people in its techniques. Confronting the media with the need for an equal exposure for films, stories, literature, etc., which will elucidate the meaning of nonviolence is also part of this need. The possible church initiatives include:

—the establishment of training processes in nonviolent action, using the various models now developed, and new ones as needed.

—education in the potential of nonviolent struggle.

—recognition of the importance of fresh literature on this issue. This might involve drawing attention to new books published, encouraging new writing, helping to promote an international English language journal for serious writing in this field, promoting further research, looking for more popular literature, promoting a photographic library for pictures of nonviolent action, publishing an issue of RISK on this subject, using WCC and the churches' channels for distribution of literature.

—many studies for the empowerment of people; study of methods of civil disobedience and how to work for constitutional changes; study of the mythology of violence and the use of "heroes."

The results of these studies should be made known in the churches especially for study at the local level.

58. No actions or programs can substitute for the clearer understanding of these issues which is urgently required within the churches, as within society at large. Assuming the Church's commitment to the promotion of social justice, we propose the following questions for Christians confronted by the dilemmas of violence and nonviolence:

a. Are there areas or situations where violence can be proved to have produced social justice?

b. Could nonviolent action have produced the same or better results?

c. Are there areas or situations where nonviolent action can be proved to have produced social justice?

d. What are the risks or dangers inherent in nonviolent action? What does nonviolent action do to (a) those who use it? (b) those against whom it is directed?

e. In those areas where nonviolent action has failed, what was the cause of the failure? Lack of preparation? or training? of continuity? of communication? of determination?

f. What areas or situations demand urgent action, if social justice is to be achieved? Can social justice be achieved in these areas by ordinary democratic processes? If not, by nonviolent action? If not—?

g. What are the basic facts regarding the full attainment of social justice in your country? How can they be resolved? What are the effects in your own country of structural and institutional violence?

h. How do your presuppositions and conclusions relate to your understanding of Biblical teaching?

23. Response to the Cardiff Report by Brethren, Friends, Mennonites *(Richmond, Indiana, December 15-17, 1972)*

Already prior to the Cardiff meeting, the Historic Peace Churches had called a study conference, April 21-23, 1972. This took place at Richmond, Indiana; twenty-three persons were present. David Gill, staff member of the WCC for the violence/nonviolence study attended the meeting. Following the Cardiff gathering, he encouraged a response from the Historic Peace Churches. Much the same group met again in December to give a detailed criticism of the document. A smaller group met in early 1973 to give final editing and to add more detail.

Response to Cardiff Report

by Brethren, Friends, Mennonites

PREFACE

Representatives of the historic peace churches, Brethren, Friends and Mennonites, have met twice at Richmond, Indiana, April 21-23, 1972, and December 15-17, 1972, to consider the Christian mandate to liberate the oppressed and to help create a reconciling fellowship working toward justice for all mankind. During the second of these consultations we were privileged to discuss these issues in relation to an early draft of the report of the Cardiff consultation between concerned Christians and participants in liberation movements called together by the World Council of Churches.

We hereby submit a summary of our reflections upon the Cardiff report in the effort to convey solidarity in the struggle for justice and concern over some aspects of the goals, motive, and tactics of the struggle. The first part of our response seeks to share our perplexities and suggestions regarding specific passages, concepts, and arguments in the Cardiff report. We seek here to understand the intent and affirm those parts of the report with which we agree. In the second part of our response (prepared by a second committee not claiming to harmonize its work entirely with that of the first committee) we seek to commend aspects of our common Christian faith and its moral imperatives which seem to us to have been under-emphasized in the report in its draft form. We recognize our own failures to live up to the high calling of Christ in working for justice and love for the oppressed. We seek to grow with Christians, and all those seeking to end oppression, in our insights and in a life which takes away the occasion of oppression.

Part I

Section I: We affirm the Cardiff report's emphasis on the need to develop a world community which transcends narrow sectarian and sociological boundaries. We value the recognition of God's concern for all mankind and that all people are God's children. We appreciate the strong concern with nonviolence that permeates the report and the way the church must be a sign and witness of this nonviolent community. We are concerned, however, that the church is a covenant community with demands upon it for purity of witness not demanded of other structures through which God is also working His will for community and humanization but which do not name Jesus as Lord. The church does not in fact include everyone; according to the New Testament it is the community of those consciously dedicated to the way of Jesus in human relations. It is the "people of God" in a special sense; not everyone belongs to it. It also is set apart in that it has a special mission to the rest of the world.

Despite reservations concerning the document's dismissal of the special role of the Church in the deliverance of mankind, we commend the understanding of violence as "any breach of community" in paragraphs 4 and its further elucidation in paragraphs 5 and 6.

Section II: The development of the concept of structural violence is a necessary and positive step. (Note: Some participants in our consultation are not yet sure that the term "structural violence" is an adequately precise instrument to guide our analysis of what we oppose.) This is the crucial issue which gives legitimacy to many revolutionary groups. Perhaps there is no more crucial issue for Western Christians to deal with than this. We agree with the unequivocal need to challenge this structural violence. Christ is relevant not only to the individual but also to the structures that men erect for the ordering of their lives. The multiple ways of discussing structural violence point to a multitude of overt and covert forms of oppression and broken community needing attention. It is likely too early to attempt definitive, concise conceptualization of structural violence. We are agreed that equality of access to and benefits from society's good is a desirable end all should seek. However, it appears that a concern for universal "participatory democracy" or an equal share for all in decision making risks being a western imposition. Many societies, often with a higher degree of sharing in their present communities not structured along democratic lines of voting or town hall discussion, are thus not appreciated as being relatively low in structural violence.

In the first sentence of paragraph 14 we feel that the crucial importance of the concept of structural violence is in indicating the presence of violence not in "clarifying its sources." The present wording seems inwardly contradictory. Still, in our present stage of seeking conceptual clarity and adequacy, we do not find it necessary to arrive at a single agreed upon definition of structural violence.

Section III: It seems to us that paragraphs 17 and 19 need to be reworked so as to emphasize overt personal and communal violence (and specifically the violence arising from nationalism), in relation to more covert forms of systemic or structural violence. If paragraph 19 is intended to show the way random violence can be harnessed to achieve social change, we feel it can be said much more clearly and discriminatingly. We feel that there are great differences from a Christian perspective between nonviolent organization of hostilities to produce change (as in M. L. King, Jr., or Gandhi) and agitation or utilization of mass hatred and mob violence to precipitate revolution. In paragraph 19 the concluding sentence well states the problem, but 19a and b are inadequate elucidations of its terms. For us they do not provide examples, or explanations, of the interaction or transmutation of communal, personal, and structural violence into creative social change. (Part of the confusion as to what is being said is the indefinite reference of this interaction and "violence of this kind interacts" in paragraphs 18 and 19.)

Section IV: We commend the recognition that the church must stand in solidarity with the poor and oppressed. It reflects the Biblical understanding of God's own championing of the disinherited. The church can do no less if it is true to its Lord.

In contrast to paragraph 19, 20c seems a very careful and discriminating discussion of the goals and use of violent and nonviolent strategies of social change. The oppressor and the oppressed cannot be reconciled without the falling away of the instrumentalities of oppression.

We believe that the church ministers primarily to people, but also in another sense to structures. It would depersonalize the Gospel and Christian witness and could allow us to neglect the obligation to minister prophetically and pastorally to people in power if the church oriented its ministry primarily to structural change. The overt and covert determining influences that social and political structures have on the lives, behavior, and attitudes of persons obliges the church to take up a ministry of confrontation and transformation of these structures, seeking greater justice, love, and concern for all. (20b)

While Jesus was constantly in conflict with religious-governmental authorities and other social-political groups (in distinction from his final confrontation which included the Roman authorities), we see no conclusive evidence in the New Testament that Jesus was, or that we as Christians should be, violent revolutionaries. It would seem that a Christian document would have given much more attention to the meaning of "taking up one's cross" in the context of the struggle for social justice. We consider the cross the central paradigm or model for the Christian. Thus the question as to whether taking up one's cross means nonviolent struggle and self-sacrifice cannot be evaded by either practitioners of violence or nonviolence. Nor for the Christian can hope in resurrection as well as for historical transformation be forgotten. The continuing work of the living Body of Christ includes the inculcation of hope and furtherance of justice.

We affirm the view of church-state relations expressed in paragraph 22, and the recognition that an uncritical identification of the interests of church and state has often led to the church's participation in structural violence. The church must be independent of the state in order to fulfill its prophetic role. Christians have a responsibility for cleansing lovelessness and injustice from the church, just as they do in correcting injustice in the state. Obedience to the law is not necessarily synonymous with obedience to Christ. We as Christians have all too often overlooked this.

Section V: We commend this section as a perceptive analysis of our situation and of questions which must be faced in relation to revolutionary change. We suggest that the questions in paragraph 27 must not only be asked by us as Christians but by all men facing violent change. One might add such specifically Christian questions as, "Is this a struggle for self- or interest-group preservation, or for Christian values? Or are these conflicting goals?" "Has my failure to stand up for the poor and oppressed in the past brought the need for struggle in the present?" "Do the methods of the struggle meet the demands of agape love?"

The paper implies a powerlessness in ordinary people which we feel indicates the need for a clearer definition and delineation of forms of power. What is the nature and use of power in both violent and nonviolent strategies and social structures? How can various forms of power be used to reconcile rather than further unproductive conflict? Power is essentially the ability to get things done and this power may be exercised through nonviolent techniques available to the so-called "powerless" as well as through military and economic force. The risks in the violent forms of power seem at least as formidable as those of nonviolent forms, but are not noted in the Cardiff report.

Section VI: We like this section particularly for the specific and detailed treatment of nonviolence which is so little understood by people in the churches. We are concerned that nonviolence be perceived not only as a tool for social change but also as a means for the preservation of humane values in violent situations. Even the power holders might better use nonviolent means to deal with criminality, juvenile delinquency, and even revolution. . . .

Section VI is limited to an evaluation of the pragmatic function of nonviolence. We recognize this is done because Christians and non-Christians alike are critical of nonviolence on the basis of efficacy. . . .

Section VII: We commend paragraphs 48 and 51 as calling attention to what might receive even more highlighting and centrality in the report. It would be consistent with our general concerns expressed to assert again that we can only recommend strategies for non-Christians but can call Christians to a more faithful fulfillment of the gospel demands for nonviolent personal, social, and political change. (50) We emphasize that many people accept violent methods of dealing with conflict without any consideration or understanding of nonviolent alternatives, nor of the uncertainty of final results of violent as well as of nonviolent strategies.

Section VIII: We commend paragraphs 53 through 55 for presenting a critique of the church's perhaps unconscious vast compromise with oppression and tendencies to bless the status quo, while participating in economic practices that contribute to oppression. We especially applaud the suggestions for mobilizing the churches to challenge structural violence by nonviolent means. The proposals for concrete action in paragraph 57 are most helpful.

In regard to paragraph 56, we want to object to the blanket approval of the rights of "freedom fighters" without reference to the rights of all men, particularly in their own societies, who may suffer in the battle between violent or nonviolent revolutionaries and present ruling elites. We do not want any implication either here or in sentence one of paragraph 37 that simply overturning present power structures will guarantee justice. Christians must side with the poor and oppressed but only so long as the poor and oppressed do not become oppressors. We affirm the rights of dissent, free speech and assembly, but we do not expect any government to recognize the right to overthrow it by either violent or nonviolent means. Such assertions of "rights" seem to make the document naïve. We would encourage dialogue with all liberation movements. The church obviously, however, cannot give unqualified support for all kinds of liberation movements and every means by which they may choose to "fight for freedom."

We feel that paragraph 58 is not a fitting conclusion to the document and that its questions where not redundant could be incorporated at other points in the document. Paragraphs 56 and 57 making suggestions to the World Council of Churches do seem appropriate as a conclusion to the document.

PART II
Section A.

Context of Ecumenical Dialog

1. The document seeks to maintain a kind of evenhandedness in the choice between strategies which include violence (23-26) and those which exclude it as a programmed option (28-45). This may be recognized as a step forward in contrast to centuries during which it has been assumed that violence is the ultimate arbiter in social conflict; yet does not a study claiming to be ecumenically Christian need to point beyond "it was not possible to reach a conclusion" (46)? If the final choice rests on "a commitment that transcends strategic considerations," should there not be some reference to the further Christian resources for such a commitment? The "further explorations" of paragraph 49 is to be welcomed in this connection.

2. On the other hand, there is no concern for evenhandedness in the tension between oppression and liberation as social values, or between "radical" and "gradualist" attitudes to liberation. From the perspective of our theology, we as Historic Peace Churches can understand this categorical opposition to oppression. But if the Cardiff document seeks to speak to the World Council of Churches, the Central Committee, and the structured member churches, this onesidedness would seem to need far more explanation. Otherwise it can be very easily brushed off as the product of:

—the professional and ideological bias, and class self-interest of the people at Cardiff, and

—catering to the *Zeitgeist*.

3. The bulk of the study compares alternative possible strategies in terms of their likely efficacy in achieving change in the direction of justice. We regret the absence of recognition that within the heritage of Christian

ethical thought there are other styles than efficacy, e.g., Torah, natural law, inspiration, intention, asceticism, spiritual as well as physical liberation, incarnation, resurrection, and hope. Interpreters of the document have told us that this occurred because Cardiff sought to meet non-Christian liberation movements halfway. If this is the intent of the document, that should be explained; then it asks to be evaluated as speaking to the movements; whereas now we are told it seeks to speak to the World Council.

4. Explicitly recognizable Christian substance is presented in the outline at three points:
—2-4, the vision of world community
—20, three dimensions of liberation
—21, whether or how Jesus was revolutionary

We doubt that this selection of a few fragments of a Christian vision of things lives up to the promise of paragraph 1: "The Christian position from which we speak." They fall short of tapping the relevant resources of the common Christian tradition and (even more) of the several Christian traditions which seek to share with one another in the ecumenical movement.

Section B

Elements of Analysis, Not Specifically Theological, Which Need More Examination

1. The document accepts or proposes a number of semantic conventions which are not of self-evident value.

　a. We understand the *intent* of the introduction of the phrases "structural violence" and "institutionalized violence" but we are not sure that they clarify moral discourse.

　b. We note a confusing variety of normative definitions of violence itself (4, 5, 6, 9). . . .

　c. The phrase "ministry to structures" may be misleading (par. 20/b) when the concrete meaning is resistance and transformation. The French version's *face aux structures* seems less confusing and does not raise the problem of multiple and quite divergent meanings of "ministry."

2. The concept of structural violence seems to be of some value in describing a phenomenon. Structures can and have violated the individuals over whom they exercise authority. However, if one is to move meaningfully toward justice within social structures, further clarification must be forthcoming. If existing structures may be described as violent, what is the alternative? One possible alternative is to eliminate all structure in order to eliminate the possibility of structured-violence. This is the anarchistic uto-

pian vision. *If,* on the other hand, the Christian concludes that there is indeed the need for exercise of legitimate authority external to the individual, for the sake of the individual's own welfare or education, or to restrain an individual from injuring others, or even for the sake of greater justice for persons whose suffering is worse, then one will need to further define the nature and style of structure he has in mind. Is one to look for structures which exercise their authority through nonviolent means? Or does one have in mind structures which still use violent means, but in some way do not violate the individual, i.e., the violence is not structured? If the latter, is there any way to prevent the violence from being misused (usually under disguises and euphemisms) both by conservative "establishments" and revolutionaries?

3. As one discusses the effectiveness of nonviolence as a means to effect social justice, it should be noted that violence often does not work either. The document is helpful in dismantling the assumption that nonviolence results from a principled unconcern for results: It could have said more fully that recourse to violence is often not pragmatically self-critical, nor particularly aware of dangers of side effects of violence.

4. The Cardiff report seems to assume a "received" system of thought on social change. This analysis leans heavily toward "radical" and "participatory, equalitarian" doctrines of goals and means of achieving justice and freedom from oppression. While we do not want to deny their importance, there might well be further thought given to the universal desirability of these processes. The conflict/transformation model seems to focus upon structural alterations to be achieved through the channeling of rage and random violence into disciplined movement or revolutionary activity. Political-social pressure is to be directed toward presently unjust systems, and presumably their manipulators and those trapped in these structures. The purpose is to force alteration of their oppressive aspects, or the destruction or amelioration of unjust systems. Are compromise, mediation, international organizations and legal means of redress rejected or seen as hopeless, or are they merely neglected as largely unavailable to liberation movements or ineffective in disputes between contenders of such disproportionate status and power? It is unclear to us whether the steam of hostility boiling up from the oppressed can be channeled (par. 19a) to run the engine of social-political transformation, or whether it will, like a volcano, destroy all around it when it erupts (par. 17), including those who are oppressed and their leaders in liberation struggles. One important element, the backlash phenomena of oppressive elites (and conservative majorities in more industrialized lands), is not explicitly dealt with.

In summary, handles of power for those now relatively powerless, or reversal of roles with those now in power, seem to be desired but there is no clear overarching strategy. Tactics of violent and nonviolent pressure are proposed and evaluated but there is lacking any overarching theoretical analysis.

5. The opportunity for illumination of the issues of liberation and systemic change from many contemporary psychological, social, and political analyses of power has been bypassed in the report. Some of the perplexities of the effect of violent or nonviolent tactics might be resolved if discriminations between cooperative, persuasive, utilitarian-compromises, manipulative and coercive forms of power were discussed. The question of moral and/or spiritual power and the demonic effects of assumed innocence on the part of the crusader for the cause of liberation, as on the part of the conscious or unconscious oppressor, is not treated. The role of the church and of individual Christians is obliquely suggested. In a document addressed to the churches it ought to have a central place. How God acts to achieve liberation and justice needs to be elaborated, for example, through proclamation of the Word, growth from a small community of faithful, apocalyptic eschatology, crucifixion and resurrection, conversion, theocracy, etc.

Section C

Further Reflections on Christian Dimensions

1. We already noted (A/4 above) a need for greater wholeness and clarity in Christian identity. Paragraph 46 speaks of commitments which transcend the strategic but does not suggest what they might be. Paragraph 27 identifies questions which "Christians must ask themselves" but limits them to humble self-examination; they are not illuminated substantially by the faith.

Our call is not for a creed or a doctrinal statement, but for attention to those specific aspects of Christian faith which are of particular relevance to the issues at hand.

Such attention is required by a document which wishes to speak from a Christian position, because the truth claim of the Gospel is, for the Christian, unavoidable. The truth of God's revelation in Jesus Christ provides a matrix from which Christian decisions are necessary and through the guidance of the Holy Spirit such decisions are possible. The incarnation is evidence of God's involvement in human struggle, decision, and victory over evil.

2. As Christians we understand that ultimately the power which will effect justice is God. God has been delivering men from oppression for a

very long time. As we find ourselves involved in the struggle for liberation and justice, this is of immediate as well as long range importance. Concretely this means that there is no such thing as hopelessness. In spite of human resources limited in power and perfection, just change can happen. Contrary to logical analysis, the future has positive possibilities.

Hence the social effect of Christian hope is not resignation, but creativity. Church history (including Historic Peace Church experience) has documented the fruitfulness of a hopeful and therefore critical stance in discovering social alternatives (prison reform, universal education, the liberation of slaves and of women, child labor laws, new mental health approaches). Instead of letting recent history suggest the available options, with Christian ethics limited to rejecting those which are "ineffective" or "illegitimate," should not Christians more hopefully invent and experiment with new models of reconciling and liberating ministry?

3. Our common need for repentance, a genuine turning from our guilty association in oppression and privilege at the expense of the poor of the earth, is a paramount priority in the churches and the powerful portions of mankind. This about-face is prerequisite to corrective action and to solidarity within the human family. Not only sorrow for sin and public confession, but action to redress the age-old effects of our wrongdoing in participating in the benefits of exploitation of men and natural resources is required of us.

4. The Cross of Christ is not only the source or means of our forgiveness and entrance into the people of God, it is also the model and the power of our obedience.

His defeat, death, and resurrection set before us in every moment the possibility that we may be called to self-forgetful, loving nonviolence, leaving questions of success (in achieving justice) in God's hands. For us as for Christ, obedience is not subject to simple calculations of foreseeable effectiveness.

At the same time it should not be assumed that such obedience sets aside all prospects of effectiveness. Often, in a paradoxical way perhaps not unrelated to the resurrection, an approach not chosen in terms of control or effectiveness nevertheless has a strong impact (e.g., the social posture of the pre-Constantinian church).

5. Jesus taught his followers to love not only their allies but also their enemies. The inclusive vision of community (par. 2-4) demands that those who unjustly hold power be included in the redemptive purpose. Past movements which have been demonstrably effective in nonviolent empowerment have consciously included the "liberation" or "humanization" *of the oppressor* as both end and means. This note is absent in 28-45. In

the section on strategies which include violence (23-27) the adversary is spoken of only destructively (25/d).

6. As Christians we find ourselves compelled to stand solidly against injustice and oppression wherever that is identified and we must respond to the situation in the interest of justice. In this we stand solidly with all persons participating in movements of liberation and social justice. However, this does not mean we find ourselves in complete agreement with the affirmative goals of all or perhaps any of the current movements. Our faith urges us to act in regard to the goal of solidarity for all people. This may and often has clashed with some of the vision and goals of revolutionary movements, e.g., nationalism, retribution, triumph of ideology. Such discontinuity must not be brushed aside in the interest of existing continuity. Even as the continuity of concern will compel Christians to join in the struggle, discontinuity of goal will control the degree and manner of involvement in any given situation.

7. The ethics of creation implied in the first sections of the report require fulfillment in God's New Creation to provide specifically Christian theological foundations for the transformation of men and structures sought by means of the tactics described in later sections. The Incarnation in Jesus in history has brought us face to face with our need of forgiveness for our complicity in oppression and violation of our fellowmen. But it also presents us with the alternative of a life creative of a New Humanity within us and among us which liberates by proclaiming hope, sharing and sacrificial love for all, but especially for the poor and dispossessed. The end is peace and justice for all; the means is sacrificial, nonviolent service, and resistance. God's coming to men in Christ provides a paradigm and power for our Christian witness and transforming love. The seeming powerlessness of Jesus on the cross must be remembered not only in the power of His resurrection (its present and future hope given to mankind) but also in His works of healing, casting out demons, proclaiming God's jubilee at hand, and the cosmic overcoming of the "principalities and powers" which are roughly equivalent to the forces of evil and oppression we seek to exorcise today. The first sections of the report call our attention to a relevant application of Irenaeus' "recapitulation" of mankind, as Christ heads a renewed humanity. We ought also to recognize a unique role for the church as the Body of Christ in this reconstituting of humanity more in keeping with God's concerns for justice and love. Thus the covenant community, conscious of its source of strength, must have a role in judging and carrying out the transforming tactics of the latter parts of the report.

An effort at "Christian secularity" seems to guide and underlie, whether consciously or not, the concern for efficacy in the Cardiff document. How should a Christian define his goals within the world? Only with tutelage of scripture, church, tradition, and the Spirit can a truly more mature mankind build on its passion and moral insight an adequate basis for the affirmation of the first four sections of the report regarding our call to action.

24. Jesus and Power (Geneva, Switzerland, May 1973)

A working party was asked to investigate the specific issue of the relationship of Jesus to political action in Palestine, as a continuation of the Cardiff consultation. John H. Yoder was a member of this group. He was designated to write up the findings of the party, which he did in an article that appeared in the Ecumenical Review.

Jesus and Power

John H. Yoder

I.

The hinge around which the two-year study on "Violence, Nonviolence, and the Struggle for Social Justice" came to turn was the consultation held at Cardiff in September 1972, gathering ethicists, theorists of social change, and participants in revolutionary struggle. Discussion ranged from the broadest theological backgrounds of the concern for social justice, through to the most concrete realism about the process of change.

A passage in its report stated an old question in a partially new shape:

> The latest stage in this discussion concerns whether Jesus did in fact exemplify nonviolence or was in broad sympathy with the violent Jewish nationalist, patriotic resistance movement of the so-called Zealots. Most of us are persuaded that the assertion that Jesus had zealot sympathies is very doubtful and that the traditional understanding of Him is much more likely.

We need not quibble about the shortcomings in phrasing inevitable when a text is written in a meeting; (Note: Is the "traditional understanding" as clear and as traditional as that? Is "broad sympathy with the Zealots" strong enough for what some people claim? The quotation is from paragraph 21 of the Cardiff report.) the question is clear and real. The claim for a justifying precedent in Jesus' Zealot sympathies was not invented self-righteously by the advocates of violent revolution today; it is a theme recently revived within serious New Testament scholarship. (Note: Hans-Ruedi Weber introduced the theme at Cardiff with a review of these studies—since published under the title "Freedom Fighter or Prince of Peace," in *Study Encounter,* Vol. VIII, No. 4, 1972, SE/32.) The issue seemed to WCC staff to be so open and so representative that a small working party of biblical scholars and theologians was convened in May 1973 under the chairmanship of the World Council's General Secretary, Philip Potter, around the theme "Jesus and Power." Despite a variety of languages and methods, the consultation justified the conclusion that the main lines of an answer, though not simple, self-evident or traditional, are accessible. If we agree for the moment to postpone debate about its meaning for today, its authority and its present application, there can be wide agreement about the canonical witness to Jesus' work. (Note: We speak here of the canonical texts; but an effort to project a "real historical Jesus" behind the texts would not change the picture radically. Weber's summary of the research data is adequate for our purpose.)

Jesus Among Conflicting Attitudes to Power
Power in the simplest sense of the word was Jesus' agenda. (Note: Etymologically, power is what it takes to make things happen. It usually includes structures to legitimate and obligate, and it distributes the economic and spiritual wherewithal for human fulfilment.) The major landmarks of His recorded ministry are public events relating to the socio-political concerns of His people:
—baptism, temptation, and public appearances among the followers of John;
—the programmatic claim of the Nazareth synagogue appearance;
—the calling and sending of disciples;
—the entry into Jerusalem and the clearing of the Temple;
—the trial and crucifixion.

Jesus could not have come into occupied Palestine talking of "Kingdom," "justice," "liberation," of God's partisanship for the poor, God's alternative to Mammon, and love for the enemy, without having to relate to the other movements and institutions already dealing with the same concerns, or to the options they represented. To schematize:

(a) In any such situation there are good reasons for "making the best of a bad deal" by working within the system to minimize its evil effects and use every chance to turn it toward the good. The Gospels tell of "Herodians" and "Sadducees" who had such a relationship to the Roman presence.

(b) One extreme alternative is radical rejection of the entire system, expressed in geographic withdrawal and the formation of autarchic countercommunities to prepare for the judgment which is sure to fall on God's enemies. A generation of archeologists have greatly clarified our picture of this option.

(c) The other logical form of radical rejection is to execute God's judgment on His enemies oneself by means of paramilitary violence against the oppressive order. Schematically we may speak of this as the "Zealot option." (Note: Josephus first uses the label "Zealot" for the movement of the late 60s which led to Jerusalem's destruction. Historians differ as to the unity, continuity and uniformity of the insurrection efforts which came and went during the preceding decades (Acts 5:36f., 21:39). Consultation participants Kenzo Tagawa (Japan) (in a paper prepared before the consultation) and Weber (WCC staff; cf. above note) considered the temporal juxtaposition of Jesus and the Zealot movement to be historically incorrect. We here follow Luke (6:12) in using the term typologically, not historically.) We may also see in it a strong analogy to today's talk of "revolution," on the simple logical level of a morally justified attack against the existing institution. (Note: In the fuller substance of definition it is evident that many strands of what is today considered revolutionary thought were not prefigured. Dr. Tagawa identified some significant differences: today's "revolutionaries" see themselves as moving forward in the dialectic of history whereas the Zealots sought to restore the Davidic theocracy; today economic structures are seen as more basic than those of political sovereignty. Such differences make the analogy modest, but it is real. The juxtaposition suggested at Cardiff is fitting and significant.)

(d) The remaining possibility is to combine serious critique on the one hand with tolerable social involvement on the other, by means of a thoroughly thought-out life-style defining the shape and the limits of participation in a fundamentally unacceptable order. The Pharisees who systematized this option were often Jesus' interlocutors.

We find in Jesus' ministry no effort to dodge the pressure to take sides, and no claim to transcend them all alike. Sometimes Jesus seems even to open the door to ambivalent interpretations of His intent. Of the available options, certainly the Zealot stance had the most sympathy among His listeners and was most analogous to His own public image and vocabulary. Zealot leanings were strongly represented among His disciples.

This option was clearly a temptation for Him from the desert to Gethsemane, and provided the grounds for His execution. (Note: The *titulon* on the Cross is evidence enough. The political dimension of Jesus' death is not dependent on the much-debated questions about the legality of the trial or the relation of Jewish and Roman responsibility.) There is thus good reason to compare and contrast Jesus' approach with that advocacy of righteous insurrection in the name of liberation/humanization/empowerment which is our theme today.

Jesus' agreement with the Zealots was far-reaching. (Note: While disavowing the Zealot label, Dr. Tagawa's characterization of Jesus' critique of oppression and of its religious and ideological justification paralleled this summary.)

(a) He shared their generally negative judgment on the existing structures on the grounds of their inhumanity.

(b) With them He saw men's power relationships as part of God's concern, ignoring any spirit/society dualism.

(c) Like them, He was ready to forsake or sacrifice other genuine but lesser values for the sake of the righteousness of the Kingdom.

(d) Like theirs, His vision of obedience was not derived from careful calculation of the probable success of particular tactics.

In these respects Jesus differed not only from the other options available in His time but also from the logic of majority views on Christian social ethics today. He did not transcend the Zealot alternative on metaphysical grounds as an *adiaphoron* or as too political: It had a real attraction for Him. If it does not for us, we may fail to understand Him.

Yet He set that temptation aside, for reasons that weigh more deeply, the more we observe the apparent proximity of the Zealot path to His own. (Note: Cf. Weber, *op. cit.*, p. 22.)

(a) He held a lower view than they of the importance of state sovereignty and the sword, either to oppress or to save, in comparison to other kinds of power.

(b) He held a higher view of the adversary; He included the outsider and the enemy in His liberating concern. The point is not the prohibition of violence as such but rather the dignity, the personhood, even of the enemy.

(c) His circle of disciples, rather than being the last of those authorized to use holy violence to inaugurate the kingdom, are the first of those privileged to live already in the freedom of the new order. Their new style of unconditional love (e.g., Luke 6:27-36) celebrates the new order even before the old has been driven out.

(d) The Zealot sword could not be set aside in favour of neutrality or "spirituality"; the alternative was servanthood and the Cross. Perhaps the clearest statement of the choice is the Upper Room statement of Luke 22:25ff.

Let it be noted that Jesus' originality is not best located in some distinctive moral principle such as, for example, the proscription of violence. If it were, later debates (law/gospel, principle/situation, rule/exception) could grasp His point and in some cases set it aside. But Jesus announces a new age, a new community, a new presence: the rest follows from that.

II.

Jesus and Our Desire for Power

That this is the most probably valid interpretation of the gospel record however does not answer the Cardiff report's question: The distance from Jesus' answer to our question is still great. It is entirely possible—in fact it has been the majority view of Christians for a millennium and a half—that the parallel we have observed between Jesus' temptation to righteous violence and our own should not be taken at face value. To leap from the canon to the present may well be historically (or should we say ahistorically?) naïve. For this reason it had to be said at the outset of this article that relative agreement on the biblical data can be attained only by postponing the question of what it means for the present. All the members of the working party tried their hand at drafting a statement on this question. All of us tried to show how Jesus' words and work both do not and yet do point to our present decision making. (Note: The phrasings of extempore drafts by E. Schweitzer and N. Nissiotis are reflected in the following lines.) Yet does not Christ's lordship, in the ecumenical conversation, mean that in some way or other there is again a valid new presentness of Christ in His call? Does not all "renewal" assume some new "leap" from Christ to us? Does not all unity trust in it? Is it not what Pentecost means?

To avoid naïvety about the "leap" one may distinguish between ends and means. We may learn from Jesus, it is argued, *that* we should take the side of the oppressed: but *how* to do so we must learn from our contemporaries. Or we learn from Him that we must love our neighbours; but what love calls us to do and to which neighbours will have to be dictated by our circumstances. There is nothing mandatory about the Cross as path if tyrannicide or some other means can do it better.

Or we can avoid the leap and free ourselves from a too crude appropriation of the ethics of Jesus by interposing a hermeneutic bridge. It may be a bridge related to the ethical agent: His "Christian liberty" or "openness to the future," His "new heart." What Jesus did about the Zealot option may be a parable for this new attitude, but not a model. The model is the belief stance of the disciple. The guidance of the Holy Spirit in the life of the community in each situation, the use of human reason's projection of the probable results of our choices, and the transformation of the "heart" through metanoia may be emphasized in varying positions. Others will use a metaphysical bridge like "Incarnation" or "apotheosis" from which ethical implications flow, or a logical-scientific one handling the distance across the centuries in cultural, linguistic, and literary terms.

The consultation could not in a few hours make its way past one barrier which I believe was partly semantic. Some would rather say Jesus was not *directly* "revolutionary" and that His pro-liberation impact must be deduced or unfolded indirectly over the bridge of the transformed personality and long-range historical development. Others would say that Jesus' presence, proclamation, and sacrifice were themselves radically critical and effective in the social *mêlée*. There was here no confirmed difference about the facts as capsuled above in terms of similarity and contrast to the "Zealot model," but neither was there consensus about whether to call that stance a social strategy, or about what dimensions we can see as fitting in other historical contexts. The concepts "direct," "social programme," and "revolution," the place of paradox and dialectic, and the self-evidence of the person/structure duality (Note: Responding to a Cardiff phrasing, Professor Schweitzer said, "The Church has no ministry to the structures—as little as it has a ministry to avalanches." Yet this negation opened the way to the call to "those who hear the appeal of Jesus" to create challenging new structures.) were seen differently. (Note: To identify a given conversational blockage as semantic does not mean to say it is unimportant, nor that all semantic frames are equally helpful. It means only that further progress in understanding would have called for other levels of analysis than those focussed on the Gospel accounts.) To the question initially proposed by the convenors, "What can be discerned from the New Testament about Jesus' own understanding of and relation to power?" the consultants as New Testament scholars did not differ. Yet about the place of Jesus in Scripture and even more about the place of Jesus and the mode of His relevance in the life of the church, they differed in very familiar ways.

Are we then sent back to just another modulation of the comparative analysis within pluralism which has so often been as far as ecumencial conversation could go? Or is there some ground to hope that, facing a contemporary question, admitting the failure of established patterns to answer it—admitting even the fact that established patterns of symbiosis between church and empire have aggravated it—hearing a canonical witness not hardened in the dogma of any one major tradition, the simplicity of the

Kingdom call could take on flesh again in a legitimate analogy between Jesus' social choices and our own?

III.

Jesus and Our Power Language

As can often happen when important but ill-defined issues are at stake, discussion of our question often turns from substance to form, from the major agenda to points of order and definitions of terms. Thus, on one hand, the advocates of subversion and terror argue that the system they wish to destroy is "violent" even though its orderly oppressiveness can get along without much direct physical abuse, and propose to call such inequities "structural violence." On the other hand, a radical critic of traditional reliance on coercion and killing like Archbishop Camara will still use terms like "revolution" and "violence" to describe the better alternative he seeks.

Such shifts in vocabulary are not "mere prolegomena"; they are intended to predispose the shape of the whole search. Cardiff recorded the variety of usages without seeking resolution. (Note: The Cardiff text itself passes on varying definitions of "violence" and "power." Sometimes "violence" is so defined as to be discrete, identifiable, avoidable. Thus there is a choice between violent and nonviolent techniques. Elsewhere it is defined as any interference with the fulfilment of human potential, i.e., as inevitable in historical existence.) The May consultation was no more conclusive: it would be presumptuous and useless to propose here yet another set of definitions. Yet it could be observed that there is biblical warrant for some of the points the shifts in usage mean to make. Jesus' words, "Those in authority are called their country's 'benefactors'" (Luke 22:25), identify the ambivalence of legitimacy. The claim to the "beneficial" made in favour of old rulers and new veils, but only partly, the violence which is their footing and their character. That insurrection is violent but oppression is not (or vice versa) or that some forms of Christian presence are "direct political action" while others are not, are terminological assumptions which need questioning. Jesus' intensification of "Thou shalt not kill" (Matt. 5:21) reaches behind pragmatism and casuistries which measure only the surface of a deed. The "power" *(exousia)* He himself exercises illustrates the broad scope of kinds of power (in the simple sense with which we began) which are not tied to violence and the state: the power of forgiveness, the power of the pilot experience, the power of peoplehood, of publicity . . . Jesus did not free His disciples from violence to make them pure and weak, but because He called them to use other, stronger resources.

The study on "Violence, Nonviolence, and the Struggle for Social

Justice" is thus improperly narrowed when against the short-range effect of rifle and bomb one weighs only the impact of a few specific nonviolent direct action techniques; the other dimensions of power which are thereby left off the balance are the ones the Church has on her side. Neither "power" nor "violence" is a univocal, unidimensional something varying only in terms of more or less; each varies in quality, in depth, in direction, in wholeness. In this awareness the technicians, both of ethical theory and of social change, must work more at refining their terms; meanwhile let not the rest of us be kept from hearing Jesus by a debate about terms. When He calls and enables us to love our enemies, neither the meaning nor the power of that call is dependent on how we define "violence." When He prefers servanthood to domination, as His path and therefore as ours, it is immaterial whether we call that "powerlessness" or "omnipotence"; it is God's way.

25. Violence, Nonviolence, and the Struggle for Social Justice (Geneva, Switzerland, August 28, 1973)

The end of the long process of drafting, consultations, critiques, and rewriting took place in the summer of 1973 when the Central Committee approved the following text of the violence/nonviolence statement. Those from the Church and Society unit working with the paper had introduced it to the committee with the comment that they had not the task of beginning the discussion, because the headlines had seen to that. Rather, their

distinctive role was that of trying to set the issue in a worldwide ecumenical context—which meant, in particular helping white, affluent Christians take seriously the perspectives of other parts of the Church.

The Central Committee commended the statement to the churches for "study, comment, and action." They noted the new context of the discussion:

... while violence is by no means a novel problem for the Christian conscience, our perception of the problem is in some respects new. In earlier years, the discussion focused almost exclusively on the "just war" and whether, or under what conditions, the Church should sanction the use of violence by sovereign states. Then Christians were deeply concerned about the morality of their individual participation in warfare, or in particular wars. The present document sets the whole issue in the wider context of the struggle for social justice, as it affects both oppressors and oppressed.

Noting appreciatively the contribution to clarification of the issue, the Committee associated itself with the call to repentance of Christians as all too often having been beneficiaries of violence. They called for further theological work on specified issues, sharpening conceptual clarity and translation of the general statements into local situations. They recognized the illustrations chosen for the report were limited in number and warned that some might misunderstand those used as leading to an imbalance.

The final recommendation was that

> WCC units and sub-units be encouraged to develop fresh initiatives appropriate to their respective programmes, to stimulate and assist churches and Christians throughout the world to more careful study of, and more courageous engagement in, nonviolent action in support of the oppressed.

The Working Committee was asked to continue its study with special attention to the "just war" concept for the role of law. Possibilities of crisis intervention were to be explored. Several recommendations of the Working Committee were not adopted. These would have created staff positions and programs for continued study and training in nonviolence.

The Statement

1. The problem of Christian responsibility in a world of force and violence is as old as the Church itself. It has appeared in ever-changing forms through the centuries: in the suffering but triumphant martyrdom of the early Church, in the question of Christian military service from the time of the Roman Empire, in the question of the "just war," in the justification of tyrannicide, or in the limits of obedience to unjust political authority and the means by which it may be resisted, to mention only a few. In all these forms the agonising question is the same: How can Christians, children of God's love and followers of Jesus Christ, live and work in a world where the use of force and violence against the countless forms of human sin seems unavoidable?

2. Today, however, this problem has taken on a new urgency for several reasons. Among them:

(a) Churches and Christians are realizing that they have too seldom been on the side of the poor and the oppressed. They have too often supported the powers of an unjust social order. They often have profited from the poverty of others. They have in the past used force when they were in power, against those who differed from them in belief or ideology. Their first word to this problem must be one of repentance. Repentance, however, means a change of mind and heart, and new forms of action for justice.

(b) Millions of Christians are confronted with the question in their own lives today: should they join the poor and oppressed of their countries in a violent movement to overthrow an unjust order that seemingly cannot be changed in any other way, or should they remain passive and therefore responsible for the continuing injustice? In their dilemma of conscience they look for guidance and help from the Church.

(c) Christians and churches find themselves engaged with those of other beliefs and ideologies in working for the whole future of mankind. They cannot be content merely with binding up human wounds. The causes of suffering in the collective selfishness and unjust structures of society must also be attacked in the name of Christian love. This leads to choices about the use of force and violence which cannot be avoided, in conditions which Christians cannot always control, but where they must act.

(d) Violence today has become demonic in its hold on human life. In the life of some nations and among many severely oppressed peoples, it seems more like an addiction than like rational behavior. Television, film, and literature have accustomed us to violent scenes and actions. Police brutality and the use of the gun have become widely accepted in civil life. In many nations military considerations increasingly dominate economic and political life. In some, military regimes have taken over. Among poor and young people in many lands there exists an unusually high rate of murder, assault, and petty crime. With such pervasiveness, violence conditions people in a fashion that makes it extremely difficult for them to see peaceful options even in personal relationships.

(e) The world and the churches have been both inspired and challenged in recent years by examples of new and sophisticated nonviolent movements for justice and freedom. Some of these—for example the Gandhian movement—have been non-Christian. Others—such as that of Martin Luther King—have been Christian. Together their witness has brought the churches of the world to examine anew the style of the involvement in the struggle for world justice and peace.

3. In response to these and other needs it is important that the World Council of Churches concern itself with the question of violence. It has done so on several occasions: in Amsterdam in 1948 where the issue was participation in war, in the Geneva Conference of 1966 which carefully focused the problem of revolutionary violence against oppressive social systems, at Uppsala in 1968 where both the violence of the status quo and the significance of nonviolent methods of social change were brought into focus, and at other meetings in between. The present study grows out of a

memorial resolution for Dr. Martin Luther King at Uppsala asking the WCC to promote studies on nonviolent methods of social change. It received further stimulus from the debate created by the WCC's help to groups combatting racism. In the present statement we build upon this heritage. (Note: For a fuller statement of this history see the Report of the Nemi Consultation.)

The Christian's Hope
   4. We believe that the fundamental reality which should govern our thinking and our acts is not some ideal form of behaviour, but the promise of God in Jesus Christ that the future is in his hands, that his kingdom is at work, and that his power will prevail over the forces of this world. This promise gives us strength and confidence for work for relative justice, liberation and peace here and now, with hope and with integrity. We believe that this promise is special good news to the poor, to the victims of injustice and to the suffering in this world, whose condition Christ shared and redeemed. We believe that for our time, "the goal of social change is a society in which all the people participate in the fruits and the decision-making processes, in which the centres of power are limited and accountable, in which human rights are truly affirmed for all, and which acts responsibly toward the whole human community of mankind, and toward coming generations." (Note: Nemi Report, para. 17c.) Such a society would not be the kingdom of God, but it might reflect within the conditions of our time that subjection of the powers of this world to the service of justice and love, which reflect God's purposes for man.
   5. The question before us then is: how do we discern God's working in this world where force and violence are so strong, and by what means can we serve him by our actions or our suffering?

The Christian's Dilemma
   6. Violence is not an abstract issue for Christians. As persons and communities, Christians live daily in the midst of violence. They often find themselves, willingly or unwillingly, participating in social organizations that embody and practise violence. They may deliberately act in violent or nonviolent ways to preserve law and order, or to bring about change. They may use the power of government or the law to promote justice, or they may fight government and break the law in the name of justice. We cannot speak in general about their dilemmas until we take account of real situations in which Christians are trying to live their faith. In 1971 the Central Committee of the WCC endorsed a letter of the General Secretary to the Secretary-General of the United Nations in which he called attention to

the increasing use of violence and brutalities within many countries in all parts of the world, belonging to various power blocs and governed by various ideologies and social systems. We cannot here speak of the dilemmas of Christians in all of these lands. In order that our reflections may be rooted in real experience, however, we remind ourselves here of a few specific areas in which Christians agonize over questions of violence today.

7. In the Republic of South Africa many Christians support a government representing a white minority that imposes its will upon a black majority by coercion, threats, and frequently overt violence, to protect their privileged status, because they are afraid of total loss and anarchy should the present power structure crumble. Other Christians seek to oppose and change the government policies in some respects, but face well-nigh complete frustration in their nonviolent and legal efforts. In the same country many black Christians and even some whites find themselves pinning their hopes on or taking part in liberation movements which aim at the overthrow of present oppressive authority, as the way to justice and freedom. These movements, which in other countries in southern Africa have liberated territory and set up de facto governments of their own, use many tactics ranging from education to military action.

8. In Latin America many Christians feel themselves to be in the midst of violence which has a long history. It shows itself in very different forms—through oppressive acts such as unjust imprisonment of opponents by the government, torture, censorship of the communications media and through economic exploitation backed by political power. Malnutrition, high infant mortality, illiteracy, cultural discrimination, exploitation of workers, and increasing inequality between rich and poor are all seen as aspects of a violent *situation* in which millions of Latin Americans are involved. The question they face is how to overthrow the forces perpetuating this situation. The consciousness of violence and injustice is rising in the masses. Ruling groups in their turn, feeling menaced in their privileges, build even more oppressive and violent systems of power. Movements for constructive change, even when legal and peaceful, may bring further repression. The Church has been challenged to denounce this situation and to define a clear option for the liberation of the people and the construction of a more just and human society. What forms should this option take? How can Christians in solidarity with the people work effectively to counter the forces of a violent status quo?

9. In Northern Ireland, Christians oppose Christians in sustained, communal violence, in which all limiting controls have broken down. Economic and political issues are being fought out and atrocities committed by groups wearing labels inherited from the Church's past. The ap-

palling irony of the situation is that those who seek justice and reconciliation find themselves accused by Christian voices at both extremes of betraying their faith.

10. In the Middle East, Arab Christians share with Muslims a burning sense of injustice in response to the occupation by Israel of some Arab homelands. Violence is the mood and spirit of the day. Successful violence has determined the status quo. Peaceful settlement seems a hopeless dream in the present circumstances. What is a Christian's duty and hope for witnessing to justice and peace in this situation?

11. In the USA most spokesmen of the Church have opposed the massive, obvious violence their country has inflicted in South East Asia, but many Christians have tacitly or openly supported it. Christians have participated in and objected to economic domination and political interventions, sometimes openly violent, in Latin America. A civil rights movement and other protest movements, often committed to nonviolent change, have sometimes adopted violence, whether by tactical choice or by uncalculated outbursts of feeling, against a systematic oppression armed with weapons both brutal and subtle. These examples illustrate the dilemma of American Christians. Some support violence by the armed forces abroad or the police at home in the name of national or local security. Some have worked to curb this violence and to achieve justice by nonviolent and legal means, but with only limited success. A few have turned to counter-violence with no more success. What is the way of hope?

12. In these and many other situations which could be described, Christians find themselves on opposing sides of conflict. In all they—at least many of them—feel a burden of conscience, an agony that cannot be healed with easy slogans, and a call to a better way of life.

Commitment to Christ

13. What guidance, then, can we find when we turn to the situation from which our faith springs?

14. As Christians we seek in Jesus Christ clarity about our action in a world of violence. We seek this clarity both in his words and in his deeds. God's love comes to all human beings in their suffering and needs, in their poverty and powerlessness, but also in the confusion which comes with wealth and power. Christ stands with the poor and suffering and he confronts with God's judgment those who are causing poverty and suffering by the selfish use of their wealth or their political or religious power.

15. We have clear evidence that Jesus of Nazareth did not use violence on behalf of the weak, the poor, and the suffering against the powerful even though he identified himself with them and found them especially

ready to hear the Gospel. The record rather shows that he himself suffered the unjust violence of the powerful to the point of dying on the Cross. This is the condition of his authority and power as the risen Lord, who overcomes all powers and all the forces of suffering, and even death itself.

16. What is the consequence of this example for us today? On this, Christians, including those in this committee, do not agree. Some argue that Jesus' renunciation of violence was incidental or situational, and that in other contexts the same commitment to justice and responsiveness to human need might lead to quite different imperatives, including violent measures either to preserve a relatively just order or to attack an unjust order. Others see in Jesus' rejection of the Zealot option a choice so basic in the definition of his ministry, so typical of the ethical problematic of every situation, and so firmly supported by the rest of Scripture and the churches' experience, as to present guidance of continuing validity.

17. We do agree, however, that Jesus' commandment to love all human beings must be the strong basis of all our action. It means love for enemies as well as friends. It excludes all hatred against persons, groups, classes, peoples, or races. "I say to you, love your enemies, bless them that curse you, do good to them that hate you and pray for them that despitefully use you." (Matt. 5:44).

18. This is a social as well as a personal commandment. Liberation of human beings is both an internal and external task. They may not be separated; neither may either be absorbed into the other. Inner freedom from hate and fear is a preparation for the work of social liberation, never a substitute for it. The destruction of structures of injustice and violence in a society prepares the way for covenants of peace among people, but these covenants must be sealed by individuals inwardly free of violence toward the neighbour.

19. We agree that all struggle against the misuse of power must include the concern to realize justice and freedom according to God's purpose for all people, even our enemies, in the present and in the future (Rom. 12:19-21).

20. We agree, furthermore, in our confidence that God himself will realize this purpose for all people. His work will be complete when his victory over all the powers of the world is made manifest. This confidence prevents us from standing aside and seeking peace only for ourselves. It leads us into the world and into the battle for justice and freedom for all people in order to have a humble part in God's work.

Human Power Under God's Commandment

21. There is still more that we can say together on the basis of our

faith, concerning human power.

22. We agree that under God's mandate governments have a legitimate function to restrain private power in the interests of justice for all, to assure human rights, and to serve public welfare. To this end they use force governed by law. When a government does this it has authority, which is to be recognized, even though we may object to some laws and seek to change them. A just government provides a legal framework within which opposing interests and points of view may work out their conflicts. Its processes are not only coercive but also persuasive and facilitating at many levels: in education, in public works and investment, in planning for and regulating the economy, in promoting peace and harmony among different groups in society.

23. All human powers, however, are tempted to misuse and exceed their authority. Government, almost by definition, is the executor of powers that it may wield violently. Government may serve the common good or may serve unjust privilege—and often serves both. Enforcement is a function of government, and the force in enforcement frequently includes the reality or the threat of violence. Since no government is ideal, citizens usually feel obliged to accept imperfections before they tear down a government— especially when they realize that the government that replaces it will also be imperfect. But government can become so tyrannical and so hostile to its own people that citizens feel a duty to resist it or overthrow it. Their decisions may depend largely upon the opportunities for free expression and peaceful change that are incorporated in the government.

24. Some forms of power, furthermore, especially economic and technological, are inadequately controlled by any just law. These forces are even more tempted to violence, and to control them requires effective opposition from those who are hurt by their actions, and from all who are concerned for justice.

25. Such powers as these are rooted in human ambitions and desires, fears and hopes. But they also transcend individual human beings and subject them. The New Testament, when it speaks of the principalities and powers of this world, recognizes this ambiguous character. The principalities and powers of the world can oppose God and human justice. They can become violent and in that case Christians must resist them (Eph. 6). At the same time Christians are called to bear witness to these powers of God's purpose for this world in Christ to which they, when redeemed, belong (Eph. 3:9-11). The Church has this ministry to the structures and powers of politics and economics, which are often violent in their way of operating. As Christians we must resist the evil of structured violence. We must stand with the poor and oppressed. We do so in obedience to our

Lord. We do so as the Church which includes the affluent and the poor. We do so as a ministry to these powers seeking their transformation into servants of the covenant relation into which God seeks to bring all people in freedom and mutual responsibility.

26. We agree therefore that the goal of resistance to unjust and illegitimate power should be not the destruction of an enemy but a more just order within which different groups and powers agree to live in peace reconciled to each other. God alone, and no human ideology or institution, is the measure of justice. None of us is righteous enough to seek total victory or to demand a society in which our ideas of justice or our ideals alone will prevail. Therefore Christians will seek a society in which all persons and groups may participate in decisions that affect the common good.

27. We also agree in recognizing that no human institution or movement is without sin. Those who uphold the powers that be as well as those who attack them bear their various measures of guilt for the evils of society. We who live by the forgiveness of our sins must translate this into a humble awareness of the judgment of God, a full sense of identity with the oppressed and an ongoing responsibility toward the enemies we fight. We expect that God will transform our struggle for justice into the realization of his justice which includes the reconciliation of all humanity in him.

Action: Violent and Nonviolent

28. It is in the context of this reality that the methods of resistance to unjust and oppressive political or economic power must be considered. There are among us three distinct points of view about methods:

(a) Some believe that nonviolent action is the only possibility consistent with obedience to Jesus Christ. They recognize that this discipline is hard and will often be unsuccessful. They object to justifying nonviolence only by its success as a strategy for solving social problems. Nonviolent action is for them a witness to the transcendent power of God in Jesus Christ, a way of faith which will be justified by him and his power alone.

(b) Some are prepared to accept the necessity of violent resistance as a Christian duty in extreme circumstances, but they would apply to it criteria similar to those governing a just war. Not only must the cause be just and all other possibilities exhausted, but also there must be reasonable expectation that violent resistance will attain the ends desired, the methods must be just and there must be a positive understanding of the order which will be established after the violence succeeds. Violence will then be understood as the *ultima ratio*. It is the act of freedom which can only be undertaken, with the guilt it brings, confident in the final judgment of God.

(c) Some find themselves already in situations of violence in which they cannot help but participate. Nonviolence does not present itself as an option unless they would withdraw totally from the struggle for justice. In this situation the problem becomes to reduce the sum total of violence in the situation and to liberate human beings for just and peaceful relations with each other. Some form of relatively just order must first be created before violence can cease. The problem of Christian responsibility, then, is to humanize the means of conflict and to build structures of peace wherever possible within it.

29. We have not been able to reduce these three radically different points of view to agreement. We are convinced however of three things:

(a) There are some forms of violence in which Christians may not participate and which the churches must condemn. There are violent causes— the conquest of one people by another or the deliberate oppression of one class or race by another—which offend divine justice. There are violent means of struggle—torture in all forms, the holding of innocent hostages and the deliberate or indiscriminate killing of innocent non-combatants for example—which destroy the soul of the perpetrator as surely as the life and health of the victim.

(b) We are convinced that far too little attention has been given by the Church and by resistance movements to the methods and techniques of non-violence, in the struggle for a just society. There are vast possibilities for preventing violence and bloodshed and for mitigating violent conflicts already in progress, by the systematic use of forms of struggle which aim at the conversion and not the destruction of the opponent and which use means which do not foreclose the possibility of a positive relationship with him. Nonviolent action represents relatively unexplored territory: Initiatives being taken by various groups and individuals to help the exploration happen deserve the strongest possible support from the WCC and the churches.

(c) We reject, however, some facile assumptions about nonviolence which have been current in the recent debate. Nonviolent action is highly political. It may be extremely controversial. It is not free of the compromise and ambiguity which accompany any attempt to embody a love-based ethic in a world of power and counter-power, and it is not necessarily bloodless. Morever, most struggles for freedom—and most government actions—have been, as a matter of fact, mixtures of violent and nonviolent action. A nonviolent movement may produce peripheral violence and have the problem of controlling it. An armed struggle may also have nonviolent dimensions such as education designed to persuade and win over the enemy. In one movement violent and nonviolent groups may be working for the same ends. In all of these Christians will have hard choices to make. The more these choices are informed by a responsible spirit and knowledge of constructive nonviolent options, the more creative they will be.

Mutual Challenge and Help

30. Christians reflecting on these dilemmas must avoid the trap of seeming to dictate strategies and tactics to people living in distant and different situations. No single one can have universal validity; and those who live outside a particular social conflict do well to be wary of handing out advice, whether towards violent or nonviolent strategies, when it is not they, but others, who will be called upon to pay the price of following it. In particular those who sit comfortably close to the top of the world's socio-economic pyramid must be sensitive to the severe limitations their affluence places on their giving moral advice to others less well placed.

31. Yet, with this qualification in mind, it is essential that the process of mutual challenge and help should continue and grow. Many of these seemingly different local situations have in fact a great deal in common, and human feelings of fear and frustration are shared the world over, and by those on both sides of conflicts. Furthermore, the dialogue between Christians needs to take place on the widest scale, because Christians associated with the world's power centres bear more responsibility for hidden or open violence in distant places than they often realize. Also the ecumenical movement has taught us the importance of hearing uncomfortable questions which challenge our facile compromises with the various cultures within which we live and witness; and it has brought home to us that Christians cannot remain indifferent to these issues of political and social justice.

32. Violence should not be equated with radicalism and revolution, nor nonviolence with gradualism and reform, nor vice versa. Either or both forms of struggle may be used with a wide range of intention, from the revolutionary overthrow of a whole system to relatively minor alterations within a social system.

33. Those who are prepared to use violence against the established order need to ask themselves such questions as:

—Have you really explored the potentialities of nonviolence for your situation, or are you simply assuming in advance that it won't work?

—Is your choice of strategies alienating public opinion more than it is enlisting support?

—How are the means you use being kept from themselves becoming an instrument of dehumanization and thus engulfing the ends you seek?

Are you contemplating too lightly the taking of life of another human being?

—Have you considered how to integrate former oppressors (and their families and friends, who may themselves have been victims of violence) into the liberated society you are fighting for?

34. Advocates of nonviolence as a matter of principle need to ask themselves such questions as:

—Are you taking with sufficient seriousness the tenacity and depth of violence in the structures of society, and the social disruption its diminution is likely to require?

—May nonviolent action emasculate effective resistance at crucial points in a struggle?

—In adhering to this as an absolute principle are you not in danger of giving the means (nonviolence, i.e., reduced revolutionary violence) priority over the end sought (justice, i.e., reduced structural violence)?

—Are you more concerned with your own "good" conscience than with the good of the oppressed?

35. Those who, by whatever means, work for the destruction of an existing power structure in order to build a better one need to face such questions as:

—Toward what expected results is your struggle directed, and how does the cost to be paid balance against the benefit expected?

—How is your power kept accountable in terms of this avowed purpose so that your victory will not mean the emergence of yet another oppressive system?

—How will those against whom the struggle is directed be integrated into the new society?

36. Those who basically are concerned with preserving the institutions of an existing society when its power structures are challenged, and commit themselves to its defence, need to face such questions as:

—Are you acting in the light of the Biblical concern for the poor and oppressed, or for the preservation of your own self- or group-interest?

—How far does your own violence differ from that of revolutionary groups?

37. Those Christians who live in countries where established institutions are open to pressure to effect change in the structures of government, industry and society in the interests of social justice, need to face such questions as:

—Do you take the tenacity and depth of structural violence seriously enough?

—Are there groups in your society permanently excluded from voice and influence? How far are the rich and powerful in fact favoured?

— How far is a fundamental dislocation of the "powers that be" needed if justice is to be achieved?

38. The most important question, however, is not raised by any one of these groups to any other, but by all of them together to the whole Church. Certainly the fact that some Christians are acting violently for justice and peace whilst others are acting nonviolently is a problem. But the greatest problem is that most of those who name Christ as Lord are not consciously acting on the matter at all. It is vital, therefore, that the widespread concern about violence and nonviolence should not obscure but rather highlight the larger challenge to which the ecumenical movement in recent years has given increasingly clear expression. This is the challenge to all Christians to become wiser and more courageous in translating their commitment to Jesus Christ into specific social and political engagement for social justice; and in this sphere to find their place as servants of the servant Lord with people of other beliefs concerned with human freedom and fulfilment.

26. The Fifth Assembly of the World Council of Churches (Nairobi, Kenya, November 23-December 10, 1975)

Very little happened in the area of nonviolence study or action within ecumenical circles between 1973 and 1975. Repeated attempts by a coalition of peace church groups and the IFOR, including offers of budgetary support met with limited or no response. The reasons for the reluctance on the part of Geneva staff to push ahead in this area were summarized on a background paper distributed to delegates to the fifth assembly in the fall of 1975. They included:

(1) The increasing shortage of funds add pressure to reduce staff and program rather than expand program;
(2) Suspicion expressed by liberationists who tend to regard the "Violence/Nonviolence" effort as a new form of Western imperialism designed to keep oppressed peoples in their place;
(3) Many in WCC regard much of the work already being done as fundamentally nonviolent in character and believe that significant "intervention ministries" are already being carried on in various countries of the world;
(4) The question whether the staff has a mandate to engage in new program between Assembly meetings, or whether such a mandate would have to come from the Fifth Assembly at Nairobi in 1975.

Therefore peace interests looked very hopefully for action at the recent world assembly. Many—one count placed them over thirty—references were made to the broad scope of peace, war, and disarmament issues at the assembly. It was agreed at the meeting that priorities would need to be established to allow the limited staff and constrained budget to select those which seemed most urgent. A specific resolution on the disarmament issue mentioned the experience of the Historic Peace Churches. The WCC staff prepared recommendations to the summer 1976 meeting of the Central

Committee in Geneva to establish which of the many Nairobi initiatives would in fact be picked up by staff for action.

Peace representatives maintained an informal meeting place at Nairobi and attempted to coordinate their efforts in a modest, non-lobbying way. The result was not entirely successful, as noted in a statement issued by John Howard Yoder and Richard Deats, of the IFOR.

An Appeal to the Churches

. . .

2. Christians must resist the temptation to resign themselves to a false sense of impotence or security. The churches should emphasize their readiness to live without the protection of armaments, and take a significant initiative in pressing for effective disarmament. Churches, individual Christians, and members of the public in all countries should press their governments to ensure national security without resorting to the use of weapons of mass destruction.

3. We call upon the new Central Committee to initiate steps to organize a consultation on disarmament. This consultation should investigate and compare available material on the factors producing the present arms race and the technological, economic, environmental, and military implications. The consultation should aim at proposing a strategy, at national and international levels, to prevent further increased military expenditure. This strategy should include, among others, the following points:

(a) Prepare educational programmes for the use of the churches.

(b) Stimulate public discussion on the matter.

(c) Review the theological teachings on the questions of war and peace.

(d) Share the experience of the Historic Peace Churches.

(e) Investigate the involvement of the churches in arms production and trade.

(f) Call for a World Disarmament Conference under UN auspices.

(g) Stress the need for retraining and re-employment of those who now make their living through the arms production industry.

The Central Committee should ensure that disarmament is a major concern of the World Council of Churches.

4. We appeal to all Christians to think, work, and pray for a disarmed world.

Pacifist Minority Still to Be Heard

(Drafted by J. Yoder and R. Deats
for the IFOR/HHC Liaison Group)

Christian pacifists, who hold all war to be morally wrong, are present within many church fellowships, in addition to the small "historic peace churches" (with seven delegates at Nairobi) for whom this conviction is a common witness.

Pacifists at Nairobi have ground for gratitude that at some points the Assembly showed awareness of their concerns. Yet this awareness could not be complete or satisfying. The mood of the Assembly was often one of caution and consolidation, rather than the kind of creativity and prophetic witness which both the biblical faith and the urgent need of our times would demand.

The Assembly spoke, as the WNC has done before, against the arms race and the arms trade, and for a modest degree of disarmament, but gave no ear to the challenging of armed national defense as such.

Assembly discussions and documents recognized—frequently—the destructiveness, inefficiency, and uncontrollability of violence, and the promise of nonviolent techniques and life-styles for bringing about desired change; yet neither the radical implications of this recognition nor the moral and theological grounds for rejecting violence were discussed in their own right.

The Assembly, representing the Universal Church, in some ways attained a genuine supra-national or transnational objectivity implicit in the Gospel. Yet there was no readiness fundamentally to challenge the moral priority of the nation-state as such. Hence national loyalties were often primary in determining positions taken on human rights or armaments or prevailing economic systems.

Assembly speeches testified to Jesus Christ as the One who frees and unites, yet in the conversation about our good deeds and moral postures, the precise content of Jesus' teaching and work were seldom assumed to be relevant.

Some pacifists at Nairobi met almost daily to keep in touch with Assembly events. They discussed such proposals as a "peace desk" in Geneva, a Program to Combat Militarism, and a Program to Promote a Nonviolent Life-style. Their agenda included such issues as the arms race and repression in many countries and how the WCC might speak to them. The International Fellowship of Reconciliation kept an information table in the Conference Centre and ran a coffee house two blocks away.

The pacifist presence and minority witness within the ecumenical council will continue, but in view of the kind of majority stance to which the WCC must be committed, they will continue to need other instruments as well to express their own, more radical convictions.

Epilogue: The Way Ahead

John H. Yoder

There is something of the treadmill in ecumenical conversation. No ecumenical meeting, nor even a firmly structured organization like the World Council of Churches has the kind of ongoing identity with which it will be possible to make substantial "progress" in a conversation. No conclusion reached in one meeting binds the participants in the next.

It would thus be unfair to the interlocutors with whom the Historic Peace Churches sought to speak, if we were to make much of the fact that in the conversations here reported "they" did not progress in their openness to or understanding of the witness of the HPC position. Many participants in these conversations had had no deep or personal acquaintance with the HPC heritage and witness before arriving at one of these meetings. If some progress in understanding was made, the next representative sent by that same mainstream church at the next conversation would again be starting at the same point. This difficulty of conversing with an ongoing "main" stream is intrinsic to the situation of the advocate of any minority position. It is, if anything, even more difficult for the minority position on war than with regard to some other points of difference (such as the Brethren conviction on adult baptism or the Quaker position on sacraments) because the subject matter of the debate correlates at the same time with the national dividedness of the churches and with non-theological antagonisms between nations and continents.

Thus the analysis of the above collection will indicate that if anything the discussants are farther from having a common vocabulary and common understandings at the end of the quarter century than they were at the beginning. This is not the result of ill will but of the expanding of the conversation. In terms of persons and perspectives, the conversation began in the North Atlantic Protestant realm, where the liberal pacifism of the period between the two world wars had obliged most thinkers to come to terms somehow with the pacifist witness. They had rejected it, and their rejection had been addressed to a kind of non-ecclesiastically-rooted pacifism somewhat different from that of the Historic Peace Churches, but nonetheless the documents of Oxford and Amsterdam and the conversations of

Puidoux occurred in a cultural arena where the memory of the case for pacifism was present.

Beginning with Bossey 1965 this was no longer the case. The explosion of the conversation to include representatives from the rest of the world's churches and to discuss the rest of the world's problems clearly left that common vocabulary behind. Thus in a world in which the destructive potential of actual warfare is greater than before, in which Vietnam, Lebanon, and southern Africa have shown us that the nuclear umbrella does not diminish the frequency nor the horror of local wars, and in which new dimensions of the ecological destructiveness of the arms race even in "peacetime" are becoming visible, Christians in the ecumenical arena are farther than they were in 1937 from being able to discuss with one another, as a theological issue on which they differ, the morality of war itself. It was dealt with head-on at Oxford, Amsterdam, and Evanston; less at Delhi, not at Uppsala and Nairobi.

This is not necessarily a step backward; it may rather represent the recognition that the statements of Oxford and Amsterdam were far ahead of where other churches really were. The numerical weakness of the Historic Peace Churches, their very spotty dispersion around the globe, their lack of practice in and commitment to ecumenical witness, and the appearance of cheap facility when critical moral convictions are communicated without being deeply present amidst the sufferings of those who feel violence is their only option, certainly have contributed to the difficulties of gaining a hearing.

There is another setback which may also be progress in disguise. The interdenominational conversations within the World Council of Churches were dominated for the first generation by a "comparative" etiquette, according to which every denomination's distinctive identity was worthy of a hearing. One needed to understand the variety of possible views before moving on to debate their possible correctness. This put a premium on those particular differences which were incarnated in denominational identity. Other questions which divided churches down the middle, such as the heritage of the liberal-fundamentalist controversy or the newer intellectual controversies (demythologizing, "Death of God") were less manageable in the World Council framework because there was no obvious way of being fair to the constituencies of each position. In that context, the Historic Peace Churches, although numerically tiny, at least had formal status which entitled them to ask for a hearing. The charismatic presence of M. R. Zigler at Geneva incarnated this demand insistently. The sizeable number of pacifists who were members of the other churches (and of the Geneva staff) had no voice in this framework.

Since the sixties, we have observed the waning of the priority of denomination-based agenda. The results of a period of mutual denominational getting-acquainted have indicated which of those hereditary issues are superficial and which are intractable. The movement has been to non-confessionally-defined issues such as racism and development, concerning which no one has any inherited answers. This setback, I suggest, may be progress since it also sets aside the assumption, superficially polite but ecumenically impolite, that concern for the morality of war is the peculiar vocation of tiny minority churches. It may give access to the conversation to the many other Christian pacifists who have come to their minority convictions on these matters through personal pilgrimage and without assistance of denominational position.

One of the unreckoned chapters in the story of the World Council of Churches is the rootage of its own history in a peace movement. It is frequently reported that the life and work movement was indirectly related to a conference held in 1914 in the interest of international understanding through the churches. It is less often reported that that meeting was also the context for the creation for the Fellowship of Reconciliation, and that through the 1920s the continuity of both concerns was carried by some of the same people. Friedrich Siegmund-Schulze, for example, was the German representative of both movements inseparably. It was only when the WCC grew from a network of renewal movements to a federation of church administrators that the anti-militarists' thrust which had marked the period between the wars had to be weakened.

Yet there remain forces in the very working of an international agency which foster cosmopolitan and anti-violence biases on the part of staff and consultants. If the Peace *Churches* need to carry less of the load in the dialog, these other voices may be stronger.

The paragraphs above have surveyed the story in terms of the identiy and style of the mainstream churches and their expression through the World Council and affiliated agencies. This is not to suggest that for the Historic Peace Churches themselves there have not been important learnings and occasions for repentance. It needs to be confessed that the number of persons and agencies within the HPC constituencies concerned to confront their non-pacifist brothers and sisters in serious conversation has always been very limited. It can hardly be claimed that in the last quarter century these churches have grown in their depth of commitment or in the articulateness with which the peace concern has been shared in deed or in word. We yet hope that the perusal of the history recorded in the preceding pages might inspire a new generation to renewed theological seriousness, that will recognize a churchly responsibility to renew the dialogue on a level commensurate with the threat to the planet and to the Gospel which is represented by Christian complacency about arms. Yet this is a hope which finds little basis in the story Dr. Durnbaugh has told. The hope is founded only in the message itself.

Notes: Introduction

1. David Paton, *Breaking Barriers: The Report of the Fifth Assembly of World Council of Churches, Nairobi, 1975* (Grand Rapids, Mich.: Eerdmans, 1976), 182.

2. For a description and analysis of the first ten years of the conferences, see Donald F. Durnbaugh, "The Puidoux Conferences," *Brethren Life and Thought,* 13 (Winter 1968), 30-40. See also Paul Peachey, "The Peace Churches as Ecumenical Witnesses" in *Kingdom, Christ and Community,* J. R. Burkholder and C. Redekop, eds. (Scottdale, Pa.: Herald Press, 1976), 249-58.

3. F. Burton Nelson, "The Ecumenical Movement and the Problem of World Peace," unpubl. Ph.D. dissertation, Northwestern University, 1965, pp. 43-45.

4. Nelson, "Ecumenical Movement," pp. 65-101.

5. J. H. Oldham, ed., *The Oxford Conference (Official Report)* (Chicago: Willett, Clark & Co., 1937), pp. 47, 162-67.

6. W. A. Visser 't Hooft, ed., *The First Assembly of the World Council of Churches,* (New York: Harper and Brothers, 1949), pp. 88-90; Edward Duff, S. J., *The Social Thought of the World Council of Churches* (New York: Association Press, 1956), p. 258.

7. *War Is Contrary to the Will of God* (Amsterdam: J. H. de Bussy, 1951), pp. 3, 4. For a perceptive analysis of the types of pacifism, see John H. Yoder, *Nevertheless* (Scottdale, Pa.: Herald Press, 1971).

8. *Peace Is the Will of God* (Amsterdam: J. H. de Bussy, 1953), also published as *Gottes Wille ist Frieden* and *Dieu veut la Paix;* Nelson, "Ecumenical Movement," p. 363.

9. "Christians Stand for Peace," *Christian Century,* 68 (August 22, 1951), 957-59; Ruth Rouse and Stephen C. Neill, eds., *A History of the Ecumenical Movement, 1517—1948* (London: SPCK, 1954), pp. 568, 716.

10. "Christian Witness to a Shaken World," *Christian Century,* 71 (September 22, 1954), 1131; Duff, *Social Thought,* p. 265.

11. N. H. Söe, "War and the Commandment of Love," *Ecumenical Review,* 6 (April 1954), 254-61; Angus Dun and Reinhold Niebuhr, "God Wills Both Justice and Love," *Christianity and Crisis,* 15 (June 13, 1955), 10: 75-78. The booklet, *The Christian and War* (Amsterdam: J. H. de Bussy, 1958) reprinted the "Peace Is the Will of God" statement and the Dun-Niebuhr critique, as well as a response "God Establishes Both Peace and Justice" (republished in 1970).

12. See Durnbaugh, "Puidoux Conferences," and Clarence Bauman, "An Introduction to Theological Discussion on Christian Participation in War and Related Concerns," mimeographed (1960); Paul Bock, "Peace Research in Old Heidelberg," *Manchester College Bulletin of the Peace Studies Institute,* 3 (October 1973), 2:14-16.

13. Fritzhermann Keienburg, "Begegnung mit den 'Schwärmern,'" *Junge Kirche,* 16 (October 1955), 431-34; Hans-Werner Bartsch, "Wieder: Begegnung mit den Schwärmern," *Junge Kirche,* 18 (October 1957), 566-70.

14. *The Christian Witness to the State* (Newton, Kans.: Faith and Life Press, 1964); *The Original Revolution: Essays on Christian Pacifism* (Scottdale, Pa.: Herald Press, 1971); *The Politics of Jesus* (Grand Rapids, Mich.: Eerdmans, 1972).

15. *The Lordship of Christ Over the World and the Church* (Geneva: World Council of Churches, 1956); *The Lordship of Christ Over the World and the Church: Study Document* (Geneva: World Council of Churches, 1957); Hans Heinrich Harms, ed., *The Lordship of Christ Over the World and the Church: Study Document* (Geneva: World Council of Churches, [1959]).

16. *Christians and the Prevention of War in an Atomic Age: A Theological Discussion* (Geneva: World Council of Churches, 1958).

17. Nelson, "Ecumenical Movement," pp. 347-56.

18. Nelson, "Ecumenical Movement," pp. 144, 276-78.

19. See the discussion of reasons for holding back in *New Delhi to Uppsala, 1961-1968* (Geneva: World Council of Churches, 1968), pp. 50-51.

20. *World Conference on Church and Society: Official Report* (Geneva: World Council of Churches, 1967), *passim.*

21. Wilmer A. Cooper, *Background Paper on World Council Program on "Violence, Nonviolence, and the Struggle for Social Justice"* (Elgin, Ill.: Church of the Brethren General Board, 1975).

22. Cooper, *Background Paper.*

23. Cooper, *Background Paper.*

24. See the special issue of the *Ecumenical Review,* 25 (October 1973), 4.

25. Peter Scherhans, "A Survey of Reactions to the World Council of Churches Statement on Violence, Nonviolence, and the Struggle for Social Justice," mimeographed, 1975.

26. Cooper, *Background Paper.*

27. Henry Okullu, "Where Was the Confrontation?" *One World,* No.13 (January-February 1976), 20.

28. Oldham, *Oxford Conference,* p. 165.

Notes: Documents

1. Principles of Christian Peace and Patriotism. Source: Archives of the Mennonite Central Committee, Akron, Pennsylvania. For a description of the conference, see Robert Kreider, "The Historic Peace Churches Meeting in 1935," *Mennonite Life,* 31 (June 1976), 2: 21-24. See also Orie O. Miller, "The Historic Peace Church Fellowship," in D. F. Durnbaugh, ed., *To Serve the Present Age: The Brethren Service Story* (Elgin, Ill.: Brethren Press, 1975), pp. 103-106.

2. World Conference on Church, Community and State. Source: Oldham, *Oxford Conference,* pp. 162-67. The quotations from the message are found on pages 45, 47. See also Nelson, "Ecumenical Movement," pp. 117-21; Duff, *Social Thought,* pp. 34-37; and Rouse and Neill, *History,* pp. 587-92.

3. The First Assembly of the World Council of Churches. Source: Visser 't Hooft, *First Assembly,* pp. 88-95. See also, *Man's Disorder and God's Design: The Amsterdam Assembly Series* (New York: Harper & Brothers, [1949]); Nelson, "Ecumenical Movement," pp. 220-43; Duff, *Social Thought, passim.*

4. War Is Contrary to the Will of God. Source: *War Is Contrary to the Will of God* (Amsterdam: J. H. de Bussy, 1951). The Quaker statement with the same title was published by the Friends Peace Committee (Oxford: Church Army Press, [n.d.]).

5. Peace Is the Will of God. Source: *Peace Is the Will of God* (Amsterdam: J. H. de Bussy, 1953).

6. The Second Assembly of the World Council of Churches. Source: W. A. Visser 't Hooft, ed., *The Evanston Report* (New York: Harper & Brothers, 1955), pp. 130-37, 141-43. The first quotation is from Nelson, "Ecumenical Movement," pp. 132-33. The second quotation is from Duff, *Social Thought,* p. 259. See also the special issue of the *Christian Century,* 71 (September 22, 1954).

7. God Wills Both Justice and Peace. Source: Angus Dun and Reinhold Niebuhr, "God Wills Both Justice and Peace," *Christianity and Crisis,* 15 (June 13, 1955), 10:75-78. N. H. Söe, "War and the Commandment of Love," *Ecumenical Review,* 6 (April 1954), 254-61. The discussion is reported in Nelson, "Ecumenical Movement," pp. 361-63. (There is some

evidence that Richard Fagley prepared the basic draft of the Dun-Niebuhr article.)

8. God Establishes Both Peace and Justice. Source: "God Establishes Both Peace and Justice," in *The Christian and War: A Theological Discussion of Justice, Peace and Love* (Amsterdam: J. H. De Bussy, 1958), pp. 33-47.

9. The Lordship of Christ Over Church and State. Source: Albert J. Meyer, ed., *The Lordship of Christ Over Church and State: Puidoux Theological Conference. Report of the First Puidoux Conference Held 15-19 August 1955, Cret-Berard, Puidoux, Switzerland* [n.p.: 1955]. There was a report in the American religious press: Alvin Pitcher, "Seek Theological Base of Pacifism," *Christian Century,* 72 (September 14, 1955), 1069-70.

10. The Lordship of Christ Over Church and State II. Source: Clarence Bauman, ed., *The Puidoux Series of Theological Conferences on the Lordship of Christ Over Church and State. Bericht der zweiten Konferenz, Iserlohn, 28. Juli—1. August, 1957* ([Basel]: Puidoux Secretariat, 1960). The addresses included here have been translated by Donald F. and Hedda Durnbaugh. Reports of the conference include: Glenn H. Bowlby, "Peace Conversations in Europe," *Gospel Messenger* (November 23, 1957); H.-W. Bartsch, "Wieder: Begegnung mit den Schwärmern," *Junge Kirche,* 18 (October 1957), 566-70; Richard K. Ullmann, "Reconciling Christians—Iserlohn Conference," *Christus Victor* (December 1957), 99: 9-12; Albert J. Meyer, "New Approaches in Theology," *Christus Victor* (June 1958), 101: 17-23; "Square Look at a Round Table," *Christian Century,* 75 (January 22, 1958), 93.

11. Christians and the Prevention of War in an Atomic Age. Source: *A Provisional Study Document on "Christians and the Prevention of War in an Atomic Age—A Theological Discussion"* (Geneva: World Council of Churches—Division of Studies, 1958). The comment is found in the report of the Central Committee to the Third Assembly: *Evanston to New Delhi, 1954-1961* (Geneva: World Council of Churches, 1961), p. 35. The document was published in revised form later: Sir Thomas Taylor and Robert S. Bilheimer, eds., *Christians and the Prevention of War in an Atomic Age* (London: SCM Press, 1961). See the discussion in Nelson, "Ecumenical Movement," pp. 347-56.

12. The Lordship of Christ Over Church and State III. Source: John H. Yoder, "Von göttlicher und menschlicher Gerechtigkeit," *Zeitschrift für evangelische Ethik,* 6 (May 1962), 166-81; Warren F. Groff, "The Sixth Commandment: Its Significance for the Christian as Citizen and for the Statesman," *Brethren Life and Thought,* 6 (1961), 1:33-44. The Yoder article was translated by Donald F. and Hedda Durnbaugh. The quotation by Douglas Steere is found in "Basis of Pacifist Witness Studied," *Quaker Life,* (October 1960), 42-43; this was reprinted in *Gospel Messenger* (November 26, 1960), 23-24. See also A. J. Muste, "Puidoux Conference

III," *Christian Century,* 77 (September 28, 1960), 1131-32; Dale Aukerman and W. Harold Row, "Talks Resumed After 360 Years: The Puidoux Theological Peace Conferences," *Brethren Life and Thought,* 6 (1961), 1:29-32.

   13. The Third Assembly of the World Council of Churches. Source: W. A. Visser 't Hooft, ed., *The New Delhi Report* (New York: Association Press, 1962), pp. 107-109, 280-81. The quotation from the Assembly Message is found on page 321. The appraisal is by F. Burton Nelson, "Ecumenical Movement," pp. 144-46. A discussion on the language of the statement on nuclear weapons is found in Nelson, "Ecumenical Movement," pp. 275-78.

   14. The Lordship of Christ Over Church and State IV. Source: "Theology and Christian Social Ethics: Papers From the Puidoux Conference on the Sources of Christian Social Ethics," *Background Information for Church and Society,* No. 32 (February 1964), published by the Department on Church and Society, Division of Studies, World Council of Churches. The conference itself is described in Dale Aukerman, ed., *The Sources of Christian Social Ethics: A Report on the Puidoux IV Conference, 9-14 July 1962, Oud Poelgeest, Holland* [Basel]: Puidoux Secretariat, 1963). Descriptions of the conference are: David J. Wieand, "Was Sagt Uns Puidoux?" *Gospel Messenger* (November 10, 1962), 6-8; Hans-Werner Bartsch, "Die Quellen der christlichen Sozialethik," *Junge Kirche,* 23 (1962), 521-24. The Lasserre theses were published in *Gospel Messenger* (April 13, 1963), 22-23.

   15. The Authority of Government and the Lordship of Christ. Source: "The Authority of Government and the Lordship of Christ: A Theological Statement Concerning the Relation of Church to State by the Faculty of Bethany Theological Seminary, 1962," unpublished mimeographed statement.

   16. God's Reconciling Work Among the Nations Today. Source: *Minutes of the Conference on God's Reconciling Work Among the Nations Today, 28th June—3rd July, 1965* (Bossey: Ecumenical Institute, 1965), mimeographed. The Kloppenburg statement was translated by Donald F. and Hedda Durnbaugh.

   17. World Conference on Church and Society. Source: "Report on Section III: Structures of International Cooperation. Living Together in Peace in a Pluralistic World Society," in *World Conference on Church and Society: Christians in the Technical and Social Revolutions of Our Time, Geneva, July 12-26, 1966* (Geneva: World Council of Churches, 1967), pp. 122-24, 128-30, 135, 143-47, 151-52. The quotation is from pages 115-16. The questions for future study are found on page 119. A searching critique of the conference and its findings was Paul Ramsey, *Who Speaks for the Church?* (Nashville: Abingdon Press, 1967).

   18. The Quaker Peace Testimony. Source: *Notes on the Quaker Peace*

Testimony. The Friends Peace Testimony—A Challenge of Our Time (Birmingham, England: Friends World Committee for Consultation, 1968), pp. 7-12.

19. Consultation on the Christian Witness to Peace. Source: *Study Encounter,* 4 (1968), 158-62; it was reprinted in *The Christian and War* (Amsterdam: De Bussy Ellerman Harms N. V., 1970), pp. 45-50.

20. The Fourth Assembly of the World Council of Churches. Source: Norman Goodall, ed., *The Uppsala Report 1968: Official Report of the Fourth Assembly of the World Council of Churches, Uppsala July 4-20, 1968* (Geneva: World Council of Churches, 1968), pp. 60-63, 65, 70-71, 270. The Oestreicher quotation is found on pages 71-72.

21. Puidoux 1955-1969. Source: "Puidoux 1955-1969: Bericht über ein Gespräch über die theologischen Grundlagen des christlichen Friedenszeugnisses," mimeographed. Translated by Donald F. and Hedda Durnbaugh. The FEST institute has sponsored a series of publications on peace research, *Studien zur Friedensforschung,* beginning in 1969. A comprehensive bibliography contains entries on the Historic Peace Churches: Gerta Scharffenorth and Wolfgang Huber, eds., *Neue Bibliographie zur Friedensforschung* (Stuttgart: Ernst Klett; Munich: Kösol, 1973), Studien zur Friedensforschung, Vol. 12.

22. Report of the Consultation on Violence, Nonviolence, and the Struggle for Social Justice. Source: "Report of the Consultation on 'Violence, Nonviolence, and the Struggle for Social Justice,' Cardiff (Wales), 3-7 September 1972," mimeographed, Church and Society, World Council of Churches, 20 November 1972. Editorial notes and an appendix are omitted.

23. Response to the Cardiff Report by Brethren, Friends, Mennonites. Source: "Response to Cardiff Report by Brethren, Friends, Mennonites," mimeographed.

24. Jesus and Power. Source: John H. Yoder, "Jesus and Power," *Ecumenical Review,* 25 (October 1973), 447-54.

25. Violence, Nonviolence, and the Struggle for Social Justice. Source: "Violence, Nonviolence, and the Struggle for Social Justice," *Ecumenical Review,* 25 (October 1973), 434-46. The Central Committee action is found on pages 430-34.

26. The Fifth Assembly of the World Council of Churches. Source: David Paton, *Breaking Barriers: The Report of the Fifth Assembly of World Council of Churches, Nairobi, 1975* (Grand Rapids, Mich.: Eerdmans, 1976), 182. The Yoder Deats statement was distributed in mimeographed form. The quotation is from Wilmer A. Cooper, *Background Paper on World Council Program on "Violence, Nonviolence, and the Struggle for Social Justice"* (Elgin, Ill.: Church of the Brethren General Board, 1975).

Index of Persons, Places, and Topics

(Note: Although this index is quite long, it is not exhaustive. Some topics—such as war, peace, New Testament, Old Testament—appear so frequently in the text that it was impossible to list every reference. In these cases, listings in the index are only suggestive. Names of biblical personalities are not included.)

Abrecht, Paul, 21
Addis Ababa (Ethiopia), 26, 329
Africa, 25, 28. *See also* South Africa.
AFSC. *See* American Friends Service Committee.
Agape, 75, 76, 109, 114-15, 121, 134, 139, 142, 217, 331. *See also* Love.
Alt, Albrecht, 214
Alternative to war, 62-63. *See also* Nonviolence, Non-violent action.
Althaus, Paul, 147, 148
American Friends Service Committee, 16, 46, 181
Amsterdam Assembly, 19, 38-45, 46-72, 73-90, 102-03, 105, 106, 118, 224, 231, 281, 294, 315-16, 375, 390-91
Anabaptists, 14, 139, 140, 152, 153ff., 156, 157, 158-59, 320, 327
Anglicanism. *See* Church of England.
Anglo-Saxon thought, 233, 284
Anhalt, Church of, 146
Antinomianism, 79-80, 159
Appeal to All Governments and Peoples, An (New Delhi), 226-28
Appeal to the Churches, An (Nairobi), 17, 387
Aquinas, Thomas, 78, 341. *See also* Thomism.
Arab Christians, 378

Arabs, 177-78, 330, 335
Arms race. *See* Disarmament.
Askov (Denmark), 21
Athanasius, 165
Atomic age, 186-95
Atomic warfare. *See* Nuclear warfare.
Augsburg Confession, 201
Augustine, 77, 126, 165, 284
Authority of Scriptures. *See* Scriptures.

Background Information for Church and Society (WCC), 229
Baillie, D. M., 219
Baker, J. Allen, 18
Baptists, 240, 280, 321
Barth, Karl, 18, 132, 170, 207, 214, 219, 237-39, 244, 256, 258, 260, 261, 320
Bartlett, Percy, 13
Bartsch, Hans-Werner, 22, 164-72, 263-69, 277, 278-79, 320
Basic Outline of Ethics (Althaus), 147
Beatitudes, 124, 263ff. *See also* Sermon on the Mount.
Beckmann, Joachim, 196, 320
Bekenntnis-Schriften der Evangelischen Kirche, 165
Berlin-Brandenburg, Church of, 146
Bethany Theological Seminary, faculty of, 272-76
Bible. *See* Scriptures.
Bièvres, (France), 21, 196, 321
Bilheimer, Robert, 21
Bodelschwingh, Friederich von, 233
Bonhoeffer, Dietrich, 53, 124, 147, 237-38, 246, 256, 320
Borovoy, Vitali, 277
Bossey (Switzerland), 24, 241, 277, 306, 391
Brethren. *See* Church of the Brethren.

Brethren Service Commission, 13, 16, 46, 63-65
Brotherhoods, in Germany, 201
Brunner, Emil, 237-38
Bultmann, Rudolf, 236, 253-56, 257
Burckhardt, E. G., 252
Butterfield, Herbert, 143, 211

Caird, G. B., 220-22
Calculation, 76, 80-82, 83, 102, 110-11. *See also* Casuistry.
Calvin, John, 132, 134, 138, 149-50. *See also* Calvinism.
Calvinism, 119, 136, 138, 139, 147, 233
Camar, Dom Helder, 371
Canon, 155, 243
Canterbury (Great Britain), 25, 329
Cardiff (Wales), 26-27, 329-52, 353-64, 365-72
Casuistry, 112, 200
Catholic Encyclopedia, 155
Catholicism. *See* Roman Catholicism.
CCIA. *See* Commission of the Churches on International Affairs.
Central Europe, 14
Central Committee (WCC), 27, 318, 329, 358, 373-85, 386-87. *See also* World Council of Churches.
Chaplaincy, 161, 167, 170, 349
Charles II, 62, 301
Chavez, Cesar, 344
Chicago, Illinois (USA), 13, 272
China, 181
Christendom, 136, 249, 288. *See also* Corpus *christianum.*
Christengemeinde und Bürgergemeinde (Barth), 170
Christian and War, The (HPC), 108, 307
Christian Century, 15, 20
Christian Conscience and War, The, 100
Christian Democratic Union, 200
Christian ethics. *See* Ethics.
Christian freedom, 148-49
Christian liberty, 125, 280
Christian pacifism, 19, 70-71, 202ff., 320-28. *See also* Non-resistance, Nonviolence, Pacifism.
Christian Peace Conferences, 21, 291

Christian peace witness, 319-28
Christian Social Union, 233
Christianity and Crisis, 21, 100
Christians and the Prevention of War in an Atomic Age (WCC), 23, 185-95
Christology, 47, 50, 260, 324ff.
Church: Anabaptist view of, 158-59; as body of Christ, 114; as community of obedience, 159; ethic of, 119-20; grace in, 274-75; Historic Peace Church view of, 84; ignored in Dun-Niebuhr report, 109; image of, 154-55; mandate of, 289; political responsibility of, 255; Reformers view of, 158; spiritual basis of society of, 156; tasks of, 288-91; wealth of, 350; witness of in face of violence, 336-38; Zwingli's view of, 156.
Church and society, 331-32. *See also* Society.
Church and Society, Conference on. *See* Conference on Church and Society.
Church and state, 40-45, 58-59, 68-69, 104, 111-15, 120, 122-45, 146-84, 191-92, 196-222, 229-71, 275-76, 277-91, 294-99, 320-28, 338, 356ff; Brethren view of, 64-65; Calvin's view of, 132; Free Church view of, 279-88; Historic Peace Church view of, 85-88; Oxford Conference on, 34-47; Protestant view of, 131; Roman Catholic view of, 130; Yoder's view of, 136-43; in Zürich, 156-57.
Church and world, 123-27
Church of England, 38, 313
Church division, 159
Church of the Brethren, 17, 38, 183, 280, 320, 327, 390; Annual Conference of, 272; in Europe, 13, 16; at Newton meeting, 30; response to Cardiff report, 353-64; statement of on peace, 63-65, 73-90, 272-76; and WCC, 19.
Church Peace Mission, 100
Citizenship, 31, 36, 43, 44, 64, 70, 87-88, 104, 115ff., 120-21, 124, 191, 209-10, 211-22, 250, 285. *See also* Patriotism.
City of God (Augustine), 126
Civil responsibility. *See* Responsibility.

Civilian Public Service camps, 30
Co-existence, 96, 315
Cold War, 57, 91-92, 181, 262. *See also* East-West struggle.
Colloquy between Anabaptists and theologians, 157
Commission of the Churches on International Affairs, 20, 45, 95, 185, 291, 299, 351
Communism, 42, 111, 188, 207, 321
Community of world, 295, 97, 305, 330-32, 354
Compendium of Theological Ethics (Luthardt), 147
Compulsory military service, 168. *See also* Military service.
Conference on Christian Politics, Economics, and Citizenship, 233
Conference on Church and Society (WCC), 24, 26, 292-99, 313, 375
Conference on Church and War, 100
Conference on Church, Community, and State. *See* Oxford Conference.
Conferences of Pacifist Churches, 30
Confessing Church, 22, 199
Conscientious objection to war, 17, 22, 30, 40, 129-30, 154, 168, 204, 290, 293, 349. *See also* Non-resistance, Non-violence, Pacifism.
Constantine, 164-65, 183, 210, 280, 281, 284. *See also* Constantinianism
Constantinianism, 203-04, 206, 278, 280, 284, 288, 289, 321, 338
Continuation committee (HPC): in USA, 13, 30; in Europe, 13, 20, 21, 46, 73, 108-21, 122, 142, 320
Coptic churches, 38
Corpus christianum, 77, 156, 203, 327. *See also* Christendom.
Counsels, 54, 78, 325
Covenant, 113-14, 116, 212-14, 241, 252, 273
Cranfield, C. B., 209
Creation, 123, 149, 214, 216, 242-43, 272-73, 308, 314, 363
Creed, 155
Croce, Benedetto, 252
Cross, 35, 48, 58, 81, 83, 294, 337, 356, 362

Crusade, 283
Cullmann, Oscar, 133, 140, 220-21, 241

Danek, Slavomil, 253
Death of God, 391
Deats, Richard, 387, 388-89
Decalogue, 132, 134, 135, 142, 162, 175, 213-14, 215, 218
Defense, 294
Democracy, 141, 167-68, 285, 355
Demythologizing, 236, 391
Department of Church and Society (WCC), 25, 26, 329, 348
Destructiveness of war, 188ff.
Deterrence, 60, 193
Detroit, Michigan (USA), 100
Development, 297-99, 313
Dibelius, Martin, 161, 164
Dibelius, Otto, 170, 207
Dignity of man, 163
Dilthey, Wilhelm, 252
Diplomats, 182
Disarmament, 17, 28, 41, 43, 92, 94, 97, 104, 200, 223ff., 224-25, 227, 296, 304, 316, 386, 387, 388
Disciples, 162, 252, 258, 280
Discipleship, 47-48, 49-56, 63, 65, 70-71, 84, 124-25, 146-60, 184, 205ff., 300-02, 320-21
Discipline, 192-93
Disobedience to Christ, 273
Dispensation: of providence, 85-86; of redemption, 85-86
Dissenters. *See* Anabaptists.
Division of Church and Society (WCC), 373
Division of Studies (WCC), 186, 223, 229, 306
Dodd, C. H., 240
Dombois, Hans, 233, 239-40
Dualism, 78-79, 118-20, 138, 198, 199ff., 204, 220, 245, 246
Duchrow, Ulrich, 322, 323
Duff, Edward, S. J., 20
Dulles, John Foster, 38
Dumas, André, 240-250
Dun, Angus, 21, 100-07, 108-21
Durnbaugh, Donald F., 17-29, 393
Dutch Anabaptism, 158

Dutch Mennonite Peace Group, 49-56
Duties, 36, 40

Early church, 263-69
East Germany, 179-80. *See also* German Democratic Republic.
East-West dialogue, 21, 182, 196, 277-78, 321, 322
East-West struggle, 41, 42, 92, 178, 188, 334. *See also* Cold War.
Eastern Europe, 182, 196
Ebeling, Gerhard, 236, 239
Ecclesiology, 22, 84, 154-55, 158-59, 230, 240, 244, 311
Ecumenical councils, 280
Ecumenical Institute (Bossey), 24, 277-91
Ecumenical movement, 18, 392. *See also* World Council of Churches, Unity of the Church.
Ecumenical Review, 27, 100
Edinburgh (Scotland), 17, 233
Elgin, Illinois (USA), 65
Ends and means, 54
Enthusiasts, 147, 152, 153, 154, 184, 203, 288
Episcopacy, 155
Erasmus, D., 198
Eschatology, 35, 205, 232, 238, 247, 254-55, 258, 261, 276, 278, 283, 326ff.
Ethics, 76; Calvinistic, 149; christological foundation of, 322; fundamental problems of, 230-40; individual and social, 58, 100-07, 109-21, 133, 230; of intent, 148; and historical events, 251-63, 321-22; international, 97-99; of medieval church, 77; of office, 201; principial, 137-38, 160, 200, 323; Protestant, 147; situational, 57-58, 67-68, 127, 153, 160, 201, 270, 323; as theological task, 307; theological problems of, 147-53; of visibility, 246.
Eusebius of Caesarea, 164
Evangelical academy, 320
Evangelische Studiengemeinschaft, 322
Evanston Assembly, 20, 47, 91-99, 231, 391
Evanston to New Delhi (WCC), 185

Evdokimov, Paul, 277
Evil, 59-61, 88
Exegesis and ethics, 241-44
Existentialism, 160, 234-35, 254
Exodus, 113, 213, 241

Faith and Order movement, 17, 19
Fall: of the church, 285; of man, 272-73.
Fast, Heinold, 319-328
Family, 235
Federal Republic of Germany, 22, 168, 200
Fellowship of Reconciliation, 100, 122. *See also* International Fellowship of Reconciliation.
FEST. *See* Research Institute of the Protestant Study Fellowship.
Fliedner, Theodor, 233
FOR. *See* Fellowship of Reconciliation.
Force, 54-55, 135. *See also* Violence.
Four Freedoms, 110
Fourth World, 26
Fox, George, 137, 160, 300, 302
Free Churches, 14, 279-88, 281-84
Freedom, 231, 280
Freedom of conscience, 43-44
Freud, Sigmund, 138
Friends Peace Committee, 46, 56-63
Friends World Committee for Consultation, 56-63, 300
Friends World Conference, Fourth, 300
Fundamentalism, 159, 242

Gandhi, M. K., 23, 25, 345, 355, 375
General Brotherhood Board, Church of the Brethren, 65
Geneva (Switzerland), 13, 27, 73, 122, 292
Geneva Conventions, 143
German Christians, 33
German Democratic Republic, 22, *See also* East Germany.
German Evangelical Churches, 22, 25, 33, 127
German Federal Republic. *See* Federal Republic of Germany.
Gide, André, 250
Gill, David, 26, 329, 353

God Establishes Both Peace and Justice (HPC), 108-121
God Wills Both Justice and Peace, 100-107
Gogarten, Friedrich, 236
Golden rule, 266
Good and evil, 56-57
Grace: antinomian concept of, 79-80; and church, 274-75; of God, 67-68.
Great Britain, 25
Grisebach, Eberhard, 236
Groff, Warren F., 196, 211-22
Grundtvig, N. F. S., 128
Guilford College, 300

H-bomb, 186ff., 194. *See also* Nuclear weapons.
Hannover, Church of, 146
Harbsmeier, Götz, 128-30, 136, 137, 320
Harnack, Adolf von, 57
Heering, G. J., 57
Hegel, G. W. F., 252
Heidegger, Martin, 236, 253
Heidelberg, 21, 319, 323
Heidelberg Theses, 319, 323
Heilsgeschichte. See Salvation history.
Herbert, Karl, 196
Hermeneutics, 22, 51, 307-08, 369. *See also* Scriptures.
Herodians, 367
Hesse and Nassau, Church of, 146
Historical discontinuity, of Bible, 243
Historical events, and ethics, 251-63, 321-22
Historic Peace Churches, 66, 108, 142, 159, 183, 280, 284, 306, 311, 320, 322, 323, 326, 329, 386-87, 389; at Amsterdam, 38; co-operation of, 16, 46; Continuation Committee, 13, 20, 21, 30, 46, 73, 108-21, 142, 320; ecumenical dialogue of, 29, 46, 73-90, 390-93; divergences of, 19, 30; meet at Newton, 13, 30-32; name given, 13; peace activities of, 13-14; position on ethics and Christology, 324ff., reception of statements by, 20; reply of to Dun and Niebuhr, 100-07; response of to Amsterdam appeal, 19; response of to Cardiff report, 353-64; response of to Nairobi Assembly, 28; shared experiences of, 17; statements by, 30, 46-72, 73-90; survey of ecumenical developments by, 27-28; at Uppsala Assembly, 25; urge implementation of non-violence report, 27.
History: as divine revelation, 257; in God's hand, 190; meaning of, 140, 285-86; meaningfulness of socio-economic type of, 285-86; mistrust of, 253; philosophy of, 253-56; polarity of, 206; theology of, 251-53.
Hitler, Adolf, 188, 207
Höchst (Germany), 21, 322
Hönigg (Switzerland), 156
Holt, Arthur E., 53
Home missions, 233
Howe, Günther, 322, 323
Hromadka, J. L., 38, 259-61, 321
Human liberation, 334-45. *See also* Human rights, Just revolution.
Human responses, to God's action, 273-74
Human rights, 39, 41, 43-44, 95, 98, 233, 317, 334, 380
Humanism, 52
Humanity, 148, 330
Hungarian revolt, 179

IFOR. *See* International Fellowship of Reconciliation.
If Soldiers Can Be in the State of Blessedness (Luther), 126
Imitation of Christ, 148, 151, 184, 320-21, 324ff.
Imperialism, 27, 41-42, 386
Individual ethic, 102-04, 109-21, 133, 230
Indonesia, 59
"Instant pacifism," 26
Institutes (Calvin), 149
Institutiones Iuris Publici Ecclesiastici, 78
Interchange of people, 227, 290
International Atomic Energy Agency, 296
International affairs, 34-37, 87, 92-99, 314-18
International community, 295-97, 305

International co-operation, 294-99
International disorder, 39-45
International Fellowship of Reconciliation, 13, 18, 19, 22, 46, 66-72, 73-90, 100, 108ff., 122, 320, 386, 387, 388, 392
International goodwill, 31
International institutions, 224
International law, 35, 42-43, 69, 98, 105, 192, 224, 295, 296
International Mennonite Peace Committee, 49-56
International Missionary Council, 20, 45, 223
International order, 94, 97-99
Interpretation of scripture. *See* Hermeneutics, Scriptures.
Interwar era, 18
Invasion, 303
Invisible church, 138, 155, 158, 159
Invisible violence. *See* Structural violence.
Irenaeus, 363
Iserlohn (Germany), 21, 146, 184, 320
Israel, 51, 85ff., 113ff., 165, 177-78, 203, 212-17, 243, 245-48, 274

Jan Matthys, 158
Jehovah's Witnesses, 131
Jerusalem, 178
Josephus, 367
Just revolution, 24, 28, 29, 292-93. 338ff., 373ff., 381ff.
Just war, 19, 23, 25, 29, 35-36, 40, 76, 77-78, 104-07, 109-11, 121, 129, 143, 192, 199-200, 259, 283, 286, 306, 341, 349, 373ff.
Justice, 40, 41, 101-07, 146-84, 190, 197-210, 276, 295, 308, 317, 334, 353ff., 363, 380; biblical concept of, 112-15; and love, 192, 320; in New Testament, 113-15; in Old Testament, 112-15; and peace, 101-07, 314-18; in society, 373-85.
Justification, 151, 175, 322-23

Käsemann, Ernst, 240
Karev, Alexander, 321
Kierkegaard, Sören, 148, 211

Kiivit, Jan, 321
King, Martin Luther, Jr., 24-25, 314, 318, 329, 355, 375, 376
Kingdom of God, 18, 50, 52, 53, 128ff., 161, 180, 211, 233, 234, 253, 294, 308
Kirchenkampf, 285
Kittel, Gerhard, 245
Kloppenburg, Heinz, 122, 196, 288-91
Köhler, Walther, 198
Köster, Reinhard, 322
Korea, 59
Korosec, V., 213
Kossen, H. B., 322
Krehbiel, H. P., 30
Kreider, Robert, 13
Küssnacht (Switzerland), 156
Kunneth, Walter, 201

Lamb's War, 15
Landeskirchen, 146, 153, 183-84, 320
Large Catechism (Luther), 165
Lassere, Jean, 22, 130-36, 137, 140, 141, 142, 221, 240, 269-71
Latin America, 342, 377
Law of God, 67, 239
Law and gospel, 79, 245
Law in Israel, 212ff.
Lebanon, 391
Left wing of the Reformation, 240. *See also* Anabaptists.
Legalism, 148, 159-60, 163-64, 310
Legitimacy, 207-09
Lesser evil, 35, 48, 60-61, 80-82
Lex talonis, 114, 116-17, 121
Liberal pacifism, 136, 390
Liberal theology, 18
Liberation movements, 25, 292ff., 334-35
Liberation theology, 292ff., 353-64, 374ff.
Life and Work movement, 17, 18, 233
Life styles of churches, 349
Literalism, 159-60
Lochmann, Jan, 251-63, 277, 321-22
Lögstrup, Knud, 236, 237, 239
Löwith, K., 252
London (Great Britain), 241
Lordship of Christ, 34, 37, 49-56, 63-64, 89, 119, 128, 129, 140, 141, 144-45,

152, 210, 221, 241, 272-76, 320, 321
Lordship of Christ Over Church and State Conferences, 18; Puidoux (I), 122-45; Iserlohn (II), 146-84; Bièvres (III), 196-222; Oud Poelgeest (IV), 229-71
Lordship of Christ Over the World and the Church (WCC) 22-23, 119
Louis XIV, 63
Love, 101-07; compatible with war, 82; distortion by pacifism, 101-02, 111-15; and justice, 173-83, 192, 320; power of, 304. *See also Agape.*
Loyalty, 31, 75-77, 83-84, 302. *See also* Citizenship, Patriotism.
Luthardt, Christoph E., 147
Luther, Martin, 119, 123-27, 134, 138, 157, 167, 320; ethics of, 78-79; 150-53; on magistrates, 167-68; on the Sixth Commandment, 165; on visible church, 155.
Lutheran churches, 38, 66, 122ff., 138, 146
Lutheranism, 123-27, 136, 147, 148-49, 163, 164, 165, 201, 321, 322, 324ff.

Maccabees, 178, 208, 283
Macgregor, G. H. C., 57
Magistrates, 133, 166, 180, 205, 209. *See also* Church and state.
Marx, Karl, 252
Marxism, 207-08. *See also* Communism.
Mao Tse-tung, 341
Marsch, W. D., 238
Means and ends, 54
Mediaeval tradition, 77-78, 209, 241
Mendenhall, G. E., 212
Menno Simons, 158
Mennonite Central Committee, 46, 56
Mennonite churches, 17, 49-56
Mennonites, 46, 183, 280, 319, 320, 326, 327; arrival of in Europe, 16; in Europe, 13; in World War I, 22, 38; at Newton, 13, 30; position of on world, 136; response of to Cardiff report, 353-64; statement of to WCC, 19, 49-56; statement agreed to by, 73-90; drafted by, 73-90.

Methodist General Conference, 30
Methodists, 280
Meyer, Albert J., 14-15, 122
Micheli, D., 277
Middle East, 378. *See also* Palestine.
Militarism, 17, 18, 28, 44, 295, 334
Military chaplaincy. *See* Chaplaincy.
Military service, 29, 35-36, 40, 70, 127, 129-130, 301-02, 374.
Minorities, 24, 25, 317
Moscow (USSR), 181
Müsterites, 158
Murder, 84-85, 373
Muslims, 182, 225, 378
Muste, A. J., 122

Nairobi Assembly, 17, 27, 28, 386-89, 391
National Service Board for Religious Objectors, 30
National Socialism, 14, 15, 33, 188, 207, 341
Nationalism, 84, 355, *See also* Patriotism.
Natural law, 170, 231, 233, 359
Natural social bonds, 75-77
Natural theology, 77-78, 170, 231ff.
Natures of Christ, 150. *See also* Christology.
Naumann, Friedrich, 233
Nazism. *See* National Socialism.
Neighbor, 150-51, 163, 190, 268
Nelson, F. Burton, 223
Nemi (Italy), 26, 329, 376
Neo-Lutheranism, 199
Neo-Reformation theology, 18, 100
New Delhi Assembly, 23-24, 223, 233, 306, 307, 391
New Delhi Report, The (WCC), 224-28
New Delhi to Uppsala (WCC), 306
New Testament: Brethren view of, 63-65; Free Church view of, 281-84; ethic of, 217-18; on Jesus and Power, 369-71; on justice, 113-15; on legitimacy, 208; and minority churches, 240; on peace, 45, 57, 67-68, 82-90, 118-19, 379; on preaching, 161-72; on state, 68; on war, 50-51. *See also* Scriptures.
Newlin, Angie, 13

Newton, Kansas (USA), 13, 30
Niebuhr, Reinhold, 18, 21, 100-07, 108-21, 133, 178-79, 189, 198
Niemöller, Martin, 22, 203
Nietzsche, F. W., 248
Nissiotis, N. A., 277, 280, 369
Non-pacifism, 307ff.
Non-resistance, 19, 25, 47-72, 82-90, 154, 183. *See also* Non-violence, Pacifism.
Non-violence, 24-25, 26-27, 56ff., 292ff., 310, 314, 342, 351-52, 353-64, 373-85. *See also* Non-resistance, Pacifism.
Non-violent actions, 341-42, 381ff.
Non-violent change, 318, 329-52
Northern Ireland, 330, 335, 377-78
Notting Hill (Great Britain), 25
NSBRO. *See* National Service Board for Religious Objectors.
Nuclear pacifism, 200, 294, 306
Nuclear warfare, 14, 23, 24, 106-07, 110, 142-43, 185-95, 200, 276, 293, 294-97, 316
Nuclear weapons, 17, 23, 40, 93, 94, 106-07, 142, 165, 185-95, 204, 224-25, 259, 276, 301, 313, 326, 387
Nyborg (Denmark), 185

Oath, 164
Obbe Phillips, 158
Obedience to Jesus Christ, 49ff., 70, 98, 129-30, 139, 148-49, 159, 172. *See also* Discipleship.
Old Testament, 203, 337-38; ethic of, 212-14; on justice, 112-15; on killing, 84-85; Reformation churches on, 240; on state, 68; on war, 51, 85. *See also* Scriptures.
Oldenburg, Church of, 146
Oldham, J. H., 18, 20, 33, 231
On the Freedom of a Christian (Luther), 125, 150
One World (WCC), 28
Order, 111-12, 127, 149, 218, 231-32, 238
Orthodox churches, 38, 223, 225, 240, 321
Ostreicher, Paul, 313
Oud Poelgeest (The Netherlands), 21, 229, 249, 321
Outline of Ethics (Althaus), 148
Oxford Conference, 17, 29, 33-37, 66-67, 74-90, 105, 106, 390-91

Pacifism, 35, 40, 73-90, 316, 321, 353-64; difficulty of, 180-81; Evanston Assembly on, 21, 91; Historic Peace Church statement on, 31-32, 46-72, 82-90; as imperialistic force, 27, 386; individualistic, 109-10, 153; liberal, 136, 390; and liberation movements, 25-26, 330-52, 357-64; and love, 101-02, 111-15; at Nairobi Assembly, 388-89; nuclear, 200, 294, 306; at Oxford conference, 19, 33, 35; in Roman Empire, 53; Society of Friends statement on, 300-05. *See also* Non-resistance, Non-violence.
Palestine, 177, 330, 335, 365ff.
Pannenberg, Wolfhart, 253
Parijskij, Leo, 321
Participation in Christ, 184, 321
Patriotism, 31-32, 59, 75-77. *See also* Citizenship, Nationalism.
Peabody, F. G., 233
Peace: biblical message of, 278-79; consultation on Christian witness to, 306-12; contribution of theology and church to, 322; desire for, 93-95; international, 295-97; and justice, 101-07, 108-21; nature of, 278; Protestant preaching on, 161-72; testimony on, 300-05; theological bases of, 320-38; and war, 315-18. *See also* Non-resistance, Non-violence, Pacifism.
Peace Committee, Mennonite, 56
Peace Is the Will of God (HPC), 20, 21, 73-90, 108
Peace Section, Friends World Conference, 300
Peachey, Paul, 108-21, 153-60
Pederson, Johannes, 214
Penn, William, 304
Pennsylvania, 304
Pentecostals, 280
People of God, 331
Perfection, 54, 116, 163, 180, 309, 310
Pharisees, 164, 174, 219, 245, 367

Pietism, 67, 147, 159, 273, 279
Pluralism, 156, 284, 294-99
Police action, 35, 59, 69
Policy Reference Committee (WCC), 318
Politics of Jesus (Yoder), 22
Political authorities, 130
Pope, 156
Positivism, 196ff.
Potter, Philip, 21, 28, 366
Poverty, 227, 304, 313, 332, 337, 355, 374ff.
Power, Jesus on, 365-72
Powers and principalities. See Principalities and powers.
Prague (Czechoslovakia), 21
Preaching on peace, 161-72
Precepts, 78, 325
Presbyterian churches, 38
Prevention of war, 185-95
Principalities and powers, 141, 147-53, 336-37, 363, 380
Principles in ethics, 137-38, 160, 200, 323
Program Guideline Committee (WCC), 28
Program to Combat Racism (WCC), 25, 29, 329, 351, 388
Prophecy, 243
Protestant Episcopal Church, 66, 100
Protestant preaching on peace, 161-72
Protestantism, 131, 202, 230, 280, 319
Public opinion, 225-26
Puidoux (Switzerland), 17, 122, 320
Puidoux Theological Conferences, 14-15, 17-18, 21-22, 122-45, 146-84, 196-222, 229-71, 290, 319-28, 391
Puritanism, 138

Quakers. *See* Society of Friends.

Racism, 24, 297, 313, 376, 377; WCC program on, 25, 29, 329, 351, 388.
Radical Reformation, 21, 22
Rage, 335
Ramsey, Paul, 24, 292
Rationalism, 129, 148
Reconciliation, 41, 44, 67-68, 69-70, 84, 88, 95-97, 121, 289, 308, 337

Redemption, 121, 123, 133, 216, 220, 272-73, 308
Reformation churches, 152-53, 240. *See also* Calvinism, Lutheranism, Reformed churches.
Reformation in Zürich, 198
Reformed Church of France, 66
Reformed churches, 66, 122, 147. *See also* Calvinism, Reformation churches.
Reformers, 138, 147-53, 154. *See also* Calvin, Luther, Zwingli.
Relief work, 16, 63, 65, 181, 304, 305
Remonstrantse Broderschap of Holland, 66
Rengstorf, Karl H., 245
Report to the Landeskirchen, 182-84, 320-21
Research Institute of the Protestant Study Fellowship, 21, 319, 322
Responsibility, 58, 102, 104, 115, 117-18, 123, 126, 128-30, 153, 209-10, 281, 295, 309, 374ff.
Resistance against state, 172. *See also* Just revolution.
Revelation by God, 128, 206
Revolution, 336, 370; conference on, 24, 25, 292ff.; and Jesus, 356ff.
Revolution of 1917, 322, 341
Revolutionary change, 24, 338-52
Revolutionary violence, 24, 338ff., 340
Rhineland, Church of, 146
Rich, A., 209
Richmond, Indiana (USA), 353
Righteousness, 112-14, 119, 173, 216
Ritschl, Albrecht, 148
Roman Catholicism, 38, 105, 110, 138, 155, 159, 170, 202, 280, 299; on church and state, 130; and duality, 138; ethics of, 232, 325; and just war, 200; in middle ages, 155; and SODEPAX, 26.
Roman empire, 58-59, 110, 117, 204, 280, 282, 356, 367ff., 374
Rules and norms. *See* Principles in ethics.
Russian Orthodox Church, 223, 240

Sacramental system, 155

Sadducees, 367
Salvation, 233
Salvation history, 232, 238-39, 252, 255, 260
Sanctification, 129
Sanctions, 303-04
Sayre, John Nevin, 72
Saxony, Church of, 146
Scharffenorth, Gerta, 322, 323
Schleiermacher, Friedrich D. E., 252
Schmidt, K. L., 245
Schwärmer. See Enthusiasts.
Schweitzer, Albert, 211
Schweitzer, E., 369, 370
Schweitzer, W., 238
Scriptures: authority of, 50, 128-30, 130-35; basis for decision, 129, 244; basis for Free Church view, 281-84; interpretation of, 51, 307-08, 369; basis of pacifism, 50-51; message of peace in, 278-79; on power, 369-71; unity of, 85. *See also* New Testament, Old Testament.
Second World War. *See* World War II.
Sects: ethic of, 119-20; view of church and state of, 131.
Security, 166, 194-97, 378
Self-defense, 61-62
Self-denial: Calvin on, 150; Luther on, 152
Separation of church and state, 287
Sermon on the Mount, 50, 62, 63, 83, 116, 118, 124, 130, 133, 164, 175, 218-19, 234-35, 245, 249, 263ff., 287. *See also* Beatitudes.
Sermon on the plain, 263ff.
Sermons, 161-72
Service programs, 65
Siegmund-Schultze, Friedrich, 18, 392
Simons, Menno. *See* Menno Simons.
Sin, 33-37, 51, 53, 74, 83, 101-04, 173ff., 201, 308. *See also* Lesser evil.
Situational ethics, 57-58, 67-68, 127, 153, 160, 201, 270, 323
Sixth Commandment, 135, 162-63, 166, 167, 196, 176, 211-22. *See also* Decalogue.
Slavery, 181, 248
Snaith, Norman, 216, 217

Social change, 329-52
Social ethics, 75-77, 78-79, 125, 197, 230-40, 234-35, 237-39, 240-50, 321. *See also* Ethics.
Social gospel, 233-34, 53
Social involvement, 309
Social justice, 111-15, 373-85
Society, 75-77, 115-18, 233
Society and church, 24, 292-99, 313, 332, 375
Society of Brothers, 183
Society of Friends, 17, 159, 179, 181, 183, 280, 301, 314, 320, 323, 390; in America, 13, 15-16, 38, 182; in Europe, 13; in Great Britain, 13, 15-16, 18, 46, 73, 301; in Japan, 66; at Newton, 13, 30; peace witness of, 15-16; relief activities of, 15, 304, 305; response to Cardiff report, 353-64; statements by, 19, 56-63, 73-90, 300-05; at Uppsala Assembly, 25; in World War II, 15-16.
SODEPAX, 26, 28
Söderblom, Nathan, 18
Söe, N. H., 21, 100, 147
Soldiers: and ethics, 269-71; Luther on, 126-27. *See also* Military service.
Sources of Christian Social Ethics, 229-71
South Africa, 25, 28, 180, 351, 377, 391
South East Asia, 378
Soviet Union, 181, 189, 321. *See also* East-West struggle.
Spinoza, Baruch, 249
Staatskirchen, 153, *See Landeskirchen, Volkskirchen.*
State, 35-36, 132-33, 151-52, 380; authority of 272-76; changes in since New Testament times 284-85; and Free Church, 287-88; submission to, 141, 281-82; and war, 85-88. *See also* Church and state.
Steere, Douglas, 196, 197
Stockholm (Sweden), 18, 233
Strobel, August, 240
Structural violence, 24, 26-27, 332-35, 354-55, 380
Studien zur Friedensforschung, 319
Study Encounter, 366

Suffering servant theme, 173-74
Surrender as option, 185ff.
Suzerainty, 213, 217
Syrian churches, 38

Tagawa, Kenzo, 367, 368
Task of Christians, 88-90
Technical-scientific world, 323
Technology, 192, 292, 294, 314, 323
Ten Commandments. *See* Decalogue.
Test ban treaty, 296, 316
Tertullian, 169-70
Theology: of history, 251-53; of liberation, 24, 292ff.; of orders, 127; of peace, 307-12; of society, 230-31; of the Word, 237
Thielicke, Helmut, 200
Thirty Years' War, 63
Thomas, Wilbur K., 30
Thomism, 77, 78, 232
Threshold, 200-201
Tödt, Heinz-Eduard, 319, 322, 323,
Tödt, Frau Dr., 322
Torture, 333, 382
Totalitarianism, 25, 33, 41, 96, 111. *See also* Communism, National Socialism.
Transitions in ethics, 323
Treysa (Germany), 162
Troeltsch, Ernst, 119-20, 233, 252, 260, 283
Tucker, Eric, 13, 15-16
Two kingdoms, 78-79, 119, 123-27, 138, 152, 199, 202, 230

Ullmann, Richard, 173-83
Una sancta, 34, 74, 84-85
Union Theological Seminary, 100
United Nations, 42, 43, 68, 94, 97, 105, 106, 182, 224, 227, 290, 295, 304, 376-77
United Nations Peace Commission, 95
United States, 13, 25, 189, 341, 342. *See also* East-West struggle.
Unity of the church, 155-56. *See also* Ecumenical Movement, World Council of Churches.
Universal church. *See Una sancta.*
Uppsala Assembly, 24-25, 313-18, 329, 375, 376, 391

Utopian theocracy of love, 197-98
Utrecht (The Netherlands), 348

Vallecrosia (Italy), 21
Van Oyen, Hendrik, 229-240
Vatican, 26, 28, 78
Verghese, Paul, 277
Vietnam, 14, 378, 342, 391
Violence, 51-52, 135, 275-76, 329-52, 381ff.; communal, 335-36; definition of, 332-33; direct, 333; nature of, 310; personal, 335-36; structural, 24, 26-27, 332-35, 354-55, 380.
Violence, Nonviolence and the Struggle for Social Justice (WCC), 26-27, 365-72, 373-85
Visible church, 138, 139, 155; Luther on, 155; Roman Catholicism on, 159.
Visser 't Hooft, W. A., 19, 46, 66, 313
Vittorini, Elio, 241
Vocation, 149, 152
Vocational pacifism, 19, 48, 59, 67, 78-79, 154
Vogel, Heinrich, 203
Volkskirchen, 320. *See also Landeskirchen, Staatskirchen.*
Volunteers, 13-14
Von Oppen, Dietrich, 235-36
Von Rad, Gerhard, 241

War, 39, 110-11, 152, 154, 169, 186-95, 259-60, 292-99, 300-05, 322; Amsterdam Assembly on, 40-45; compatible with Christian love, 82; Evanston Assembly on, 91; fear of, 93-95; renounced by Historic Peace Churches, 31-32; in nuclear age. 186-95; Oxford Conference on, 18-19, 33; sinfulness of, 31; Society of Friends statement on, 300-05; in twentieth century, 14. *See also* Violence.
War and the Christian Ethic (Lassere), 269-71
War crimes trial, 168
War Is Contrary to the Will of God (HPC), 19-20, 46-72, 118
Wealth of churches, 350
Weber, Hans-Ruedi, 366, 368
Weber, Max, 250

Welch, Claude, 219
Wellhausen, Julius, 212
Wendland, H. D., 232, 234
Westphalia, Church of, 146
Wichern, J. H., 233
Wilkens, Ernst, 277
Windisch, Hans, 218-19
Wittenberg, Church of, 146
Wolf, Ernst, 22, 123-27, 129, 147-53, 162, 196, 240, 320
Women, identity of, 334
Woolman, John, 62, 181, 304
World Alliance for Promoting International Friendship Through the Churches, 18
World Conference on Church, Community, and State. *See* Oxford Conference.
World community, 92-99
World Council of Churches, 38-45, 46, 66, 118, 142, 299, 329, 358, 366; Brethren representative to, 13; and CCIA, 20, 45, 95, 185, 291, 351; Central Committee of, 17, 23, 24-26, 28, 105, 185, 329, 351, 373-74; consultation on peace, 24, 306-12; Conference on Church and Society, 24, 292-99, 313, 375; Department of Church and Society, 25, 26, 329; Division of Studies, 23-24, 186, 223, 229, 306-12; Ecumenical Institute, 241, 277-91, 306, 391; First Assembly, 19, 38-45, 46-72, 58, 66, 73-90, 102-03, 118, 231, 281, 294, 315-16, 375, 390-91; Fifth Assembly, 17, 28, 386-89, 391; formation of, 19; Fourth Assembly, 24-25, 313-18, 329, 376, 391; and Historic Peace Churches, 14, 15, 20, 29, 46, 66, 185, 313, 390-93; and international problems, 44-45; and non-violence, 24-25, 26-27, 329-52, 353-64; and peace, 351, 392; Policy Reference Committee, 314; in Process of Formation, 34; and Puidoux conference, 21, 22, 229; Program to Combat Racism, 24-25, 29, 329, 351, 388; and responsible society, 20, 29, 115-16, 204, 231-33, 241, 281, 286-87; Second Assembly, 20, 47, 91-99, 231, 391; and SODEPAX, 26, 28; Study Department, 20; Third Assembly, 23-24, 223, 237, 306, 307, 392; and war, 23, 185-95.
World development, 227
World War I, 18, 22, 109, 110, 135, 252, 301
World War II, 14, 15-16, 20, 34, 38, 41, 110-11, 231, 252, 301
"Worldly Christianity," 234

Yoder, John H., 22, 28, 122, 136-43, 153, 196, 197-210, 229-230, 277, 279-88, 322, 303, 365-72, 287, 288-89, 290-93
Youth, as peacemakers, 13-14

Zealots, 117, 208, 281, 337, 365ff., 379
Zeist (The Netherlands), 46, 49
Zigler, M. R., 13-14, 17, 46, 49, 66, 391
Zimmerli, Walther, 243
Zofingen (Switzerland), 157
Zürich (Switzerland), 156-57, 197-98
Zwei Reiche. See Two Kingdoms
Zwingli, Huldreich, 155, 156-57, 197-98